FOOD LAW
CASES AND MATERIALS

2017-18 Edition

Lisa Heinzerling
Georgetown University Law Center

To the reader:

In these materials, I have omitted most citations and footnotes from cases and articles without using ellipses to indicate the omissions. The numbers of the retained footnotes correspond to the numbers in the original documents.

LH

Table of Contents

Part Three
Safety

Chapter 6
The Varieties of Adulteration 186

Chapter 7
The Challenges of Food Additives 232

Chapter 8
Modernizing Food Safety 267

Chapter 9
Genetically Engineered Food 296

Part Four
Food Security

Chapter 10
Food Assistance Programs 340

Chapter 11
The Environmental Dimension of Food Security 366

Part Five

CHAPTER 1
WHAT IS FOOD LAW?

The Law of the Horse?

What is Food Law? This turns out to be an interesting question, and one that is harder to answer than you might expect.

In recent years, a rich nonfiction literature relating to food and food policy has emerged. Barry Estabrook, Jonathan Safran Foer, Barbara Kingsolver, Mark Kurlansky, Frances Moore Lappé, Marion Nestle, Michael Pollan, Vandana Shiva, and many others have contributed to an outpouring of writing on food production, food consumption, food labeling, food security, food justice, local food, global food markets, and more. So much attention, in fact, has lately focused on food-related issues that the rather loose assemblage of causes embraced by these writers has been dubbed a "food movement." A striking fact about these writers and many others in the field is that none is a lawyer and thus, although all write about food policy in one sense or another, none writes from the perspective of a lawyer.

At the same time, no lawyer or law professor has yet set out to define and conceptualize with any precision the emerging field of Food Law. The traditional course on Food and Drug Law does not treat Food Law as a distinct field, and often covers only the federal regulatory regime codified in the Food, Drug, and Cosmetic Act and administered by the Food and Drug Administration. This structure makes a good deal of sense in many ways, but it fails to capture the richness of the emerging field and identify the strands that tie together seemingly disparate legal regimes relating to food.

One could treat the field much more broadly, and say that all law relating to how food is grown, produced, processed, transported, marketed, labeled, paid for, consumed, and disposed of should be covered in a course on Food Law. Such a course would span a huge range, from environmental rules for agriculture to food safety rules for food processors to subsidies for producers to special rules for food trucks to laws on the humane treatment of agricultural animals to limits on deceptive marketing and labeling. The course would need to last more than a semester. It would also seem a little like a course on what Judge Frank Easterbrook criticized years ago as "The Law of the Horse." In dismissing attempts to stake out a special field of "cyberlaw," Judge Easterbrook wrote: "Lots of cases deal with sales of horses; others deal with people kicked by horses; still more deal with the licensing and racing of horses, or with the care veterinarians give to horses, or with prizes at horse shows. Any effort to collect these strands into a course on 'The Law of the Horse' is doomed to be shallow and to miss unifying principles."[1] One could say that a course simply canvasing all of the law that relates in any way to food would succumb to the problem of The Law of the Horse: it would have no core.

Knowledge, Safety, and Security

Properly conceived, however, Food Law does have a core. This book embraces a conception of Food Law as a distinct field, with a distinctive set of regulatory goals and strategies. As we will see, the regulatory regime created by federal statutes on food is exceedingly complex, but the law's basic structure is quite simple. The federal law on food aims to achieve knowledge on the part of consumers about the food they buy and eat; the safety of that food; and reliable access to adequate and nutritious food. These three goals – knowledge, safety, and security – tie together and define the many different federal statutes, enacted across a period of more than a century, governing our food.

The goals of knowledge and safety – denominated as prohibitions on "misbranding" and "adulteration" – appear in numerous federal and state regulatory regimes relating to food. The central legal commands of the federal Food, Drug, and Cosmetic Act (FDCA), as it relates to food, are the prohibitions on misbranding and adulteration. The federal Meat Inspection Act, the Poultry Products Inspection Act, and the Egg Products Inspection Act contain, for meat, poultry, and eggs, respectively, the same basic injunctions against adulterated and misbranded food as are contained in the FDCA (although they are implemented by the U.S. Department of Agriculture rather than the Food and Drug Administration). The federal Lacey Act prohibits the false labeling of seafood. The Federal Trade Commission Act prohibits "unfair or deceptive acts or practices in or affecting commerce," including such acts or practices that relate to food. The Federal Insecticide, Fungicide, and Rodenticide Act aims to ensure that pesticides are properly labeled and do not pose an unacceptable risk to humans or the environment. As you can see, it is possible to connect many seemingly disparate federal laws relating to food by emphasizing the goals of knowledge and safety. The

---

[1] Frank H. Easterbrook, *Cyberspace and the Law of the Horse*, U. CHI. LEGAL FORUM 207 (1996).

same goes for numerous food-related laws at the state level; these laws, too, tend to focus on knowledge and safety.

Thus, although we will mostly be occupied here with study of the FDCA, lessons we learn from studying this law apply generally to many different laws related to food. Difficulties in determining the kind of information that consumers should receive about food and in determining the limits of legal prohibitions on misleading information recur throughout the field of food law. Challenges in defining and ensuring food safety also recur throughout this field. Moreover, many (though by no means all) of the concerns of the so-called "food movement" – exemplified in the writings of the nonfiction authors mentioned previously – are, at their core, concerns about knowledge and safety.

A third goal also runs through U.S. food law. This is the goal of providing food "security," that is, reliable access to an adequate quantity of nutritious food. Many laws – and the government programs that spring from them – have food security as a central purpose. The School Lunch Act, Healthy Hunger-Free Kids Act, Food Conservation and Energy Act, laws governing the Supplemental Nutrition Assistance Program (SNAP), and numerous agricultural appropriations bills aim to improve food security.

The Food, Drug, and Cosmetic Act

The main focus of our studies will be the Food, Drug, and Cosmetic Act and its amendments. The FDCA regulates numerous major categories of products, including food, dietary supplements, prescription and non-prescription drugs, medical devices, radiological products, blood products, vaccines, tissues for transplantation, animal drugs, animal feed, cosmetics, and tobacco products. As a consequence, the FDA, charged with implementing the FDCA, has jurisdiction over products representing about a quarter of all consumer spending in the United States.

The FDCA has its origins in the Pure Food and Drug Act of 1906, passed in the wake of the publication of Upton Sinclair's *The Jungle*. The statute has been amended many times since its initial passage, but it retains the original aims of preventing misbranding and adulteration. The law can be enforced through criminal penalties, civil penalties, and/or seizing of prohibited items. Thanks to the passage of the Food Safety Modernization Act of 2010, the FDA now also has the authority to issue mandatory recalls of unsafe food.

The FDCA and its predecessor, the Pure Food and Drug Act, have been amended many times. The following list shows just the major amendments over the years:

1906 – Pure Food and Drug Act, Meat Inspection Act
1938 – Federal Food, Drug, and Cosmetic Act
1958 – Food Additives Amendment (Delaney clause)
1960 – Color Additive Amendment
1962 – Kefauver-Harris Amendments
1990 – Nutrition Labeling and Education Act (NLEA)
1994 – Dietary Supplement Health and Education Act (DSHEA)
1996 – Food Quality Protection Act (FQPA)
1997 – Food and Drug Administration Modernization Act
2004 – Food Allergy Labeling and Consumer Protection Act
2011 – Food Safety Modernization Act (FSMA)

The amendments to the original statute have made requirements relating to consumer knowledge far more detailed and complex and have for the most part strengthened requirements relating to safety. In most instances, Congress has amended the law by adding requirements while leaving older provisions in place. The FDCA has, as a consequence, become something of a palimpsest: the original text is still visible, but it has been obscured by later additions.

The Relevant Agencies

Although we will spend considerable time on the FDCA and its implementation by the FDA, you should be aware that there is a complicated, even dizzying, overlap among federal regulatory agencies when it comes to regulating food products. A 2010 article in the Los Angeles Times put it this way: "In the U.S. cheese pizza is regulated by one federal agency, but a pepperoni pizza is overseen by another. An open-faced turkey sandwich, likewise, falls under the purview of the U.S. Department of Agriculture, but one with two slices of bread is under the jurisdiction of the FDA. Liquid beef broth and dehydrated chicken broth? USDA. Liquid chicken broth and dehydrated beef broth? FDA." A perennial recommendation for reform of federal food law is to locate the regulatory authority over food within one agency.

Fifteen federal agencies have some role in the federal regulatory system for food, but two institutions predominate: the FDA and USDA. It is worth knowing something about these agencies as you begin to study the field of

Food Law. The FDA is one of the oldest public health agencies in the United States, with more than 15,000 employees and a budget of almost $5 billion. As you might imagine, given its wide-ranging regulatory authority, the agency has organized itself into several different offices and centers focusing on different kinds of products. The agency's regulatory activities relating to food primarily emerge from the Office of Foods and Veterinary Medicine and its Center for Food Safety and Applied Nutrition (CFSAN) and Center for Veterinary Medicine (CVM). The head of the Office of Foods and Veterinary Medicine is a political appointee (appointed by the President, not requiring Senate confirmation). The heads of CVM and CFSAN are career professionals at the FDA.

The scope and nature of the FDA's regulatory authority depends crucially on the kind of product in question. Drugs are subject to a much stricter regulatory regime than are food and dietary supplements. In the next chapter, we will see how the FDCA defines these different products. This will give us an opportunity to think more deeply about what "food" is.

The USDA, created in 1862, has the complicated task of both promoting and regulating agriculture. With over 100,000 employees and a budget of over $150 billion, the Department has 33 separate agencies within it. The most important of these for our purposes are the Food Safety and Inspection Service, which regulates and inspects meat, and the Food and Nutrition Service, which oversees food assistance programs like SNAP and the school lunch program. Both of these agencies are overseen by politically appointed USDA undersecretaries.

The Food Movement

Let us consider a sampling of the causes that some have labeled the "food movement." Can we see a coherent shape to this movement? What does it have to do with law?

If the contemporary food movement has a high priest, it may well be Wendell Berry. And if it has a signal essay, it may well be Berry's "The Pleasures of Eating," which begins:

> Many times, after I have finished a lecture on the decline of American farming and rural life, someone in the audience has asked, "What can city people do?"
>
> "Eat responsibly," I have usually answered. Of course, I have tried to explain what I mean by that, but afterwards I have invariably felt there was more to be said than I had been able to say. Now I would like to attempt a better explanation.

I begin with the proposition that eating is an agricultural act....

Please read Berry's essay for our first class. The essay is available here: **http://www.ecoliteracy.org/essays/pleasures-eating**.

Michael Pollan has said that Berry's observation, "eating is an agricultural act," "formed a template" for much of Pollan's own work. Through books like *The Ominivore's Dilemma*, Pollan himself has been a major force in increasing the prominence of issues related to food.

Before the fall 2016 election, Pollan wrote an appraisal of the aspirations and political challenges of the food movement. Please read his essay, "Big Food Strikes Back: Why did the Obamas fail to take on corporate agriculture?," available here: **http://www.nytimes.com/interactive/2016/10/09/magazine/obama-administration-big-food-policy.html?_r=0**.

Who Made Your Food? farm exemptions

One of the challenges of the food movement, when it comes to law, is that so many laws in the U.S. have carved out agriculture as a special category, often explicitly exempting agricultural activities from legal requirements. In environmental law, for example, as law professor J.B. Ruhl has observed, "the active and passive safe harbors farms enjoy in most environmental laws amount to an 'anti-law' that finds no rational basis given the magnitude of harms farms cause."[2] The same is true – perhaps even more so – in the realm of worker protection. Most federal labor laws exclude farm workers, resulting in an "agricultural exceptionalism" that leaves farm workers outside common legal protections. Sometimes the consequences are horrible, as described in the essay that follows.

Politics of the Plate: The Price of Tomatoes

Barry Estabrook
Gourmet Magazine
March 2009

---

[2] J.B. Ruhl, *Farms, Their Environmental Harms, and Environmental Law*, 27 ECOL. L.Q. 263 (2000).

...

Immokalee is the tomato capital of the United States. Between December and May, as much as 90 percent of the fresh domestic tomatoes we eat come from south Florida, and Immokalee is home to one of the area's largest communities of farmworkers. According to Douglas Molloy, the chief assistant U.S. attorney based in Fort Myers, Immokalee has another claim to fame: It is "ground zero for modern slavery."

The beige stucco house at 209 South Seventh Street is remarkable only because it is in better repair than most Immokalee dwellings. For two and a half years, beginning in April 2005, Mariano Lucas Domingo, along with several other men, was held as a slave at that address. At first, the deal must have seemed reasonable. Lucas, a Guatemalan in his thirties, had slipped across the border to make money to send home for the care of an ailing parent. He expected to earn about $200 a week in the fields. Cesar Navarrete, then a 23-year-old illegal immigrant from Mexico, agreed to provide room and board at his family's home on South Seventh Street and extend credit to cover the periods when there were no tomatoes to pick.

Lucas's "room" turned out to be the back of a box truck in the junk-strewn yard, shared with two or three other workers. It lacked running water and a toilet, so occupants urinated and defecated in a corner. For that, Navarrete docked Lucas's pay by $20 a week. According to court papers, he also charged Lucas for two meager meals a day: eggs, beans, rice, tortillas, and, occasionally, some sort of meat. Cold showers from a garden hose in the backyard were $5 each. Everything had a price. Lucas was soon $300 in debt. After a month of ten-hour workdays, he figured he should have paid that debt off.

But when Lucas—slightly built and standing less than five and a half feet tall—inquired about the balance, Navarrete threatened to beat him should he ever try to leave. Instead of providing an accounting, Navarrete took Lucas's paychecks, cashed them, and randomly doled out pocket money, $20 some weeks, other weeks $50. Over the years, Navarrete and members of his extended family deprived Lucas of $55,000.

Taking a day off was not an option. If Lucas became ill or was too exhausted to work, he was kicked in the head, beaten, and locked in the back of the truck. Other members of Navarrete's dozen-man crew were slashed with knives, tied to posts, and shackled in chains....

What happened at Navarrete's home would have been horrific enough if it were an isolated case. Unfortunately, involuntary servitude—slavery—is alive and well in Florida. Since 1997, law-enforcement officials have freed more than 1,000 men and women in seven different cases. And those are only the instances that resulted in convictions. Frightened, undocumented, mistrustful of the police, and speaking little or no English, most slaves refuse to testify, which means their captors cannot be tried....

[W]hen asked if it is reasonable to assume that an American who has eaten a fresh tomato from a grocery store or food-service company during the winter has eaten fruit picked by the hand of a slave, Molloy said, "It is not an assumption. It is a fact."...

Note

Are the strands of discontent with the food system cohesive enough to be a "movement"? Are reformers trying to do too much at once? Or is part of their point that we must look at the food system holistically, not atomistically, in order to improve it? If you had to prioritize the various aspirations of the food movement, which would you choose to pursue first?

What is the role of law in achieving the goals of the food movement? Is law by nature too specialized and atomized to realize the kind of wholeness and unity Berry describes? Is it to politicized to achieve the discrete goals Pollan describes? What can lawyers do to help?

CHAPTER 2
WHAT IS "FOOD"?

Food Rules

As we discussed in our first class, navigating the complexity of the modern food marketplace can be daunting. What is in our food? Is it healthy, safe, and nutritious? What combination of industrial processes and human labor brought it to our plates?

Michael Pollan has famously offered three simple rules for deciding what to eat: "Eat food. Not too much. Mostly plants."

But what is "food"? In *Food Rules: An Eater's Manual* (Penguin Books 2009), Pollan offers guidelines for distinguishing food from what he calls "edible food-like substances," which include rules of thumb such as the following:

- Don't eat anything your great-grandmother wouldn't recognize as food
- Avoid food products containing ingredients that no ordinary human would keep in the pantry
- Avoid food products that have more than 5 ingredients
- Avoid food products containing ingredients that a third-grader cannot pronounce
- Avoid food products that make health claims
- Avoid food products with the word "lite" or the terms "low fat" or "nonfat" in their names
- Avoid foods that are pretending to be something they are not
- Avoid foods you see advertised on television
- Shop the peripheries of the supermarket and stay out of the middle
- Eat only foods that will eventually rot
- Eat foods made from ingredients that you can picture in their raw state or growing in nature
- Get out of the supermarket whenever you can
- Eat only foods that have been cooked by humans
- Don't ingest foods made in places where everyone is required to wear a surgical cap
- If it came from a plant, eat it; if it was made in a plant, don't
- It's not food if it arrived through the window of your car

- It's not food if it's called by the same name in every language (Think Big Mac, Cheetos or Pringles)
- Don't eat breakfast cereals that change the color of the milk

Pollan's defense of food is in part a critique of "nutritionism" – the idea that the value of food comes from the specific nutrients we have identified in it. Taken to its extreme, nutritionism might persuade us that we can manufacture "edible food-like products" that are better for us than unprocessed foods are. It might also persuade us that dietary supplements can make up for an otherwise unhealthy diet. These ideas would ignore the possibility that we have not identified all of the ways in which whole food is good for us and dismiss the other benefits – in culture, conviviality, and sheer pleasure – that come with eating real food.

In this light, what do you make of Soylent™, described by its producers as an "open sourced nutritional drink" and accompanied by the tagline, "What if you never had to worry about food again?" The Soylent website describes the product as "a food, not a supplement," that is "designed for use as a staple meal by all adults." The idea is that, with Soylent, you don't need to eat anything else. The nutrition facts panel for Soylent is reproduced below. Consider whether Soylent is "food" in Pollan's sense.

As you read the materials that follow on the legal definitions of food, consider as well whether Soylent is "food" in a legal sense. To the extent that your answers differ depending on whether you are thinking about this issue through Pollan's lens or through the law's, what does that tell us about food? About law?

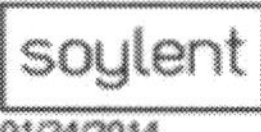

01/24/2014

Nutrition Facts

Serving Size (148g)
Servings Per Container 3

Amount Per Serving	Soylent Powder	with Oil Packets
Calories	510	670
Calories from Fat	45	210
		% Daily Value**
Total Fat 5g*	8%	37%
Saturated Fat 1g	5%	19%
Trans Fat 0g		
Cholesterol 0mg	0%	5%
Sodium 350mg	15%	15%
Potassium 1155mg	33%	33%
Total Carbohydrate 84g	28%	28%
Dietary Fiber 8g	32%	32%
Sugars 2g		
Protein 38g		
Vitamin A	33%	33%
Vitamin C	33%	33%
Calcium	40%	40%
Iron	40%	40%
Vitamin D	33%	35%
Vitamin E	33%	47%
Vitamin K	37%	52%
Thiamin	33%	33%
Riboflavin	33%	33%
Niacin	33%	33%
Vitamin B6	33%	33%
Folate	33%	33%
Vitamin B12	33%	33%
Biotin	33%	33%
Pantothenic Acid	33%	33%
Iodine	57%	57%
Magnesium	33%	33%
Zinc	33%	33%
Selenium	33%	33%
Copper	37%	37%
Manganese	33%	33%
Chromium	33%	33%
Molybdenum	33%	33%

*Amount in Soylent Powder with Oil Packets contributes an additional [illegible] Calories, [illegible] g Total Fat ([illegible] g Saturated Fat), [illegible] mg Cholesterol.
**Percent Daily Values are based on a 2,000 calorie diet. Your daily values may be higher or lower depending on your calorie needs:

	Calories:	2,000	2,500
Total Fat	Less than	[illegible]	[illegible]
Saturated Fat	Less than	[illegible]	[illegible]
Cholesterol	Less than	[illegible]	[illegible]
Sodium	Less than	2,400mg	2,400mg
Potassium		3,500 mg	3,500 mg
Total Carbohydrate		[illegible]	[illegible]
Dietary Fiber		[illegible]	[illegible]

Calories per gram:
Fat 9 • Carbohydrate 4 • Protein 4

INGREDIENTS: Maltodextrin, Rice Protein, Oat Flour, Vitamin and Mineral Blend [Potassium (as Potassium gluconate), choline bitartrate, Calcium (as calcium carbonate), Magnesium (as magnesium oxide), Vitamin C (as ascorbic acid), Vitamin E (as dl-alpha-tocopheryl acetate), Vitamin B3 (as niacinamide), Zinc (as zinc sulfate), Vitamin B5 (as calcium D-pantothenate), Vitamin B6 (as pyridoxine HCL), Copper (as copper gluconate), Manganese (as manganese sulfate), Vitamin B2 (as riboflavin), Vitamin A (as palmitate), Vitamin B1 (as thiamin HCL), Folic Acid , Biotin, Iodine (as potassium iodide), Chromium (as chromium chloride), Vitamin K1 (as phytonadione), Selenium (as sodium selenite), Vitamin D2 (as ergocalciferol), Molybdenum (as sodium molybdate), Vitamin B2 (as riboflavin)], Gum Acacia, Soybean Lecithin, Salt, Artificial Flavor, Sucralose.

INGREDIENTS: Canola Oil, Fish Oil

Contains: Soy

The Legal Definition of "Food"

In U.S. law, the most important definition of "food" comes from the federal Food, Drug, and Cosmetic Act (FDCA). Several important legal consequences flow from the determination of whether a food-like item is "food" in a legal sense. Items not covered by the FDCA's definitions for regulated products are outside the legal jurisdiction of the Food and Drug Administration (FDA). In addition, requirements under the FDCA vary considerably depending on which legal category fits a particular product. The legal categories of most relevance to us in studying Food Law are food, drugs, and dietary supplements. These categories bring with them very different regulatory regimes. For example, "food" need not undergo the rigorous premarket approval process applicable to "drugs." Dietary supplements also do not need to undergo this process, nor do they have to satisfy all of the requirements that apply to food.

Thus, identifying the categories of products regulated by the FDCA and determining the legal boundaries for these categories are tasks of great importance for lawyers in this field. They can mean the difference between regulation and no regulation, or between strict regulation and relatively lenient regulation. We begin, then, by considering the regulatory dividing lines created by the FDCA. In particular, we consider the definitional divide between food, drugs, and dietary supplements.

The definitions quoted immediately below are from the current version of the FDCA. Provisions of the FDCA are known, alternately, by their U.S. Code numbers and by the numbered sections of the original bill that became the FDCA. I provide both numbers when I include lengthy quotes from the FDCA, as below.

Food, Drug, and Cosmetic Act

21 U.S.C. § 321

SEC. 201. DEFINITIONS

For the purposes of this Act—...

(f) The term "food" means

(1) articles used for food or drink for man or other animals,

(2) chewing gum, and

(3) articles used for components of any such article.

(g)(1) The term "drug" means ...

(B) articles intended for use in the diagnosis, cure, mitigation, treatment, or prevention of disease in man or other animals; and

(C) articles (other than food) intended to affect the structure or any function of the body of man or other animals...

(ff) The term "dietary supplement" –

(1) means a product (other than tobacco) intended to supplement the diet that bears or contains one or more of the following dietary ingredients:

(A) a vitamin;

(B) a mineral;

(C) an herb or other botanical;

(D) an amino acid;

(E) a dietary substance for use by man to supplement the diet by increasing the total dietary intake; or

(F) a concentrate, metabolite, constituent, extract, or combination of any ingredient described in clause (A), (B), (C), (D), or (E);

(2) means a product that -

(A)(i) is intended for ingestion in a form described in section 411(c)(1)(B)(i); or (ii) complies with section 411(c)(1)(B)(ii);

(B) is not represented for use as a conventional food or as a sole item of a meal or the diet; and

(C) is labeled as a dietary supplement...

Except for purposes of section 201(g), a dietary supplement shall be deemed to be a food within the meaning of this Act.

See how much these short, even if dry, passages tell us about the meaning of "food" under the FDCA. Food is to be distinguished from dietary supplements and drugs. Food includes drink – and food and drink for other animals, not just humans. Food includes chewing gum, which – one hopes – is not ingested. Food includes components of food. With regard to the latter proposition, notice that the inclusion of "components" of food within the definition of "food" suggests that Congress had in mind a notion of "food" that exists apart from the components we might add to it – that is, perhaps, it believed that "food" was not the same as the additives we include in it.

Notice that, in defining drugs, Congress took care to exempt food from the definition that turns on an intent to affect that "structure or any function of the body of man." Why do you think Congress exempted food from this definition of drugs? Without this exemption, might every food be considered a drug?

The definition of dietary supplements was added in 1994 amendments to the FDCA, known as the Dietary Supplement Health and Education Act (DSHEA). These amendments generally weakened regulation of dietary supplements. For example, they allowed health-protective claims for dietary supplements without requiring supplement manufacturers to go through the robust approval process required for drugs. The amendments also provided, in section 411(c)(1) (21 U.S.C. 350), that FDA could not place limits on the potency of vitamins or minerals in "a food to which this section applies," defining this term as follows:

[T]he term "food to which this section applies" means a food for humans which is a food for special dietary use-

(A) which is or contains any natural or synthetic vitamin or mineral, and

> (B) which-
>
> > (i) is intended for ingestion in tablet, capsule, powder, softgel, gelcap, or liquid form, or
> >
> > (ii) if not intended for ingestion in such a form, is not represented as conventional food and is not represented for use as a sole item of a meal or of the diet.

This provision appears to give us yet another definition of food: a "food to which this section applies."

The cases that follow trace a history that has involved varying FDCA definitions over time. The first two cases illustrate the marvelous alchemy the law can perform, transforming ordinary water and ordinary honey into "drugs."

Bradley v. United States

264 F. 79 (5th Cir. 1920)

CALL, District Judge.

Libel was filed in the United States District Court for the Western District of Louisiana against 275 cases of mineral water, praying for confiscation and condemnation of same for having been shipped in interstate commerce in violation of the Food and Drugs Act.

The libel, after alleging the shipment of the cases of mineral water in interstate commerce and the presence of the same within the jurisdiction of the court, alleges that the same were misbranded in the following respects:

That the following statements regarding the therapeutic or curative effects thereof, appearing on the label aforesaid, to wit: 'Robinson Springs Water. Springs at Pocahontas, Miss. Recommended in the treatment of Bright's Disease, Diabetes, Dropsy, Cystitis, Gout, Rheumatism, Indigestion, Kidney and Bladder troubles. Directions: * * * Robinson Springs and Sanitarium Co., Pocahontas, Miss.' -- were false and fraudulent, in that the same were applied to said articles knowingly and in a reckless and wanton disregard of their truth or falsity, so as to represent falsely and fraudulently to the purchaser thereof, and create in the minds of purchasers thereof, the impression and belief that it was in whole or in part composed of or contained ingredients or medical agents, effective, among other things, as a remedy for Bright's disease, diabetes, dropsy, cystitis, gout rheumatism, indigestion, kidney and bladder troubles, when in truth and in fact said article was not in whole or in part composed of and did not contain ingredients, nor a combination of ingredients, capable of producing the therapeutic effects claimed on the labels, and therefore not effective as a treatment for said abovementioned ailments.

C. L. Bradley put in a claim to the water seized by the marshal, and excepted to the libel...

The exceptions were overruled, and the cause went to trial before a jury. After the government case was in, the claimant moved for an instructed verdict. This motion was renewed at the close of the entire evidence. Each of said motions were refused, and the jury returned a verdict in favor of the government, upon which a judgment was entered condemning said water....

The contention is made that the water condemned in this case is not a drug, within the meaning as used in the act. To confine the meaning of the word "drugs"[*] ... to any definition of "drug" found in dictionaries or pharmacopoeias, would in our judgment be entirely too narrow. As Justice Hughes says, in Seven Cases v. U.S., 239 U.S. 517 (1916), "That false and fraudulent representations may be made with respect to the curative affect of substances is obvious," and when so made of water it seems to us it would be trifling to say that water ordinarily is not a drug in the true meaning of the word, and therefore does not fall within the condemnation of the third subdivision of section 8 of the act. If the allegations of the libel are true, the claimant has put the substance, water, in interstate commerce with the recommendation that it possesses certain elements or ingredients which are curative, or at least alleviative, for the diseases named in the label. He will not be heard now to say the substance recommended is water, and not a drug. Such a construction would nullify the act of Congress....

United States v. An Article...U.S. Fancy Pure Honey

218 F. Supp. 208 (E.D. Mich. 1963)

FREEMAN, District Judge.

---

[*] Editor's note: the statute at the time defined "drug" as follows: "all medicines and preparations recognized in the United States Pharmacopoeia or National Formulary for internal or external use, and any substance or mixture of substances intended to be used for the cure, mitigation, or prevention of disease of either man or other animals."

This matter is before the Court on a libel proceeding brought by the United States for the condemnation under §304(a) of the Federal Food, Drug and Cosmetic Act, of a quantity of allegedly misbranded honey, sold by the claimant, Detroit Vital Foods, Inc., at one of its stores located at 22,200 Grand River Avenue, Detroit, Michigan.

The parties have entered into a stipulation of facts which was presented to this Court on the day this case was orally argued. The essential facts are as follows. On October 12, 1961, Food and Drug Inspector, Gerald E. Vince, visited claimant's store and, posing as an ordinary or prospective customer, asked a clerk on duty whether they had any material about honey. In response to this request, the clerk pointed out a booklet entitled 'About Honey' by P. E. Norris and gave Inspector Vince a copy of a newspaper mailing piece containing an article entitled 'Eat Honey and Increase Your Vitality,' which was sent to the customers on claimant's mailing list.

On November 8, 1961, the government seized some 198 jars and tins of honey, along with six copies of the booklet by Norris and 71 copies of the newspaper-type mailing leaflet, which were the same articles that were pointed out and given to Inspector Vince. The seized honey, which had been shipped from other states and countries in interstate commerce, was located in the store on shelves displaying honey, jams, jellies, etc., along the wall to the right and left and in the center of the store, in a storeroom at the back of the main store premises, and in the hallway near the basement stairs. The six booklets 'About Honey', which sold at $ 1.00 per copy, were displayed with other books upon a fiber pegboard rack atop stock shelves containing honey along the wall on the right side of the store as one faces the back. The newspaper mailing pieces were located on a table in a small room in back of the cash register, which was located at the rear of the store and constituted a surplus of copies sent to claimant's customers.

The claimant makes no contention with respect to the medicinal and curative properties of honey for the prevention and treatment of diabetes, high blood pressure, arthritis, kidney and bladder ailments, nervous conditions, weakening of potency and virility, loss of appetite, heartburn, gastric catarrh, obesity, throat and bronchial ills, premature death, lack of vitality, gout, digestive upsets, sciatica, rheumatism, arteriosclerosis, weak heart, or for any medical purposes. The claimant did consent to the libelant's introducing into evidence affidavits of medical doctors attesting to the fact that honey is not adequate and effective for these purposes, waiving any right to cross-examination of the affiants.

Both the claimant and the libelant agree that in order for the latter to properly condemn the seized goods, it must establish that the honey was a drug and that the literature constituted labeling, as these terms are respectively defined by Title 21 U.S.C.A. § 321(g) and (m)....

Title 21 U.S.C.A. §321(g), defines a drug to include '...(2) articles intended for use in the diagnosis, cure, mitigation, treatment, or prevention of diseases in man or other animals.'

In determining that a particular article was intended to be used as a drug, a court is not limited to the labels on such article or to the labeling which accompanies it, but may look at all relevant sources. Therefore, in the present case, this Court may utilize the newspaper leaflet and the booklet, regardless of whether they constitute labeling under the Act, in order to determine whether the seized honey was intended to be used as a drug. A reading of the booklet and mailing leaflets results in the inescapable conclusion that such honey was intended to be used as a drug, since this literature makes the rather remarkable claim that honey is a panacea for various diseases and ailments that have plagued man from time immemorial. The fact that the seized honey is a food cannot take it out of the statutory definition of the word 'drug', since such honey was intended to be used in the capacity of a drug....

[The court goes on to hold that the seized literature constituted labeling within the meaning of the Act.]

Vitamins and Minerals as "Foods"

National Nutritional Foods Association v. Mathews

557 F.2d 325 (2d Cir. 1977)

ANDERSON, Circuit Judge.

Plaintiffs-appellants, producers and vendors of vitamin preparations, appeal the dismissal of their action seeking declaratory and injunctive relief against regulations promulgated by the Food and Drug Administration (FDA) which classified preparations of Vitamins A and D in excess of 10,000 IU (international units) per dosage unit and 400 IU per dosage unit, respectively, as "drugs" under §201(g)(1) of the Federal Food, Drug and Cosmetic Act, and which restricted them to prescription sale under §503(b)(1) of the Act. The district court upheld the regulations as not "arbitrary, capricious, an abuse of discretion or otherwise not in accordance with law" under the standard of review prescribed by 5 U.S.C. §706(2)(A)....

Acting under the rule-making power vested in the Secretary of Health, Education and Welfare, § 701(a) of the Act, 21 U.S.C. § 371(a), and delegated to the Commissioner of Food and Drugs (Commissioner), 21 C.F.R. § 2.120(a)(1), the latter, on December 14, 1972, announced his proposal to adopt regulations restricting the sale of Vitamins A and D in dosages exceeding 10,000 IU and 400 IU, respectively, to prescription sales. 37 Fed. Reg. 26618. Employing the notice-and-comment procedure of the Administrative Procedure Act, 5 U.S.C. § 553(c), the Commissioner solicited comments from interested persons concerning the proposed regulations. Over 2,500 written comments were received. On August 2, 1973, the Commissioner summarized the comments, answered the criticisms of the proposed regulations, and, upon determining that the regulations were in the public interest and should be adopted, ordered that they become effective on October 1, 1973. 38 Fed. Reg. 20723.

During the period when the proposed Vitamins A and D regulations were under consideration by the FDA, formal administrative hearings were held on proposed labeling statements and standards of identity for "Food for Special Dietary Uses." These regulations, covering the vast array of vitamin and mineral preparations, were adopted as parts 80 and 125 of 21 C.F.R. on August 2, 1973, 38 Fed. Reg. 20708-18, 20730-40, to become effective January 1, 1975. As part of the FDA's regulatory scheme for the sale of vitamin and mineral dietary supplements, the Commissioner promulgated new U.S. Recommended Daily Allowances for the vitamins and minerals considered essential to human nutrition and for which there was available scientific evidence to show the level of ingestion nutritionally necessary. 21 C.F.R. § 80.1(f)(1). The U.S. RDA upper limits for Vitamin A is 2,500 IU for children under four years of age, 5,000 IU for adults, and 8,000 IU for pregnant and lactating women. The upper limit for Vitamin D is 400 IU for all age groups. As part of the general Dietary Supplement regulations, the FDA determined that all preparations containing more than the upper limit of the U.S. RDA per serving for any vitamin or mineral on the list is a "drug," 21 C.F.R. § 125.1(h),[2] thus subjecting such products to the rigorous provisions of subchapter V of the Act. When the Commissioner promulgated the specific Vitamins A and D regulations, therefore, the levels restricted to prescrip-

[2] The regulations contained exceptions for conventional foods containing naturally-occurring amounts in excess of the U.S. RDA limits and for special dietary foods such as infant formulas.

tion sale under these regulations were already denominated "drugs" under the general Dietary Supplement regulations.

In *National Nutritional Foods Association v. Food & Drug Administration*, 504 F.2d 761 (2d Cir. 1974), this court, on a petition to review the general dietary supplement regulations under § 701(f) of the Act, 21 U.S.C. § 371(f), determined that the evidence supporting 21 C.F.R. § 125.1(h), classifying as "drugs" all vitamin and mineral preparations containing dosages in excess of the U.S. RDA's upper limits, was insufficient to bring such preparations within the statutory definition of "drug" in § 201(g) of the Act, 21 U.S.C. § 321(g)....

When the Commissioner adopted the Vitamins A and D regulations, he concluded that the available evidence showed that the U.S. RDA upper limits were adequate for all known nutritional needs; and, in view of the fact that there was no evidence to establish a food value or nutritional use for Vitamins A and D at higher levels, the ingestion of these vitamins at the regulated levels is "appropriate only for therapeutic uses and thus are properly classed as drugs." 38 Fed. Reg. 2073 (Aug. 2, 1973). The Commissioner based the drug classification for all vitamin and mineral preparations in excess of the U.S. RDA contained in 21 C.F.R. §125.1(h) solely upon lack of nutritional usefulness for most people. This court, however, held in the course of invalidating the general drug classification in [a separate rulemaking proceeding], that "demonstrated uselessness as a food for most people" is an insufficient basis upon which to establish a drug classification under §201(g)(1)(B) of the Act. National Nutritional Foods Association v. Food & Drug Administration, 504 F.2d 761 (2d Cir. 1974).[4]

---

[4] Since the decision in National Nutritional Foods Association v. Food & Drug Administration, 504 F.2d 761 (2d Cir. 1974), Congress enacted §411 of the Act, which provides, in relevant part, that except as provided in paragraph (2):

> (B) the Secretary may not classify any natural or synthetic vitamin or mineral (or combination thereof) as a drug solely because it exceeds the level of potency which the Secretary determines is nutritionally rational or useful.

Paragraph (2) renders paragraph (1) inapplicable when a vitamin or mineral is represented for use in the treatment of "specific diseases or disorders" or for use by children or pregnant or lactating women. This section elevates this court's holding in *National Nutritional Foods Association v. Food & Drug Administration*...to an affirmative statutory limitation upon the Commissioner's power to regulate vitamins as drugs and clearly retains "therapeutic intent" as the primary factor in drug classification under §201(g) of the Act.

...In proposing the Vitamin A and D regulations, ...the Commissioner indicated that an additional basis for the drug classification was the widespread promotion of the products for therapeutic uses....

...[T]he Commissioner determined that the circumstances surrounding the use of Vitamins A and D at the regulated levels indicated an intended therapeutic use under §201(g)(1)(B). The vendors' intent in selling the product to the public is the key element in this statutory definition.

In determining whether an article is a "drug" because of an intended therapeutic use, the FDA is not bound by the manufacturer's subjective claims of intent but can find actual therapeutic intent on the basis of objective evidence. Such intent also may be derived or inferred from labeling, promotional material, advertising, and "any other relevant source." See, e.g., United States v. An Article...Consisting of 216 Cartoned Bottles..."Sudden Change," 409 F.2d at 739. In remanding this case, this court expressly indicated that evidence that Vitamins A and D at the regulated levels were used "almost exclusively for therapeutic purposes" when coupled with lack of a recognized nutritional use, would be sufficient to show that high dosage Vitamins A and D products were intended for use in the treatment of disease.

In proposing the regulations, the Commissioner emphasized the potential for toxicity and the widespread promotion of the intake of high doses of Vitamins A and D to cure a variety of ills.[5] To show objective therapeutic intent, the Commissioner[]...relied upon three factors: (1) widespread promotion to the public in the use of high potency Vitamins A and D preparations for the treatment of various ailments; (2) lack of recognized nutritional usefulness; and (3) potential for toxicity from the ingestion of large doses of these vitamins over extended periods of time.

Potential for toxicity was cited in the statements of proposal and adoption of the regulations as supporting the limitation of high-dosage Vitamins A and D preparations to prescription sale in the interest of public safety.... [T]he Commissioner admitted that "in promulgating these regulations, concern over the public harm that could be done by these high potency therapeutic preparations weighed more heavily upon my mind than any other

---

[5] This court determined that there was ample evidence that Vitamins A and D can be toxic if consumed in large quantities over a period of time and, therefore, upheld the Commissioner's determination under §503(b) of the Act as not being arbitrary and capricious. To limit an article to prescription sale under §503(b), however, it must first be properly classified as a drug under §201(g) of the Act.

single factor[]." The Commissioner also indicated that evidence of toxicity was further objective evidence of therapeutic intent because it was unreasonable to believe that one could intend that a toxic product be used as a food.

Plaintiffs assert that toxicity is irrelevant to the issue of therapeutic intent and, although the key element in determining that a drug should be limited to prescription use under §503(b) of the Act, it has no bearing upon whether an article is a drug. The Government argues, on the other hand, that toxicity is relevant to therapeutic intent and that the Commissioner must make the decision of whether there should be a regulation which classifies an article as a food or as a drug, for the purposes of the Act. Although an article may be recognized as a food, this does not preclude it from being regulated as a drug. The determination that an article is properly regulated as a drug, however, is not left to the Commissioner's unbridled discretion to act to protect the public health but must be in accordance with the statutory definition. Toxicity is not included as an element in the statutory definition of a drug. It is relevant as a factor supporting the Commissioner's classification under §201(g)(1)(B), but only to the extent that it constitutes objective evidence of therapeutic intent. Toxicity is cited by the Commissioner as constituting objective evidence of "something more" than lack of nutritional usefulness in an attempt to distinguish the general drug classification invalidated in National Nutritional Foods Ass'n v. FDA, 504 F.2d at 789. Such evidence, however, only presents a further indication that the excessive intake of Vitamins A and D may not be nutritionally useful and does not provide the objective evidence of therapeutic intent necessary to support these regulations.

There is no evidence in the administrative record that the manufacturers and vendors of Vitamins A and D preparations, at the regulated dosages, represent through labeling, promotional materials, or advertising that these products are effective in the cure or treatment of disease. They are sold as "dietary supplements."

The district court dismissed the complaint on the ground that the record evidence of lack of nutritional usefulness, when coupled with the evidence of widespread promotion of high-dosage preparations of Vitamins A and D for therapeutic purposes, established that the drug classification was not arbitrary or capricious. The district court relied upon three sources for its determinations that there was widespread promotion of these products for therapeutic purposes: (1) the Commissioner's experience;[8] (2) the medical and popular literature in the record advocating the therapeutic use of these vitamins; and (3) the large number of comments to the proposed regulations which indicated a desire to continue using Vitamins A and D for therapeutic purposes. None of the promotions for therapeutic use in the record was attributed to the manufacturers or vendors.

The main issue on this appeal is whether the evidence of the extensive use of large doses of Vitamins A and D to treat or prevent diseases and the promotion of such usage by persons not associated with the manufacturers or vendors establishes such widespread therapeutic use at the regulated levels as to overcome the plaintiffs' claim of the lack of an intended use to cure or prevent disease and thus justifies the Commissioner's determination.

The Commissioner admits that below the stated levels of potency, Vitamins A and D are foods. The evidence relied upon to show therapeutic intent, therefore, must be related to the potency level chosen to differentiate between the use of Vitamins A and D as foods and the use of these vitamins as drugs. The administrative record clearly establishes that the factors involved in choosing the levels at which Vitamins A and D become drugs were solely related to the Commissioner's fear of potential toxic effect and his belief that the ingestion of vitamins at levels above the U.S. RDA is not nutritionally useful. No further record evidence has been produced on the remand to show that the 10,000 IU and 400 IU levels were chosen because at those potencies, consumption of them is almost exclusively for therapeutic purposes. A sampling of the comments submitted to the FDA after publication of the proposed regulations reveals that people believe that a wide range of doses of these vitamins are therapeutically useful. A large group of individuals indicated that they ingested these vitamins at various dosages solely to supplement their daily diet in the belief that more Vitamins A and

8 The FDA can rely upon its experience to support its regulations. When experience is relied upon to provide a factual basis for a regulation, it must be made part of the administrative record to enable effective judicial review. The Commissioner's experience relied upon in this case is a general awareness of the "numerous and widespread" therapeutic usages for high dosage Vitamins A and D preparations. This experience was not made part of the administrative record and, therefore, cannot provide factual support for the Commissioner's conclusion that Vitamins A and D preparations in dosage units of 10,000 IU and 400 IU, respectively, are objectively intended for therapeutic use.

D were needed to maintain optimal health than the upper limits in the U.S. RDA.

In remanding this case, this court suggested that proof in the record demonstrating that, at the 10,000 IU and 400 IU levels, respectively, these vitamins were taken "almost exclusively" for therapeutic purposes, would tend to show that the regulations were not arbitrary or capricious. There was no evidence, however, supporting the Commissioner's conclusion that, when sold at the regulated, *i.e.* prescription, levels, therapeutic usage of these vitamins so far outweighed their use as dietary supplements, it showed an objective intent that these products were used in the mitigation and cure of diseases. This claim furnished no contradiction to the charge that the FDA's regulations are arbitrary and capricious and not in accordance with law.

Moreover, the potency level chosen for drug classification was based upon factors that are not relevant to the statutory definition of a drug. Although the Commissioner's application of the statutory provision is to be given great weight, see, NLRB v. Hearst Publications, 322 U.S. 111, 130-32 (1944), the statutory provision at issue here strictly limits the FDA's authority to regulate items as drugs to those that fall within the specific provision of § 201(g)(1)(B). The drug definition is to be given a liberal interpretation in light of the remedial purposes of the legislation, see, United States v. An Article of Drug...Bacto-Unidisk, 394 U.S. 784, 792, 798 (1968), but when an FDA determination that an article is a "drug" is so directly in conflict with the statutory definition, it must be invalidated as arbitrary and capricious and not in accordance with law.

The Commissioner also seeks to justify the Vitamins A and D regulations on the basis of §201(g)(1)(A), which defines as drugs, articles "recognized" in the United States Pharmacopoeia (USP) or National Formulary (NF). Both Vitamins A and D are included in the USP and NF. The Eighteenth Revision of the USP, official from September 1, 1970, listed the usual daily dosage of Vitamin A for prophylactic uses at 5,000 U.S.P. vitamin A units[10] and for therapeutic uses at 25,000 U.S.P. vitamin A units. For Vitamin D, the respective daily dosages were 400 U.S.P. vitamin D units for prophylactic uses and 1,200 U.S.P. vitamin D units for therapeutic uses. Olive oil and salt are also included within the pages of these compendia. To construe §201(g)(1)(A) so as to grant the Commissioner the power to regu-

---

[10] The "U.S.P. units" in the United States Pharmacopoeia are treated by the FDA as substantially equivalent to the "international units" in the regulations for both Vitamins A and D.

late as drugs every item mentioned in the USP and NF solely on the basis of such inclusion would give the FDA virtually unlimited discretion to regulate as drugs a vast range of items. In National Nutritional Foods Ass'n v. FDA (504 F.2d 761), the court concluded that a claim that a vitamin is a drug solely because of a listing in the USP and NF "would prove too much, for it would lead to the conclusion that all vitamin and mineral preparations even within the [U.S. RDA] limits are drugs – a position that would run counter to the regulations." 504 F.2d at 789. An administrator's decision under a regulatory statute, such as the Food, Drug, and Cosmetic Act, must be governed by an intelligible statutory principle. If §201(g)(1)(A) defines as drugs every item included in the USP and NF, the FDA is not being consistent in its treatment of other items similarly recognized. The Commissioner, therefore, has not applied the §201(g)(1)(A) definition to every item in the compendia. Rather he has singled out for drug classification items included in the USP and NF on the basis of factors, such as toxicity in this case, that are not relevant to the statutory criteria in §201(g).

The Commissioner admitted...that mere inclusion in the USP and NF is an insufficient basis for drug classification after the decision in National Nutritional Foods Ass'n v. FDA (504 F.2d 761). He attempts to distinguish that case on the ground that Vitamins A and D are recognized at therapeutic dosages in the compendia and are regulated as drugs in this case only at levels in excess of the recognized food levels in the USP. Other articles, however, are recognized in the compendia at therapeutic levels and not regulated as drugs, for example Vitamin C. The Commissioner must, therefore, show that the conflicting treatment in the regulations of items similarly classified in the USP and NF is not arbitrary under the applicable criteria. The FDA regulates Vitamin C preparations at the USP's therapeutic level as food. To justify the regulation of Vitamins A and D as drugs by relying on §201(g)(1)(A) the Commissioner would have to distinguish his treatment of Vitamin C as food.

In proposing and adopting these regulations for Vitamins A and D, the Commissioner did not rely upon or cite the recognition of these vitamins in the USP and NF. He may not at this late hour on appeal rely upon them as the basis for his drug classification because it is sheer *post hoc* rationalization.

Inclusion in the USP or NF does not automatically establish that the classification of such an article as a drug is reasonable. To invoke the §201(g)(1)(A) definition as justifying a drug classification, the Commissioner must conform with the rule-making procedure and, through a clear exposition of his rationale, state the justification for his reliance upon recognition in the USP and NF.

The district court's dismissal of this action is reversed and the case is remanded with directions to enter an order granting summary judgment in plaintiffs' favor declaring 21 C.F.R. §§250.09 and 250.10 invalid as arbitrary and capricious and not in accordance with law.

The Common Sense of Food: Taste, Aroma, and Nutritive Value

Nutrilab, Inc. v. Schweiker

713 F.2d 335 (7th Cir. 1983)

CUMMINGS, Chief Judge.

Plaintiffs manufacture and market a product known as "starch blockers" which "block" the human body's digestion of starch as an aid in controlling weight. On July 1, 1982, the Food and Drug Administration ("FDA") classified starch blockers as "drugs" and requested that all such products be removed from the market until FDA approval was received. The next day plaintiffs filed two separate complaints in the district court seeking declaratory judgments that these products are foods under 21 U.S.C. §321(f) and not drugs under 21 U.S.C. §321(g). The cases were consolidated and the government counterclaimed for a temporary restraining order, which was denied. At the close of the hearing on the preliminary injunction, the parties stipulated to advancing the hearing as a trial on the merits. On October 5, 1982, the district court held that starch blockers were drugs under 21 U.S.C. §321(g), plaintiffs were permanently enjoined from manufacturing and distributing the products, and they were ordered to destroy existing inventories. The portion of the order requiring destruction of the products was stayed pending appeal.

The only issue on appeal is whether starch blockers are foods or drugs under the Federal Food, Drug, and Cosmetic Act. Starch blocker tablets and capsules consist of a protein which is extracted from a certain type of raw kidney bean. That particular protein functions as an alpha-amylase inhibitor; alpha-amylase is an enzyme produced by the body which is utilized in digesting starch. When starch blockers are ingested during a meal, the protein acts to prevent the alpha-amylase enzyme from acting, thus allowing the undigested starch to pass through the body and avoiding the calories that would be realized from its digestion.

Kidney beans, from which alpha-amylase inhibitor is derived, are dangerous if eaten raw. By August 1982, FDA had received seventy-five reports of adverse effects on people who had taken starch blockers, including complaints of gastro-intestinal distress such as bloating, nausea, abdominal pain, constipation and vomiting. Because plaintiffs consider starch blockers to be food, no testing as required to obtain FDA approval as a new drug has taken place. If starch blockers were drugs, the manufacturers would be required to file a new drug application pursuant to 21 U.S.C. §355 and remove the product from the marketplace until approved as a drug by the FDA.

The statutory scheme under the Food, Drug, and Cosmetic Act is a complicated one. Section 321(g)(1) provides that the term "drug" means

> ...(B) articles intended for use in the diagnosis, cure, mitigation, treatment, or prevention of disease in man or other animals; and (C) articles (other than food) intended to affect the structure or any function of the body of man or other animals; and (D) articles intended for use as a component of any article specified in clauses (A), (B), or (C) of this paragraph; but does not include devices or their components, parts, or accessories.

The term "food" as defined in Section 321(f) means

> (1) articles used for food or drink for man or other animals, (2) chewing gum, and (3) articles used for components of any such article.

Section 321(g)(1)(C) was added to the statute in 1938 to expand the definition of "drug." The amendment was necessary because certain articles intended by manufacturers to be used as drugs did not fit within the "disease" requirement of Section 321(g)(1)(B). Obesity in particular was not considered a disease. Thus "anti-fat remedies" marketed with claims of "slenderizing effects" had escaped regulation under the prior definition. See Food, Drugs, and Cosmetics: Hearings on S. 1944 before Subcomm. of Sen. Comm. on Commerce, 73d Cong., 2d Sess. 15-16 (1933) (Statement of Walter G. Campbell, Chief of FDA), reprinted in 1 Legislative History of Food, Drug and Cosmetic Act 105, 107-108 (hereinafter "L.H.F.D.C.A."). The purpose of part C in Section 321(g)(1) *supra* was "to make possible the regulation of a great many products that have been found on the market that cannot be alleged to be treatments for diseased conditions." Id.

It is well established that the definitions of food and drug are normally not mutually exclusive; an article that happens to be a food but is intended for use in the treatment of disease fits squarely within the drug definition in part B of Section 321(g)(1) and may be regulated as such. See, e.g., National Nutritional Foods Ass'n v. Mathews, 557 F.2d 325, 334 (2d Cir. 1977);

United States v. Hohensee, 243 F.2d 367 (3d Cir. 1957) (tea leaves); United States v. 250 Jars of United States Fancy Pure Honey, 218 F. Supp. 208, 211 (E. D. Mich. 1963). See also S. Rep. No. 493, 73d Cong., 2d Sess. 2 (1934) (provision providing that the definition of food, drug, and cosmetic not be construed as mutually exclusive was deleted because language was superfluous); S. Rep. No. 361, 74th Cong., 1st Sess. 4 (1935). Under part C of the statutory drug definition, however, "articles (other than food)" are expressly excluded from the drug definition (as are devices) in Section 321(g)(1). In order to decide if starch blockers are drugs under Section 321(g)(1)(C), therefore, we must decide if they are foods within the meaning of the part C "other than food" parenthetical exception to Section 321(g)(1)(C). And in order to decide the meaning of "food" in that parenthetical exception, we must first decide the meaning of "food" in Section 321(f).

Congress defined "food" in Section 321(f) as "articles used as food." This definition is not too helpful, but it does emphasize that "food" is to be defined in terms of its function as food, rather than in terms of its source, biochemical composition or ingestibility. Plaintiffs' argument that starch blockers are food because they are derived from food – kidney beans – is not convincing; if Congress intended food to mean articles derived from food it would have so specified. Indeed some articles that are derived from food are indisputably not food, such as caffeine and penicillin. In addition, all articles that are classed biochemically as proteins cannot be food either, because for example insulin, botulism toxin, human hair and influenza virus are proteins that are clearly not food.

Plaintiffs argue that 21 U.S.C. §343(j) specifying labeling requirements for food for special dietary uses indicates that Congress intended products offered for weight conditions to come within the statutory definition of "food." Plaintiffs misinterpret that statutory Section. It does not define food but merely requires that if a product is a food and purports to be for special dietary uses, its label must contain certain information to avoid being misbranded. If all products intended to affect underweight or overweight conditions were *per se* foods, no diet product could be regulated as a drug under Section 321(g)(1)(C), a result clearly contrary to the intent of Congress that "anti-fat remedies" and "slenderizers" qualify as drugs under that Section.

If defining food in terms of its source or defining it in terms of its biochemical composition is clearly wrong, defining food as articles intended by the manufacturer to be used as food is problematic. When Congress meant to define a drug in terms of its intended use, it explicitly incorporated that element into its statutory definition. For example, Section 321(g)(1)(B) defines drugs as articles "intended for use" in, among other things, the treatment of disease; Section 321(g)(1)(C) defines drugs as "articles (other than food) intended to affect the structure or any function of the body of man or other animals." The definition of food in Section 321(f) omits any reference to intent. But see United States v. Articles of Drug, No. CV74-L-136 (D. Neb. Sept. 1, 1976), where the court noted the intended use of the product in considering a defense that Zymaferm was a food. Further, a manufacturer cannot avoid the reach of the FDA by claiming that a product which looks like food and smells like food is not food because it was not intended for consumption. In United States v. Technical Egg Prods., Inc., 171 F. Supp. 326 (N.D. Ga. 1959), the defendant argued that the eggs at issue were not adulterated food under the Act because they were not intended to be eaten. The court held that there was a danger of their being diverted to food use and rejected defendant's argument.

Although it is easy to reject the proffered food definitions, it is difficult to arrive at a satisfactory one. In the absence of clearcut Congressional guidance, it is best to rely on statutory language and common sense. The statute evidently uses the word "food" in two different ways. The statutory definition of "food" in Section 321(f) is a term of art and is clearly intended to be broader than the common-sense definition of food, because the statutory definition of "food" also includes chewing gum and food additives. Food additives can be any substance the intended use of which results or may reasonably result in its becoming a component or otherwise affecting the characteristics of any food. See 21 U.S.C. §321(s). Paper food-packaging when containing polychlorinated biphenyls (PCB's), for example, is an adulterated food because the PCB's may migrate from the package to the food and thereby become a component of it. Natick Paperboard Corp. v. Weinberger, 525 F.2d 1103, 1106 (1st Cir. 1975). Yet the statutory definition of "food" also includes in Section 321(f)(1) the common-sense definition of food. When the statute defines "food" as "articles used for food," it means that the statutory definition of "food" includes articles used by people in the ordinary way most people use food – primarily for taste, aroma, or nutritive value. To hold as did the district court that articles used as food are articles used solely for taste, aroma or nutritive value is unduly restrictive since some products such as coffee or prune juice are undoubtedly food but may be consumed on occasion for reasons other than taste, aroma, or nutritive value.

Defining food as articles used primarily for taste, aroma, or nutritive value would not be contrary to National Nutritional Foods Ass'n v. FDA, 504 F.2d 761 (2d Cir. 1974). In that case, the FDA attempted to regulate as drugs all vitamin and mineral products in excess of the upper limits of the U.S. Recommended Daily Allowances ("RDA"). To bring these products within the Section 321(g)(1)(B) drug definition, the FDA had to show that the manufacturer's intended use was for treatment of a disease. Because the hearing record disclosed no food or nutrition use of nutrients at such high levels, the FDA inferred that the products were intended for therapeutic use. The court found first, that a significant number of persons have indisputable nutritional need for potencies exceeding the upper limits; and second, that to find actual therapeutic intent under part B of Section 321(g)(1) requires something more than evidence of uselessness as a food for most people. This holding does not invalidate a definition of food that is based in part on consumption for nutritive value.

This double use of the word "food" in Section 321(f) makes it difficult to interpret the parenthetical "other than food" exclusion in the Section 321(g)(1)(C) drug definition. As shown by that exclusion, Congress obviously meant a drug to be something "other than food," but was it referring to "food" as a term of art in the statutory sense or to foods in their ordinary meaning? Because all such foods are "intended to affect the structure or any function of the body of man or other animals" and would thus come within the part C drug definition, presumably Congress meant to exclude common-sense foods. Fortunately, it is not necessary to decide this question here because starch blockers are not food in either sense.* The tablets and pills at issue are not consumed primarily for taste, aroma, or nutritive value under Section 321(f)(1); in fact, as noted earlier, they are taken for their ability to block the digestion of food and aid in weight loss. In addition, starch blockers are not chewing gum under Section 321(f)(2) and are not components of food under Section 321(f)(3). To qualify as a drug under Section 321(g)(1)(C), the articles must not only be articles "other than food," but must also be "intended to affect the structure or any function of the body of man or other animals." Starch blockers indisputably satisfy this requirement

* The FDA urges an interpretation of the statute that would allow drug regulation of a product if, for example, an appetite suppressant were added to a recognized food. According to the FDA, addition of the drug might make it a "component" and therefore subject to regulation as a statutory "food". As such, the literal language of Section 321(g)(1)(C) would preclude regulation as a drug because the product would qualify as a statutory "food". Even if Section 321(g)(1)(C) meant only to exclude common-sense foods, an article might still be considered food unless addition of an appetite suppressant so changed its nature that it was no longer used primarily for taste, aroma or nutritional value. The FDA submits that a drug manufacturer could easily escape drug regulation by simply adding the drug to a food.

It is not necessary to resolve this problem in order to resolve this case. We merely note the possibility that the word "component" might be interpreted to exclude substances specifically added to a food to avoid bringing the substance within the drug definition, and, as noted above, a food may lose its food character if a drug is added.

for they are intended to affect digestion in the people who take them. Therefore, starch blockers are drugs under Section 321(g)(1)(C) of the Food, Drug, and Cosmetic Act.

Note

In *American Health Products Co. v. Hayes*, 574 F. Supp. 1498 (SDNY 1983), the court faced the same basic setting as in *Nutrilab*. There, though, the government argued that even a product that meets the common sense definition of "food" can be classified as a drug if the product is accompanied by a claim that the product affects the structure or function of the human body. The court rejected the government's claim that there could be dual classification (classification of a product as a food and as a drug) in this situation, reasoning that "[t]hough most sections of the Act countenance dual classification, no other contains a parenthetical like that Congress inserted in part (C). Ignoring that parenthetical would render meaningless the distinctions Congress has attempted to delineate." (Recall that section 321(g)(C) of the FDCA defines "drugs" to include "articles (other than food) intended to affect the structure or any function of the body of man or other animals.") The government nevertheless won the case, as it did in *Nutrilab*, because, the court explained, "the pills are not a 'food' in any sense cognizable under the statute...." The appeals court affirmed without reaching the issue of dual classification.

Under the FDCA as amended by the Dietary Supplement Health and Education Act of 1994 (DSHEA), products that fit within the new statutory definition for dietary supplements are classified as food even if they do not fit within a "common sense" understanding of food.

The following case involves the question whether the method of intake matters in determining whether an item is "food" within the meaning of the FDCA. Note that here we will have our first encounter with a legal principle common to all administrative regulatory regimes in the current period: the idea, associated with the Supreme Court's famous "Chevron" case, that an agency's interpretation a statute it administers is, if the statute is ambiguous, to be given deference by the courts so long as it is reasonable. The *Chevron* doctrine is under attack from a variety of directions at the moment, but for now it remains the dominant interpretive principle applied in judicial review of agencies' interpretive choices.

The Importance of Ingestion

United States v. Ten Cartons, More or Less, of an Article of Drug...Ener-B Nasal Gel

888 F. Supp. 381 (E.D.N.Y. 1995)

SPATT, District Judge:

BACKGROUND

The defendant markets Ener-B, which is intended to be applied to the inside of one's nose. As intended to be used, the vitamin B-12 contained in Ener-B bypasses digestion through the gastrointestinal tract, where it would be absorbed into the body through the intestines. Instead, Ener-B's vitamin B-12 is absorbed directly into the blood stream through the nasal mucosa.

On February 26, 1987, the FDA notified Nature's Bounty that the FDA considered Ener-B to be a "drug" under the FDCA, and that Ener-B was being marketed illegally because it had not received recognition or approval as a "new drug" under the Act. The FDA also alleged that Ener-B was misbranded and improperly labelled under the Act. The FDA's notice informed Nature's Bounty that the Act provided for the seizure of illegal products, and for an injunction against the distributor of such products.

Nature's Bounty responded to the FDA's letter, and on April 2, 1987 filed a Citizen Petition with the FDA pursuant to 21 C.F.R. § 10.30. In its petition Nature's Bounty essentially contended that Ener-B was a dietary supplement which was considered a "food" under the Act, and Ener-B's route of administration into the body bypassing digestion through the gastrointestinal tract did not reconstitute it as a "drug" under the Act. The petition requested (i) that the FDA establish and make public its policy regarding whether the method of ingestion of a substance otherwise classified as a food may make it a drug under the Act; (ii) promulgate a rule or guideline subject to notice and comment with respect to its policy; and (iii) refrain from taking any administrative or enforcement action against Ener-B in the absence of any policy delineated by a rule or guideline.

On May 24, 1988, the FDA denied Nature's Bounty's petition. As described in greater detail later in this Opinion, the FDA explained its denial on the grounds that it considered Ener-B to be a "drug" within the meaning of the Act because Ener-B affected the structure of the human body, and that Ener-B could not be a "food" within the meaning of the relevant statutory section because it was not ingested -- namely, it was not enterally administered into the gastrointestinal tract....

Subsequent to the denial of Nature's Bounty's Citizen Petition, the United States ("Government" or "plaintiff"), on behalf of the FDA, instituted an *in rem* proceeding against Ener-B pursuant to 21 U.S.C. § 334 on September 28, 1988, and seized ten cartons of Ener-B from Nature's Bounty. Approximately eighteen months later, on May 11, 1990, the Government brought a second action against Nature's Bounty *in personam,* pursuant to 21 U.S.C. § 332(a), seeking to permanently enjoin Nature's Bounty from selling Ener-B.

In October of 1991 the Government moved for summary judgment in its favor on the complaints in both of these cases....

FINDINGS AND CONCLUSIONS BY JUDGE ROSS

Judge Ross conducted a five-day evidentiary hearing.... Seven expert witnesses were called, three by the Government and four by the defendant.

Judge Ross found that the credible expert testimony offered at the hearing, by both the Government's and the defendant's experts, strongly supported the conclusion that the common sense and scientific definitions of "food" entail two elements: (i) nutrient intake, and (ii) ingestion into the gastrointestinal tract of such nutrients, also known as enteral administration of nutrients. According to Judge Ross, ingestion into the gastrointestinal tract was viewed as a necessary element of a food by the medical and scientific communities:

> [The] common sense and scientific definitions of "food...for man" that incorporate as a necessary element ingestion into the gastrointestinal tract are both reasonable and accepted by a substantial segment of the medical and scientific community. As evidenced by certain defense expert definitions, other respectable segments of the scientific community apparently adopt a more expansive definition that includes parenterally administered nutrients as well. This showing, however, does not impeach the evidence that a definition requiring enteral administration is reasonable and is also well accepted by credible scientists.

Report at 9-10.

Indeed, to highlight the point Judge Ross cited to the testimony of the defendant's expert Dr. Raymond R. Brown, retired Professor Emeritus at the University of Wisconsin Medical School, who acknowledged in his testimony that "whether Ener-B is drug is a question as to which reasonable scientists could reasonably disagree." Report at 12, 27 (citing Tr. at 545).

Judge Ross also found that the Government adduced substantial evidence through learned treatises and expert testimony regarding the different physiologies of the digestive and respiratory systems, including the mechanisms present in the gastrointestinal tract for the transport, storage and absorption of nutrients. This evidence was not disputed by the defendant's experts.

According to Judge Ross, the experts also agreed "virtually unanimously" that the mucosa lining the nasal cavity are functionally dissimilar to the membranes lining the gastrointestinal tract. As a result of this difference, Judge Ross found that both parties' experts acknowledged (1) "that parenteral administration bypasses the normal physiological safety mechanisms present in the gastrointestinal tract," and (2) that the route of exposure to the nutrients, namely whether absorption occurs through the nasal mucosa or through ingestion, has an impact on toxicity. Report at 11-12.

Based on these findings, Judge Ross concluded that the agency's determination that Ener-B is not a food based on its route of administration into the body is reasonable, and in accord with the Second Circuit's interpretation of the term "food" in the parenthetical exception to section 321(g)(1)(C); namely, that Congress intended the term to have "the everyday meaning of food." Report at 25 (citing *American Health Products v. Hayes,* 574 F. Supp. 1498, 1504 (S.D.N.Y. 1983) (construing the term "food" in the parenthetical exception to section 321(g)(1)(C) as having been intended by Congress to refer to its "common usage"), *aff'd,* 744 F.2d 913 (2d Cir. 1984))....

Based on her findings and conclusions, Judge Ross recommended that this Court (1) defer to the agency's determination that Ener-B is an unapproved "new drug" pursuant to 21 U.S.C. § 321(p), (2) that as such, Ener-B is subject to condemnation under 21 U.S.C. § 334, and (3) that Nature's Bounty be permanently enjoined from selling Ener-B, pursuant to 21 U.S.C. § 332....

DISCUSSION

...

In 1976, Congress amended the FDCA by enacting section 411 of the Act, 21 U.S.C. § 350, governing the regulation of vitamins and minerals. *See* Pub. L. 94-278, § 501(a), 90 Stat. 410 (1976), commonly known as the Proxmire Amendments. The underlying purpose of this amendment involves the promotion of concentrated vitamins to help supplement peoples' diets. Basically, section 350 precludes the FDA from regulating a vitamin or mineral solely on the basis of its potency or combination with another vitamin or mineral. The provisions of section 350 apply to certain vitamins or minerals which meet the definition in section 350(c) of a "food to which [section 350] applies." Up until the enactment of the DSHEA, Nature's

Bounty contended that Ener-B met the criteria set forth in section 350(c) of a "food to which [section 350] applies."

In order to further facilitate the use of vitamins and minerals to combat nutritional deficiencies and disease, portions of the FDCA, including section 350, were amended by the DSHEA in October, 1994. The basic purpose of the DSHEA amendments to the FDCA is to ensure that the public has over-the-counter access to "dietary supplements," which include vitamins, minerals, amino acids and herbs. In order to accomplish this, the DSHEA precludes the FDA from regulating "dietary supplements" as a "drug" under section 321(g)(1)(C) solely because of any statements on the products' labelling regarding claims that the product can treat or affect a nutritional deficiency or disease, unless the FDA determines that the product is not safe.

Following the enactment of the DSHEA amendments to sections 321(g) and 350, Nature's Bounty now contends that Ener-B is a "dietary supplement" as that term is defined in the DSHEA, and as such is excluded from regulation as a drug under the FDCA. The Court disagrees with both of Nature's Bounty's contentions, and believes that Ener-B is neither a food to which section 350 applies, nor a dietary supplement under the DSHEA.

A. Ener-B is Not a Food to which Section 350 Applies.

In order to be excluded from regulation as a "drug" under the provisions of sections 350(a) and (b) -- in other words, in order to be a "food to which this [section 350] applies" -- a product must, under the definition of that phrase in section 350(c) prior to the DSHEA amendments, be a "food for humans which is a food for special dietary use" which (A) is a vitamin or mineral, and (B) "which is (i) intended for ingestion in tablet, capsule, or liquid form, or (ii) if not intended for ingestion in such a form, does not simulate and is not represented as conventional food...[or] for use as a sole item of a meal or of a diet."

As explained earlier, Nature's Bounty contends that Ener-B meets the definition of a "food to which [section 350] applies," because Ener-B is a food for special dietary use which is a vitamin, and which, according to the defendant, is "not intended for ingestion" within the meaning of section 350(c)(1)(B)(ii).

While the defendant is correct to assert that Ener-B may be used for a "special dietary use" as that term is defined in section 350(c)(3)(B), namely "to supply a vitamin for use by man to supplement his [or her] diet," the defendant's contention that Ener-B is subject to the protection of section 350 ultimately fails, because the remaining requirements that are necessary for Ener-B to be a "food" to which section 350 applies are not met. Specifically, under section 350(c)(1)(B) Ener-B must be "intended for ingestion" either in a tablet, capsule or liquid form, or if not in that form, than it must be "intended for ingestion" in some other form. Ener-B however, is not intended for "ingestion" as that term is meant to be used in the statute. The defendant's construction of section 350(c)(1)(B)(ii) to apply to foods for special dietary use that are "not intended for ingestion" is erroneous, because it reads out of the statute the words "in such form."...

The ordinary and plain meaning of the term "ingestion" means to take into the stomach and gastrointestinal tract by means of enteral administration. *See* Stedman's Medical Dictionary (4th Lawyer's Ed. 1976) (defining ingestion as "the introduction of food and drink into the stomach."); Webster's Third New International Dictionary (1976) (defining ingestion as "the taking of material (as food) into the digestive system."). Two of Nature's Bounty's expert witness agreed with this definition. *See* testimony of Richard S. Litman, M.D., Tr. at 678 (agreeing that ingestion means to take into the gastrointestinal tract for absorption in the digestive system), and testimony of Dr. Edward James Calabrese, Tr. at 859-60 (agreeing that the standard meaning of ingestion is to take food into the gastrointestinal tract for processing and absorption)....

B. Ener-B is Not a Dietary Supplement.

The DSHEA defines a "dietary supplement" in relevant part, as follows:

> The term "dietary supplement" --
>
> (1) means a product (other than tobacco) intended to supplement the diet that bears or contains one or more of the following dietary ingredients:
>
> (A) a vitamin....
>
> (2) means a product that –
>
> (A)(i) is intended for ingestion in a form described in section 411(c)(1)(B)(i); or (ii) complies with section 411(c)(1)(B)(ii);
>
> (B) is not represented for use as a conventional food or as a sole item of a meal or the diet....
>
> Except for purposes of section 201(g) [21 U.S.C. § 321(g)], a dietary supplement shall be deemed to be a food within the meaning of this Act.
>
> DSHEA § 3(a) (codified at 21 U.S.C. § 321(ff)).

Further, section 3(a) of the DSHEA amends section 350(c)(1)(B) by enumerating several additional forms of ingestion applicable to the definition of a food to which section 350 applies. The amendment reads:

> FORM OF INGESTION. -- Section 411(c)(1)(B) [21 U.S.C. § 350(c)(1)(B)] is amended --
>
> (1) in clause (i) , by inserting "powder, softgel, gelcap," after "capsule,"; and
>
> (2) in clause (ii), by striking "does not simulate and".

As amended, the language of section 350(c)(1) that is relevant to this case now reads:

> The term "food to which this section applies" means a food for humans which is a food for special dietary use --
>
> (A) which is [a] vitamin..., and
>
> (B) which –(i) is intended for ingestion in tablet, capsule, powder, softgel, gelcap, or liquid form, or (ii) if not intended for ingestion in such a form, is not represented as conventional food and is not represented for use as a sole item of a meal or of a diet.

21 U.S.C. § 350(c)(1).

Thus, the definition of a "dietary supplement" in the DSHEA incorporates part of the definition of a "food" to which section 350 applies: namely, the part which provides that the vitamin must be a product that is (i) "intended for ingestion in tablet, capsule, powder, softgel, gelcap, or liquid form," or (ii) "if not intended for ingestion in such a form, is not represented as a conventional food and is not represented for use as a sole item of a meal or of a diet."

Accordingly, Ener-B cannot be a dietary supplement because, as shown earlier, Ener-B is not "intended for ingestion" and, therefore, does not meet the criteria of section 350(c)(1)(B)(i) or (ii). Nature's Bounty's contention that Ener-B is perforce excluded from regulation as a drug under section 321(g)(1)(C), because it is a dietary supplement that the DSHEA defines as a food not subject to regulation under section 321(g)(1)(C), is a tautology. In order to be outside the reach of section 321(g)(1)(C), Ener-B must first meet the definition of a "dietary supplement." It does not meet the definition, and unless Ener-B falls within the parenthetical exception in the statute -- which it does not -- the FDA can regulate Ener-B as a drug under section 321(g)(1)(C)....

The FDA's Determination that Ener-B is Not a Food is Reasonable.

Nature's Bounty contends that the FDA's determination that Ener-B is not a food is irrational and contrary to the holdings in *Nutrilab* and *Am. Health Prods.* Essentially, Nature's Bounty contends that (1) the ingestibility of an article was explicitly excluded by the *Nutrilab* court as a factor by which to determine whether a particular article is food, (2) the fact that Ener-B is not consistent with the traditional notion of a "food" does not preclude its being regulated as a food, and (3) the FDA's determination that Ener-B is not a food is irrational and arbitrary.

A. Ingestibility as a Factor.

In the Court's opinion, Nature's Bounty misinterprets the holding of *Nutrilab* with regard to ingestibility. In *Nutrilab,* the Court considered a challenge to the FDA's classification of starchblockers as a drug. The starchblockers at issue in that case were in tablet and capsule form and used to control weight by blocking the digestion of starch. *Id.,* 713 F.2d at 335-36. The district court construed section 321(f)(1) to mean that articles were used for food if they were solely used for taste, aroma or nutritive value. *Id.* at 338. The Seventh Circuit disagreed, and held that the district court's interpretation was unduly restrictive, since foods like prune juice and coffee could be used for reasons other than taste, aroma and nutritive value. Instead, the Seventh Circuit held that the common-sense definition of a food under section 321(f)(1) encompassed "articles used by people in the ordinary way most people use food -- *primarily* for taste, aroma, or nutritive value." *Id.* (emphasis supplied). (To these uses the Court would also add aphrodisiacal purposes).

In arriving at its decision, the Seventh Circuit rejected the industry's argument that starchblockers were food because they were derived from a food, namely kidney beans. The Seventh Circuit held that the congressional intent underlying the definition of food in section 321(f)(1) indicates that "'food' is to be defined in terms of its function as food, rather than in terms of its source, biochemical composition or ingestibility." *Id.* at 337. As an example, the court stated that although caffeine and penicillin are derived from foods, they are not foods. The *Nutrilab* court was, thus, emphasizing that neither an article's source nor its ingestibility can be the sole criterion for classifying it as a food.

However, stating that the ingestibility of an article cannot be the sole basis for classifying it as a food does not mean that an article's administration through a route other than ingestion cannot be a basis for determining that it is a non-food. The two propositions are exclusive. Moreover, this

Court does not read the Seventh Circuit's holding as excluding consideration of ingestibility as a *functional factor* when determining whether a particular article is a food. In the Court's view, ingestion has everything to do with the common place and everyday meaning of "food," and it is completely rational to use non-ingestion as a factor for determining that something is not as food. The mistake Nature's Bounty makes here is in contending that (1) the *Nutrilab* court's preclusion of ingestibility as a basis for determining whether an article is a food also precludes the converse, namely that non-ingestibility can be the basis for determining that an article is not a food, and (2) ingestion has nothing to do with the functional aspects of the everyday meaning of a food.

For these reasons -- and especially in light of the very clear holding in *Am. Health Prods.* that the term "food" in the parenthetical exception of section 321(g)(1)(C) refers to the term's common usage -- Nature's Bounty's contention that the FDA and Judge Ross erred in determining that Ener-B is not a food because it does not meet the traditional notion of a "food," is untenable.

Equally unconvincing is the defendant's contention that nasal administration of a vitamin is no more unusual than administration by capsules and tablets once was. Assuming that one day in the future administration of vitamins through the nose will be as common as the taking of vitamin capsules and tablets now is, the decision to expedite the process is not for the Court to make in the first instance by declaring that Ener-B is a "food." Rather, in this very nebulous area of the law where an article can be both a food and a drug, the Court believes that the decision is for the FDA to make in the first instance, as it is the agency containing specialized knowledge that is charged with administering the statutory provisions of the FDCA.

B. The FDA's Determination is Not Irrational.

The statutory language in sections 321(g)(1)(C) and 321(f)(1) regarding what is meant by the term "food" is ambiguous. Moreover, Congress has not directly addressed whether a nasal gel is a food, or whether route of administration of an article affects its classification as a food or drug. Accordingly, substantial deference to the FDA's interpretation of the statute is warranted, so long as its interpretation is based on a permissible construction of the statute....

Here, the FDA's determination that the term "food" in sections 321(g)(1)(C) and 321(f)(1) is to be interpreted according to the ordinary meaning of the term, and is to include foods that provide nutrition by enteral administration into the gastrointestinal tract -- in other words, that the food is ingested -- is a permissible construction of the statute: it reflects a plausible construction of the plain language of the statute, and does not conflict in any way with the limited Congressional intent that can be gleaned regarding sections 321(g)(1)(C) and 321(f)(1).

In addition to contending that the FDA has impermissibly used ingestion as a factor in determining that Ener-B is a not a food, Nature's Bounty makes two more claims in support of its contention that the FDA's determination is unreasonable. These are: (i) adopting the FDA's and Judge Ross's interpretation would render all dietary supplements in tablet and capsule form as drugs, because they are not "foods" in the common sense meaning of the term; and (ii) the FDA's interpretation of the word "food" is in direct contradiction to the agency's determination that nasal, esophagal and jejunal tubes used to feed people are "food," even though these methods cannot be considered "ingesting food" in the common, everyday meaning of the term.

The Court finds these contentions unconvincing. The first claim is rendered moot by the DSHEA, because under the DSHEA vitamins, minerals and other dietary supplements are expressly deemed to be a "food" within the meaning of the FDCA. *See* DSHEA § 3(a) (codified at 21 U.S.C. § 321(ff)). Moreover, in order to ensure that a dietary supplement is not regulated as a drug under section 321(g)(1)(C), the DSHEA amends section 321(g)(1) and related labelling provisions of the FDCA to expressly provide that a dietary supplement cannot be regulated as a drug under section 321(g)(1)(C) on the basis of any claims in its labelling regarding benefits related to a disease or the process by which the supplement affects the structure of the body, provided the claim is truthful and not misleading. *See* DSHEA §§ 6 and 10 (codified at 21 U.S.C. §§ 343(r)(6) and 321(g)(1)).

With regard to the second claim, the Court believes that the defendant is confusing different definitions of "food" under the FDCA. The FDCA establishes a separate category of "medical foods" in order to accommodate the enteral feeding and dietary management of people who are ill or injured. The definition of a "medical food" provides in relevant part: "the term medical food means a food which is formulated to be consumed or administered enterally under the supervision of a physician[.]" 21 U.S.C. § 360ee(b)(3). In the Court's view, there is no contradiction between Congress's special designation of a food that is formulated for enteral administration through devices such as nasal, esophagal or jejunal tubes to be a "medical food," and the FDA's determination that Ener-B is not a "food" because it is not "ingested." In the former case, Congress simply created a special category of "food," notwithstanding the unconventional method of delivery into the body, in order to serve a special medical purpose.

Moreover, the statute's premising of a "medical food" on enteral administration undercuts the defendant's contention that a parenterally administered nutrient like Ener-B should also be considered a "food." The regulatory interpretation of "medical food" makes it very clear that if the nutrient is not administered enterally, it is not a food: "parenteral nutrients...are drugs and not medical foods. By definition, medical foods are consumed or administered enterally." 56 Fed. Reg. 60377-78 (Nov. 27, 1991). *See also id.* ("enteral nutrition is defined as nutrition provided through the gastrointestinal tract, taken by mouth or provided through a tube[.]").

Accordingly, the FDA's determination that Ener-B is neither a "food" within the parenthetical exception of section 321(g)(1)(C) nor within the definition of that term in section 321(f)(1) is reasonable. Certainly, the FDA's determination is not "so directly in conflict with the statutory definition, [that] it must be invalidated as arbitrary and capricious and not in accordance with law." *Mathews,* 557 F.2d at 336. As a result, the Court determines that Judge Ross was correct in recommending that the Court defer to the FDA's determination and interpretation of the statute....

CONCLUSION AND ORDER

In the modern technocratic state where regulatory implementation and enforcement of scientifically technical and complex legislation is delegated to administrative agencies, the courts must beware of usurping the prerogative of Congress that permits the agencies in the first instance to interpret legislation concerning the subject matter of their expertise.

The issue raised by the present cases is novel, and has not been squarely addressed by Congress in either the language of the statute or in the deliberations of Congress prior to enacting the legislation. Deference to the FDA's interpretation of the statute is, thus, appropriate. Perhaps some day in the future, as Nature's Bounty predicts, society will cross a threshold where administration of vitamins via a nasal gel will be as commonplace as the taking of vitamin tablets is today. At that time, Congress and/or the FDA may wish to regulate Ener-B as a food or dietary supplement. However, until that time the Court believes it is not this Court's function to do so....

Accordingly, it is the determination of this Court that Ener-B is not a food, but rather is a drug within the meaning of 21 U.S.C. § 321(g)(1)(C). Moreover, Ener-B is a new drug within the meaning of 21 U.S.C. § 321(p) that is unapproved, and therefore subject to condemnation under 21 U.S.C. § 334....

Notes

1. The Second Circuit upheld the district court's judgment on appeal, in United States v. Ten Cartons, More or Less, of an Article...Ener-B Vitamin B-12, 72 F.3d 285 (2d Cir. 1995). The court found it unnecessary to decide whether Ener-B was a dietary supplement, as it determined that this decision would not be relevant to deciding whether Ener-B was a drug within the meaning of § 321(g)(1)(C). The court emphasized that section 321(g)(1) provides that a dietary supplement "is not a drug under clause (C) *solely* because the label or the labeling contains" certain "truthful and not misleading statements" regarding the supplement's benefits related to classical nutrient deficiency diseases. The court thought that "this language clearly implies that a dietary supplement can be a drug under § 321(g)(1)(C) for other reasons, such as its method of intake." The court also stressed that Congress had, in enacting DSHEA, rejected a provision that would have excluded dietary supplements from the definition of drugs.

2. Coco Loko is a snortable chocolate. Marketed as "raw cacao snuff," it contains cacao powder, which contains caffeine. Is it a food? Dietary supplement? Drug? Senator Schumer has urged FDA to investigate.

3. The next document for our consideration is a warning letter from the FDA to the maker of "Larry Larry" brownies. The FDA uses warning letters as one device for obtaining compliance with the FDCA. Warning letters are published on the FDA's website and thus may have consequences for a firm's reputation and financial standing even though they do not follow from a formal process of rulemaking or adjudication. They may be issued – pardon the pun – without warning.

Warning Letter

From Michael W. Roosevelt, Center for Food Safety and Applied Nutrition
To Terry Harris, Baked World, Memphis, Tenn.
July 28, 2011

Dear Mr. Harris:

The Food and Drug Administration (FDA) has reviewed the regulatory status of your product, "Lazy Larry" (formerly "Lazy Cakes"). Your "Lazy Larry" product is adulterated under section 402(a)(2)(C) of the Federal Food, Drug, and Cosmetic Act (FDCA) [21 U.S.C. § 342(a)(2)(C)] because it bears or contains an unsafe food additive. Specifically, it contains melatonin (5-methoxy-N-acetyltryptamine, CAS Reg. No. 73-31-4), which is a neurohormone and is an unapproved food additive under section 409 of the FDCA [21 U.S.C. § 348]. The regulations pertaining to the general provisions for food additives are located in Title 21, Code of Federal Regulations (21 CFR), Part 170. You can find copies of the FDCA and these regulations through links on FDA's home page at http://www.fda.gov.

Your "Lazy Larry" product is represented for use as a conventional food, and accordingly is not a dietary supplement, as defined under Section 201(ff) of the FDCA [21 U.S.C. § 321(ff)]. The FDCA excludes from the definition of a dietary supplement a product represented for use as a conventional food or as a sole item of a meal or the diet [21 U.S.C. § 321(ff)(2)(B)]. Your use of the term "dietary supplement" in the statement of identity and your use of a "Supplement Facts" panel for nutrition labeling do not make your product a dietary supplement, because your "Lazy Larry" product is represented for use as a conventional food. Examples of factors and information that establish that the product is represented as a conventional food are as follows:

- the product is marketed alongside snack foods;
- the name of a URL, www.mylazycakes.com (accessed 7-14-11), that directs people to your product website, refers to a conventional food (cake);
- the product is described on your website (accessed 7-14-11) as having "the same ingredients your mother uses to make brownies," which is a conventional food;
- the use of a combination of ingredients particular to a brownie (including sugar, flour, oil, cocoa, egg, and salt, in order of predominance by weight);
- the appearance and packaging of the product as a brownie.

As previously sold, your "Lazy Cakes" product additionally was represented for use as conventional food, for example, by the use of the words "cakes" in the product name and use of the word "brownie" in the statement of identity on the package label.

Any substance added to a conventional food, such as your "Lazy Larry" product must be used in accordance with a food additive regulation, unless the substance is the subject of a prior sanction or is generally recognized as safe (GRAS) among qualified experts for its use in foods [21 CFR 170.30(g)]. There is no food additive regulation that authorizes the use of melatonin. We are not aware of any information to indicate that melatonin is the subject of a prior sanction [see 21 CFR Part 181].... [W]e are not aware of any basis to conclude that melatonin is GRAS for use in conventional foods....

Melatonin is a neurohormone that is used for medicinal purposes, primarily as a sleep aid in the treatment of sleep-related disorders.... [R]eports in the scientific literature have raised safety concerns about the use of melatonin. Among these are concerns about effects on blood glucose homeostasis, and effects on the reproductive/developmental, cardiovascular, ocular and neurological systems. Therefore, the use of melatonin in your "Lazy Larry" product does not satisfy the criteria for GRAS status under 21 CFR 170.30.

FDA is not aware of any other exemption from the food additive definition that would apply to melatonin for use as an ingredient in a conventional food, such as your brownie product. Therefore, melatonin added to a conventional food is a food additive under section 201(s) of the FDCA [21 U.S.C § 321(s)] and is subject to the provisions of section 409 of the FDCA [21 U.S.C. § 348]. Under section 409, a food additive is deemed unsafe unless it is approved by FDA for its intended use prior to marketing. Melatonin is not approved for use in any food, including brownies. Therefore, your "Lazy Larry" product is adulterated within the meaning of section 402(a)(2)(C) of the FDCA [21 U.S.C. § 342(a)(2)(C)].

You should take prompt action to correct this violation and prevent its future recurrence. Failure to do so may result in enforcement action without further notice....

Notes

1. Lazy Larry brownies have been reborn as "Mellow Munchies," marketed as "relaxation products" and "chocolate supplement snacks." Their label says "not suitable for children," and advises: "Chill Out Dude." Are Mellow Munchies food?

2. In states that have legalized marijuana use, a burgeoning market in "edibles" has developed. State-law restrictions on sales in some respects mimic federal, FDCA-based restrictions. Rules implementing the Colorado Retail Marijuana Code, for example, require, for all retail marijuana products, an ingredient list (including a list of potential allergens), a statement regarding refrigeration (if necessary), a serving size statement, and a statement of expiration date.

Are marijuana-containing foods "food" within the meaning of the FDCA? Are they drugs? Dietary supplements?

3. Going back to the question posed at the outset of this chapter, is Soylent food? Put differently, does Soylent spell the end of food? Consider the following passage ("Rhinehart" is Rob Rhinehart, the co-founder CEO of the company that produces Soylent):

> Soylent has been heralded by the press as "the end of food," which is a somewhat bleak prospect. It conjures up visions of a world devoid of pizza parlors and taco stands – our kitchens stocked with beige powder instead of banana bread, our spaghetti nights and ice-cream socials replaced by evenings slipping sludge. But, Rhinehart says, that's not exactly his vision. "Most of people's meals are forgotten," he told me. He imagines that, in the future, "we'll see a separation between our meals for utility and function, and our meals for experience and socialization." Soylent isn't coming for our Sunday potlucks. It's coming for our frozen quesadillas.[3]

[3] Lizzie Widdicombe, *The End of Food*, THE NEW YORKER (May 12, 2014).

PART II
KNOWLEDGE

CHAPTER 3
PROHIBITIONS AGAINST FRAUD AND COMPELLED DISCLOSURES

One of the main purposes of the Food, Drug, and Cosmetic Act and other federal statutes relating to food is to facilitate knowledge on the part of consumers about the food they buy and eat. Indeed, a prominent prohibition in the FDCA is that against "misbranding," which not only proscribes "misleading" claims but also affirmatively requires the provision of certain, highly specific information on product labels. Likewise, the Meat Inspection Act of 1967 gives the Department of Agriculture the authority to prevent labeling that is false or misleading. Numerous other federal statutes contain the same basic requirement.

In this chapter, we first consider what makes for a "misleading" claim. We then turn to a discussion of the kind of consumer – careful? unthinking? skeptical? credulous? – protected by the FDCA and other federal statutes.

Food, Drug, and Cosmetic Act

21 U.S.C. §§ 343, 301

SEC. 403. MISBRANDED FOOD

A food shall be deemed to be misbranded—

(a) If

(1) its labeling is false or misleading in any particular...

(b) If it is offered for sale under the name of another food.

(c) If it is an imitation of another food, unless its label bears, in type of uniform size and prominence, the word "imitation" and, immediately thereafter, the name of the food imitated.

(d) If its container is so made, formed, or filled as to be misleading.

(e) If in package form unless it bears a label containing (1) the name and place of business of the manufacturer, packer, or distributor; and (2) an accurate statement of the quantity of the contents in terms of weight, measure, or numerical count, except that under clause (2) of this paragraph reasonable variations shall be permitted, and exemptions as to small packages shall be established, by regulations prescribed by the Secretary.

(f) If any word, statement, or other information required by or under authority of this Act to appear on the label or labeling is not prominently placed thereon with such conspicuousness (as compared with other words, statements, designs, or devices, in the labeling) and in such terms as to render it likely to be read and understood by the ordinary individual under customary conditions of purchase and use.

SEC. 201. DEFINITIONS

(n) If an article is alleged to be misbranded because the labeling or advertising is misleading, then in determining whether the labeling or advertising is misleading there shall be taken into account (among other things) not only representations made or suggested by statement, word, design, device, or any combination thereof, but also the extent to which the labeling or advertising fails to reveal facts material in the light of such representations or material with respect to consequences which may result from the use of the article to which the labeling or advertising relates under the conditions of use prescribed in the labeling or advertising thereof or under such conditions of use as are customary or usual.

Unites States v. An Article...Candy Lollipops

292 F.Supp. 839 (S.D.N.Y. 1968)

MANSFIELD, District Judge.

This is a libel for condemnation instituted under the Federal Food, Drug, and Cosmetic Act, 21 U.S.C.A. §334(a), on the ground that the article of food seized was misbranded when introduced into interstate commerce. The complaint for forfeiture alleges that the labeling of the article is false or misleading and that therefore the food is misbranded under 21 U.S.C.A. §343(a). Claimant, the owner of the goods, has admitted the jurisdiction of the Court over this matter, but denies that the article of food is misbranded. It also raises two affirmative defenses. The United States has moved for a judgment of condemnation on the pleadings pursuant to Rule 12(c), F.R.Civ.P. Since matters outside the pleadings have been presented to and not excluded by the Court, the motion pursuant to Rule 12(c) can and shall be treated as one for summary judgment under Rule 56, F.R.Civ.P.

The article of food in question consists of about 432 cartons each containing six lollipops. On the outside the carton is labeled on top "Candy...for one with Sophisticated Taste," on one side, "A. Freed Novelty, Inc.,

N.Y.C.," and on the other side, "Ingredients: Sugar, corn syrup, citric acid, natural and artificial flavors." The inside of the box contains the legend, "Liquor Flavored Lollypops," and the slogan, "Take Your Pick of a Liquor Stick." In addition the lollipops themselves are labeled, both in the box and on the cellophane in which they are individually wrapped, as "Scotch," "Bourbon," and "Gin."

The Government contends that the internal labeling is false or misleading in that it implies and represents that "the article is flavored with liquor, which it is not." In response claimant does not allege that the lollipops are flavored with liquor, but by way of affirmative defenses contends that they are not misbranded because the cartons are clearly labeled "candy" and the ingredients are distinctly set forth, and that the ordinary purchaser would not read or understand it to represent that the lollipops contain any alcohol or liquor.

In approaching the question of whether the labeling here was false and misleading within the meaning of the statute, we recognize that the statute does not provide for much flexibility in interpretation, since it requires only that the labeling be false or misleading "*in any particular.*" 21 U.S.C.A. §343(a). This represents a stricter substantive standard than that applied with respect to false advertising, which in order to be prohibited must be "misleading in a *material respect.*" 15 U.S.C.A. §55(a). Furthermore the statute says "false *or* misleading." For instance, the use of the term "fruit flavored" on a pudding product has been held after a trial on the merits to be false and misleading even though the product was manufactured from grain which, while botanically a fruit, was not a fruit in common parlance. United States v. 150 Cases of Fruit Puddine, 211 F. 360 (D.Mass.1914).

The issue of whether a label is false or misleading may not be resolved by fragmentizing it, or isolating statements claimed to be false from the label in its entirety, since such statements may not be deemed misleading when read in the light of the label as a whole. However, even though the actual ingredients are stated on the outside of a carton, false or misleading statements inside the carton may lead to the conclusion that the labeling is misleading, since a true statement will not necessarily cure or neutralize a false one contained in the label. Furthermore, the fact that purchasers of a product have not been misled, while admissible on the issue of whether the label is false or misleading, would not constitute a defense.

Applying these principles here, it cannot be concluded as a matter of law that no material issue exists with respect to the alleged false and misleading character of the label here before us. Although the labeling on the inside of each box of "candy," when read alone, might be misleading, the detailed description of the contents of the box listed on the outside of the carton could convince a jury, when the labeling or literature is read as a whole, that it is not "misleading in any particular," as that term is used in 21 U.S.C. §343(a)....

It appears that the Government, although it has not so indicated in its papers, may be concerned with some potential abuse in the distribution of this product that has not been drawn to the attention of this Court. If this is so, it would seem appropriate for this factual aspect of the case to be developed at trial rather than to grant a judgment on the pleadings in favor of the Government on the basis of a completely rigid reading of the words of the statute and a fragmentization of the labeling under attack here. The Government's motion for a judgment on the pleadings is therefore denied.

Federation of Homemakers v. Butz

466 F.2d 462 (D.C. Cir. 1972)

ROBB, Circuit Judge:

The appellee, Federation of Homemakers, brought this action in the district court to challenge a regulation promulgated by the Secretary of Agriculture, 9 C.F.R. §319.180. The regulation, prescribing the labeling to be employed on certain sausage products, permits frankfurters to be labeled "All Meat," "All Beef," "All Pork," or "All [species]"[4] as the case may be, although they contain, in addition to meat, 10 percent water and 5 percent other ingredients, including corn syrup, spice flavoring and curing additives. At the same time the regulation prohibits the use of the "All Meat" label on frankfurters containing binders and extenders,[5] such as dried milk, cereal or

---

[4] Species permitted under the regulation include beef, pork, veal, mutton, lamb, goat meat, chicken, or turkey, with limitations as prescribed therein. 9 C.F.R. §319.180. For convenience we will refer to the "All Meat" label throughout this opinion, although our holding applies to the various species labels as well.

[5] Binders include such products as dried milk and cereal, which are necessary in some production processes to provide the necessary cohesiveness to the frankfurter, although some companies have eliminated them through the development of new production techniques. Extenders include meat by-products mixed with the other ingredients of the frankfurter.

meat by-products aggregating not more than 3-1/2 percent of the ingredients of the frankfurters.

On cross motions for summary judgment the district court granted the plaintiff's motion, held the regulation invalid, and permanently enjoined the Secretary from enforcing the labeling policy which it embodied.[6]

The Secretary of Agriculture under the Meat Inspection Act of 1967, 21 U.S.C. §§601 et seq., may prescribe the labeling of meat or meat food products in order to avoid the use of a label which would be false or misleading to the consumer. 21 U.S.C. §607(d), (e). Pursuant to this authority, the Secretary promulgated the challenged regulation. That regulation establishes, among other things, standards governing the use of the "All Meat" label on frankfurters and other cooked or smoked sausage products. For purposes of this case the relevant parts of the regulation can be summarized as follows: Sausage products labeled "All Meat" may contain, in addition to meat, added water, corn syrup, salt, spices, and curing agents in designated quantities. The non-meat ingredients in "All Meat" sausages constitute approximately 15 percent of the finished product. Frankfurters which cannot be labeled "All Meat" differ from the "All Meat" variety in that they contain binders and extenders such as dried milk, cereal, or meat by-products. These added ingredients cannot constitute in the aggregate more than 3-1/2 percent of the total ingredients of the frankfurters. Thus, the only difference between "All Meat" frankfurters and other frankfurters is the existence of up to 3-1/2 percent binders and extenders in the latter; in all other respects the two products are subject to identical standards of composition under the applicable regulations.

The question presented here is whether the label "All Meat," applied to a product containing 85 percent meat, and employed to distinguish such products from those containing 3-1/2 percent binders and extenders and 81-1/2 percent meat, is false or misleading under 21 U.S.C. §607(d), which provides that:

> No article subject to this subchapter shall be sold or offered for sale by any person, firm, or corporation, in commerce, under any name or other marking or labeling which is false or misleading, or in any container of a mis-

---

[6] The complaint alleges that the Federation of Homemakers is a non-profit educational association of individual consumers, dedicated "to protecting the national integrity of food products and to assuring the food consumer informative and non-deceptive labeling." No question of the standing of the Federation has been raised by the government on appeal. The district court faced this issue and decided it in favor of the appellee....

> leading form or size, but established trade names and other marking and labeling and containers which are not false or misleading and which are approved by the Secretary are permitted.

If the "All Meat" label is false or misleading, the challenged regulation must be invalidated, for the Secretary's action in promulgating such a regulation would be in excess of his authority and "arbitrary, capricious, an abuse of discretion, or otherwise not in accordance with law." 5 U.S.C. §706(2)(A).

It is indisputable that the label "All Meat" as employed in this case is inaccurate. The words used are clear and unequivocal, and they import a description which cannot be attached to a product which is "Part Meat" or "All Meat, Water, Condiments, and Curing Agents." The fact is that frankfurters labeled "All Meat" are simply not all meat.

The Secretary points out, and it is conceded by the Federation, that because of technical limitations no frankfurter can contain more than 85 percent meat. Additional ingredients, such as condiments and water, are essential to supply the properties of taste and texture that are common to frankfurters and without which they would not be recognized as frankfurters. In other words, the Secretary says that by definition a frankfurter is a product containing not more than 85 percent meat. From this premise the Secretary argues that he reasonably determined that the term "all meat frankfurter" is not misleading when applied to a product having all the meat a frankfurter can technically contain.

If frankfurters containing 85 percent meat were the only kind known to man the Secretary's argument might be persuasive, particularly to one familiar with the niceties of frankfurter composition and production. Our difficulty is that there are other frankfurters, specifically those containing 81-1/2 percent meat and 3-1/2 percent binders and extenders; and the regulation forbids the use of the "All Meat" label on such frankfurters. We are thus confronted with the question whether there is a rational basis for the distinction in the labels that may be applied to the two types of frankfurters. If a frankfurter containing 85 percent meat may be labeled all meat, then why must a frankfurter containing 81-1/2 percent meat be denied that label? The Secretary answers in his brief that "...the 'all meat' label affirmatively has assisted the consumer in rapidly distinguishing such a frankfurter [the 85 percent meat frankfurter] from those which contain cereal, milk products or other ingredients which are neither meat nor processing agents essential to the manufacture of what is commonly accepted to be a frankfurter." We are not persuaded by the Secretary's argument.

The record discloses that in 1955 about one-third of the total frankfurter production in this country was of the "All Meat" type, the remaining two-thirds consisting of sausage with binders or extenders added. As of 1970, however, nearly 70 percent of the total sausage production was of the "All Meat" type. We think it plain from this that "All Meat" frankfurters are preferred by consumers. The "All Meat" label is therefore an indication that a frankfurter bearing it occupies a preferred status, or is at least considered to be in some way superior to a frankfurter not so labeled. The Secretary says that the element of superiority is the absence of extenders or binders in the "All Meat" frankfurter, and that the distinction is made plain by the "All Meat" label. Thus the issue presented by the Secretary's argument is whether there is a reasonable basis for his conclusion that the label "All Meat" conveys to an ordinary consumer the message that a frankfurter so labeled, while containing only 85 percent meat, does not contain cereal or milk products or other binders and extenders.

Do the words "All Meat" mean to an ordinary consumer, as distinguished from an expert, that a frankfurter in a package on which these words appear contains 85 percent meat and other components, and not 81-1/2 percent meat and other components? We think the answer to the question is plain, that the words do not convey that meaning and distinction, and that the Secretary could not reasonably conclude that they do. As employed, therefore, the "All Meat" label is misleading and deceptive.

The Secretary argues that the meaning of the words "All Meat" and the calculation of their effect upon a consumer are matters for him to determine in the exercise of his expert judgment. We must disagree, for the common meaning of the words is clear and unequivocal, and we find no basis in the record for the Secretary's conclusion that these words, in a label intended for the ordinary consumer, convey the kind of technical and esoteric message that the Secretary finds in them. Nor is the vice of the label cured by the accompanying language which identifies the processing agents contained in "All Meat" frankfurters. Few purchasers read such detailed specifications.

The Secretary relies upon Armour & Co. v. Freeman, 304 F.2d 404 (1962). In that case we held that a ham containing 10 percent added water was nevertheless a ham so that a regulation requiring it to be labeled "Imitation Ham" could not be sustained. The Secretary reasons that a frankfurter may still be an "All Meat" frankfurter notwithstanding a similar content of water. The argument misses the mark. We do not suggest that a frankfurter containing 85 percent meat, 10 percent water and 5 percent other ingredients is not a frankfurter; we hold only that the label "All Meat" is deceptive and misleading when used to distinguish such a frankfurter from one containing

81-1/2 percent meat, together with water, condiments, curing agents and binders and extenders.

The district court ordered the Secretary to discontinue the use of the "All Meat" label within six months.... [I]n the interim the Secretary should develop, prescribe and submit to the district court revised labels that accurately and without deception distinguish the different types of frankfurters from each other and from competitive meats.... [S]uch a revision would have made this litigation unnecessary. Accordingly...while the district court retains jurisdiction, the Secretary shall develop, prescribe and submit to the court such revised labels.

United States v. Farinella

558 F.2d 695 (7th Cir. 2009)

POSNER, Circuit Judge:

The defendant was convicted by a jury of wire fraud, and of introducing into interstate commerce a misbranded food with intent to defraud or mislead. The judge sentenced him to five years' probation (including six months of home confinement) and to pay a $75,000 fine and forfeit the net gain from the offense, which was in excess of $400,000. The government's cross-appeal challenges the sentence as too lenient. The defendant's appeal primarily argues that there was insufficient admissible evidence to convict him of misbranding....

The facts, stated as favorably to the government as the record permits, but without extraneous detail, are as follows. In May 2003 the defendant bought 1.6 million bottles of "Henri's Salad Dressing" from ACH Foods, which in turn had bought it from Unilever, the manufacturer. The label on each bottle said "best when purchased by" followed by a date, which had been picked by Unilever, ranging from January to June 2003. ACH had purchased Henri's Salad Dressing from Unilever when the "best when purchased by" date was approaching. The intention was to sell the salad dressing to consumers through discount outlets. The defendant accordingly resold the salad dressing he bought from ACH to "dollar stores," which are discount stores, but before doing so he pasted, over the part of the label that contains the "best when purchased by" date, on each bottle, a new label changing the date to May or July 2004. The government calls these the dates on which "the dressing would expire." That is itself false and misleading, and is part of a pattern of improper argumentation in this litigation that does no credit to the Justice Department. The usage echoes the indictment and was employed repeatedly by the prosecution at trial; in her opening argument the principal prosecutor said that "it's a case about taking nearly two million bottles of old, expired salad dressing and relabeling it with new expiration dates to pass it off as new and fresh . . . . [N]obody wants to eat foul, rancid food." The term "expiration date" (or "sell by" date, another date that the government's brief confuses with "best when purchased by" date) on a food product, unlike a "best when purchased by" date, has a generally understood meaning: it is the date after which you shouldn't eat the product. Salad dressing, however, or at least the type of salad dressing represented by Henri's, is what is called "shelf stable"; it has no expiration date....

It is important to understand what else this case does not involve, and also what is not in the record—the omissions are more interesting than the scanty contents of the government's threadbare case. There is no suggestion that selling salad dressing after the "best when purchased by" date endangers human health; so far as appears, Henri's Salad Dressing is edible a decade or more after it is manufactured. There is no evidence that the taste of any of the 1.6 million bottles of Henri's Salad Dressing sold by the defendant had deteriorated by the time of trial—four years after the latest original "best when purchased by" date—let alone by the latest relabeled "best when purchased by" date, which was 18 months after Unilever's original "best when purchased by" date. There is no evidence that any buyer of any of the 1.6 million bottles sold by the defendant has ever complained about the taste.

The term "misbranded food" is defined in some detail in 21 U.S.C. § 343, but there is nothing there about dates on labels, so that the defendant's conduct if illegal is so only if it can be said to be "false or misleading in any particular." § 343(a)(1). No regulation issued by the Food and Drug Administration, or, so far as we are informed, by the Federal Trade Commission or any other body, official or unofficial, defines "best when purchased by" or forbids a wholesaler (as here) or retailer to change the date. There is evidence that Unilever picked the "best when purchased by" dates on the basis of tests that it conducted, but the tests were not described at the trial and we do not know whether for example they are taste tests.

There is also and critically nothing in the record concerning consumers' understanding of the significance of "best when purchased by." Without evidence of that understanding, whether the defendant's redating was misleading cannot be determined. No consumer evidence was presented, whether as direct testimony or in survey form....

No evidence was presented that "best when purchased by" has a uniform meaning in the food industry. The government wants us to believe that it is a synonym for "expires on" but presented no evidence for this interpretation, and indeed argues the point by innuendo, simply by substituting in its brief, as in the indictment and in the prosecution's statements at the trial in the hearing of the jury, "expires on" for "best when purchased by."

The parties have found no previous case, either criminal or civil, and no administrative proceeding, in which alteration of the "best when purchased by" date was challenged as unlawful. As far as the evidence shows, any firm in the chain of production and distribution that leads from the manufacturer to the ultimate consumer can make its own judgment of when the taste of the product is likely to deteriorate. For all we know, the date is determined less by a judgment about taste than about concern with turnover. The manufacturer might want to affix an early "best when purchased by" date so that his distributors would be more inclined to repurchase the product within a reasonably short time, so that he has more sales. Admittedly, this is speculation, for while a date in the near future will increase turnover it will do so at the cost of making each bottle less likely to be sold at retail, and hence less valuable. Grocery stores pay less for bottles that are less likely to be sold. The cost of restocking shelves more frequently also would drive down the price to the manufacturer....

All this is speculation, but it is less implausible speculation than the government's that consumers think "best when purchased by" means "expires on," so that if they knew that the manufacturer's "best when purchased by" date had passed they would not dream of buying the product no matter how steeply it was discounted.

In mid-trial the government was permitted to call as an expert witness an employee of the Food and Drug Administration. He testified that the FDA has a database of inquiries regarding the relabeling of food products, that he had looked in the database, and that he had found no record of an inquiry from the defendant concerning the relabeling of salad dressing. The implication was that changing the "best when purchased by" date on a label requires the FDA's permission, and he added that the FDA requires supporting data before approving a request to change the date. This evidence, to which the defendant vociferously objected, should not have been admitted. If there is a requirement that the FDA's approval must be obtained before a "best when purchased by" date may be changed, it would, to be a lawful predicate of a criminal conviction, have to be found in some statute or regulation, or at least in some written interpretive guideline or opinion, and not just in the oral testimony of an agency employee. It is a denial of due process of law to convict a person of a crime because he violated some bureaucrat's secret understanding of the law. "The idea of secret laws is repugnant. People cannot comply with laws the existence of which is concealed." Torres v. INS, 144 F.3d 472, 474 (7th Cir. 1998)....

The testimony of the FDA's employee was not just improper and inadmissible but incoherent. He testified that he did not know what "the FDA say[s] about best when purchased by dates." When shown the "best when purchased by" date on a bottle and asked what it meant he said he did not know. He also said—contradicting his own testimony that altering the date is misbranding— that "the FDA doesn't have the authority to regulate expiration dates." Then he said that it did. He never explained the basis for either of his contradictory statements concerning his agency's authority.

The prosecutor told the judge that if there is a "best when purchased by" date on the label of a food product "and it's changed[,] that is a violation of the Food, Drug and Cosmetic Act." That is false.

The government is left to argue that any change on the label of a food product is misbranding, whatever consumers understand....

We do not suggest that a novel fraud can never be punished as a crime. But to prove a person guilty of having made a fraudulent representation, a jury must be given evidence about the meaning (unless obvious) of the representation claimed to be fraudulent, and that was not done here. We remind that one possible meaning of "best when purchased by" is that it is a guarantee by the seller that if purchased by then (and, presumably, eaten within a reasonable time afterward) it will taste as good as when it was first sold; if this is the meaning that consumers attach to the phrase, there was no misrepresentation.

Because the government presented insufficient evidence that the defendant engaged in misbranding, he is entitled to be acquitted. But since there was insufficient evidence, why did the jury convict? Perhaps because of a series of improper statements by prosecutor Juliet Sorensen in her rebuttal closing argument, for which the government in its brief (which she signed) belatedly apologizes (belatedly because the government defended the remarks emphatically in the district court)....

The prosecutor told the jury that the "best when purchased by" date "allows a manufacturer to trace the product if there is a consumer complaint, if there is illness, if there is a need to recall the product." The implication is that by altering the "best when purchased by" date the defendant had prevented the manufacturer from tracing the product in order to prevent it from causing illness. If that were true, the FDA presumably would require that the date not be altered, and it does not require that; in any event there was no evidence that a bottle of Henri's Salad Dressing consumed before or for that matter after the altered "best when purchased by" date could make anybody ill.

In like vein the prosecutor told the jury that if what the defendant "did was business as usual in the food industry, I suggest we stop going to the store right now and start growing our own food." That was a veiled reference to the nonexistent issue of safety, which she pressed further when she said that "in spite of all this talk about the quality of the dressing, I don't see them opening any of these bottles and taking a whiff." The implication, which has no basis in the evidence, was that the dressing in some of the bottles was rotten. She told the jury that the defendant was indifferent to "safety" and that "the harm caused by the fraud was to public confidence in the safety of the food supply." (The government repeats this in its brief; there is no basis in the evidence for the remark.) She also called the bottles of salad dressing "truckfulls of nasty, expired salad dressing," which was another groundless comment about quality and safety. She said that after the "expiration date" the salad dressing was no longer "fresh" and that the defendant had "had to convert the expired dressing into new, fresh product," a proposition that is not completely intelligible, but sounds ominous.

The government could have performed tests on the salad dressing to determine its freshness—perhaps the same tests that Unilever had performed. It did not do so, or, if it did, it did not present the results at trial. In her closing argument the prosecutor 14 times substituted "expiration date" or "expires" for "best when purchased by"—14 further improprieties, which grew to 20 in the government's main appeal brief by virtue of its using "sell-by date" as a synonym for "expiration date."

We asked the government's lawyer at argument what an appropriate sanction for the prosecutor's misconduct might be. We are not permitted to reverse a judgment on the basis of a lawyer's misconduct that would not have caused a reasonable jury to acquit, but in this case, had the government presented enough evidence to sustain a conviction, we would have reversed the judgment and ordered a new trial on the basis of the prosecutor's misconduct. That sanction is not available only because the government presented so little evidence that the defendant is entitled to an acquittal. That does not detract from the gravity of the prosecutor's misconduct and the need for an appropriate sanction. The government's appellate lawyer told us that the prosecutor's superior would give her a talking-to. We are not impressed by the suggestion.

Since we are directing an acquittal on all counts, the sentencing issues are academic and we do not address them, beyond expressing our surprise that the government would complain about the leniency of the sentence for a crime it had failed to prove.

Note

What sort of consumer is to be protected from being misled by labeling on products regulated by the FDA? The reasonable consumer? The gullible and credulous consumer? The following case arose in the context of determining whether a lotion called "Sudden Change" was a "drug" within the meaning of the FDCA due to the advertising claims its sellers made on its behalf. Thus the case does not arise in the context of food. Nevertheless, the decision provides some important insights into how courts have viewed the consumer the FDCA protects.

United States v. An Article...Sudden Change

409 F.2d 734 (2d Cir. 1969)

ANDERSON, Circuit Judge.

This is an appeal in a seizure action from an order of the United States District Court for the Eastern District of New York entered on July 30, 1968, denying the Government's motion for summary judgment and granting summary judgment for the claimant. The seizure concerned 216 bottles of a cosmetic product called "Sudden Change" which is a clear liquid lotion consisting primarily of two ingredients: bovine albumen (15%) and distilled water (over 84%). It is meant to be applied externally to the surface of the facial skin, and it is claimed, *inter alia*, in its labeling and advertising that it will provide a "Face Lift Without Surgery." The court below described the effects of the product as follows:

> Allowed to dry on the skin, it leaves a film which (1) masks imperfections, making the skin look smoother and (2) acts mechanically to smooth and firm the skin by tightening the surface. Both effects are temporary. There is apparently no absorption by, or changes in, skin tissue resulting from its applications; it washes off.

The central issue presented in this appeal is whether Sudden Change is, within the meaning of the Federal Food, Drug and Cosmetic Act, 21 U.S.C. §321(g)(1), a "drug." That Section, in pertinent part, provides: "The term 'drug' means...(C) articles (other than food) intended to affect the structure...of the body of man...." The question posed is whether, by reason of its labeling and promotional claims, Sudden Change is to be deemed a drug for purposes of the Act....

Claimant...contends that the article is solely a cosmetic which functions simply as a mask for facial lines and wrinkles and that the product's labeling claims were not understood otherwise by cosmetic consumers. It argues that the Government's construction of 21 U.S.C. §321(g)(1)(C) is so broad that every "cosmetic" would automatically be a "drug," since by definition a cosmetic must have some "effect" on the human body, even though that effect is only a change of appearance....

Claimant also filed a statement of claimed uncontested facts..., which admits, *inter alia*:...

The box in which Sudden Change is sold bears the capitalized words "SUDDEN CHANGE"..."THE PERFECTED ANTI-WRINKLE FACE LIFT." Another side of the box bears the following description:

> SUDDEN CHANGE by Lanolin Plus is the new and improved, dramatically different wrinkle-smoothing cosmetic. By simple, dynamic contraction, it lifts, firms, tones slack skin...smoothes out wrinkles, lifts the puffs under eyes, leaving your contours looking beautifully defined. It acts noticeably, visibly...and so quickly you will see and feel results minutes after you apply it. Not a hormone or chemical astringent, SUDDEN CHANGE is a concentrated purified natural protein, a clear invisible liquid cosmetic that can be used as often as you like.
>
> Because there never has been a cosmetic exactly like SUDDEN CHANGE before, we suggest you read the directions carefully before applying. For best results, use SUDDEN CHANGE often. The more you use, the longer your wrinkle-free look will last.

The face of the leaflet insert bears the following words, capitalized and displayed prominently: "FACE LIFT WITHOUT SURGERY" - "The Perfected Anti-Wrinkle Face Lift Acts in Minutes Lasts for Hours." It also repeats the descriptive material that appears on the box and contains directions for use.

The advertising claims for Sudden Change (newspaper, magazine, store placard, television) include the prominently displayed capitalized words "Now...a face lift without surgery!" together with "before" and "after" poses of a model and the following words:

> 'Sudden Change' - the new antiwrinkle face lift - works in minutes...lasts for hours...gives you a noticeably smoother younger look.
>
> Sudden Change is the one cosmetic that can make you look years younger for hours...although it cannot eliminate wrinkles permanently. Just smooth it on and watch it smooth away crowsfeet, laugh and frown lines - even under-eye puffiness. In minutes. Sudden Change helps keep fatigue lines,

> wrinkles and 'that tired look' away for hours. Sudden Change is pure natural protein – contains no hormones – does not change the structure or function of your skin in any way. Try Sudden Change. As long as you are using Sudden Change, you have nothing to lose but your wrinkles.
>
> 'Sudden Change' by Lanolin Plus $2.95 plus tax.

[T[he applicable section of the Federal Food, Drug and Cosmetic Act, §321(g)(1)(C), defines "drug" for purposes of the Act in pertinent part as follows:

> (g)(1) The term 'drug' means...(C) articles (other than food) intended to affect the structure...of the body of man....

It is clear that the fact that an article is a cosmetic does not preclude its being a drug for purposes of the Act.

It is well settled that the intended use of a product may be determined from its label, accompanying labeling, promotional material, advertising and any other relevant source. Regardless of the actual physical effect of a product, it will be deemed a drug for purposes of the Act where the labeling and promotional claims show intended uses that bring it within the drug definition. Thus, Congress has made a judgment that a product is subject to regulation as a drug if certain promotional claims are made for it.

The mere statement of this rule poses a crucial issue: by what standards are these claims to be evaluated? Or, to put it another way, what degree of sophistication or vulnerability is to be ascribed to the hypothetical potential consumer in order to understand how these claims are understood by the buying public? The District Court answered this question as follows:

> Such seller's claims [as that of "face lift without surgery"] must be considered in the special context of late twentieth century American mores. The labeling of Sudden Change is directed to women who are potential consumers of the article. Subjected to the incessant advertising campaigns of the cosmetic industry, a potential buyer can be expected to have achieved some immunity to the beautifiers' hyperbole.

And further:

> Against this background of constant exposure to puffing and extravagant claims, we cannot believe that a prospective purchaser of Sudden Change – faced with instructions advising her that she can repeat the process in a few hours – expects anything other than a possibility that she may look better. She would view the promise of 'face lift' with the same skepticism – or lack of it – as she would view other promises offering her beauty, loveliness, rejuvenation or a young look. She would not expect a structural change of the kind available through plastic surgery.

Although this analysis properly focuses on the relevant question by inquiring into the subjective understanding of potential consumers, it appears to us to hypothesize an unduly high level of sophistication and skepticism. A primary purpose of the Act is the protection of the ultimate consumer's economic interests. See Federal Security Administrator v. Quaker Oats Co., 318 U.S. 218, 230 (1943).[6] Considering the remedial purposes of the Act and particularly of the 1938 amendments, the Supreme Court declared:

> The purposes of this legislation thus touch phases of the lives and health of people which, in the circumstances of modern industrialism, are largely beyond self-protection. Regard for these purposes should infuse construction of the legislation if it is to be treated as a working instrument of government and not merely as a collection of English words.[7]

Accepting this admonition, we conclude that the purposes of the Act will best be effected by postulating a consuming public which includes "the ignorant, the unthinking and the credulous...." Florence Mfg. Co. v. J. C. Dowd & Co., 178 F. 73, 75 (2d Cir. 1910).[8] See, United States v. 62 Packag-

---

[6] The legislative history supports the view that both health and economic interests of the consumer were considered. Thus, S.Rep.No.361, 74 Cong., 1st Sess., indicates that Congress was concerned with "unscrupulous" persons "endangering the public health and defrauding the consumer." H.Rep. 2755, 74 Cong., 2d Sess., indicates that Congress was concerned with "abuses of the consumer's health and pocketbook...." Finally, Senator Copeland, a sponsor of the expansion of the definition of drug in the 1938 revision of the Act, stated that the former "narrow definition" permits the escape of preparations which are intended to alter the structure or some function of the body, as for example, preparations intended to reduce excessive weight. There are *many worthless* and some dangerous devices and preparations falling within these classifications. (Emphasis added.)

[Editor's Note: Before 1938, the definition of "drugs" included "any substance or mixture of substances intended to be used for the cure, mitigation or prevention of disease of either man or other animals"; the definition did not include substances intended to affect the structure or function of the human body.]

[7] United States v. Dotterweich, 320 U.S. 277, 280 (1943).

[8] The court was discussing likelihood of confusion of trademarks in an action alleging infringement and unfair competition. This Circuit subsequently extended this protective view of the consuming public to cases arising under the Federal Trade Commission Act. In Charles of the Ritz Dist. Corp. v. Federal Trade Commission, 143 F.2d 676, 679 (2d Cir. 1944), Judge Clark, speaking for the court of which the other members of the panel were Judge Learned Hand and Judge Swan, wrote:

es...Marmola, etc., 48 F. Supp. 878, 887 (W.D. Wis.1943). See also United States v. 250 Jars..."Cal's Tupelo Blossom U.S. Fancy Pure Honey," 344 F.2d 288, 289 (6th Cir. 1965), which held that "...the Act was passed to protect unwary customers in vital matters of health and, consequently, must be given a liberal construction to effectuate this high purpose, and [this court should] not open a loophole through which those who prey upon the weakness, gullibility, and superstition of human nature can escape the consequences of their actions."

While it is not altogether clear what standard the court below applied, the reasoning appears to assume something like a "reasonable woman" standard. Thus, the District Court assumes that the "constant exposure to puffing and extravagant claims" has induced "some immunity to the beautifiers' hyperbole" which is such that the court "cannot believe" that the potential consumer of Sudden Change "expects anything other than a possibility that she may look better." We agree that certain claims which arguably would bring the product within §321(g)(1)(C) have so drenched the potential consumer that even the "ignorant, the unthinking and the credulous" must be presumed able to discount their promises as typical of cosmetic advertising puffery. We cannot agree, however, with the conclusion that such immunity or skepticism somehow transfers to the promise to "lift out puffs" or give a "face lift without surgery." The references to "face lift" and "surgery" carry distinctly physiological connotations, suggesting, at least to the vulnerable consumer, that the product will "affect the structure...of the body..." in some way other than merely temporarily altering the appearance. We do not accept the concept that skepticism toward familiar claims necessarily entails skepticism toward unfamiliar claims; the theory of the legislation is that someone might take the claim literally.

> [The Federal Trade Commission Act] was not 'made for the protection of experts, but for the public – that vast multitude which includes the ignorant, the unthinking and the credulous,' Florence Mfg. Co. v. J. C. Dowd & Co., 2d Cir., 178 F. 73, 75; and the 'fact that a false statement may be obviously false to those who are trained and experienced does not change its character, nor take away its power to deceive others less experienced.' ...The important criterion is the net impression which the advertisement is likely to make upon the general populace.

We believe that the remedial purpose of the Federal Trade Commission Act is sufficiently analogous to that of the Federal Food, Drug and Cosmetics Act to justify the application of Judge Clark's reasoning to the case at bar.

In other words, with the exception of those claims which have become so associated with the familiar exaggerations of cosmetics advertising that virtually everyone can be presumed to be capable of discounting them as puffery, the question of whether a product is "intended to affect the structure...of the body of man..." is to be answered by considering, first, how the claim might be understood by the "ignorant, unthinking or credulous" consumer, and second, whether the claim as so understood may fairly be said to constitute a representation that the product will affect the structure of the body in some medical – or drug-type fashion, i.e., in some way other than merely "altering the appearance."

We hold, therefore, that so long as Sudden Change is claimed to give a "face lift without surgery" and to "lift out puffs" it is to be deemed a drug within the meaning of 21 U.S.C. §321(g)(1)(C). It should be understood, however, that if the claimant ceases to employ these promotional claims and avoids any others which may fairly be interpreted as claiming to affect the structure of the skin in some physiological, though temporary, way, then, assuming *arguendo* that no actual physical effect exists, the product will not be deemed a drug for purposes of the Act. While there may be merit in the cause of those who seek to require pretesting of new cosmetics, it is not for the courts to legislate such a requirement; rather it must rest in the hands of Congress to decide whether such an amendment to the statute should be enacted or not.

MANSFIELD, District Judge sitting by designation, dissenting.

...

Applying the basic standard that the advertising and labelling must be viewed as a whole, the product "Sudden Change" appears as nothing more than a superficial wrinkle smoothing cosmetic or beautifier intended to give the surface of a lady's skin a smoother or more attractive appearance for a few hours. Although the labelling refers to "Face Lift Without Surgery," it also prominently states in bold print that the product "lasts for hours." The advertising further emphasizes the temporary nature of the product's effect upon the skin by stating that it "wears off gradually," that it "does not change the structure or function of the skin in any way," that "it will not eliminate them [wrinkles] permanently," and that if the product is applied "several hours later...your skin is firmed and tightened again, and the more you use, the longer your wrinklefree look will last." The price is $2.95 per bottle.

I find it difficult to believe that any of the fairer sex, whether described as "gullible" or "reasonable," would be led by the description of the product in its entirety, including the puffery, to believe that it is anything more than another one of the many lotions, creams, oils or similar cosmetics which are claimed by vendors to "lift," "tone," "smooth" or "moisturize" the skin....

It may well be that the existence of fraud upon consumers of such products (whether drugs or cosmetics) should depend upon whether "the ignorant, the unthinking and credulous" would be deceived. The issue before us, however, is not whether consumers may be defrauded by the labelling and enclosures used in connection with the sale of "Sudden Change." The issue is whether the product must be classified as a "drug" which must be pretested, cleared and bear a label listing its components. Since that issue turns upon whether the article is "*intended* to affect the structure of the body" (emphasis added), it seems to me that the "gullible" woman standard is both irrelevant and unnecessary, and that the standard should be whether a reasonable person would construe the labelling and advertising as showing that the product was so intended....

Notes

1. In *Sudden Change*, the court invoked the "unthinking" consumer in determining whether the product in question was a drug or a cosmetic. The courts have also had to decide what standard to apply to claims that labeling is "misleading." Some courts have adopted the kind of standard embraced by the court in *Sudden Change* – protecting the ignorant, unthinking, and credulous consumer (see, e.g., United States v. El-O-Pathic Pharmacy, 192 F.2d 62, 75 (9th Cir. 1951)), while others have concluded that courts should have the "ordinary person" in mind when considering whether a label is misleading (see, e.g., United States v. 88 Cases, Bireley's Orange Beverage, 187 F.2d 967, 971 (3d Cir. 1951)).

2. *In its 1993 final regulations implementing the Nutrition Labeling and Education Act of 1990, the* FDA announced that it would regulate "implied health claims," and defined these as: "...those statements, symbols, vignettes, or other forms of communication that a manufacturer intends, or *would be likely to be understood*, to assert a direct beneficial relationship between the presence or level of any substance in the food and a disease or health-related condition." *Department of Health and Human Services, Food and Drug Administration,* Food Labeling; General Requirements for Health Claims for Food, Final Rule, *58 Fed. Reg. 2478, 2482 (Jan. 6, 1993) (emphasis added). In determining what constitutes an implied health claim, the FDA declined to adopt the "reasonable*

person" standard; that is, it declined to say that a health claim would be inferred only if a reasonable person would understand a statement to be asserting a direct beneficial relationship between the product and a disease or health-related condition. The agency noted that "courts have construed the act as protecting not just the reasonable person but also the "ignorant, the unthinking and the credulous." Id. at 2483, citing "Sudden Change," 409 F.2d at 741. Given this case law, FDA concluded, "it is unnecessary to look to the standard applied by FTC for guidance," a standard which one comment had described as applying the "reasonable consumer" test. 58 Fed. Reg. at 2483.

3. Without mentioning the rule just discussed, the following excerpt from an FDA guidance seeks to lay this issue to rest by adopting the "reasonable consumer" standard. Note that the agency now invokes the FTC's approach in adopting this standard.

Guidance for Industry: Qualified Health Claims in the Labeling of Conventional Foods and Dietary Supplements

U.S. Food and Drug Administration
Center for Food Safety and Applied Nutrition
Office of Nutritional Products, Labeling and Dietary Supplements
December 18, 2002

...

As FDA facilitates the provision of scientifically supported health information for food products, the agency must also increase its enforcement of the rules prohibiting unsubstantiated or otherwise misleading claims in food labeling. In assessing whether food labeling is misleading, FDA will use a "reasonable consumer" standard, as discussed below. Use of this standard will contribute to the rationalization of the legal and regulatory environment for food promotion, by making FDA's regulation of dietary supplement and conventional food labeling consistent with the FTC's regulation of advertising for these products.

The FTC's jurisdiction over food advertising derives from sections 5 and 12 of the FTC Act (15 USC 45 and 52), which broadly prohibit unfair or deceptive commercial acts or practices and specifically prohibit the dissemination of false advertisements for foods, drugs, medical devices, or cosmetics. The FTC has issued two policy statements, the Deception Policy Statement and the Statement on Advertising Substantiation, that articulate the basic elements of the deception analysis employed by the Commission in advertising cases. According to these policies, in identifying deception in an advertisement, the FTC considers the representation from the perspective of a consumer acting reasonably under the circumstances: "The test is whether the consumer's interpretation or reaction is reasonable."

FDA's general statutory authority to regulate food labeling derives from section 403(a)(1) of the Federal Food, Drug, and Cosmetic Act (FDCA or Act), which deems a food misbranded if its labeling is false or misleading "in any particular."[7] The FDCA contains similar provisions for drugs and medical devices (21 USC 352(a)) and cosmetics (21 USC 362(a)). In some cases, the courts have interpreted the FDCA to protect "the ignorant, the unthinking, and the credulous" consumer. See, e.g., United States v. El-O-Pathic Pharmacy, 192 F.2d 62, 75 (9th Cir. 1951); United States v. An Article of Food..."Manischewitz...Diet Thins," 377 F. Supp. 746, 749 (E.D.N.Y. 1974). In other cases, the courts have interpreted the Act to require evaluation of claims from the perspective of the ordinary person or reasonable consumer. See, e.g., United States v. 88 Cases, Bireley's Orange Beverage, 187 F.2d 967, 971 (3d Cir.). FDA believes that the latter standard is the appropriate standard to use in determining whether a claim in the labeling of a dietary supplement or conventional food is misleading.

The reasonable consumer standard is consistent with the FTC deception analysis, which means its use by FDA will contribute to the rationalization of the legal and regulatory environment for food promotion. The standard is also consistent with the governing First Amendment case law precluding the government from regulating the content of promotional communication so that it contains only information that will be appropriate for a vulnerable or unusually credulous audience. Cf. Bolger v. Youngs Drug Prods. Corp., 463 U.S. 60, 73-74 (1983) ("the government may not 'reduce the adult population...to reading only what is fit for children.'") (quoting Butler v. Michigan, 352 U.S. 380, 383 (1957)). Finally, the reasonable consumer standard more accurately reflects FDA's belief that consumers are active partners in their own health care who behave in health-promoting ways when they are given accurate health information.

---

[7] The FDCA does not require FDA to have survey evidence or other data before the agency is entitled to proceed under section 403(a)(1). FDA nevertheless recognizes that survey data and other evidence will be helpful in evaluating whether consumers are misled by a particular claim. For example, surveys, copy tests, and other reliable evidence of consumer interpretation can be helpful in assessing the particular message conveyed by a statement that FDA believes constitutes an implied claim.

Based on the FTC's success in policing the marketplace for misleading claims in food advertising, FDA believes that its own enforcement of the legal and regulatory requirements applicable to food labeling will not be adversely affected by use of the "reasonable consumer" standard in evaluating labeling for dietary supplements and conventional foods. Explicit FDA adoption of the reasonable consumer standard will rationalize the regulatory environment for food promotion while both protecting and enhancing the public health....

Notes

1. What is the standard now – the "unthinking consumer" or the "reasonable consumer"? In Chevron U.S.A. Inc. v. NRDC, 467 U.S. 837 (1984), the Supreme Court held that an agency's interpretation of an ambiguous statute is entitled to judicial deference so long as it is reasonable. Is the FDCA ambiguous on this point? Is FDA's latest interpretation reasonable? Note that the Court has also held than agency interpretation can receive *Chevron* deference even if the courts have previously interpreted the relevant statute differently from the agency's current interpretation – so long as the courts' prior decisions did not rest on a finding that the statute in question was unambiguous. Nat'l Cable & Telecomms. Ass'n v. Brand X Internet Servs., 125 S.Ct. 2688 (2005). Did the courts interpreting the FDCA to protect the "unthinking" consumer hold that the statute unambiguously required this result? Would it have been appropriate for them to so hold?

2. Claims that products are "all natural," "whole grain," "0 trans fat," or the like are increasingly subject to litigation. In November 2011, the FDA sent the following warning letter to a company that had labeled its products as "all natural" despite the presence of a synthetic preservative in them. The FDA offers one way to decide whether an "all natural" label is false or misleading – the presence of artificial or synthetic substances that would not normally be expected to be in the food in question. What else might you add to the considerations that might make such a label false or misleading? During the Obama administration, the FDA opened for public comment the question of how to define "natural" in food labeling. (In case you want to check it out, the docket for this proceeding is here: **https://www.regulations.gov/docket?D=FDA-2014-N-1207**.) If the FDA continues with this initiative in the present administration, what should it say?

Warning Letter

From U.S. Food and Drug Administration
To Alex Dziedusycki, Alexia Foods, Long Island City, N.Y.
November 16, 2011

Dear Mr. Dziedusycki:

The U.S. Food and Drug Administration (FDA) has reviewed the labels for your Alexia brand Roasted Red Potatoes & Baby Portabella Mushrooms products. Based on our review, we have concluded that these products are in violation of the Federal Food, Drug, and Cosmetic Act (the Act). You can find copies of the Act and the FDA regulations through links in FDA's home page at http://www.fda.gov.

Your Alexia brand Roasted Red Potatoes & Baby Portabella Mushrooms product is misbranded within the meaning of section 403(a)(1) of the Act [21 U.S.C. 343(a)(1)], which states that a food shall be deemed to be misbranded if its labeling is false or misleading in any particular. The phrase "All Natural" appears at the top of the principal display panel on the label. FDA considers use of the term "natural" on a food label to be truthful and non-misleading when "nothing artificial or synthetic...has been included in, or has been added to, a food that would not normally be expected to be in the food." [58 FR 2302, 2407, January 6, 1993.]

Your Alexia brand Roasted Red Potatoes & Baby Portabella Mushrooms product contains disodium dihydrogen pyrophosphate, which is a synthetic chemical preservative. Because your products contain this synthetic ingredient, the use of the claim "All Natural" on this product label is false and misleading, and therefore your product is misbranded under section 403(a)(1) of the Act.

We note that your Alexia brand products market a number of food products with the "All Natural" statement on the label. We recommend that you review all of your product labels to be consistent with our policy to avoid additional misbranding of your food products.

This letter is not intended to be an all-inclusive review of your products and their labeling. It is your responsibility to ensure that all of your products and labeling comply with the Act and its implementing regulations. You should take prompt action to correct the violations cited in this letter. Failure to do so may result in enforcement action without further notice. Such action may include, but is not limited to, seizure or injunction....

Compelled Disclosures: Food Ingredients

Beyond prohibiting fraudulent statements about food, federal statutes also compel numerous disclosures about our food. Next we turn to the provisions added to the FDCA by the Nutrition Labeling and Education Act (NLEA) of 1990. The most visible consequence of the NLEA is the nutrition facts panel, shown here and now ubiquitous in the food marketplace. The statutory provisions following the nutrition facts panel set out the requirements for the nutrition facts panel.

Nutrition Facts

Serving Size 1/2 cup (about 82g)
Servings Per Container 8

Amount Per Serving

Calories 200	Calories from Fat 130
	% Daily Value*
Total Fat 14g	**22%**
Saturated Fat 9g	**45%**
Trans Fat 0g	
Cholesterol 55mg	**18%**
Sodium 40mg	**2%**
Total Carbohydrate 17g	**6%**
Dietary Fiber 1g	**4%**
Sugars 14g	
Protein 3g	

Vitamin A 10% • Vitamin C 0%
Calcium 10% • Iron 6%

*Percent Daily Values are based on a 2,000 calorie diet. Your daily values may be higher or lower depending on your calorie needs:

	Calories:	2,000	2,500
Total Fat	Less than	65g	80g
Saturated Fat	Less than	20g	25g
Cholesterol	Less than	300mg	300 mg
Sodium	Less than	2,400mg	2,400mg
Total Carbohydrate		300g	375g
Dietary Fiber		25g	30g

Calories per gram:
Fat 9 • Carbohydrate 4 • Protein 4

Food, Drug, and Cosmetic Act

21 U.S.C. § 343

SEC. 403. MISBRANDED FOOD

A food shall be deemed to be misbranded—

(q) Nutrition Information

(1) Except as provided in subparagraphs (3), (4), and (5), if it is a food intended for human consumption and is offered for sale, unless its label or labeling bears nutrition information that provides—

(A)(i) the serving size which is an amount customarily consumed and which is expressed in a common household measure that is appropriate to the food, or (ii) if the use of the food is not typically expressed in a serving size, the common household unit of measure that expresses the serving size of the food,

(B) the number of servings or other units of measure per container,

(C) the total number of calories—

(i) derived from any source, and

(ii) derived from the total fat,

in each serving size or other unit of measure of the food,

(D) the amount of the following nutrients: Total fat, saturated fat, cholesterol, sodium, total carbohydrates, complex carbohydrates, sugars, dietary fiber, and total protein contained in each serving size or other unit of measure,

(E) any vitamin, mineral, or other nutrient required to be placed on the label and labeling of food under this Act before October 1, 1990, if the Secretary determines that such information will assist consumers in maintaining healthy dietary practices.

The Secretary may by regulation require any information required to be placed on the label or labeling by this subparagraph or subparagraph (2)(A) to be highlighted on the label or labeling by larger type, bold type, or contrasting color if the Secretary determines that such highlighting will assist consumers in maintaining healthy dietary practices....

(2)(A) If the Secretary determines that a nutrient other than a nutrient required by subparagraph (1)(C), (1)(D), or (1)(E) should be included in the label or labeling of food subject to subparagraph (1) for purposes of providing information regarding the nutritional value of such food that will assist consumers in maintaining healthy dietary practices, the Secretary may by regulation require that information relating to such additional nutrient be included in the label or labeling of such food.

(5)

(A) Subparagraphs (1), (2), (3), and (4) shall not apply to food—

(i) which is served in restaurants or other establishments in which food is served for immediate human consumption or which is sold for sale or use in such establishments,

(ii) which is processed and prepared primarily in a retail establishment, which is ready for human consumption, which is of the type described in subclause (i), and which is offered for sale to consumers but not for immediate human consumption in such establishment and which is not offered for sale outside such establishment....

(D) If a person offers food for sale and has annual gross sales made or business done in sales to consumers which is not more than $500,000 or has annual gross sales made or business done in sales of food to consumers which is not more than $50,000, the requirements of subparagraphs (1), (2), (3), and (4) shall not apply with respect to food sold by such person to consumers unless the label or labeling of food offered by such person provides nutrition information or makes a nutrition claim....

The Food Label

U.S. Food and Drug Administration
FDA Backgrounder, May 1999

Grocery store aisles are avenues to greater nutritional knowledge.

Under regulations from the Food and Drug Administration of the Department of Health and Human Services and the Food Safety and Inspection Service of the U.S. Department of Agriculture, the food label offers more complete, useful and accurate nutrition information than ever before.

With today's food labels, consumers get:

- nutrition information about almost every food in the grocery store
- distinctive, easy-to-read formats that enable consumers to more quickly find the information they need to make healthful food choices
- information on the amount per serving of saturated fat, cholesterol, dietary fiber, and other nutrients of major health concern
- nutrient reference values, expressed as % Daily Values, that help consumers see how a food fits into an overall daily diet
- uniform definitions for terms that describe a food's nutrient content--such as "light," "low-fat," and "high-fiber"--to ensure that such terms mean the same for any product on which they appear
- claims about the relationship between a nutrient or food and a disease or health-related condition, such as calcium and osteoporosis, and fat and cancer. These are helpful for people who are concerned about eating foods that may help keep them healthier longer.

- standardized serving sizes that make nutritional comparisons of similar products easier
- declaration of total percentage of juice in juice drinks. This enables consumers to know exactly how much juice is in a product.

NLEA

These and other changes are part of final rules published in the *Federal Register* in 1992 and 1993. FDA's rules implement the provisions of the Nutrition Labeling and Education Act of 1990 (NLEA), which, among other things, requires nutrition labeling for most foods (except meat and poultry) and authorizes the use of nutrient content claims and appropriate FDA-approved health claims....

Nutrition Information Panel

Under the label's "Nutrition Facts" panel, manufacturers are required to provide information on certain nutrients. The mandatory (underlined) and voluntary components and the order in which they must appear are:

- total calories
- calories from fat
- calories from saturated fat
- total fat
- saturated fat
- polyunsaturated fat
- monounsaturated fat
- cholesterol
- sodium
- potassium
- total carbohydrate
- dietary fiber
- soluble fiber
- insoluble fiber
- sugars
- sugar alcohol (for example, the sugar substitutes xylitol, mannitol and sorbitol)
- other carbohydrate (the difference between total carbohydrate and the sum of dietary fiber, sugars, and sugar alcohol if declared)
- protein
- vitamin A

- percent of vitamin A present as beta-carotene
- vitamin C
- calcium
- iron
- other essential vitamins and minerals

If a claim is made about any of the optional components, or if a food is fortified or enriched with any of them, nutrition information for these components becomes mandatory.

These mandatory and voluntary components are the only ones allowed on the Nutrition Facts panel. The listing of single amino acids, maltodextrin, calories from polyunsaturated fat, and calories from carbohydrates, for example, may not appear as part of the Nutrition Facts on the label.

The required nutrients were selected because they address today's health concerns. The order in which they must appear reflects the priority of current dietary recommendations.

Nutrition Panel Format

All nutrients must be declared as percentages of the Daily Values which are label reference values. The amount, in grams or milligrams, of macronutrients (such as fat, cholesterol, sodium, carbohydrates, and protein) are still listed to the immediate right of these nutrients. But, for the first time, a column headed "% Daily Value" appears on the far right side.

Declaring nutrients as a percentage of the Daily Values is intended to prevent misinterpretations that arise with quantitative values. For example, a food with 140 milligrams (mg) of sodium could be mistaken for a high-sodium food because 140 is a relatively large number. In actuality, however, that amount represents less than 6 percent of the Daily Value for sodium, which is 2,400 mg.

On the other hand, a food with 5 g of saturated fat could be construed as being low in that nutrient. In fact, that food would provide one-fourth the total Daily Value because 20 g is the Daily Value for saturated fat.

Nutrition Panel Footnote

The % Daily Value listing carries a footnote saying that the percentages are based on a 2,000-calorie diet. Some nutrition labels--at least those on larger packages--have these additional footnotes:

- a sentence noting that a person's individual nutrient goals are based on his or her calorie needs
- lists of the daily values for selected nutrients for a 2,000- and a 2,500-calorie diet.

An optional footnote for packages of any size is the number of calories per gram of fat (9), and carbohydrate and protein (4)....

Serving Sizes

The serving size remains the basis for reporting each food's nutrient content. However, unlike in the past, when the serving size was up to the discretion of the food manufacturer, serving sizes now are more uniform and reflect the amounts people actually eat. They also must be expressed in both common household and metric measures.

FDA allows as common household measures: the cup, tablespoon, teaspoon, piece, slice, fraction (such as "1/4 pizza"), and common household containers used to package food products (such as a jar or tray). Ounces may be used, but only if a common household unit is not applicable and an appropriate visual unit is given--for example, 1 oz (28g/about 1/2 pickle)....

NLEA defines serving size as the amount of food customarily eaten at one time. The serving sizes that appear on food labels are based on FDA-established lists of "Reference Amounts Customarily Consumed Per Eating Occasion."

These reference amounts, which are part of the regulations, are broken down into 139 FDA-regulated food product categories, including 11 groups of foods specially formulated or processed for infants or children under 4. They list the amounts of food customarily consumed per eating occasion for each category, based primarily on national food consumption surveys. FDA's list also gives the suggested label statement for serving size declaration. For example, the category "breads (excluding sweet quick type), rolls" has a reference amount of 50 g, and the appropriate label statement for sliced bread or roll is "___ piece(s) (__ g)" or, for unsliced bread, "2 oz (56 g/__ inch slice)."

The serving size of products that come in discrete units, such as cookies, candy bars, and sliced products, is the number of whole units that most closely approximates the reference amount. Cookies are an example. Under the "bakery products" category, cookies have a reference amount of 30 g. The household measure closest to that amount is the number of cookies that comes closest to weighing 30 g. Thus, the serving size on the label of a package of cookies in which each cookie weighs 13 g would read "2 cookies (26 g)."

If one unit weighs more than 50 percent but less than 200 percent of the reference amount, the serving size is one unit. For example, the reference amount for bread is 50 g; therefore, the label of a loaf of bread in which each slice weighs more than 25 g would state a serving size of one slice.

Certain rules apply to food products that are packaged and sold individually. If such an individual package is less than 200 percent of the applicable reference amount, the item qualifies as one serving. Thus, a 360-mL (12-fluid-ounce) can of soda is one serving, since the reference amount for carbonated beverages is 240 mL (8 ounces).

However, if the product has a reference amount of 100 g or 100 mL or more and the package contains more than 150 percent but less than 200 percent of the reference amount, manufacturers have the option of deciding whether the product can be one or two servings.

An example is a 15-ounce (420 g) can of soup. The serving size reference amount for soup is 245 g. Therefore, the manufacturer has the option to declare the can of soup as one or two servings.

Daily Values--DRVs

The new label reference value, Daily Value, comprises two sets of dietary standards: Daily Reference Values (DRVs) and Reference Daily Intakes (RDIs). Only the Daily Value term appears on the label, though, to make label reading less confusing.

DRVs have been established for macronutrients that are sources of energy: fat, saturated fat, total carbohydrate (including fiber), and protein; and for cholesterol, sodium and potassium, which do not contribute calories.

DRVs for the energy-producing nutrients are based on the number of calories consumed per day. A daily intake of 2,000 calories has been established as the reference. This level was chosen, in part, because it approximates the caloric requirements for postmenopausal women. This group has the highest risk for excessive intake of calories and fat.

DRVs for the energy-producing nutrients are calculated as follows:

- fat based on 30 percent of calories
- saturated fat based on 10 percent of calories
- carbohydrate based on 60 percent of calories
- protein based on 10 percent of calories. (The DRV for protein applies only to adults and children over 4. RDIs for protein for special groups have been established.)
- fiber based on 11.5 g of fiber per 1,000 calories.

Because of current public health recommendations, DRVs for some nutrients represent the uppermost limit that is considered desirable. The DRVs for total fat, saturated fat, cholesterol, and sodium are:

- total fat: less than 65 g
- saturated fat: less than 20 g
- cholesterol: less than 300 mg
- sodium: less than 2,400 mg

Daily Values--RDIs

"Reference Daily Intake" replaces the term "U.S. RDA," which was introduced in 1973 as a label reference value for vitamins, minerals and protein in voluntary nutrition labeling. The name change was sought because of confusion that existed over "U.S. RDAs," the values determined by FDA and used on food labels, and "RDAs" (Recommended Dietary Allowances), the values determined by the National Academy of Sciences for various population groups and used by FDA to figure the U.S. RDAs.

However, the values for the new RDIs remain the same as the old U.S. RDAs for the time being.

Notes

1. In 2016, the FDA finalized revisions to the nutrition facts panel. (If you are interested in seeing the details, they are here: **http://www.fda.gov/Food/GuidanceRegulation/GuidanceDocumentsRegulatoryInformation/LabelingNutrition/ucm385663.htm**.) Among the FDA's major revisions are the addition of a separate line on "added sugars," a new requirement to declare the amount of potassium and Vitamin D in food products, updated serving size requirements to reflect more realistically the amount people actually eat in one sitting (e.g., no one eats only half a cup of ice cream...), and a "refreshed" design for the whole nutrition facts label. In 2017, the Trump administration extended the compliance date for this rule while it reconsiders it.

2. Are there other revisions you would make to the nutrition facts panel? What more would you like to know about your food? How helpful do you think the "added sugars" line would be? Critics have charged that there is no chemical difference between natural and added sugars. Proponents have asserted that it makes sense to disclose to consumers how much "unnecessary" sugar – and calories – they are getting in the foods they buy. What do you think?

Letter

From John D. Graham, Administrator, Office of Information and Regulatory Affairs
To Hon. Tommy G. Thompson, Secretary of Health and Human Services
September 18, 2001

Dear Mr. Secretary:

The purpose of this letter is to request that the Department of Health and Human Services and the Food and Drug Administration (FDA) consider giving greater priority to an existing rulemaking concerning the *trans* fatty acid content of foods. There is a growing body of scientific evidence, both experimental and epidemiological, suggesting that consumption of *trans* fatty acids in foods increases the consumer's risk of developing coronary heart disease (CHD). We refer to evidence published in quality medical journals such as LANCET, ARTERIOSCLEROSIS, THROMBOSIS, AND VASCULAR BIOLOGY, CIRCULATION, and THE NEW ENGLAND JOURNAL OF MEDICINE. We encourage FDA to review carefully the public comments on its 1999 proposed rulemaking concerning consumer labeling of trans fatty acids and, if appropriate, proceed to a final rulemaking.

As you know, on November 17, 1999, FDA published a proposed rule entitled "Food Labeling: Trans Fatty Acids in Nutrition Labeling, Nutrient Content Claims, and Health Claims." The rule would amend the current nutrition labeling regulations by requiring the amount of *trans* fatty acids present in food to be included in the product's Nutrition Facts panel. The proposal also would create a new nutrient content claim defining "*trans* fat free" and require a limit on *trans* fatty acids whenever there are limits on saturated fat in nutrient content claims or health claims. The proposal was mainly based on studies that indicate that consumption of *trans* fatty acids contributes to increased blood LDL-cholesterol levels, which increase the risk of CHD. As indicated above, recent studies have strengthened that conclusion and shown that *trans* fatty acids may also work through other mechanisms to increase the risk of CHD.

Based on assumptions that the proposal will assist consumers in their efforts to reduce their risk of CHD and provide incentives to producers to reformulate food products to reduce the trans fat content, FDA's preliminary Regulatory Impact Analysis estimated that, 10 years after the effective date, the rule would prevent 7,600 to 17,100 cases of CHD and avert 2,500 to 5,600 deaths per year. Over a 20-year period, FDA estimated the benefits of the proposed rule would range from $25 to $59 billion, while the costs were only $400 million to $850 million.

In light of these estimates and the recent scientific findings, OMB believes there may be an opportunity here to pursue cost-effective rulemaking that provides significant net benefits to the American people. At the time OMB reviewed the proposed rule, OMB was impressed with the magnitude of the potential net benefits estimated by the underlying analysis. We understand that FDA has gathered additional information from the public as part of the public comment period, and that FDA is in the process of drafting a final rule in response to the comments received. If the regulatory impact analysis still suggests that the potential benefits of this rule far exceed the costs, then I strongly encourage you to finalize this rule or explain the rationale for not moving it forward. This rulemaking appears to be a tremendous opportunity for the FDA to address the nation's leading cause of death – coronary heart disease – and to save thousands of lives.

If you should decide to submit a draft final rule to OMB for review, we will conduct a rigorous, careful, and expeditious review. Prior to the review, my staff is eager to work with you to ensure the best possible rule and supporting analysis. At your earliest convenience, my staff would like to meet with FDA's staff to discuss the comments FDA received on the proposal and the agency's current thinking on how it plans to proceed.

Final Rule: Food Labeling: Trans Fatty Acids in Nutrition Labeling, Nutrient Content Claims, and Health Claims

Department of Health and Human Services (HHS)
Food and Drug Administration (FDA)
68 Fed. Reg. 41434
July 11, 2003

SUMMARY: The Food and Drug Administration (FDA) is amending its regulations on nutrition labeling to require that *trans* fatty acids be declared in the nutrition label of conventional foods and dietary supplements on a separate line immediately under the line for the declaration of saturated fatty acids. This action responds, in part, to a citizen petition from the Center for Science in the Public Interest (CSPI). This rule is intended to provide information to assist consumers in maintaining healthy dietary practices. Those sections of the proposed rule pertaining to the definition of nutrient content claims for the "free" level of *trans* fatty acids and to limits on the amounts of *trans* fatty acids wherever saturated fatty acid limits are placed on nutrient content claims, health claims, and disclosure and disqualifying levels are being withdrawn. Further, the agency is withdrawing the proposed requirement to include a footnote stating: "Intake of *trans* fat should be as low as possible." Issues related to the possible use of a footnote statement in conjunction with the *trans* fat label declaration or in the context of certain nutrient content and health claims that contain messages about cholesterol-raising fats in the diet are now the subject of an advance notice of proposed rulemaking (ANPRM) which is published elsewhere in this issue of the Federal Register.

II. Highlights of the Final Rule

In this final rule and given the current state of scientific knowledge, FDA is requiring the mandatory declaration in the nutrition label of the amount of *trans* fatty acids present in foods, including dietary supplements. The declaration of this nutrient must be on a separate line immediately under the declaration for saturated fat but it will not include a %DV that is required for some of the other mandatory nutrients, such as saturated fat. ... [T] he agency is withdrawing the proposed requirement to include a footnote stating: "Intake of *trans* fat should be as low as possible."...

III. Legal Authority

...

FDA believes it has adequate authority to adopt this rule. FDA's authority under the act to require *trans* fat labeling includes sections 201(n), 403(a)(1) and (q), and 701(a) of the act. FDA has authority under section 701(a) of the act to issue regulations for the efficient enforcement of the act. FDA can require labeling of certain facts that are material in light of representations made in the labeling or with respect to consequences which may result from the use of the article in order for a product not to be misbranded under sections 201(n) and 403(a) of the act. Further, under section 403(q)(2)(A) of the act, the Secretary (and FDA, by delegation) may require that information relating to a nutrient be in the labeling of food for the purpose of "providing information regarding the nutritional value of such food that will assist consumers in maintaining healthy dietary practices."

The agency believes that the data in the record supports mandatory *trans* fat labeling to ensure that consumers are not misled and are adequately informed about the product's attributes. Accordingly, FDA believes that mandatory *trans* fat labeling is necessary for foods not to be misbranded under section 403(a) of the act. The absence of information about the content of *trans* fat in foods that are subject to mandatory labeling would constitute an omission of a material fact under section 201(n) of the act.

Under the act, the agency has the mandate to ensure that labeling provides truthful and nonmisleading information to consumers. Thus, the law provides the agency with authority to require specific label statements when needed for reasons other than to ensure the safe use of food. Under section 403(a)(1) of the act, a food is misbranded if its labeling is false or misleading in any particular. Section 201(n) of the act amplifies what is meant by "misleading" in section 403(a)(1) of the act. Section 201(n) of the act states that, in determining whether labeling is misleading, the agency shall take into account not only representations made about the product, but also the extent to which the labeling fails to reveal facts material in light of such representations made or suggested in the labeling or material with respect to consequences which may result from use of the article to which the labeling relates under the conditions of use prescribed in the labeling or under such conditions of use as are customary or usual. Thus, the omission of certain material facts from the label or labeling of a food causes the product to be misbranded within the meaning of 21 U.S.C. 343(a)(1) and 321(n)....

Consumption of *trans* fat results in consequences to the consumer. Consumers may increase or decrease their risk of CHD based on the level of *trans* fat in their diets. Thus, the presence or absence of *trans* fat in a food product is a material fact under section 201(n) of the act.

Consumers must know--and the agency believes is material information that the reasonable consumer should know--the amount of *trans* fat in food products that they select as part of their total daily diet to choose products that would allow them to reduce their intake of *trans* fat, and thus, reduce the risk of CHD....

V. Nutrition Labeling of Trans Fats

...

In response to the November 2002 reopening of the comment period on the November 1999 proposal to require a footnote stating "Intake of *trans* fat should be as low as possible" when *trans* fat is listed, FDA received some comments that supported the proposed footnote statement. A few comments noted that the proposed footnote was needed to raise consumer awareness and understanding about the relevance of *trans* fat in the diet and to assist them in making healthy food choices. Another comment stated that the footnote is consistent with the IOM/NAS report on macronutrients. Two of the comments strongly recommended that the footnote be modified to state that "Combined total intake of saturated and *trans* fats should be as low as possible." The comments argued that the footnote proposed by FDA gives undue emphasis to *trans* fat and will cause some consumers to evaluate products based on the content of *trans* fat instead of on the content of both *trans* and saturated fats, as is recommended in dietary guidance....

Similarly, several comments described the proposed footnote statement as an unjustified warning statement on the label of foods that contain *trans* fat. Some of these comments stated that consumers will perceive the footnote as a de facto % DV of zero and will not understand the meaning of the portion of the proposed footnote statement "as low as possible"; consumers will perceive it as a warning to avoid *trans* fat-containing foods at all costs. Several comments stated that the footnote would be misleading because consumers would be confused about the relative impact of saturated fat (by thinking up to 20 g, i.e., the DV for saturated fat, is heart healthy) compared to *trans* fat (thinking *trans* fat intake must be kept to zero to be heart healthy). Some of these comments mentioned that the dietary recommendation to reduce saturated fat is a well established goal of federal agencies and other health organizations and that Americans consume much more saturated fat than *trans* fat. The comments stressed, therefore, that any footnote statement on the nutrition label about *trans* fat should not undermine the important health message consumers have learned over the years about limiting saturated fat intake.

Comments also criticized the proposed footnote for being more prescriptive than, and inconsistent with, other Federal Government dietary recommendations, such as the Dietary Guidelines for Americans 2000 and the NCEP Adult Treatment Panel III Report, 2001. According to the comments, the recommendations of these reports support the need for Americans to choose diets that are low in saturated fat and cholesterol and moderate in fat while reducing, not eliminating, dietary consumption of *trans* fat.

Comments also pointed out that the IOM/NAS report gives essentially identical advice for saturated fat and cholesterol as it gives for *trans* fat, yet FDA's proposed footnote singled out only their recommendation for *trans* fat. The comments argued that this placed undue emphasis on the role of *trans* fat in heart health.

Some comments expressed concern that the proposed footnote statement would provide a disincentive to the industry such that many foods would be reformulated to reduce or remove *trans* fat but, as a result, saturated fat content would be increased....

The agency is persuaded by comments that the statement it proposed may have unintended consequences. It was not FDA's intent to distract consumers from dietary guidance to minimize intake of saturated fat, but rather, in the absence of a DV for *trans* fat, to inform consumers of recommendations concerning its consumption....

The agency agrees with comments that support consumer testing to ensure that information on the food label provides meaningful guidance to consumers and drives the market in a nutritionally beneficial direction. FDA concludes, therefore, that based on arguments presented in the comments, that while the footnote would provide guidance on dietary recommendations for *trans* fat, it is premature to require the use of the proposed footnote statement in the nutrition label without further research. Consumer research would likely need to provide information on the impact of the statement in a footnote on consumers' food selections.

Accordingly, as a result of concerns expressed in the comments, asserting that consumers may place undue emphasis on *trans* fat information relative to other heart-unhealthy fats from the presence of the *trans* fat proposed footnote, the agency is not proceeding at this time to incorporate a requirement for a footnote statement in this final rule....

In the meantime, as noted in the preceding comment, FDA is issuing this final rule to require the quantitative declaration of *trans* fat in the Nutrition Facts panel. To help consumers understand more about this heart-unhealthy fat, the agency plans to initiate consumer education programs about this final rule following publication. As noted earlier, most comments that opposed the proposed footnote stated a belief that even in the absence of a DV, consumers can still find quantitative information useful, and pointed to current labeling of mono- and polyunsaturated fats. In light of previous research that shows that consumers often use information on the Nutrition Facts panel to compare levels of nutrients in two or more foods, FDA concludes that it is important to proceed to list the quantitative information on *trans* fat at this time so that consumers will have information to use in comparing products and making dietary selections to reduce their intake of *trans* fat. The agency believes a footnote or other labeling approach about saturated fat, cholesterol, and *trans* fat may provide additional assistance to convey the relative importance of each of these fats to consumers in a manner which enables them to understand their relative significance, to each other and in the context of a total daily diet. However, because of the public health impact of CHD in the United States and the additional time it will take to conduct the necessary consumer research, the agency concludes that it is essential to proceed at this time to mandate the listing of the quantitative information on *trans* fat so that consumers will be able to use that information to help maintain healthy dietary practices and to address an added footnote statement at a later time....

Notes

1. In June 2015, the FDA announced a final determination that partially hydrogenated oils (the primary source of trans fats in our diets) are not "generally recognized as safe" (GRAS) for use in food and that they are therefore food additives. This means that if a food manufacturer wants to keep using them in food, it must obtain prior approval from the FDA.

2. The Food Allergen Labeling and Consumer Protection Act (FALCPA) of 2004 amended the FDCA to require that food containing "major food allergens" be labeled to indicate this fact. The Act identifies eight foods or food groups as "major food allergens": milk, eggs, fish, Crustacean shellfish, tree nuts, peanuts, wheat, and soybeans. Food manufacturers can meet the labeling requirements in one of two ways: they can either include the allergenic ingredient in the list of ingredients or include a "contains" statement noting the presence of the allergenic ingredient.

Here are examples of both means of complying with FALCPA:

1. **Ingredients**: Enriched flour (**wheat** flour, malted barley, niacin, reduced iron, thiamin mononitrate, riboflavin, folic acid), sugar, partially hydrogenated soybean oil, and/or cottonseed oil, high fructose corn syrup, whey **(milk), eggs**, vanilla, natural and artificial flavoring, salt, leavening (sodium acid pyrophosphate, monocalcium phosphate), lecithin (**soy**), mono-and diglycerides.

2. Contains Wheat, Milk, Egg, and Soy

3. The eight allergens initially covered by FALCPA account for some 90 percent of documented food allergies. In addition to requiring disclosure of the presence of these allergens in food, FALCPA also directed the FDA to propose a rule that define "gluten free" and allow food manufacturers to use this term on labeling if their food products met the FDA's definition. People who have celiac disease – recent estimates are that some 2 million people in the U.S. have celiac disease – need to avoid gluten because it triggers an

immune reaction in the small intestine and the ensuing damage to the small intestine can lead to a variety of adverse reactions and conditions.

The FDA issued a final rule on gluten-free labeling in 2013. The FDA defined "gluten-free" to mean that the relevant food contains less than 20 parts per million of gluten. FDA explains its choice to allow the label "gluten-free" for foods that do indeed contain gluten, as follows:

> FDA used an analytical methods-based approach to define the term gluten-free and adopted < 20 ppm gluten as one of the criteria for a food labeled gluten-free because the agency relies upon scientifically validated methods for enforcing its regulations. Analytical methods that are scientifically validated to reliably detect gluten at a level lower than 20 ppm are not currently available.
>
> In addition, some celiac disease researchers and some epidemiological evidence suggest that most individuals with celiac disease can tolerate variable trace amounts and concentrations of gluten in foods (including levels that are less than 20 ppm gluten) without causing adverse health effects.

What does this mean? Was the FDA correct to allow the "gluten-free" label for foods containing gluten?

CHAPTER 4
COMPELLED DISCLOSURES: NAMING FOOD

A little-known but nevertheless important (and fascinating!) aspect of the FDCA are the provisions relating to food names. The Act empowers the FDA to set "standards of identity" for food – standards that fix not only the name of a food but also its required and optional ingredients. The FDCA's provision on misbranding contains specific requirements for naming food products. For many years, these requirements were a centerpiece of the agency's efforts to control both the nomenclature surrounding food products and the composition of the products themselves.

Ask yourselves: why do we require that foods be named at all? Won't food producers naturally do this, without government intervention? And why wouldn't we allow food producers to call their products anything they want, and to add any ingredients they want, so long as they are safe? Do limits on food names and composition help mostly consumers, or are they a way of limiting competition by specifying, for example, that the name "milk" can be attached only to the product that comes from cows?

Food, Drug, and Cosmetic Act

21 U.S.C. §§ 341, 343

SEC. 401. DEFINITIONS AND STANDARDS FOR FOOD

Whenever in the judgment of the Secretary such action will promote honesty and fair dealing in the interest of consumers, he shall promulgate regulations fixing and establishing for any food, under its common or usual name so far as practicable, a reasonable definition and standard of identity.... In prescribing a definition and standard of identity for any food or class of food in which optional ingredients are permitted, the Secretary shall, for the purpose of promoting honesty and fair dealing in the interest of consumers, designate the optional ingredients which shall be named on the label....

SEC. 403. MISBRANDED FOOD

A food shall be deemed to be misbranded...

(b) If it is offered for sale under the name of another food.

(c) If it is an imitation of another food, unless its label bears, in type of uniform size and prominence, the word "imitation" and, immediately thereafter, the name of the food imitated....

(g) If it purports to be or is represented as a food for which a definition and standard of identity has been prescribed by regulations as provided by section 341 of this title, unless

(1) it conforms to such definition and standard, and

(2) its label bears the name of the food specified in the definition and standard, and, insofar as may be required by such regulations, the common names of optional ingredients (other than spices, flavoring, and coloring) present in such food.

(i) Unless its label bears the common or usual name of the food, if any there be...

What do these provisions together accomplish?

The first, section 401, directs the Secretary (or FDA, under the delegation agreements in place at the agency) to promulgate regulations "fixing and establishing for any food, under its common or usual name so far as practicable, a reasonable definition and standard of identity," if doing so would "promote honesty and fair dealing in the interest of consumers." The result has been to create one of the most ubiquitous but obscure regulatory programs in the food law world. In the 1970s, approximately half of the U.S. food supply (excluding fruits and vegetables) was covered by a standard of identity. Even today, there remain almost 300 standards of identity for everything from milk and cream to fruit pies and frozen peas. The standards prescribe not only the name to be used for the covered products, but also their exact ingredients and detailed specifications for any variation in ingredients. Clearly, however, in a food marketplace that features tens of thousands of products, 300 standards of identity will cover only a fraction of the products sold.

The second provision quoted above, section 403, provides an enforcement mechanism for the standards of identity. It deems "misbranded" any food covered by a standard of identity unless its label and contents conform to the standard. A person who violates the statute's prohibition on misbranding may be imprisoned or fined, and the misbranded food may be seized by the government.

Section 403 also provides that a food that is an imitation of another food must be labeled as such and that food labels must include the "common or usual name of the food, if any there be." Again, why do you suppose we need a federal law telling food producers to include the names of their products on their product labels? What if the food is an entirely novel collection of ingredients? A theme that runs throughout discussions of legal restrictions on food names is the potential tension between consumer protection and product innovation.

The article that follows provides historical background on food identity standards, including an account of the proceedings on the FDA's standard of identity for peanut butter. These proceedings, famous among students of administrative law, took a decade to answer this fundamental question: what percentage of peanuts must "peanut butter" contain?

The Rise and Fall of Federal Food Standards in the United States: The Case of the Peanut Butter and Jelly Sandwich

Suzanne White Junod, Ph.D., Historian
U.S. Food and Drug Administration
April 9, 1999

In 1906, the United States Congress, after more than 25 years of proposals, counterproposals, bills defeated, and bills allowed to die in benevolent and sometimes not so benevolent desuetude, passed the U.S. Pure Food and Drugs Act. It was one of the first consumer protection acts passed in the United States--the first if you ignore an 1878 Tea Act, designed to protect the U.S. from inferior teas. For an act propelled into law through a focus on food, the law was surprisingly and seriously flawed in its food provisions. The first flaw was apparent even before the law was passed. Offshoots of the food industry (principally manufacturers of rectified or blended whiskey and chemical preservatives including formaldehyde, borax, copper salts, salicylates, saccharin, and sodium benzoate) defeated a provision which would have allowed the government to set standards for food products. These manufacturers rightly feared that if Chief Chemist Harvey Wiley had had his way in administering a law with food standards provisions, chemical preservatives would not be allowed in food products. Beginning in 1898, Wiley himself had pioneered in the establishment of the nation's first food standards as a member of the Food Standard Committee of the Association of Official Agricultural Chemists (AOAC), so the nation's food industries had enjoyed a preview of what food standards might look like. Concerned that the established standards might be so strict as to eliminate some products from the marketplace entirely, these food industries inserted a so-called "distinctive name proviso" into the law. This second flaw was not quite so obvious until the 1920s brought a heyday in inventive advertising, and the Great Depression of the 1930s created a market for cheap, inferior products. And this is where jelly first enters my sandwich standards analogy.

This distinctive name proviso permitted the marketing of foods that would have otherwise been illegal under the 1906 Act. In the case of jam and jelly, they would have been considered adulterated or misbranded under the law since they had so little fruit. Beautiful food dye hues, artificial pectin, and grass seeds, accompanied by expensive yet tasteful packaging, and promoted through clever advertising, all created a new kind of fabricated product. Given a fanciful and "distinctive" yet meaningless name BRED-SPRED, this product typifies the kind of inferior product which began to gain a foothold in the U.S. marketplace beginning in the 1920s.

How did this happen? In World War I, there had been quite a marked expansion in the industry to supply our Allies, esp. the British, as well as our own military with jams, jellies, and preserves. After the war, the overbuilt industry had to go after volume sales with low prices. The development of refined pectin under the Douglas patents made it possible to make much better preserves without using green fruit, but it also make it possible to make sugar and water alone jell. In the marketplace, standards spiraled downward. The consumer could not depend on the labeling or the appearance of the product to guarantee its contents or quality. The only official food standards were voluntary "advisory" standards of the Bureau of Chemistry, forerunner of the present U.S. Food and Drug Administration. As an old-timer described the situation, "there never was a product made but some gosh darn fool could make it worse and sell it for less." The market for fabricated foods under this "distinctive name" proviso grew rapidly following the 1929 stock market crash.

Preserves were not the only consumer products caught in a downward economic spiral in which the incentive was to make products worse. Canned fruit and vegetable manufacturers finally went to Congress and got the so-called “Canner's Amendment” (McNary-Mapes) enacted in 1930 which allowed the establishment and enforcement of canned foods, excluding meat and milk products. Substandard products could be sold but did have to carry a so-called "crepe" label--a black label announcement that announced that while a product was good food, it was poor quality.

The preserving industry tried to get standards for its products ushered in under this law, but the Secretary of Agriculture refused. Meanwhile the government lost its legal cases against Bred Spred. In 1933, as part of President Franklin Roosevelt's New Deal, the National Recovery Act was passed, and the preserve industry quickly adopted a Code of Fair Practices, which included product standards. But the NRA was short lived, its Blue Eagle symbol brought down by the U.S. Supreme Court, in the infamous "sick chicken" case. In 1936, the preserve industry tried to get another agency, the Federal Trade Commission to enact product standards. FTC held hearings and issued rules which did contain product standards. A series of court decisions were upheld, but the fight to get to court was an uphill battle.

In the end, it was the U.S. Food and Drug Administration that rescued the preserves industry. Beginning in 1933, the agency had begun the lengthy and politically treacherous process of replacing the 1906 Pure Food and Drugs Act with a new act.

In support of its case, it assembled a collection of problem products against which FDA had been unable to act under its 1906 statute.

President Roosevelt's wife, Eleanor, a tireless advocate of causes, toured the exhibit [on these problem products].

A reporter accompanying her dubbed the exhibit the "American Chamber of Horrors." The name stuck, a book was written by the same name and promoted by consumer advocacy groups--the so-called guinea pig muckrakers, the law passed, and the exhibit itself was so persuasive that Congress enacted a law prohibiting agencies from expending funds to lobby Congress in the future.

Ultimately, the 1938 Food, Drug, and Cosmetic Act would provide for the establishment of 3 kinds of food standards 1) standards of identity 2) standards of quality and 3) standards regulating the fill-of-container. All of these standards were to be established "whenever in the judgment of the Secretary such action will promote honesty and fair dealing in the interest of consumers." In short, these standards were to ensure value to the consumer of the foods....

More consumer oriented than its 1906 predecessor, the 1938 Food, Drug, and Cosmetic Act represents a true watershed in U.S. food policy....

The 1938 Food, Drug, and Cosmetic Act simply eliminated the "distinctive name proviso" and required instead that the label of a food "bear its common or usual name." The food would be illegal (misbranded under the law) if it represented itself as a standardized food unless it conformed to that standard.

But what was a food standard to look like? Congress thought that standards of identity would resemble a "recipe." Foods would be defined in terms of home recipes or standards with which the consumer could readily identify. They were generally established for goods one would find in any well-stocked pantry. By 1957, standards had been set for many varieties of chocolate, flour, cereals and cereal grains, macaroni products, bakery products, milk and cream, cheese, butter, non-fat milk solids, dressings (mayonnaise), canned fruits and fruit juices, fruit preserves and jellies, shellfish, canned tuna, eggs and egg products, margarine, and canned vegetables. The first standards issued covered tomato products. The second set of standards established under the 1938 law, however, was for jams and jellies. In setting this standard, FDA accepted evidence from cookbooks and family recipes dating back at least 200 years. It was pretty clear that jams and jellies should be about half fruit or fruit juice and half sugar. It was a relatively easy standard to establish, but its symbolic value was high.

FDA initiated and supported the concept of a recipe approach to establishing food standards because it made enforcement very easy. Lawyers for major food companies and ingredient manufacturers had no objections because in many cases it recognized and even promoted use of their client's or their company's products. Competitors had few objections because it meant that they met on a level playing field and both foreign and domestic producers had to meet the same guidelines. Unfortunately, however, the recipe concept did little to promote innovation in the food industry and nothing to inform consumers about the composition of standardized foods. Under the 1938 Act, standardized foods had to list only the optional ingredients that they used in the product on the label, but not the mandated ingredients. Ironically, then, consumers knew less about the contents of standardized foods than about non-standardized products that had to list all of their ingredients on the label.

The recipe approach not only worked well during the 1940s and early 1950s, it was upheld by the courts. The U.S. government was able to eliminate a number of nutritional deficiency diseases in the post-war era by promulgating standards for enriched food products. The courts upheld the FDA's enrichment formula and ruled that the government had a rationale for its actions and that manufacturers had to adhere to the mandated formula or cease to enrich their foods altogether. Catsup that had some benzoate of soda which was not provided for in the standards for canned tomato products, including catsup, was ruled illegal. In a crushing blow, however, the Supreme Court ruled that a product labeled "Delicious Brand Imitation Jam" which contained only 25% fruit, instead of the 45% required under the standard, could nonetheless be marketed as long as it was conspicuously labeled as an "imitation." FDA had argued, that despite the accuracy of the term "imitation" in its name, Congress had not intended that such a product be marketed at all since it did not meet the standard and was marketed in competition with standardized products. This case proved to be the lone exception to the general rule that a truthful labeling cannot render a debased version of a standardized food legal.

In 1953, the Hale amendment modified the food standards hearing procedures, waiving a hearing altogether in cases in which there was no dispute. This amendment, however, served as an early warning that the hearing process was beginning to become unwieldy. By allowing "any interested person" to initiate the standard-making process, FDA's own standard setting agenda was undermined. What Congress and FDA had intended to be a fact-finding process, began to resemble a trial between adversaries. The hearings to set standards for enriched white bread provide the best illustration of the new complexities that confronted the U.S. standards setting process by the mid-twentieth century.

FDA officials had a saying based on years of regulatory work that anyone who came up with a new food additive or ingredient tried it first in bread. With little information about the safety of some of these proposed new ingredients, FDA turned to the standards hearings as one way to limit the introduction of new chemical substances into the food supply. In the earliest bread hearings, begun in 1941, there had been minor disputes over the suitability of several new ingredients including mono and di-glycerides, hydrogenated shortening, soy lecithin, and some so-called dough "conditioners." The final standards allowed most of the former ingredients, but disallowed some of the dough conditioners. World War II intervened, however, and these standards were put on hold. During the war, bread was subject to a war food order mandating enrichment. After the war, when the bread hearings were re-opened, FDA elected not to mandate enrichment, but rather to write separate standards for enriched and for non-enriched products. The bread standards hearings, however, quickly began to revolve around the admission as optional ingredients in standardized bread of a new class of additives, known as polyoxyethylene monostearates. The product was variously described as an emulsifier, a "crumb softener" a "staling retardant" and an additive "to prolong palatability and softness." Had the manufacturer limited its petition to a few products from this new line of chemical additives, observers felt that they might have been successful. It was painfully clear to everyone at the hearings, however, that all twenty-seven emulsifiers had not been subjected to the same level of scientific scrutiny for either safety or suitability for use in bread. Of course, the Institute of Shortening Manufacturers and Edible Oils opposed the inclusion of this new class of competitive ingredients in the standards for white bread, and ably represented by a future Supreme Court Justice, Potter Stewart, they successfully converted the hearings into a full-fledged trade war.

The government, in a thankless attempt to locate more neutral grounds for debate, could not simply express its concerns about the safety of the new emulsifiers and the adequacy of their testing. Instead, under the law, the government had to show that the new ingredients would not promote "honesty and fair dealing in the interests of consumers." FDA, therefore, began to build its case trying to show that the softeners deceived customers as to the freshness of a loaf of bread. It was this issue, more than any other that led the hearings into absurdity. It was universally acknowledged that consumers tested bread by squeezing the loaf and that the bread softeners kept bread softer longer. The question in dispute, therefore, became "Did consumers conclude from squeezing, that a softer loaf was a fresher loaf?" All the tools of modern psychology and social science were brought to bear on the task of dissociating softness and freshness. In one consumer preference test, researchers asserted that they had used numbers 16 and 24 to designate the test slices because "they were found psychologically correct." In a supervised taste test, women were simply asked to indicate a preference, if they had one, for one of two slices of bread, and to choose which one seemed fresher to them. In a seemingly straightforward conclusion, it was reported that four of five women chose the bread with the softener as the fresher loaf. A defense witness, however, a statistician, challenged the survey's conclusions by insisting that the more accurate conclusion was that "1100 consumers preferred soft bread and those who preferred soft bread preferred the bread made with the softener. Those who preferred firm bread, however, had noticed no differences between the control bread and the test bread." Finally, when the statistician summarized his modification of the original survey results he noted that "for those who prefer the soft bread, the test bread is preferred both for its softness and for the factors other than softness (presumably taste, texture, grain, etc.) while the control bread is preferred for its firmness." This profound conclusion so confounded lawyers and listeners alike that the statistician was held over for cross-examination the next day. And so it went for day after day of the bread hearings. It was not until 1950 that a Federal Register notice formally announced the exclusion of [polyoxyethylene monostearates] from the standards of identity for white bread. In the meantime, Frank Keefe, a member of Congress, had introduced a resolution in the House of Representatives providing for the establishment of a Select Committee to Investigate the Use of Chemicals in Food Products. This committee's work led to the passage of the 1958 Food Additives Amendment which established a pre-market approval process for new food additives similar to that applied to new drugs, requiring new food additives to be shown safe and suitable before they were allowed in food products. Scientific petitions on food safety replaced pitched battles over food standards. Although the new law removed the need to debate the safety of additives from the standards setting process, it did not guarantee that food standard hearings would be shorter or that food standards would be issued more quickly. As we will see, even after food additive issues were removed from the food standards process, it still took over a decade to issue standards for peanut butter.

By 1958, the definition of pantry goods had changed substantially. New food products and a newly competitive refrigerated and frozen goods industry that developed in the domestic marketplace after World War II had literally redefined the household pantry. As the number of new processed and fabricated foods grew, the government spent less time issuing refined standards for products such as raisin bread and egg bread, and more time establishing new standards for products such as frozen orange juice, frozen "TV" dinners, frozen breaded shrimp, freeze dried coffee, and "instant chocolate drinks." As soon as the Food Additives Amendment was in place, FDA began to experiment with less restrictive food standards than the strict "recipe standards" that had predominated in the standards program. In 1961, FDA first deviated from the recipe approach when it issued standards for "frozen raw breaded shrimp" which simply provided for the use of "safe and suitable" batter and breading ingredients, rather than listing all optional ingredients individually. A legal definition of "safe and suitable" was later codified and used to allow "safe and suitable preservatives" or "safe and suitable emulsifiers."

The peanut butter hearings, however, were launched before this period of regulatory innovation and relaxation of standards. In 1940, peanut butter manufacturers had inquired about the addition of glycerin to peanut butter to prevent oil separation. FDA's response was ambivalent: IF glycerin could be added without rendering the food adulterated, its addition would have to be set forth prominently on the product label, according to regulators. The term "peanut butter," wrote the agency, "is generally understood by the consuming public to mean a product consisting solely of ground roasted peanuts, with or without a small quantity of added salt." Perhaps fearing another bread battle over ingredients, FDA waited until 1959, the year after the Food Additives Amendment was enacted, to launch its assault on inferior peanut butters. In a press release in 1959, FDA announced that a survey had shown that products labeled peanut butter had reduced the peanut content as much as 20% by substituting cheaper vegetable oils or hydrogenated oils for more expensive peanuts and peanut oil. FDA proposed a standard for peanut butter consisting of 95% peanuts and 5% optional ingredients including salt, sugar, dextrose, honey or hydrogenated or partially hydrogenated peanut oil. Although the FDA considered this an adulteration issue, it was clear that consumers often preferred peanut butter that spread more easily as well as peanut butter that had some sweetening. In 1961, therefore, FDA proposed a standard recognizing 90% peanuts as well as some additional sweeteners. Three competitive brands of peanut butter then entered the standards battle: Skippy, Jif, and Peter Pan. The public evidentiary hearing alone, a small fragment in the decade long process, took 20 weeks and produced a transcript of nearly 8,000 pages. A prominent attorney on the case wryly observed that the peanut butter standards "put many lawyers' children through college." Participants began to feel that they were close to arguing about the number of angels that could dance on the head of a pin when it became clear that the differences between the industrial protagonists came down to a mere 3% difference in proposed peanut content. In the end, the government did prevail as the U.S. Appeals Court affirmed the FDA order setting standards for peanut butter at no less than 90% for peanuts and no more than 55% fat. The court concluded that the Commissioner's findings were based upon substantial evidence and that the promulgation of such standards was within his authority. It was not a sweet victory, however. The peanut butter standards had merely underscored growing concerns that the food standards program in the U.S. had outgrown its usefulness. As the standards setting process had grown increasingly complex and time-consuming, it was the peanut butter hearings that made it clear that strict standards were not only becoming a waste of time and money, but actually and ultimately worked to the detriment of both business and consumers.

The experimentation and innovation in the food standards process which had been launched in 1961 with the raw frozen breaded shrimp standards, was propelled forward in 1969 following the White House Conference on Food, Nutrition, and Health convened by President Richard Nixon. An era of regulatory reform followed which transformed and modernized the food standards program with a new emphasis on nutrition. FDA, led by an energetic General Counsel, Peter Barton Hutt, took steps to insure that the agency's regulatory practices did not stand in the way of innovative food products, provided such new products were safe and informatively labeled. Freed from formulas, the ideals of a free food marketplace were close to being met during the 1970s. The agency encouraged more extensive ingredient labeling in general, and it amended food standards to require the labeling of non-mandatory ingredients. A substitute food had to carry the "crepe label" imitation only if it was nutritionally inferior to the original product. In the case of jams and jellies, this opened up the market for "fruit spreds" which had less sugar and more fruit--a far cry from the era of BRED-SPRED. Non-standardized products were authorized to state exactly what the product was, so that a food standard would be unnecessary. Seafood cocktail, contains X% seafood, for example.

Increased industry and consumer concerns about healthy diets led to 1978 regulations specifying on-the-label requirements of a reduced calorie and low-calorie food. In 1994, when Skippy, Jif, and Peter Pan all developed lower-fat peanut butters, FDA agreed with their competitors that the product did not meet FDA's hard fought standards. The agency notified the makers that the new products could be called "spreads" and compared with regular peanut butter on the label, or they could petition FDA to change the standard definition. In an era of affluence accompanied by increased concerns about the relation between nutrition, heart disease, stroke and obesity, the reduced fat peanut spreads have found a steady market and the standard has remained intact. Basic foods are still both wholesome and competitive. They are competitive, now, however, not by strictly regulating every ingredient, optional and otherwise in the finished product, but rather by the imposition of mandatory nutritional food labels specifying the competitive components valued by consumers. Fat, fiber, sugar, and sodium specifications have made this label the most widely read standard in American history....

Note

Is the peanut butter saga mostly a story about a misconceived process (formal rulemaking), a misconceived substantive policy, or both?

A bill now circulating in the Senate – the Regulatory Accountability Act – would amend the Administrative Procedure Act to add procedures to notice and comment rulemaking that would make this process look more like formal rulemaking than it does now. Is this a good idea? What might be said in favor of and against this proposal?

The following entry from the Code of Federal Regulations is one of the food identity standards set by the FDA (and still in effect). Do not read it for the specific requirements for sherbet; instead, while you are reading the standard, consider what purposes are served by its requirements and whether there might be other regulatory (or non-regulatory) strategies that would serve the same purposes as this detailed "recipe" for sherbet does.

Standards of Identity

Frozen Desserts

U.S. Food and Drug Administration
21 C.F.R. Part 135

Subpart B — Requirements for Specific Standardized Frozen Desserts

Sec. 135.140. Sherbet.

(a) Description.

(1) Sherbet is a food produced by freezing, while stirring, a pasteurized mix consisting of one or more of the optional dairy ingredients specified in paragraph (b) of this section, and may contain one or more of the optional caseinates specified in paragraph (c) of this section subject to the conditions hereinafter set forth, and other safe and suitable nonmilk-derived ingredients; and excluding other food fats, except such as are added in small amounts to accomplish specific functions or are natural components of flavoring ingredients used. Sherbet is sweetened with nutritive carbohydrate sweeteners and is characterized by the addition of one or more of the characterizing fruit ingredients specified in paragraph (d) of this section or one or more of the nonfruit-characterizing ingredients specified in paragraph (e) of this section.

(2) Sherbet weighs not less than 6 pounds to the gallon. The milkfat content is not less than 1 percent nor more than 2 percent, the nonfat milk-derived solids content not less than 1 percent, and the total milk or milk-derived solids content is not less than 2 percent nor more than 5 percent by weight of the finished food. Sherbet that is characterized by a fruit ingredient shall have a titratable acidity, calculated as lactic acid, of not less than 0.35 percent.

(b) Optional dairy ingredients. The optional dairy ingredients referred to in paragraph (a) of this section are: Cream, dried cream, plastic cream (sometimes known as concentrated milkfat), butter, butter oil, milk, concentrated milk, evaporated milk, superheated condensed milk, sweetened condensed milk, dried milk, skim milk, concentrated skim milk, evaporated skim milk, condensed skim milk, sweetened condensed skim milk, sweetened condensed part-skim milk, nonfat dry milk, sweet cream buttermilk, condensed sweet cream buttermilk, dried sweet cream buttermilk, skim milk that has been concentrated and from which part of the lactose has been removed by crystallization, and whey and those modified whey products (e.g., reduced lactose whey, reduced minerals whey, and whey protein concentrate) that have been determined by FDA to be generally recognized as safe (GRAS) for use in this type of food. Water may be added, or water may be evaporated from the mix. The sweet cream buttermilk and the concentrated sweet cream buttermilk or dried sweet cream buttermilk, when adjusted with water to a total solids content of 8.5 percent, has a titratable acidity of not more than 0.17 percent calculated as lactic acid. The term "milk" as used in this section means cow's milk.

(c) Optional caseinates. The optional caseinates referred to in paragraph (a) of this section which may be added to sherbet mix are: Casein prepared by precipitation with gums, ammonium caseinate, calcium caseinate, potassium caseinate, and sodium caseinate. Caseinates may be added in liquid or dry form, but must be free of excess alkali, such caseinates are not considered to be milk solids.

(d) Optional fruit-characterizing ingredients. The optional fruit-characterizing ingredients referred to in paragraph (a) of this section are any mature fruit or the juice of any mature fruit. The fruit or fruit juice used may be fresh, frozen, canned, concentrated, or partially or wholly dried. The fruit may be thickened with pectin or other optional ingredients. The fruit is prepared by the removal of pits, seeds, skins, and cores, where such removal is usual in preparing that kind of fruit for consumption as fresh fruit. The fruit may be screened, crushed, or otherwise comminuted. It may be acidulated. In the case of concentrated fruit or fruit juices, from which part of the water is removed, substances contributing flavor volatilized during water removal may be condensed and reincorporated in the concentrated fruit or fruit juice. In the case of citrus fruits, the whole fruit, including the peel but excluding the seeds, may be used, and in the case of citrus juice or concentrated citrus juices, cold-pressed citrus oil may be added thereto in an amount not exceeding that which would have been obtained if the whole fruit had been used. The quantity of fruit ingredients used is such that, in relation to the weight of the finished sherbet, the weight of fruit or fruit juice, as the case may be (including water necessary to reconstitute partially or wholly dried fruits or fruit juices to their original moisture content), is not less than 2 percent in the case of citrus sherbets, 6 percent in the case of berry sherbets, and 10 percent in the case of sherbets prepared with other fruits. For the purpose of this section, tomatoes and rhubarb are considered as kinds of fruit.

(e) Optional nonfruit characterizing ingredients. The optional nonfruit characterizing ingredients referred to in paragraph (a) of this section include but are not limited to the following:

(1) Ground spice or infusion of coffee or tea.

(2) Chocolate or cocoa, including syrup.

(3) Confectionery.

(4) Distilled alcoholic beverage, including liqueurs or wine, in an amount not to exceed that required for flavoring the sherbet.

(5) Any natural or artificial food flavoring (except any having a characteristic fruit or fruit-like flavor).

(f) Nomenclature. (1) The name of each sherbet is as follows:

(i) The name of each fruit sherbet is "____ sherbet", the blank being filled in with the common name of the fruit or fruits from which the fruit ingredients used are obtained. When the names of two or more fruits are included, such names shall be arranged in order of predominance, if any, by weight of the respective fruit ingredients used.

(ii) The name of each nonfruit sherbet is "____ sherbet", the blank being filled in with the common or usual name or names of the characterizing flavor or flavors; for example, "peppermint", except that if the characterizing flavor used is vanilla, the name of the food is "____ sherbet", the blank being filled in as specified by Sec. 135.110[(e)](5)(i).

(2) When the optional ingredients, artificial flavoring, or artificial coloring are used in sherbet, they shall be named on the label as follows:

(i) If the flavoring ingredient or ingredients consists exclusively of artificial flavoring, the label designation shall be "artificially flavored".

(ii) If the flavoring ingredients are a combination of natural and artificial flavors, the label designation shall be "artificial and natural flavoring added".

(iii) The label shall designate artificial coloring by the statement "artificially colored", "artificial coloring added", "with added artificial coloring", or "____, an artificial color added", the blank being filled in with the name of the artificial coloring used.

(g) Characterizing flavor(s). Wherever there appears on the label any representation as to the characterizing flavor or flavors of the food and such flavor or flavors consist in whole or in part of artificial flavoring, the statement required by paragraph (f)(2) (i) and (ii) of this section, as appropriate, shall immediately and conspicuously precede or follow such representation, without intervening written, printed, or graphic matter (except that the word "sherbet" may intervene) in a size reasonably related to the prominence of the name of the characterizing flavor and in any event the size of the type is not less than 6-point on packages containing less than 1 pint, not less than 8-point on packages containing at least 1 pint but less than one-half gallon, not less than 10-point on packages containing at least one-half gallon but less than 1 gallon, and not less than 12-point on packages containing 1 gallon or over.

(h) Display of statements required by paragraph (f)(2). Except as specified in paragraph (g) of this section, the statements required by paragraph (f)(2) of this section shall be set forth on the principal display panel or panels of the label with such prominence and conspicuousness as to render them likely to be read and understood by the ordinary individual under customary conditions of purchase and use.

(i) Label declaration. Each of the ingredients used in the food shall be declared on the label as required by the applicable sections of parts 101 and 130 of this chapter.

Note

Have you been in the frozen desserts section of a grocery store lately? Have you noticed how many products there seem to resemble sherbet, or ice cream, which also has a precise standard of identity, but are not called sherbet or ice cream? Gelatos, sorbets, frozen dairy desserts, frozen nondairy desserts, and more may be found in the grocery aisles today. Why might there be a proliferation of products that do not use the name associated with an existing standard of identity? Who might worry about this proliferation?

The following case shows how powerful standards of identity can be in determining the actual composition of food products.

Federal Security Administrator v. Quaker Oats Co.

318 U.S. 218 (1943)

MR. CHIEF JUSTICE STONE delivered the opinion of the Court.

The Federal Security Administrator, acting under §§401 and 701 (e), of the Federal Food, Drug and Cosmetic Act, promulgated regulations establishing "standards of identity" for various milled wheat products, excluding vitamin D from the defined standard of "farina" and permitting it only in "enriched farina," which was required to contain vitamin B1, riboflavin, nicotinic acid and iron. The question is whether the regulations are valid as applied to respondent. The answer turns upon (a) whether there is substantial evidence in support of the Administrator's finding that indiscriminate enrichment of farina with vitamin and mineral contents would tend to confuse and mislead consumers; (b) if so, whether, upon such a finding, the Administrator has statutory authority to adopt a standard of identity, which excludes a disclosed non-deleterious ingredient, in order to promote honesty and fair dealing in the interest of consumers; and (c) whether the Administrator's treatment, by the challenged regulations, of the use of vitamin D as an ingredient of a product sold as "farina" is within his statutory authority to prescribe "a reasonable definition and standard of identity."

Section 401 of the Act provides that "Whenever in the judgment of the Administrator such action will promote honesty and fair dealing in the interest of consumers, he shall promulgate regulations fixing and establishing for any food, under its common or usual name so far as practicable, a reasonable definition and standard of identity.... In prescribing a definition and standard of identity for any food or class of food in which optional ingredients are permitted, the Administrator shall, for the purpose of promoting honesty and fair dealing in the interest of consumers, designate the optional ingredients which shall be named on the label." By §701 (e) the Administrator, on his own initiative or upon application of any interested industry or a substantial part of it, is required to "hold a public hearing upon a proposal to issue, amend, or repeal any regulation contemplated by" §401. At the hearing "any interested person may be heard." The Administrator is required to promulgate by order any regulation he may issue, to "base his order only on substantial evidence of record at the hearing," and to "set forth as part of his order detailed findings of fact on which the order is based."[1]

Any food which "purports to be or is represented as a food for which a definition and standard of identity has been prescribed" pursuant to §401 is declared by §403 (g) to be misbranded "unless (1) it conforms to such definition and standard, and (2) its label bears the name of the food specified in the definition and standard, and, insofar as may be required by such regulations, the common names of optional ingredients...present in such food." The shipment in interstate commerce of "misbranded" food is made a penal offense by §§301 and 303.... On [judicial] review the findings of the Administrator "as to the facts, if supported by substantial evidence, shall be conclusive." §701(f)(1), (f)(3).

After due notice and a hearing in which respondent participated, the Administrator by order promulgated regulations establishing definitions and standards of identity for sixteen milled wheat products, including "farina" and "enriched farina." Regulation 15.130 defined "farina" as a food prepared by grinding and bolting cleaned wheat, other than certain specified kinds, to a prescribed fineness with the bran coat and germ of the wheat berry removed to a prescribed extent. The regulation made no provision for the addition of any ingredients to "farina." Regulation 15.140 defined "enriched farina" as conforming to the regulation defining "farina," but with added prescribed minimum quantities of vitamin B1, riboflavin,[3] nicotinic acid (or nicotinic acid amide) and iron. The regulation also provided that minimum quantities of vitamin D, calcium, wheat germ or disodium phosphate might be added as optional ingredients of "enriched farina," and required that ingredients so added be specified on the label. In support of the regulations the Administrator found that "unless a standard" for milled wheat products "is promulgated which limits the kinds and amounts of enrichment, the manufacturers' selection of the various nutritive elements and combinations of elements on the basis of economic and merchandising considerations is likely to lead to a great increase in the diversity, both qualitative and quantita-

---

[1] As enacted, the Act vested the foregoing powers in the Secretary of Agriculture. By §§12 and 13 of Reorganization Plan No. IV, approved April 11, 1940, the Federal Food and Drug Administration and all functions of the Secretary of Agriculture relating thereto were transferred to the Federal Security Agency and the Federal Security Administrator.

[3] The effective date of the riboflavin requirement has been postponed until April 20, 1943, because it appeared that the available supply was inadequate.

tive, in enriched flours offered to the public. Such diversity would tend to confuse and mislead consumers as to the relative value of and need for the several nutritional elements, and would impede rather than promote honesty and fair dealing in the interest of consumers."

On respondent's appeal from this order the Court of Appeals for the Seventh Circuit set it aside, holding that the regulations did not conform to the statutory standards of reasonableness, that the Administrator's findings as to probable consumer confusion in the absence of the prescribed standards of identity were without support in the evidence and were "entirely speculative and conjectural," and that in any case such a finding would not justify the conclusion that the regulations would "promote honesty and fair dealing in the interest of consumers." We granted certiorari...because of the importance of the questions involved to the administration of the Food, Drug and Cosmetic Act.

Respondent, The Quaker Oats Company, has for the past ten years manufactured and marketed a wheat product commonly used as a cereal food, consisting of farina as defined by the Administrator's regulation, but with vitamin D added. Respondent distributes this product in packages labeled "Quaker Farina Wheat Cereal Enriched with Vitamin D," or "Quaker Farina Enriched by the Sunshine Vitamin." The packages also bear the label "Contents 400 U.S.P. units of Vitamin D per ounce, supplied by approximately the addition of 1/5 of 1 percent irradiated dry yeast."

Respondent asserts, and the Government agrees, that the Act as supplemented by the Administrator's standards will prevent the marketing of its product as "farina" since, by reason of the presence of vitamin D as an ingredient, it does not conform to the standard of identity prescribed for "farina," and that respondent cannot market its product as "enriched farina" un-

less it adds the prescribed minimum quantities of vitamin B1, riboflavin, nicotinic acid and iron. Respondent challenges the validity of the regulations on the grounds sustained below and others so closely related to them as not to require separate consideration.

As appears from the evidence and the findings, the products of milled wheat are among the principal items of the American diet, particularly among low income groups.[84] Farina, which is a highly refined wheat prod-

[4] One witness at the hearing referred to estimates that over 95% of human consumption of wheat products is in the form of white flour.

uct resembling flour but with larger particles, is used in macaroni, as a breakfast food, and extensively as a cereal food for children. It is in many cases the only cereal consumed by them during a period of their growth. Both farina and flour are manufactured by grinding the whole wheat and discarding its bran coat and germ. This process removes from the milled product that part of the wheat which is richest in vitamins and minerals, particularly vitamin B1, riboflavin, nicotinic acid and iron, valuable food elements which are often lacking in the diet of low income groups. In their diet, especially in the case of children, there is also frequently a deficiency of calcium and vitamin D, which are elements not present in wheat in significant quantities. Vitamin D, whose chief dietary value is as an aid to the metabolism of calcium, is developed in the body by exposure to sunlight. It is derived principally from cod liver and other fish oils. Milk is the most satisfactory source of calcium in digestible form, and milk enriched by vitamin D is now on the market.

In recent years millers of wheat have placed on the market flours and farinas which have been enriched by the addition of various vitamins and minerals. The composition of these enriched products varies widely.[5] There was testimony of weight before the Administrator, principally by expert nutritionists, that such products, because of the variety and combination of added ingredients, are widely variable in nutritional value; and that con-

---

[5] The report of the officer presiding at the hearing enumerates the following varieties disclosed by the testimony:

Flours, phosphated flours, and self-rising flours –

1. One with added vitamin D;
2. One with added calcium;
3. One with added vitamin B1, nicotinic acid, and calcium [produced by some 23 mills];
4. One with added vitamin B1, calcium, and iron;
5. One containing wheat germ and wheat germ oil, said to furnish vitamin B1, vitamin E and riboflavin;
6. One 'long extraction' flour containing B1, riboflavin, calcium and iron.

Farinas --

7. One with added vitamin D;
8. One with added vitamin B1, calcium and iron.

The labels used, and advertising claims made, for those products were not in the record. However, there was testimony that certain of them were sold under such names as "Sunfed," "Vitawhite," "Holwhite."

sumers generally lack knowledge of the relative value of such ingredients and combinations of them.

These witnesses also testified, as did representatives of consumer organizations which had made special studies of the problems of food standardization, that the number, variety and varying combinations of the added ingredients tend to confuse the large number of consumers who desire to purchase vitamin-enriched wheat food products but who lack the knowledge essential to discriminating purchase of them; that because of this lack of knowledge and discrimination they are subject to exploitation by the sale of foods described as "enriched," but of whose inferior or unsuitable quality they are not informed. Accordingly a large number of witnesses recommended the adoption of definitions and standards for "enriched" wheat products which would ensure fairly complete satisfaction of dietary needs, and a somewhat lesser number recommended the disallowance, as optional ingredients in the standards for unenriched wheat products, of individual vitamins and minerals whose addition would suggest to consumers an adequacy for dietary needs not in fact supplied.

The court below characterized this evidence as speculative and conjectural, and held that because there was no evidence that respondent's product had in fact confused or misled anyone, the Administrator's finding as to consumer confusion was without substantial support in the evidence. It thought that, if anything, consumer confusion was more likely to be created, and the interest of consumers harmed, by the sale of farinas conforming to the standard for "enriched farina," whose labels were not required to disclose their ingredients, than by the sale of respondent's product under an accurate and informative label such as that respondent was using.

The Act does not contemplate that courts should thus substitute their own judgment for that of the Administrator. As passed by the House it appears to have provided for a judicial review in which the court could take additional evidence, weigh the evidence, and direct the Administrator "to take such further action as justice may require." H. R. Rep. No. 2139, 75th Cong., 3d Sess., pp. 11-12. But before enactment, the Conference Committee substituted for these provisions those which became §701(f) of the Act. While under that section the Administrator's regulations must be supported by findings based upon "substantial evidence" adduced at the hearing, the Administrator's findings as to the facts if based on substantial evidence are conclusive. In explaining these changes the chairman of the House conferees stated on the floor of the House that "there is no purpose that the court shall exercise the functions that belong to the executive or the legislative branches." 83 Cong. Rec., p. 9096.

The review provisions were patterned after those by which Congress has provided for the review of "quasi-judicial" orders of the Federal Trade Commission and other agencies, which we have many times had occasion to construe. Under such provisions we have repeatedly emphasized the scope that must be allowed to the discretion and informed judgment of an expert administrative body. These considerations are especially appropriate where the review is of regulations of general application adopted by an administrative agency under its rule-making power in carrying out the policy of a statute with whose enforcement it is charged. Section 401 calls for the exercise of the "judgment of the Administrator." That judgment, if based on substantial evidence of record, and if within statutory and constitutional limitations, is controlling even though the reviewing court might on the same record have arrived at a different conclusion.

...The exercise of the administrative rule-making power necessarily looks to the future. The statute requires the Administrator to adopt standards of identity which in his judgment "will" promote honesty and fair dealing in the interest of consumers. Acting within his statutory authority he is required to establish standards which will guard against the probable future effects of present trends. Taking into account the evidence of public demand for vitamin-enriched foods, their increasing sale, their variable vitamin composition and dietary value, and the general lack of consumer knowledge of such values, there was sufficient evidence of "rational probative force" (see Consolidated Edison Co. v. Labor Board, 305 U.S. 197, 229, 230), to support the Administrator's judgment that, in the absence of appropriate standards of identity, consumer confusion would ensue.

Respondent insists, as the court below held, that the consumer confusion found by the Administrator affords no basis for his conclusion that the standards of identity adopted by the Administrator will promote honesty and fair dealing. But this is tantamount to saying, despite the Administrator's findings to the contrary, either that in the circumstances of this case there could be no such consumer confusion or that the confusion could not be deemed to facilitate unfair dealing contrary to the interest of consumers. For reasons already indicated we think that the evidence of the desire of consumers to purchase vitamin-enriched foods, their general ignorance of the composition and value of the vitamin content of those foods, and their consequent inability to guard against the purchase of products of inferior or unsuitable vitamin content, sufficiently supports the Administrator's conclusions.

We have recognized that purchasers under such conditions are peculiarly susceptible to dishonest and unfair marketing practices. In United States v. Carolene Products Co., 304 U.S. 144, 149, 150, we upheld the constitutionality of a statute prohibiting the sale of "filled milk" – a condensed milk product from which the vitamin content had been extracted – although honestly labeled and not in itself deleterious. Decision was rested on the ground that Congress could reasonably conclude that the use of the product as a milk substitute deprives consumers of vitamins requisite for health and "facilitates fraud on the public" by "making fraudulent distribution easy and protection of the consumer difficult."

Both the text and legislative history of the present statute plainly show that its purpose was not confined to a requirement of truthful and informative labeling. False and misleading labeling had been prohibited by the Pure Food and Drug Act of 1906. But it was found that such a prohibition was inadequate to protect the consumer from "economic adulteration," by which less expensive ingredients were substituted, or the proportion of more expensive ingredients diminished, so as to make the product, although not in itself deleterious, inferior to that which the consumer expected to receive when purchasing a product with the name under which it was sold. Sen. Rep. No. 493, 73d Cong., 2d Sess., p. 10; Sen. Rep. No. 361, 74th Cong., 1st Sess., p. 10. The remedy chosen was not a requirement of informative labeling. Rather it was the purpose to authorize the Administrator to promulgate definitions and standards of identity "under which the integrity of food products can be effectively maintained" (H. R. Rep. 2139, 75th Cong., 3d Sess., p. 2; H. R. Rep. 2755, 74th Cong., 2d Sess., p. 4), and to require informative labeling only where no such standard had been promulgated, where the food did not purport to comply with a standard, or where the regulations permitted optional ingredients and required their mention on the label. §§403(g), 403(i); see Sen. Rep. No. 361, 74th Cong., 1st Sess., p. 12; Sen. Rep. No. 493, 73d Cong., 2d Sess., pp. 11-12.

The provisions for standards of identity thus reflect a recognition by Congress of the inability of consumers in some cases to determine, solely on the basis of informative labeling, the relative merits of a variety of products superficially resembling each other.[7] We cannot say that such a standard of

---

[7] A Message of the President, dated March 22, 1935, urging passage of the bill and particularly of the standard of identity provision, pointed out that "The various qualities of goods require a kind of discrimination which is not at the command of consumers. They are likely to confuse outward appearances with inward integrity. In such a situation as has grown up through our rising level of living and our multiplication of goods, consumers are prevented from choosing intelligently and producers are handicapped in any attempt to maintain higher standards." H. R. Rep. No. 2755,

identity, designed to eliminate a source of confusion to purchasers – which otherwise would be likely to facilitate unfair dealing and make protection of the consumer difficult – will not "promote honesty and fair dealing" within the meaning of the statute.

Respondent's final and most vigorous attack on the regulations is that they fail to establish reasonable definitions and standards of identity, as §401 requires, in that they prohibit the marketing, under the name "farina," of a wholesome and honestly labeled product consisting of farina with vitamin D added, and that they prevent the addition of vitamin D to products marketed as "enriched farina" unless accompanied by the other prescribed vitamin ingredients which do not co-act with or have any dietary relationship to vitamin D. Stated in another form, the argument is that it is unreasonable to prohibit the addition to farina of vitamin D as an optional ingredient while permitting its addition as an optional ingredient to enriched farina, to the detriment of respondent's business.

The standards of reasonableness to which the Administrator's action must conform are to be found in the terms of the Act construed and applied in the light of its purpose. Its declared purpose is the administrative promulgation of standards of both identity and quality in the interest of consumers. Those standards are to be prescribed and applied, so far as is practicable, to food under its common or usual name, and the regulations adopted after a hearing must have the support of substantial evidence. We must reject at the outset the argument earnestly pressed upon us that the statute does not contemplate a regulation excluding a wholesome and beneficial ingredient from the definition and standard of identity of a food. The statutory purpose to fix a definition of identity of an article of food sold under its common or usual name would be defeated if producers were free to add ingredients, however wholesome, which are not within the definition. As we have seen, the legislative history of the statute manifests the purpose of Congress to substitute, for informative labeling, standards of identity of a food, sold under a common or usual name, so as to give to consumers who purchase it under that name assurance that they will get what they may reasonably expect to receive. In many instances, like the present, that purpose could be achieved only if the definition of identity specified the number, names and proportions of ingredients, however wholesome other combinations might be. The statute accomplished that purpose by authorizing the Administrator to adopt a definition of identity by prescribing some ingredients, including some

---

74th Cong., 2d Sess., pp. 1-2....

which are optional, and excluding others, and by requiring the designation on the label of the optional ingredients permitted.[8]

Since the definition of identity of a vitamin-treated food, marketed under its common or usual name, involves the inclusion of some vitamin ingredients and the exclusion of others, the Administrator necessarily has a large range of choice in determining what may be included and what excluded. It is not necessarily a valid objection to his choice that another could reasonably have been made. The judicial is not to be substituted for the legislative judgment. It is enough that the Administrator has acted within the statutory bounds of his authority, and that his choice among possible alternative standards adapted to the statutory end is one which a rational person could have made.

The evidence discloses that it is well known that the milling process for producing flours and farinas removes from the wheat a substantial part of its health-giving vitamin contents, which are concededly essential to the maintenance of health, and that many consumers desire to purchase wheat products which have been enriched by the restoration of some of the original vitamin content of the wheat. In fixing definitions and standards of identity in conformity with the statutory purpose the Administrator was thus confronted with two related problems. One was the choice of a standard which would appropriately identify unenriched wheat products which had long been on the market. The other was the selection of a standard for enriched wheat products which would both assure to consumers of vitamin-enriched products some of the benefits to health which they sought, and protect them from exploitation through the marketing of vitamin-enriched foods of whose dietary value they were ignorant. In finding the solution the Administrator could take into account the facts that whole wheat is a natural and common source of the valuable dietary ingredients which he prescribed for enriched farina; that wheat is not a source of vitamin D; that milk, a common article of diet, is a satisfactory source of an assimilable form of calcium; that the

---

[8] The standard of identity provision was repeatedly stated in the Committee reports to have been patterned on the Butter Standards Act of 1923. That Act was entitled "An Act to define butter and provide a standard therefor," and establish a legislative definition and standard for butter. The Chairman of the House Committee which reported it said "The only things you can put into [butter] are salt, casein, the butter fat, and water. That is what the definition provides." Hearings, House Committee on Agriculture on H. R. 12053, 67th Cong., 2nd Sess., p. 25....

principal function of vitamin D is to aid in the metabolism of calcium; and that milk enriched with vitamin D was already on the market.

We cannot say that the Administrator made an unreasonable choice of standards when he adopted one which defined the familiar farina of commerce without permitting addition of vitamin enrichment, and at the same time prescribed for "enriched farina" the restoration of those vitamins which had been removed from the whole wheat by milling, and allowed the optional addition of vitamin D, commonly found in milk but not present in wheat. Consumers who buy farina will have no reason to believe that it is enriched. Those who buy enriched farina are assured of receiving a wheat product containing those vitamins naturally present in wheat, and, if so stated on the label, an additional vitamin D, not found in wheat.

Respondent speaks of the high cost of vitamin B1 ($700 per pound), but there was evidence that the cost of adding to flour the minute quantities of the four ingredients required for enriched farina would be about 75 cents per barrel, and respondent concedes that the cost to it may be but a fraction of a cent per pound. The record is otherwise silent as to the probable effect of the increased cost on the marketing of respondent's product. On this record it does not appear that the increased cost has any substantial bearing on the reasonableness of the regulation.

We conclude that the Administrator did not depart from statutory requirements in choosing these standards of identity for the purpose of promoting fair dealing in the interest of consumers, that the standards which he selected are adapted to that end, and that they are adequately supported by findings and evidence.

"Imitation" Foods

The FDCA provides an escape hatch for food producers that want to market a food product that is similar but not identical to another food product, yet still use the same name for that product. In that case, the food name must bear the less-than-appealing qualifier "imitation." The following case concerns the interaction between the provision on "imitation" products and the standards of identity.

62 Cases of Jam et al. v. United States

340 U.S. 593 (1951)

MR. JUSTICE FRANKFURTER delivered the opinion of the Court.

The Federal Food, Drug, and Cosmetic Act authorizes the United States to bring a libel against any article of food which is "misbranded" when using the channels of interstate commerce. The Act defines "misbranded" in the eleven paragraphs of §403. The question before us is raised by two apparently conflicting paragraphs.

One of them, subsection (c), comes from the original Pure Food and Drugs Act of 1906. It directs that a food shall be deemed "misbranded" if it "is an imitation of another food, unless its label bears, in type of uniform size and prominence, the word 'imitation' and, immediately thereafter, the name of the food imitated." The other, subsection (g), was added by the enlargement of the statute in 1938. It condemns as "misbranded" a product which "purports to be or is represented as a food," the ingredients of which the Administrator has standardized, if the product does not conform in all respects to the standards prescribed. The Administrator has authority to promulgate standards when in his judgment "such action will promote honesty and fair dealing in the interest of consumers." §401.

The proceeding before us was commenced in 1949 in the District Court for the District of New Mexico. By it the United States seeks to condemn 62 cases of "Delicious Brand Imitation Jam," manufactured in Colorado and shipped to New Mexico. The Government claims that this product "purports" to be fruit jam, a food for which the Federal Security Administrator has promulgated a "definition and standard of identity." The regulation specifies that a fruit jam must contain "not less than 45 parts by weight" of the fruit ingredient. The product in question is composed of 55% sugar, 25% fruit, 20% pectin, and small amounts of citric acid and soda. These specifications show that pectin, a gelatinized solution consisting largely of water, has been substituted for a substantial proportion of the fruit required. The Government contends that the product is therefore to be deemed "misbranded" under §403(g).

On the basis of stipulated testimony the District Judge found that although the product seized did not meet the prescribed standards for fruit jam, it was "wholesome" and "in every way fit for human consumption." It was found to have the appearance and taste of standardized jam, and to be used as a less expensive substitute for the standard product. In some instances, products similar to those seized were sold at retail to the public in response to telephone orders for jams, and were served to patrons of restaurants, ranches and similar establishments, who had no opportunity to learn the quality of what they received. But there is no suggestion of misrepresentation. The judge found that the labels on the seized jars were substantially accurate; and he concluded that since the product purported to be only an imitation fruit preserve and complied in all respects with subsection (c) of §403 of the Act, it could not be deemed "misbranded."

The Court of Appeals for the Tenth Circuit, one judge dissenting, reversed this judgment. It held that since the product seized closely resembled fruit jam in appearance and taste, and was used as a substitute for the standardized food, it "purported" to be fruit jam, and must be deemed "misbranded" notwithstanding that it was duly labeled an "imitation." The court therefore remanded the cause with instructions to enter a judgment for condemnation. We granted certiorari because of the importance of the question in the administration of the Federal Food, Drug, and Cosmetic Act.

1. By the Act of 1906, as successively strengthened, Congress exerted its power to keep impure and adulterated foods and drugs out of the channels of commerce. The purposes of this legislation, we have said, "touch phases of the lives and health of people which, in the circumstances of modern industrialism, are largely beyond self-protection. Regard for these purposes should infuse construction of the legislation if it is to be treated as a working instrument of government and not merely as a collection of English words." United States v. Dotterweich, 320 U.S. 277, 280. This is the attitude with which we should approach the problem of statutory construction now presented. But our problem is to construe what Congress has written. After all, Congress expresses its purpose by words. It is for us to ascertain – neither to add nor to subtract, neither to delete nor to distort.

2. Misbranding was one of the chief evils Congress sought to stop. It was both within the right and the wisdom of Congress not to trust to the colloquial or the dictionary meaning of misbranding, but to write its own. Concededly we are not dealing here with misbranding in its crude manifestations, what would colloquially be deemed a false representation. Compare §403(a), (b), (d). Our concern is whether the article of food sold as "Delicious Brand Imitation Jam" is "deemed to be misbranded" according to §403(c) and (g) of the Federal Food, Drug, and Cosmetic Act of 1938.

3. The controlling provisions of the Act are as follows:...

> SEC. 401. Whenever in the judgment of the [Administrator] such action will promote honesty and fair dealing in the interest of consumers, he shall promulgate regulations fixing and establishing for any food, under its common or usual name so far as practicable, a reasonable definition and standard of identity, a reasonable standard of quality, and/or reasonable standards of fill of container: .... In prescribing a definition and standard of identity for any food or class of food in which optional ingredients are permitted, the [Administrator] shall, for the purpose of promoting honesty and

> fair dealing in the interest of consumers, designate the optional ingredients which shall be named on the label....
>
> SEC. 403. A food shall be deemed to be misbranded--...
>
> (c) If it is an imitation of another food, unless its label bears, in type of uniform size and prominence, the word 'imitation' and, immediately thereafter, the name of the food imitated....
>
> (g) If it purports to be or is represented as a food for which a definition and standard of identity has been prescribed by regulations as provided by section 401, unless (1) it conforms to such definition and standard, and (2) its label bears the name of the food specified in the definition and standard, and, insofar as may be required by such regulations, the common names of optional ingredients (other than spices, flavoring, and coloring) present in such food.

4. By §§401 and 403(g), Congress vested in the Administrator the far-reaching power of fixing for any species of food "a reasonable definition and standard of identity." In Federal Security Administrator v. Quaker Oats Co., 318 U.S. 218, we held that this means that the Administrator may, by regulation, fix the ingredients of any food, and that thereafter a commodity cannot be introduced into interstate commerce which "purports to be or is represented as" the food which has been thus defined unless it is composed of the required ingredients. The Administrator had prescribed the ingredients of two different species of food – "farina" and "enriched farina." The former was an exclusively milled wheat product; the latter included certain additional ingredients, one of which optionally could be vitamin D. The Quaker Oats Company marketed a product it called "Quaker Farina Wheat Cereal Enriched with Vitamin D," which did not conform to either standard. Because it contained an additional vitamin it was not "farina"; because it lacked certain of the essential ingredients it could not be called "enriched farina." It was concededly a wholesome product, accurately labeled; but under the Administrator's regulations it could not be sold. We sustained the regulations, holding that Congress had constitutionally empowered the Administrator to define a food and had thereby precluded manufacturers – or courts – from determining for themselves whether some other ingredients would not produce as nutritious a product. "The statutory purpose to fix a definition of identity of an article of food sold under its common or usual name would be defeated if producers were free to add ingredients, however wholesome, which are not within the definition." 318 U.S. at 232.

5. Our decision in the *Quaker Oats* case does not touch the problem now before us. In that case it was conceded that although the Quaker product did

not have the standard ingredients, it "purported" to be a standardized food. We did not there consider the legality of marketing properly labeled "imitation farina." That would be the comparable question to the one now here.

According to the Federal Food, Drug, and Cosmetic Act, nothing can be legally "jam" after the Administrator promulgated his regulation in 1940, 5 Fed. Reg. 3554, 21 C.F.R. §29.0, unless it contains the specified ingredients in prescribed proportion. Hence the product in controversy is not "jam." It cannot lawfully be labeled "jam" and introduced into interstate commerce, for to do so would "represent" as a standardized food a product which does not meet prescribed specifications.

But the product with which we are concerned is sold as "imitation jam." Imitation foods are dealt with in §403 (c) of the Act. In that section Congress did not give an esoteric meaning to "imitation." It left it to the understanding of ordinary English speech. And it directed that a product should be deemed "misbranded" if it imitated another food "unless its label bears, in type of uniform size and prominence, the word 'imitation' and, immediately thereafter, the name of the food imitated."

In ordinary speech there can be no doubt that the product which the United States here seeks to condemn is an "imitation" jam. It looks and tastes like jam; it is unequivocally labeled "imitation jam." The Government does not argue that its label in any way falls short of the requirements of §403(c). Its distribution in interstate commerce would therefore clearly seem to be authorized by that section. We could hold it to be "misbranded" only if we held that a practice Congress authorized by §403(c) Congress impliedly prohibited by §403(g).

We see no justification so to distort the ordinary meaning of the statute. Nothing in the text or history of the legislation points to such a reading of what Congress wrote. In §403(g) Congress used the words "purport" and "represent" – terms suggesting the idea of counterfeit. But the name "imitation jam" at once connotes precisely what the product is: a different, an inferior preserve, not meeting the defined specifications. Section 403(g) was designed to protect the public from inferior foods resembling standard products but marketed under distinctive names. See S. Rep. No. 361, 74th Cong., 1st Sess. 8-11. Congress may well have supposed that similar confusion would not result from the marketing of a product candidly and flagrantly labeled as an "imitation" food. A product so labeled is described with precise accuracy. It neither conveys any ambiguity nor emanates any untrue innuendo, as was the case with the "Bred Spred" considered by Congress in its deliberation on §403(g). See H. R. Rep. No. 2139, 75th Cong., 3d Sess. 5; House Hearings on H. R. 6906, 8805, 8941 and S. 5, 74th Cong., 1st Sess. 46-47. It purports and is represented to be only what it is – an imitation. It does not purport nor represent to be what it is not – the Administrator's genuine "jam."

In our anxiety to effectuate the congressional purpose of protecting the public, we must take care not to extend the scope of the statute beyond the point where Congress indicated it would stop. The Government would have us hold that when the Administrator standardizes the ingredients of a food, no imitation of that food can be marketed which contains an ingredient of the original and serves a similar purpose. If Congress wishes to say that nothing shall be marketed in likeness to a food as defined by the Administrator, though it is accurately labeled, entirely wholesome, and perhaps more within the reach of the meager purse, our decisions indicate that Congress may well do so. But Congress has not said so. It indicated the contrary. Indeed, the Administrator's contemporaneous construction concededly is contrary to what he now contends. We must assume his present misconception results from a misreading of what was written in the *Quaker Oats* case.

MR. JUSTICE DOUGLAS, with whom MR. JUSTICE BLACK concurs, dissenting.

The result reached by the Court may be sound by legislative standards. But the legal standards which govern us make the process of reaching that result tortuous to say the least. We must say that petitioner's "jam" purports to be "jam" when we read §403(g) and purports to be not "jam" but another food when we read §403(c). Yet if petitioner's product did not purport to be "jam" petitioner would have no claim to press and the Government no objection to raise.

Note

Did the Court get it right? What effect might its ruling have on the effectiveness of the FDA's standards of identity regime? What effect might the opposite ruling have had on the availability of wholesome but "inferior" – and less costly – food? Consider, in addition to the reasoning of the Supreme Court, the views of the judge who dissented from the Tenth Circuit's decision upholding the government's position:

> It is clear to me that the very purpose of Section 343(c) is to permit on the market a wholesome and nutritious food which is within the means of a great mass of our people who are unable to purchase the standard products....

> A large portion of the food consumed today comes within the provisions of the Act. To sustain the government's position here gives the Federal Security Administrator absolute control over the ingredients of all such foods. He will have the right to standardize the same, which will mean virtually a standardization of the price. It will remove from the market a nutritious and wholesome food which sells for approximately one-half the price of standard product. The purchasing public, regardless of their ability to pay, will be forced to purchase the same quality of food. I cannot believe Congress had any such intent....

Below is another case on the FDCA's provision on "imitation" foods.

United States v. 651 Cases, More or Less, of Chocolate Chil-Zert

114 F. Supp. 430 (N.D.N.Y. 1953)

BRENNAN, District Judge:

On September 30, 1952, about 650 cases of Rich's Chocolate Chil-Zert was seized at New Orleans, Louisiana, under the provisions of the Federal Food, Drug and Cosmetic Act. The libel alleged that the food product known as "Chil-Zert" is misbranded in that it is an imitation of another food to-wit, chocolate flavored ice cream and fails to bear the word "imitation" followed by the name of the food imitated as required by the provisions of [§403(c)] and that it was further misbranded in that its label fails to bear the name of each ingredient as required by the provisions of [§403(i)(2)]....

The problem here involved the construction and application of that part of the section of the Federal Food, Drug and Cosmetic Act quoted below:

> Sec. 403. A food shall be deemed to be misbranded--...
>
> (c) If it is an imitation of another food, unless its label bears, in type of uniform size and prominence, the word "imitation" and, immediately thereafter, the name of the food imitated.

Imitation is initially a question of fact, but both parties agree that there are no material facts in dispute, and the question becomes one of law.

Chil-Zert is a food product manufactured at Buffalo, New York, and the cases seized were shipped in interstate commerce to New Orleans, Louisiana, in the latter half of the year 1952. It is a comparatively new product, having been offered for sale in only two cities. It contains the usual ingredients of chocolate-flavored ice cream in approximately the same proportions, except that soy fat and soy protein are used therein in place of milk fat and milk protein. The product is similar in taste and appearance to chocolate ice cream. It has the same characteristics such as color, taste, texture, body and melting qualities. It is manufactured substantially in the same manner as chocolate flavored ice cream, and with the use of similar machinery. It is appropriate for use for the same purposes for which ice cream is used and is packaged and offered for sale in containers or cartons of the same size, shape and description as those used in the packaging and selling of ice cream. The retail price of pint packages of chocolate Chil-Zert is substantially lower than the average retail price of a pint of ice cream, as shown by Labor Department statistics for 1951, cited by the claimant.

The food sought to be condemned is packaged in pint carton containers with the words "Rich's Chocolate Chil-Zert" prominently printed on the four sides of the container and on the top and bottom thereof. Immediately below the words quoted above and in prominent letters the words "not an ice cream" appear, and on two sides of the carton there also appear the words "contains no milk or milk fat." The ingredients are printed on two sides of the carton, and the product is referred to as "The Delicious New Frozen Dessert." Advertising copy is attached to the moving papers which need not be described in detail. It is sufficient to say that there is no claim made here as to deceptive or misleading statements as to the advertising of the product.

The government contends that Chocolate Chil-Zert is an imitation of another food; to-wit, chocolate ice cream, and is, therefore, misbranded, since the word "imitation" followed by the name of the food imitated does not appear upon the container in which the food is packed, shipped and offered for sale. The claimant contends that Chocolate Chil-Zert is a new distinctive product composed of natural rather than artificial ingredients; that, as labeled, no element of deception is involved, and it is, therefore, not an imitation within the meaning of the statute. Claimant further contends that, since no legal standard has been promulgated for chocolate ice cream, the test of imitation may not be applied.

Congress has not defined the word "imitation" as it is used in the present section of the law set forth above. Judicial precedent does not confine its meaning within a rigid mould. Ordinary understanding of the term appears to be the test of its meaning.

"Imitation foods are dealt with in Sec. 403(c) of the Act. In the section Congress did not give an esoteric meaning to 'imitation.' It left it to the understanding of ordinary English speech." 62 Cases of Jam v. United States, 340 U.S. 593, 599.

It is plain that no all-inclusive test of imitation can be prescribed. Resemblance and taste are elements.... Smell is included as one of the elements. The word connotes inferiority, in the sense that it is cheapened by the substitution of ingredients. Resemblance alone is not enough to constitute imitation. It would seem that imitation is tested not by the presence or absence of any one element of similarity, but rather by the effect of a composite of all such elements. As indicated above, Chil-Zert is identical with ice cream in its method of manufacture, packaging and sale. It is similar in taste, appearance, color, texture, body and melting qualities. It has identical uses; its composition differs only from ice cream in the substitution of a cheaper ingredient; namely, vegetable oil in place of milk products. It is, therefore, something less than the genuine article chocolate ice cream. It is inescapable that the ordinary understanding of English speech would denominate it as an imitation of ice cream.

The claimant's contentions have not been overlooked and will be briefly discussed. The following quotation taken from claimant's brief appears to the Court to be the sum total of claimant's contention. "We predicate our case, however, in the last analysis, upon the principle that the manufacturer of Chil-Zert has a right to market the product, if he does so honestly, regardless of whether it has greater or less merit than an existing product such as ice cream."...

Claimant does not purport to pass off its product as ice cream. The labeling of the product in language negates any such contention. It may be debatable whether or not the words "not an ice cream" will act as a warning or as a snare for the unwary purchaser. In any event, it is not for the claimant to choose the means or method to advise the public that his product is not in fact the one which is imitated. The statute in explicit terms makes a provision therefor. It may be that the requirement of the statute would be less effective than the means adopted by the claimant. Such an argument is one for Congress and not for the Court. Truthful labeling does not exempt Chil-Zert from the requirement of the statute. Neither is deception nor intent to mislead necessary to establish that claimant's product is an imitation. The Court is impressed that claimant's argument proceeds as if the distinctive name provision of the 1906 Act is still in force, and claimant seeks to use the fanciful name of Chil-Zert with informative labeling to escape the provisions of the present statue. (The distinctive name provision was eliminated in the 1938 Act.)

Claimant's contention to the effect that chocolate ice cream is not imitated by Chil-Zert because no legal standard has been promulgated therefor will be briefly referred to. In other words, it is contended that a food may not be imitated until it is defined. A short answer to such an argument is that the statute does not refer to an imitation only to foods for which a standard has been set. If Congress has intended to so limit the law, it is reasonable to conclude that it would have so stated. The statutory provisions as to adulterations apply to non-standardized food. The same reasoning would seem to apply to the misbranding provisions of the law.

Research fails to disclose that the section of the statute invoked here has been extensively used. In fact, no case has been cited by either counsel in which Section [403(c)] has been invoked under circumstances comparable to those which exist here. The Court has tried to keep in mind the beneficial purposes of the statute and at the same time not to unduly restrict the marketing of the many variations of well known food products. It is difficult to conceive that the statute invoked has any purpose unless it is applicable here. It is concluded that...the libellant's motion for a summary judgment is granted....

Notes

Critics charged that a strict definition of "imitation" thwarted innovation in the food marketplace. Companies desiring to create healthier versions of particular foods faced a difficult choice of either refraining from this innovation or labeling the new products "imitation" – not exactly an appealing term. Eventually, the FDA stated that a product did not need to be labeled "imitation" so long as it was not "nutritionally inferior" to the product it was imitating.

Critics also maintained that rigid standards of identity thwarted innovation. The FDA now allows "safe and suitable" ingredients, even if not provided for in the relevant standard of identity, when there is a nutrient content claim for the food product (such as "reduced calorie") and the additional ingredient ensures that the food product is not inferior to the standardized food. For example, the standard of identity for milk allows a "nutritive sweetener" (such as sugar) as a flavoring ingredient. If a company sells milk as "reduced calorie," it may add a non-nutritive sweetener (such as aspartame) without running afoul of the standard of identity for milk.

Even so, critics believe that the system remains too rigid. Dairy trade groups have recently petitioned the FDA to amend the standard of identity for milk and other dairy products to allow any safe and suitable sweetener as an optional ingredient. They contend, among other things, that claims such as "reduced calorie" are not attractive to children and that it would be best to exclude such a claim from the label. Indeed, the petitioners say that since consumers do not recognize milk – even flavored milk – as containing sugar, milk flavored with non-nutritive sweeteners should be labeled simply as milk so that consumers can "more easily identify its overall nutritional value."

Pause for a moment to marvel (or wince?) at the complexity of a system aimed at making food labels simple for ordinary consumers to understand.

As the following warning letter from the FDA observes, the standard of identity for milk provides that milk is "the lacteal secretion, practically free from colostrum, obtained by the complete milking of one or more healthy cows." After reading the following warning letter from the FDA, ask yourself: Is soymilk "milk"? Is goat's milk "milk"? Milk producers have asked that FDA to take enforcement action against the use of the nomenclature "soymilk" to describe beverages made from soy. Although the agency has occasionally issued warning letters to companies that use the term "milk" for products that do not contain milk as that term has been defined by the FDA, these efforts have been sporadic. A soyfoods trade group has, for its part, petitioned the FDA to recognize that "soymilk" is the "common or usual name" for certain soy-based beverages and that this term "should be officially recognized by FDA as the correct name for the product." The petition has been pending since 1997.

A bill pending in Congress – the "DAIRY PRIDE Act" – would, according to sponsor Senator Tammy Baldwin,

> protect the integrity of milk by requiring foods that make an inaccurate claim about milk contents to be considered "misbranded" and subject to enforcement. The *DAIRY PRIDE Act* would require the FDA to issue guidance for nationwide enforcement of mislabeled imitation dairy products within 90 days and require the FDA to report to Congress two years after enactment to hold the agency accountable for this update in their enforcement obligations.

Good idea? Who would be helped by this bill?

The warning letter that follows reflects one of the FDA's intermittent forays into this controversy.

Warning Letter

From Barbara Cassens, FDA District Director, San Francisco, Cal.
To Michael Pickett, CytoSport, Benicia, Cal.
June 29, 2011

Dear Mr. Pickett:

The Food and Drug Administration (FDA) has reviewed the labels for your "Chocolate Muscle Milk Protein Nutrition Shake" (14 fl. oz.), "Vanilla Crème Muscle Milk Light Nutritional Shake" (4-8.25 oz. servings), and "Chocolate Peanut Caramel Muscle Milk" (5.57 oz.) products. Based on our review, we have concluded that these products are in violation of the Federal Food, Drug, and Cosmetic Act (the Act) and the applicable regulations in Title 21, Code of Federal Regulations, Part 101 (21 CFR Part 101). These products are misbranded within the meaning of section 403 of the Act [21 U.S.C. § 343]. You can find copies of the Act and these regulations through links on FDA's home page at http://www.fda.gov.

1. Your "Chocolate Muscle Milk Protein Nutrition Shake" and "Vanilla Crème Muscle Milk Light Nutritional Shake" products are misbranded within the meaning of section 403(a)(1) of the Act [21 U.S.C. § 343(a)(1)] in that the labels are false or misleading. For example:

- These product labels prominently feature the word "MILK," however these products contain no milk. The actual statements of identity, "Protein Nutrition Shake" and "Nutritional Shake" are in significantly smaller and less prominent type than the words "MUSCLE MILK" on these product labels.
- These product labels include the statement "Contains No Milk" on the principal display panel; however, according to the ingredient statements, these products contain the following milk-derived ingredients: calcium and sodium caseinate, milk protein isolate, and whey. The allergen statement printed on both of these products states "This product contains ingredients derived from milk . . . ." The "Contains No Milk" statement could give consumers the impression that these products are free of milk-derived ingredients.

2. Your "Chocolate Muscle Milk Protein Nutrition Shake" and "Vanilla Crème Muscle Milk Light Nutritional Shake" products are misbranded within the meaning of section 403(g)(1) of the Act [21 U.S.C. § 343(g)(1)] because they purport to be a food for which a definition and standard of identity has been prescribed by regulation but they fail to conform to such definition and standard. Specifically, these products purport to be milk by prominently featuring the word "MILK" on the labels. Milk is a food for which a definition and standard of identity has been prescribed by regulation. The standard of identity for milk (21 CFR 131.110) describes milk as "the lacteal secretion, practically free from colostrum, obtained by the complete milking of one or more healthy cows" and it lists the vitamins and other ingredients that may be added. According to the ingredient list on your

product labels, your products contain no milk and contain numerous ingredients not permitted by the standard; therefore, your products do not conform to the standard of identity for milk....

This letter is not intended to be an all-inclusive review of your products and their labeling. It is your responsibility to ensure that all of your products comply with the Act and its implementing regulations. You should take prompt action to correct these violations. Failure to do so may result in regulatory action without further notice. Such action may include, but is not limited to, seizure or injunction....

"COMMON OR USUAL" NAMES

Recall that the FDCA requires a food product label to include the "common or usual name of the food, if any there be." Sometimes a food does not have a common or usual name; sometimes a food product is so novel that no name exists for it outside of the name its producer invents for it. In that situation, the FDA has sometimes found it useful to settle upon the name to be used for such a product.

So it was that the FDA came to spend 25 years considering the appropriate name for beverages that are blends of several different kinds of juices. What, for example, should the name be for a beverage that contains multiple juices in varying amounts? What if the beverage is predominantly made of, say, apple juice, but contains a tiny amount of pomegranate juice as well? Can it be named "pomegranate juice"? The FDA settled on a rule that a blend of juices that has a name that does not include all of the juices in the blend and indeed includes only juices that do not predominate in the blend must either declare the percentage content of the named juice(s) or "[i]ndicate that the named juice is present as a flavor or flavoring." Thus, a beverage that contained raspberry and cranberry juice but also contained – as a predominant ingredient – apple juice would need either to declare the percentage of the raspberry and cranberry juices or be called something like "raspberry and cranberry flavored juice drink."

Confused yet?

So, apparently, are consumers. That, at least, is the premise of the lawsuit underlying the following decision on the interaction between the FDCA and the Lanham Act.

POM Wonderful LLC v. Coca-Cola Co.

134 S.Ct. 2228 (2014)

JUSTICE KENNEDY delivered the opinion of the Court.

POM Wonderful LLC makes and sells pomegranate juice products, including a pomegranate-blueberry juice blend. One of POM's competitors is the CocaCola Company. Coca-Cola's Minute Maid Division makes a juice blend sold with a label that, in describing the contents, displays the words "pomegranate blueberry" with far more prominence than other words on the label that show the juice to be a blend of five juices. In truth, the Coca-Cola product contains but 0.3% pomegranate juice and 0.2% blueberry juice.

Alleging that the use of that label is deceptive and misleading, POM sued Coca-Cola under §43 of the Lanham Act. That provision allows one competitor to sue another if it alleges unfair competition arising from false or misleading product descriptions. The Court of Appeals for the Ninth Circuit held that, in the realm of labeling for food and beverages, a Lanham Act claim like POM's is precluded by a second federal statute. The second statute is the Federal Food, Drug, and Cosmetic Act (FDCA), which forbids the misbranding of food, including by means of false or misleading labeling.

The ruling that POM's Lanham Act cause of action is precluded by the FDCA was incorrect. There is no statutory text or established interpretive principle to support the contention that the FDCA precludes Lanham Act suits like the one brought by POM in this case. Nothing in the text, history, or structure of the FDCA or the Lanham Act shows the congressional purpose or design to forbid these suits. Quite to the contrary, the FDCA and the Lanham Act complement each other in the federal regulation of misleading food and beverage labels. Competitors, in their own interest, may bring Lanham Act claims like POM's that challenge food and beverage labels that are regulated by the FDCA.

I

A

This case concerns the intersection and complementarity of these two federal laws. A proper beginning point is a description of the statutes.

. . .

The Lanham Act creates a cause of action for unfair competition through misleading advertising or labeling. Though in the end consumers also benefit from the Act's proper enforcement, the cause of action is for competitors, not consumers....

The cause of action the Act creates imposes civil liability on any person who "uses in commerce any word, term, name, symbol, or device, or any combination thereof, or any false designation of origin, false or misleading description of fact, or false or misleading representation of fact, which . . . misrepresents the nature, characteristics, qualities, or geographic origin of his or her or another person's goods, services, or commercial activities." 15 U. S. C. §1125(a)(1).... POM's cause of action would be straightforward enough but for Coca-Cola's contention that a separate federal statutory regime, the FDCA, allows it to use the label in question and in fact precludes the Lanham Act claim.

So the FDCA is the second statute to be discussed. The FDCA statutory regime is designed primarily to protect the health and safety of the public at large. See 62 Cases of Jam v. United States, 340 U. S. 593, 596 (1951); FDCA, §401, 52 Stat. 1046, 21 U. S. C. §341 (agency may issue certain regulations to "promote honesty and fair dealing in the interest of consumers"). The FDCA prohibits the misbranding of food and drink. A food or drink is deemed misbranded if, inter alia, "its labeling is false or misleading," §343(a), information required to appear on its label "is not prominently placed thereon," §343(f), or a label does not bear "the common or usual name of the food, if any there be," §343(i). To implement these provisions, the Food and Drug Administration (FDA) promulgated regulations regarding food and beverage labeling, including the labeling of mixes of different types of juice into one juice blend. See 21 CFR §102.33 (2013). One provision of those regulations is particularly relevant to this case: If a juice blend does not name all the juices it contains and mentions only juices that are not predominant in the blend, then it must either declare the percentage content of the named juice or "[i]ndicate that the named juice is present as a flavor or flavoring," e.g., "raspberry and cranberry flavored juice drink." §102.33(d). The Government represents that the FDA does not preapprove juice labels under these regulations. That contrasts with the FDA's regulation of other types of labels, such as drug labels, see 21 U. S. C. §355(d), and is consistent with the less extensive role the FDA plays in the regulation of food than in the regulation of drugs.

Unlike the Lanham Act, which relies in substantial part for its enforcement on private suits brought by injured competitors, the FDCA and its regulations provide the United States with nearly exclusive enforcement authority, including the authority to seek criminal sanctions in some circumstances. Private parties may not bring enforcement suits. §337. Also unlike the Lanham Act, the FDCA contains a provision pre-empting certain state laws on misbranding. That provision, which Congress added to the FDCA in the Nutrition Labeling and Education Act of 1990, forecloses a "State or political subdivision of a State" from establishing requirements that are of the type but "not identical to" the requirements in some of the misbranding provisions of the FDCA. 21 U. S. C. §343–1(a). It does not address, or refer to, other federal statutes or the preclusion thereof.

B

POM Wonderful LLC is a grower of pomegranates and a distributor of pomegranate juices. Through its POM Wonderful brand, POM produces, markets, and sells a variety of pomegranate products, including a pomegranate blueberry juice blend.

POM competes in the pomegranate-blueberry juice market with the Coca-Cola Company. Coca-Cola, under its Minute Maid brand, created a juice blend containing 99.4% apple and grape juices, 0.3% pomegranate juice, 0.2% blueberry juice, and 0.1% raspberry juice. Despite the minuscule amount of pomegranate and blueberry juices in the blend, the front label of the Coca-Cola product displays the words "pomegranate blueberry" in all capital letters, on two separate lines. Below those words, Coca-Cola placed the phrase "flavored blend of 5 juices" in much smaller type. And below that phrase, in still smaller type, were the words "from concentrate with added ingredients"—and, with a line break before the final phrase— "and other natural flavors." Ibid. The product's front label also displays a vignette of blueberries, grapes, and raspberries in front of a halved pomegranate and a halved apple.

Claiming that Coca-Cola's label tricks and deceives consumers, all to POM's injury as a competitor, POM brought suit under the Lanham Act. POM alleged that the name, label, marketing, and advertising of Coca-Cola's juice blend mislead consumers into believing the product consists predominantly of pomegranate and blueberry juice when it in fact consists predominantly of less expensive apple and grape juices. That confusion, POM complained, causes it to lose sales. POM sought damages and injunctive relief.

The District Court granted partial summary judgment to Coca-Cola on POM's Lanham Act claim, ruling that the FDCA and its regulations preclude challenges to the name and label of Coca-Cola's juice blend. The District Court reasoned that in the juice blend regulations the "FDA has directly spoken on the issues that form the basis of Pom's Lanham Act claim against the naming and labeling of" Coca-Cola's product, but has not pro-

hibited any, and indeed expressly has permitted some, aspects of CocaCola's label.

The Court of Appeals for the Ninth Circuit affirmed in relevant part. Like the District Court, the Court of Appeals reasoned that Congress decided "to entrust matters of juice beverage labeling to the FDA"; the FDA has promulgated "comprehensive regulation of that labeling"; and the FDA "apparently" has not imposed the requirements on Coca-Cola's label that are sought by POM. "[U]nder [Circuit] precedent," the Court of Appeals explained, "for a court to act when the FDA has not—despite regulating extensively in this area— would risk undercutting the FDA's expert judgments and authority." For these reasons, and "[o]ut of respect for the statutory and regulatory scheme," the Court of Appeals barred POM's Lanham Act claim.

II

A

This Court granted certiorari to consider whether a private party may bring a Lanham Act claim challenging a food label that is regulated by the FDCA. The answer to that question is based on the following premises.

First, this is not a pre-emption case. In pre-emption cases, the question is whether state law is pre-empted by a federal statute, or in some instances, a federal agency action. This case, however, concerns the alleged preclusion of a cause of action under one federal statute by the provisions of another federal statute. So the state-federal balance does not frame the inquiry. Because this is a preclusion case, any "presumption against pre-emption" has no force.... Although the Court's pre-emption precedent does not govern preclusion analysis in this case, its principles are instructive insofar as they are designed to assess the interaction of laws that bear on the same subject.

Second, this is a statutory interpretation case and the Court relies on traditional rules of statutory interpretation. That does not change because the case involves multiple federal statutes. Nor does it change because an agency is involved. Analysis of the statutory text, aided by established principles of interpretation, controls....

B

Beginning with the text of the two statutes, it must be observed that neither the Lanham Act nor the FDCA, in express terms, forbids or limits Lanham Act claims challenging labels that are regulated by the FDCA. By its terms, the Lanham Act subjects to suit any person who "misrepresents the nature, characteristics, qualities, or geographic origin" of goods or services. 15 U. S. C. §1125(a). This comprehensive imposition of liability extends, by its own terms, to misrepresentations on labels, including food and beverage labels. No other provision in the Lanham Act limits that understanding or purports to govern the relevant interaction between the Lanham Act and the FDCA. And the FDCA, by its terms, does not preclude Lanham Act suits. In consequence, food and beverage labels regulated by the FDCA are not, under the terms of either statute, off limits to Lanham Act claims. No textual provision in either statute discloses a purpose to bar unfair competition claims like POM's.

This absence is of special significance because the Lanham Act and the FDCA have coexisted since the passage of the Lanham Act in 1946. If Congress had concluded, in light of experience, that Lanham Act suits could interfere with the FDCA, it might well have enacted a provision addressing the issue during these 70 years. Congress enacted amendments to the FDCA and the Lanham Act, including an amendment that added to the FDCA an express pre-emption provision with respect to state laws addressing food and beverage misbranding. Yet Congress did not enact a provision addressing the preclusion of other federal laws that might bear on food and beverage labeling....

The structures of the FDCA and the Lanham Act reinforce the conclusion drawn from the text. When two statutes complement each other, it would show disregard for the congressional design to hold that Congress nonetheless intended one federal statute to preclude the operation of the other. The Lanham Act and the FDCA complement each other in major respects, for each has its own scope and purpose. Although both statutes touch on food and beverage labeling, the Lanham Act protects commercial interests against unfair competition, while the FDCA protects public health and safety. The two statutes impose "different requirements and protections." J.E.M. Ag Supply v. Pioneer Hi-Bred In'tl, 534 U.S. 124, 144].

The two statutes complement each other with respect to remedies in a more fundamental respect. Enforcement of the FDCA and the detailed prescriptions of its implementing regulations is largely committed to the FDA. The FDA, however, does not have the same perspective or expertise in assessing market dynamics that day-to-day competitors possess. Competitors who manufacture or distribute products have detailed knowledge regarding how consumers rely upon certain sales and marketing strategies. Their awareness of unfair competition practices may be far more immediate and accurate than that of agency rulemakers and regulators. Lanham Act suits draw upon this market expertise by empowering private parties to sue competitors to protect their interests on a case-by-case basis. By "serv[ing] a distinct compensatory function that may motivate injured persons to come forward," Lanham Act suits, to the extent they touch on the same subject matter as the FDCA, "provide incentives" for manufacturers to behave well. [Wyeth v. Levine, 555 U.S. 555, 579 (2009)]. Allowing Lanham Act suits takes advantage of synergies among multiple methods of regulation. This is quite consistent with the congressional design to enact two different statutes, each with its own mechanisms to enhance the protection of competitors and consumers.

A holding that the FDCA precludes Lanham Act claims challenging food and beverage labels would not only ignore the distinct functional aspects of the FDCA and the Lanham Act but also would lead to a result that Congress likely did not intend. Unlike other types of labels regulated by the FDA, such as drug labels, it would appear the FDA does not preapprove food and beverage labels under its regulations and instead relies on enforcement actions, warning letters, and other measures. Because the FDA acknowledges that it does not necessarily pursue enforcement measures regarding all objectionable labels, if Lanham Act claims were to be precluded then commercial interests—and indirectly the public at large—could be left with less effective protection in the food and beverage labeling realm than in many other, less regulated industries. It is unlikely that Congress intended the FDCA's protection of health and safety to result in less policing of misleading food and beverage labels than in competitive markets for other products.

C

Coca-Cola argues the FDCA precludes POM's Lanham Act claim because Congress intended national uniformity in food and beverage labeling. Coca-Cola notes three aspects of the FDCA to support that position: delegation of enforcement authority to the Federal Government rather than private parties; express pre-emption with respect to state laws; and the specificity of the FDCA and its implementing regulations. But these details of the FDCA do not establish an intent or design to preclude Lanham Act claims.

Coca-Cola says that the FDCA's delegation of enforcement authority to the Federal Government shows Congress' intent to achieve national uniformity in labeling. But POM seeks to enforce the Lanham Act, not the FDCA or its regulations. The centralization of FDCA enforcement authority in the Federal Government does not indicate that Congress intended to foreclose private enforcement of other federal statutes....

[I]t is far from clear that Coca-Cola's assertions about national uniformity in fact reflect the congressional design. Although the application of a federal statute such as the Lanham Act by judges and juries in courts throughout the country may give rise to some variation in outcome, this is the means Congress chose to enforce a national policy to ensure fair competition. It is quite different from the disuniformity that would arise from the multitude of state laws, state regulations, state administrative agency rulings, and state-court decisions that are partially forbidden by the FDCA's pre-emption provision. Congress not infrequently permits a certain amount of variability by authorizing a federal cause of action even in areas of law where national uniformity is important. The Lanham Act itself is an example of this design: Despite Coca-Cola's protestations, the Act is uniform in extending its protection against unfair competition to the whole class it describes. It is variable only to the extent that those rights are enforced on a case-by-case basis. The variability about which Coca-Cola complains is no different than the variability that any industry covered by the Lanham Act faces. And, as noted, Lanham Act actions are a means to implement a uniform policy to prohibit unfair competition in all covered markets.

Finally, Coca-Cola urges that the FDCA, and particularly its implementing regulations, addresses food and beverage labeling with much more specificity than is found in the provisions of the Lanham Act. That is true. The pages of FDA rulemakings devoted only to juice-blend labeling attest to the level of detail with which the FDA has examined the subject. E.g., Food Labeling; Declaration of Ingredients; Common or Usual Name for Non-standardized Foods; Diluted Juice Beverages, 58 Fed. Reg. 2897–2926 (1993). Because, as we have explained, the FDCA and the Lanham Act are complementary and have separate scopes and purposes, this greater specificity would matter only if the Lanham Act and the FDCA cannot be implemented in full at the same time. But neither the statutory structure nor the empirical evidence of which the Court is aware indicates there will be any difficulty in fully enforcing each statute according to its terms.

D

The Government disagrees with both Coca-Cola and POM. It submits that a Lanham Act claim is precluded "to the extent the FDCA or FDA regulations specifically require or authorize the challenged aspects of [the] label." Applying that standard, the Government argues that POM may not bring a Lanham Act challenge to the name of Coca-Cola's product, but that other aspects of the label may be challenged. That is because, the Government argues, the FDA regulations specifically authorize the names of juice blends but not the other aspects of the label that are at issue.

In addition to raising practical concerns about drawing a distinction between regulations that "specifically ... authorize" a course of conduct and those that merely tolerate that course, the flaw in the Government's intermediate position is the same as that in CocaCola's theory of the case. The Government assumes that the FDCA and its regulations are at least in some circumstances a ceiling on the regulation of food and beverage labeling. But, as discussed above, Congress intended the Lanham Act and the FDCA to complement each other with respect to food and beverage labeling.

The Government claims that the "FDA's juice-naming regulation reflects the agency's 'weigh[ing of] the competing interests relevant to the particular requirement in question.'" [U.S. Brief] at 19 (quoting Medtronic, Inc. v. Lohr, 518 U. S. 470, 501 (1996)). The rulemaking indeed does allude, at one point, to a balancing of interests: It styles a particular requirement as "provid[ing] manufacturers with flexibility for labeling products while providing consumers with information that they need." 58 Fed. Reg. 2919–2920. But that rulemaking does not discuss or even cite the Lanham Act, and the Government cites no other statement in the rulemaking suggesting that the FDA considered the full scope of the interests the Lanham Act protects. In addition, and contrary to the language quoted above, the FDA explicitly encouraged manufacturers to include material on their labels that is not required by the regulations. Id., at 2919. A single isolated reference to a desire for flexibility is not sufficient to transform a rulemaking that is otherwise at best inconclusive as to its interaction with other federal laws into one with preclusive force, even on the assumption that a federal regulation in some instances might preclude application of a federal statute....

It is necessary to recognize the implications of the United States' argument for preclusion. The Government asks the Court to preclude private parties from availing themselves of a well-established federal remedy because an agency enacted regulations that touch on similar subject matter but do not purport to displace that remedy or even implement the statute that is its source. Even if agency regulations with the force of law that purport to bar other legal remedies may do so, it is a bridge too far to accept an agency's after-the-fact statement to justify that result here. An agency may not reorder federal statutory rights without congressional authorization.

***

Coca-Cola and the United States ask the Court to elevate the FDCA and the FDA's regulations over the private cause of action authorized by the Lanham Act. But the FDCA and the Lanham Act complement each other in the federal regulation of misleading labels. Congress did not intend the

FDCA to preclude Lanham Act suits like POM's. The position Coca-Cola takes in this Court that because food and beverage labeling is involved it has no Lanham Act liability here for practices that allegedly mislead and trick consumers, all to the injury of competitors, finds no support in precedent or the statutes. The judgment of the Court of Appeals for the Ninth Circuit is reversed, and the case is remanded for further proceedings consistent with this opinion.

Note

Does the Court accurately describe the purpose of the Food, Drug, and Cosmetic Act? With this decision, does the Court effectively undo the FDA's rule on naming juice blends? Does the Court's decision favor competitors over consumers?

CHAPTER 5
HEALTH CLAIMS AND "QUALIFIED" HEALTH CLAIMS

Have you ever seen a food label like the following: "Green tea may reduce the risk of breast or prostate cancer. FDA has concluded that there is very little scientific evidence for this claim." Or this: "Whole grains may reduce the risk of type 2 diabetes, although the FDA has concluded that there is very limited scientific evidence for this claim." What on earth are such labels supposed to convey? Aren't they self-contradictory? And how could the FDA – the agency charged by statute with ensuring that food labels are not misleading – allow such labels to persist? The materials for today will help you to understand the answers to these questions.

Recall that the Food, Drug, and Cosmetic Act defines "drugs" as "articles intended for use in the diagnosis, cure, mitigation, treatment, or prevention of disease in man or other animals" and "articles (other than food) intended to affect the structure or any function of the body of man or other animals." A "health claim" – that is, a claim asserting a relationship between a food or dietary supplement and the risk of particular diseases or health-related conditions – could move a food or dietary supplement into the highly regulated category of "drugs."

Before the Nutrition and Labeling Education Act of 1990 (NLEA), the FDA had no explicit authority to permit health claims for foods or dietary supplements. The NLEA gave the agency this authority. In 1994, the Dietary Supplement Health and Education Act (DSHEA) gave the FDA authority to allow "structure/function" claims for dietary supplements – that is, claims describing the role of a nutrient or dietary ingredient in the structure or functioning of the human body. "Calcium builds strong bones" is an example of a structure/function claim. Crucially, these statutory revisions allowed marketers of food and dietary supplements to make claims about the beneficial properties of these products for human health, without satisfying the more stringent regulatory requirements for drugs.

The NLEA also gave the agency the power to regulate "nutrient content" claims for foods. Nutrient content claims emphasize the levels of important nutrients, cholesterol, fiber, or calories in foods. "Low-fat," "low-sodium," "lean," and "low-calorie" are just a few of the nutrient content claims now regulated by the FDA.

Here, our main focus will be on health claims and on a new category of claims – "qualified" health claims – necessitated by the D.C. Circuit's 1999 decision in *Pearson v. Shalala*. In that case, the court held that the first amendment requires the FDA to allow certain health- or disease-related claims if accompanied by a suitable disclaimer – thus ushering in an era of internally inconsistent labels like the ones for green tea and whole grains, noted above.

In the statutory provisions below, note the different legal treatment of health-related claims made for food and dietary supplements. Is this difference justified?

Food, Drug, and Cosmetic Act

21 U.S.C. § 343

SEC. 403. MISBRANDED FOOD

A food shall be deemed to be misbranded—

(a) If

(1) its labeling is false or misleading in any particular...

(r)

(1)...it is a food intended for human consumption which is offered for sale and for which a claim is made in the label or labeling of the food which expressly or by implication—...

(B) characterizes the relationship of any nutrient which is of the type required by paragraph (q)(1) or (q)(2) to be in the label or labeling of the food to a disease or a health-related condition unless the claim is made in accordance with subparagraph (3)....

(3)

(A)...a claim described in subparagraph (1)(B) may only be made—

(i) if the claim meets the requirements of the regulations of the Secretary promulgated under clause (B)...

(B)

(i) The Secretary shall promulgate regulations authorizing claims of the type described in subparagraph (1)(B) only if the Secretary determines, based on the totality of publicly available scientific evidence (including evidence from well-designed studies conducted in a manner which is consistent with generally recognized scientific procedures and principles), that there is significant scientific agreement, among experts qualified by scientific training and experience to evaluate such claims, that the claim is supported by such evidence.

(ii) A regulation described in subclause (i) shall describe—

(I) the relationship between a nutrient of the type required in the label or labeling of food by paragraph (q)(1) or (q)(2) and a disease or health-related condition, and

(II) the significance of each such nutrient in affecting such disease or health-related condition.

(iii) A regulation described in subclause (i) shall require such claim to be stated in a manner so that the claim is an accurate representation of the matters set out in subclause (ii) and so that the claim enables the public to comprehend the information provided in the claim and to understand the relative significance of such information in the context of a total daily diet....

(5)(D) A subparagraph (1)(B) claim made with respect to a dietary supplement of vitamins, minerals, herbs, or other similar nutritional substances shall not be subject to subparagraph (3) but shall be subject to a procedure and standard, respecting the validity of such claim, established by regulation of the Secretary.

(6) For purposes of paragraph (r)(1)(B), a statement for a dietary supplement may be made if—

(A) the statement claims a benefit related to a classical nutrient deficiency disease and discloses the prevalence of such disease in the United States, describes the role of a nutrient or dietary ingredient intended to affect the structure or function in humans, characterizes the documented mechanism by which a nutrient or dietary ingredient acts to maintain such structure or function, or describes general well-being from consumption of a nutrient or dietary ingredient,

(B) the manufacturer of the dietary supplement has substantiation that such statement is truthful and not misleading, and

(C) the statement contains, prominently displayed and in boldface type, the following: "This statement has not been evaluated by the Food and Drug Administration. This product is not intended to diagnose, treat, cure, or prevent any disease."

A statement under this subparagraph may not claim to diagnose, mitigate, treat, cure, or prevent a specific disease or class of diseases. If the manufacturer of a dietary supplement proposes to make a statement described in the first sentence of this subparagraph in the labeling of the dietary supplement, the manufacturer shall notify the Secretary no later than 30 days after the first marketing of the dietary supplement with such statement that such a statement is being made.

Pearson v. Shalala

164 F.3d 650 (D.C. Cir. 1999)

SILBERMAN, Circuit Judge.

Marketers of dietary supplements must, before including on their labels a claim characterizing the relationship of the supplement to a disease or health-related condition, submit the claim to the Food and Drug Administration for preapproval. The FDA authorizes a claim only if it finds "significant scientific agreement" among experts that the claim is supported by the available evidence. Appellants failed to persuade the FDA to authorize four such claims and sought relief in the district court, where their various constitutional and statutory challenges were rejected. We reverse.

I.

Dietary supplement marketers Durk Pearson and Sandy Shaw, presumably hoping to bolster sales by increasing the allure of their supplements' labels, asked the FDA to authorize four separate health claims. (Pearson and Shaw are supported by two other appellants, the American Preventive Medical Association, a health care advocacy organization whose members are health care practitioners, and Citizens for Health, a health care advocacy organization whose members are consumers of dietary supplements.) A "health claim" is a "claim made on the label or in labeling of...a dietary supplement that expressly or by implication...characterizes the relationship of any substance to a disease or health-related condition." 21 C.F.R. §101.14(a)(1) (1998). Each of appellants' four claims links the consumption of a particular supplement to the reduction in risk of a particular disease:

(1) "Consumption of antioxidant vitamins may reduce the risk of certain kinds of cancers."

(2) "Consumption of fiber may reduce the risk of colorectal cancer."

(3) "Consumption of omega-3 fatty acids may reduce the risk of coronary heart disease."

(4) ".8 mg of folic acid in a dietary supplement is more effective in reducing the risk of neural tube defects than a lower amount in foods in common form."

Understanding the preapproval requirement for health claims on dietary supplements requires a brief excursus on the broader regulatory framework applicable to dietary supplements, foods, and drugs. A "dietary supplement" is a "product (other than tobacco) *intended to supplement the diet*" that contains one or more of certain dietary ingredients, including a vitamin, a mineral, an herb or other botanical, or an amino acid, 21 U.S.C. §321(ff)(1)(A)-(D) (emphasis added), "is not represented for use as a conventional food or as a sole item of a meal or the diet," id. §321(ff)(2)(B), and "is labeled as a dietary supplement," id. §321(ff)(2)(C). A "drug" includes, *inter alia*, "articles intended for use in the diagnosis, cure, mitigation, treatment, or prevention of disease." 21 U.S.C. §321(g)(1)(B). If the product is a "new drug," the product must survive the arduous drug approval process, see 21 U.S.C. §355, before the manufacturer may introduce it into interstate commerce, id. §355(a); see also 21 U.S.C. §343(r)(1)(B) (deeming "misbranded" a dietary supplement whose label includes a health claim); 21 U.S.C. §331 (prohibiting the introduction of a misbranded product into interstate commerce); 21 U.S.C. §333 (prescribing penalties for violations of §331).

Although there is apparently some definitional overlap between drugs and dietary supplements under the statute, it creates a safe harbor from designation as a "drug" for certain dietary supplements whose labels or labeling advertise a beneficial relationship to a disease or health-related condition: If the FDA authorizes a label claim under 21 U.S.C. §343(r), the product is not considered a drug under 21 U.S.C. §321(g)(1). The FDA authorizes a claim only

> when it determines, based on the totality of publicly available scientific evidence (including evidence from well-designed studies conducted in a manner which is consistent with generally recognized scientific procedures and principles), that there is significant scientific agreement among experts qualified by scientific training and experience to evaluate such claims, that the claim is supported by such evidence.

21 C.F.R. §101.14(c). The FDA's authorization comes by an informal rulemaking under the Administrative Procedure Act. See 21 C.F.R. §101.70 (1998); 5 U.S.C. §553. This choice of a rulemaking rather than an adjudication – which would seem a more natural fit for this individualized determination – was mandated by Congress for the regulation of health claims on *food* labels, see 21 U.S.C. §343(r)(3)(B)(i), and then adopted by the FDA as well for the regulation of health claims on dietary supplement labels, see id. §343(r)(5)(D) (authorizing but not specifying regulatory procedure); 21 C.F.R. §101.70.

The requirement that health claims be approved before being added to the label of a dietary supplement constitutes the primary regulatory hurdle faced by marketers of dietary supplements. The actual *sale* of dietary supplements is regulated only when the supplement contains a "new dietary ingredient," 21 U.S.C. §350b, or poses a safety risk, id. §342(f).

The safe harbor from "drug" status for dietary supplements bearing FDA-approved health claims did not always exist. Prior to 1984, the FDA took the position that a statement that consumption of a *food* could prevent a particular disease was "tantamount to a claim that the food was a drug...and therefore that its sale was prohibited until a new drug application had been approved." H.R. REP. NO. 538, 101st Cong., 2d Sess. 9 (1990). But during the mid-1980s, companies began making health claims on foods without seeking new drug approval, a practice that the FDA supported in regulations proposed in 1987. Congress became concerned that health claims were increasingly common in the marketplace, and that the FDA had not issued clear, enforceable rules to regulate such claims.

Against this background, and in light of the further concern that the FDA might lack statutory authority to permit health claims on foods without also requiring that the claim meet the premarket approval requirements applicable to drugs, Congress enacted the Nutrition Labeling and Education Act of 1990 (NLEA). The NLEA addressed foods and dietary supplements separately. Health claims on foods may be made without FDA approval as a new drug, or the risk of sanctions for issuing a "misbranded" product, if it has been certified by the FDA as supported by "significant scientific agreement." Id. §343(r)(3)(B)(i). Congress created a similar safe harbor for health claims on dietary supplements, but delegated to the FDA the task of establishing a "procedure and standard respecting the validity of [the health] claim." Id. §343(r)(5)(D).

The FDA has since promulgated 21 C.F.R. §101.14 – the "significant scientific agreement" "standard" (quoted above) – and 21 C.F.R. §101.70 – a "procedure" (not particularly relevant to this case) – for evaluating the validity of health claims on dietary supplements.[2] In doing so, the agency rejected arguments asserted by commenters – including appellants – that the "significant scientific agreement" standard violates the First Amendment because it precludes the approval of less-well supported claims accompanied by a disclaimer and because it is impermissibly vague. The FDA explained that, in its view, the disclaimer approach would be ineffective because "there would be a question as to whether consumers would be able to ascertain which

---

[2] The FDA uses the same substantive standard and procedure for the regulation of health claims on foods, see 21 C.F.R. §101.14, 101.70 (1998), even though the substantive standard and procedure for foods, unlike dietary supplements, was prescribed by statute, see 21 U.S.C. §343(r)(3)(B)(i).

claims were preliminary [and accompanied by a disclaimer] and which were not," and concluded that its prophylactic approach is consistent with applicable commercial speech doctrine. The agency, responding to the comment that "significant scientific agreement" is impermissibly vague, asserted that the standard is "based on objective factors" and that its *procedures* for approving health claims, including the notice and comment procedure, sufficiently circumscribe its discretion.

Then the FDA rejected the four claims supported by appellants. See 21 C.F.R. §101.71(a) (dietary fiber-cancer), §101.71(c) (antioxidant vitamins-cancer), §101.71(e) (omega-3 fatty acids-coronary heart disease); id. §101.79(c)(2)(i)(G) (claim that 0.8 mg of folic acid in a dietary supplement is more effective in reducing the risk of neural tube defects than a lower amount in foods in common form). The problem with these claims, according to the FDA, was not a dearth of supporting evidence; rather, the agency concluded that the evidence was inconclusive for one reason or another and thus failed to give rise to "significant scientific agreement." But the FDA never explained just how it measured "significant" or otherwise defined the phrase. The agency refused to approve the dietary fiber-cancer claim because "a supplement would contain *only* fiber, and there is no evidence that any specific fiber itself caused the effects that were seen in studies involving fiber-rich [foods]." 58 Fed. Reg. 53,296, 53,298 (1993) (emphasis added). The FDA gave similar reasons for rejecting the antioxidant vitamins-cancer claim, and the omega-3 fatty acids-coronary heart disease claim. As for the claim that 0.8 mg of folic acid in a dietary supplement is more effective in reducing the risk of neural tube defects than a lower amount in foods in common form, the FDA merely stated that "the scientific literature does not support the superiority of any one source over others." 61 Fed. Reg. 8752, 8760. The FDA declined to consider appellants' suggested alternative of permitting the claim while requiring a corrective disclaimer such as "The FDA has determined that the evidence supporting this claim is inconclusive."[3]

---

[3] In general, the FDA appears quite reluctant to approve health claims on dietary supplements; only two are currently authorized. See 21 C.F.R. §101.72(c)(2)(ii)(C) (calcium-osteoporosis); id. §101.79(c)(2)(ii)(B) (folate-neural tube defects). The FDA has, however, approved several health claims on *foods*. See, e.g., id. §101.72(c)(2)(ii) (calcium-osteoporosis); id. §101.76 (fiber-containing products-cancer); id. §101.78 (fruits and vegetables-cancer); id. §101.79 (folate-neural tube defects); id. §101.81 (soluble fiber-coronary heart disease).

A more general folate-neural tube defect claim supported by appellants – that consumption of folate reduces the risk of neural tube defects – was initially rejected but ultimately approved for both dietary supplement and food labels. The parties disagree on what caused the FDA's change of position on this claim. Appellants contend that political objections – Senator Hatch was one of the complainers – concentrated the agency's mind. The FDA insists that its initial denial of the claim was based on a concern that folate consumption might have harmful effects on persons suffering from anemia, and that its concern was alleviated by new scientific studies published after the initial denial of the claim.

Appellants sought relief in the district court, raising APA and other statutory claims as well as a constitutional challenge, but were rebuffed.

II.

Appellants raise a host of challenges to the agency's action. But the most important are that their First Amendment rights have been impaired and that under the Administrative Procedure Act the FDA was obliged, at some point, to articulate a standard a good deal more concrete than the undefined "significant scientific agreement." Normally we would discuss the non-constitutional argument first, particularly because we believe it has merit. We invert the normal order here to discuss first appellants' most powerful constitutional claim, that the government has violated the First Amendment by declining to employ a less draconian method – the use of disclaimers – to serve the government's interests, because the requested remedy stands apart from appellants' request under the APA that the FDA flesh out its standards. That is to say, even if "significant scientific agreement" were given a more concrete meaning, appellants might be entitled to make health claims that do not meet that standard – with proper disclaimers....

A. Disclaimers

It is undisputed that FDA's restrictions on appellants' health claims are evaluated under the commercial speech doctrine. It seems also undisputed that the FDA has unequivocally rejected the notion of requiring disclaimers to cure "misleading" health claims for dietary supplements. (Although the general regulation does not *in haec verba* preclude authorization of qualified claims, the government implied in its statement of basis and purpose that disclaimers were not adequate, and did not consider their use in the four sub-regulations before us). The government makes two alternative arguments in response to appellants' claim that it is unconstitutional for the government to refuse to entertain a disclaimer requirement for the proposed health claims: first, that health claims lacking "significant scientific agreement" are *inherently* misleading and thus entirely outside the protection of the First Amendment; and second, that even if the claims are only *potentially* misleading, under Central Hudson Gas & Elec. Corp. v. Public Serv. Comm'n of New York, 447 U.S. 557, 566 (1980), the government is not obliged to consider requiring disclaimers in lieu of an outright ban on all claims that lack significant scientific agreement.

If such health claims could be thought inherently misleading, that would be the end of the inquiry.... As best we understand the government, its first argument runs along the following lines: that health claims lacking "significant scientific agreement" are inherently misleading because they have such an awesome impact on consumers as to make it virtually impossible for them to exercise any judgment *at the point of sale*. It would be as if the consumers were asked to buy something while hypnotized, and therefore they are bound to be misled. We think this contention is almost frivolous. We reject it. But the government's alternative argument is more substantial. It is asserted that health claims on dietary supplements should be thought at least potentially misleading because the consumer would have difficulty in independently verifying these claims. We are told, in addition, that consumers might actually assume that the government has approved such claims.

Under *Central Hudson*, we are obliged to evaluate a government scheme to regulate potentially misleading commercial speech by applying a three-part test. First, we ask whether the asserted government interest is substantial. The FDA advanced two general concerns: protection of public health and prevention of consumer fraud. The Supreme Court has said "there is no question that [the government's] interest in ensuring the accuracy of commercial information in the marketplace is substantial," Edenfield v. Fane, 507 U.S. 761, 769 (1993), and that government has a substantial interest in "promoting the health, safety, and welfare of its citizens," Rubin v. Coors Brewing Co., 514 U.S. 476, 485 (1995). At this level of generality, therefore, a substantial governmental interest is undeniable.

The more significant questions under *Central Hudson* are the next two factors: "whether the regulation *directly* advances the governmental interest asserted," Central Hudson, 447 U.S. at 566 (emphasis added), and whether the fit between the government's ends and the means chosen to accomplish those ends "is not necessarily perfect, but reasonable," Board of Trustees of the State University of New York v. Fox, 492 U.S. 469, 480 (1989). We think that the government's regulatory approach encounters difficulty with both factors.

It is important to recognize that the government does not assert that appellants' dietary supplements in any fashion *threaten* consumer's health and safety.[6] The government simply asserts its "common sense judgment" that the health of consumers is advanced *directly* by barring any health claims not approved by the FDA. Because it is not claimed that the product is harmful, the government's underlying – if unarticulated – premise must be that consumers have a limited amount of either attention or dollars that could be devoted to pursuing health through nutrition, and therefore products that are not indisputably health enhancing should be discouraged as threatening to crowd out more worthy expenditures. We are rather dubious that this simplistic view of human nature or market behavior is sound, but, in any event, it surely cannot be said that this notion – which the government does not even dare openly to set forth – is a *direct* pursuit of consumer health; it would seem a rather indirect route, to say the least.

On the other hand, the government would appear to advance directly its interest in protecting against consumer *fraud* through its regulatory scheme. If it can be assumed – and we think it can – that some health claims on dietary supplements will mislead consumers, it cannot be denied that requiring FDA pre-approval and setting the standard extremely, perhaps even impossibly, high will surely prevent any confusion among consumers. We also recognize that the government's interest in preventing consumer fraud/confusion may well take on added importance in the context of a product, such as dietary supplements, that can affect the public's health.

The difficulty with the government's consumer fraud justification comes at the final *Central Hudson* factor: Is there a "reasonable" fit between the government's goals and the means chosen to advance those goals? The government insists that it is never obliged to utilize the disclaimer approach, because the commercial speech doctrine does not embody a preference for disclosure over outright suppression. Our understanding of the doctrine is otherwise. In Bates v. State Bar of Arizona, 433 U.S. 350 (1977), the Supreme Court addressed an argument similar to the one the government advances. The State Bar had disciplined several attorneys who advertised their fees for certain legal services in violation of the Bar's rule, and sought to justify the rule on the ground that such advertising is inherently misleading "because advertising by attorneys will highlight irrelevant factors and fail to

---

[6] Drugs, on the other hand, appear to be in an entirely different category – the potential harm presumably is much greater.

show the relevant factor of skill." Id. at 372. The Court observed that the Bar's concern was "not without merit," but refused to credit the notion that "the public is not sophisticated enough to realize the limitations of advertising, and that the public is better kept in ignorance than trusted with correct but incomplete information." Id. at 374-75. Accordingly, the Court held that the "incomplete" attorney advertising was not inherently misleading and that "the preferred remedy is more disclosure, rather than less." Id. at 376. In more recent cases, the Court has reaffirmed this principle, repeatedly pointing to disclaimers as constitutionally preferable to outright suppression....[7]

Our rejection of the government's position that there is no general First Amendment preference for disclosure over suppression, of course, does not determine that any supposed weaknesses in the claims at issue can be remedied by disclaimers and thus does not answer whether the subregulations are valid. The FDA deemed the first three claims – (1) "Consumption of antioxidant vitamins may reduce the risk of certain kinds of cancers," (2) "Consumption of fiber may reduce the risk of colorectal cancer," and (3) "Consumption of omega-3 fatty acids may reduce the risk of coronary heart disease" – to lack significant scientific agreement because existing research had examined only the relationship between consumption of *foods* containing these components and the risk of these diseases. The FDA logically determined that the specific effect of the *component* of the food constituting the dietary supplement could not be determined with certainty. (The FDA has approved similar health claims on *foods* containing these components. See, e.g., 21 C.F.R. §101.79 (folate-neural tube defects).) But certainly this concern could be accommodated, in the first claim for example, by adding a prominent disclaimer to the label along the following lines: "The evidence is inconclusive because existing studies have been performed with *foods* containing antioxidant vitamins, and the effect of those foods on reducing the

---

[7] The government is correct to observe that the existence of sufficient alternative channels of communication would count in its favor at the final step of *Central Hudson*, but we do not think it is possible to so characterize the situation here. Although a dietary supplement manufacturer remains free to publish articles and books concerning health claims, and may market its dietary supplements with certain physically separate peer-reviewed scientific literature, see 21 U.S.C. §343-2, those channels of communication reach consumers less effectively than does a claim made directly on the label because they impose higher search costs on consumers, see John E. Calfee & Janis K. Pappalardo, *How Should Health Claims for Foods Be Regulated?* 26-27 (Bureau of Economics, Federal Trade Commission 1989).

risk of cancer may result from other components in those foods." A similar disclaimer would be equally effective for the latter two claims.

The FDA's concern regarding the fourth claim – "0.8 mg of folic acid in a dietary supplement is more effective in reducing the risk of neural tube defects than a lower amount in foods in common form" – is different from its reservations regarding the first three claims; the agency simply concluded that "the scientific literature does not support the superiority of any one source [of folic acid] over others." 61 Fed. Reg. at 8760. But it appears that credible evidence did support this claim, see, e.g., DIET AND HEALTH: IMPLICATIONS FOR REDUCING CHRONIC DISEASE RISK 67 (Committee on Diet and Health, Food and Nutrition Board 1989) (concluding that "losses [of folic acid] in cooking and canning [foods] can be very high due to heat destruction"), and we suspect that a clarifying disclaimer could be added to the effect that "The evidence in support of this claim is inconclusive."[8]

The government's general concern that, given the extensiveness of government regulation of the *sale* of drugs, consumers might assume that a claim on a supplement's label is approved by the government, suggests an obvious answer: The agency could require the label to state that "The FDA does not approve this claim." Similarly, the government's interest in preventing the use of labels that are true but do not mention adverse effects would seem to be satisfied – at least ordinarily – by inclusion of a prominent disclaimer setting forth those adverse effects.

The government disputes that consumers would be able to comprehend appellants' proposed health claims in conjunction with the disclaimers we have suggested – this mix of information would, in the government's view, create confusion among consumers. But all the government offers in support is the FDA's pronouncement that "consumers would be considerably confused by a multitude of claims with differing degrees of reliability." 59 Fed. Reg. at 405. Although the government may have more leeway in choosing suppression over disclosure as a response to the problem of consumer confusion where the product affects health, it must still meet its burden of justifying a restriction on speech – here the FDA's conclusory assertion falls far short.

We do not presume to draft precise disclaimers for each of appellants' four claims; we leave that task to the agency in the first instance. Nor do we

---

[8] As we noted in Part I there is no indication that the FDA even considered disclaimers in the context of evaluating these four health claims.

rule out the possibility that where evidence in support of a claim is outweighed by evidence against the claim, the FDA could deem it incurable by a disclaimer and ban it outright.[10] For example, if the weight of the evidence were against the hypothetical claim that "Consumption of Vitamin E reduces the risk of Alzheimer's disease," the agency might reasonably determine that adding a disclaimer such as "The FDA has determined that *no* evidence supports this claim" would not suffice to mitigate the claim's misleadingness. Finally, while we are skeptical that the government could demonstrate with empirical evidence that disclaimers similar to the ones we suggested above would bewilder consumers and fail to correct for deceptiveness, we do not rule out that possibility.

B. The Unarticulated Standard

Wholly apart from the question whether the FDA is obliged to consider appropriate disclaimers is appellants' claim that the agency is obliged to give some content to the phrase "significant scientific agreement."...

[W]e agree with appellants that the APA requires the agency to explain why it rejects their proposed health claims – to do so adequately necessarily implies giving some definitional content to the phrase "significant scientific agreement." We think this proposition is squarely rooted in the prohibition under the APA that an agency not engage in arbitrary and capricious action. See 5 U.S.C. §706(2)(A). It simply will not do for a government agency to declare – without explanation – that a proposed course of private action is not approved. See Motor Vehicle Mfrs. Ass'n v. State Farm Mut. Auto. Ins. Co., 463 U.S. 29, 43 (1983) ("The agency must...articulate a satisfactory explanation for its action...."). To refuse to define the criteria it is applying is equivalent to simply saying no without explanation. Indeed, appellants' suspicions as to the agency's real reason for its volte-face on the general folate-neural tube defect claim highlight the importance of providing a governing rationale for approving or rejecting proposed health claims.

To be sure, Justice Stewart once said, in declining to define obscenity, "I know it when I see it," Jacobellis v. Ohio, 378 U.S. 184, 197 (1964) (Stewart, J., concurring), which is basically the approach the FDA takes to the term "significant scientific agreement." But the Supreme Court is not subject to the Administrative Procedure Act. Nor for that matter is the Congress. That

---

[10] Similarly, we see no problem with the FDA imposing an outright ban on a claim where evidence in support of the claim is *qualitatively* weaker than evidence against the claim – for example, where the claim rests on only one or two old studies.

is why we are quite unimpressed with the government's argument that the agency is justified in employing this standard without definition because Congress used the same standard in 21 U.S.C. §343(r)(3)(B)(i). Presumably – we do not decide – the FDA in applying that statutory standard would similarly be obliged under the APA to give it content.

That is not to say that the agency was necessarily required to define the term in its initial general regulation – or indeed that it is obliged to issue a comprehensive definition all at once. The agency is entitled to proceed case by case or, more accurately, sub-regulation by sub-regulation, but it must be possible for the regulated class to perceive the principles which are guiding agency action. Accordingly, on remand, the FDA must explain what it means by significant scientific agreement or, at minimum, what it does not mean....

Note

In 2009, responding to the D.C. Circuit's decision in *Pearson v. Shalala*, the FDA published guidance on the meaning of "significant scientific agreement" under section 403(r)(3) of the FDCA. In the guidance, FDA described this standard as follows:

> Significant scientific agreement refers to the extent of agreement among qualified experts in the field. On the continuum of scientific evidence that extends from very limited to inconclusive [sic?] evidence, SSA lies closer to consensus. FDA's determination of SSA represents the agency's best judgment as to whether qualified experts would likely agree that the scientific evidence supports the substance/disease relationship that is the subject of a proposed health claim. The SSA standard is intended to be a strong standard that provides a high level of confidence in the validity of the substance/disease relationship. SSA means that the validity of the relationship is not likely to be reversed by new and evolving science, although the exact nature of the relationship may need to be refined. SSA does not require a consensus based on unanimous and incontrovertible scientific opinion. SSA occurs well after the stage of emerging science, where data and information permit an inference, but before the point of unanimous agreement within the relevant scientific community that the inference is valid.

How helpful is this guidance? How challenging would it be to define this standard more precisely?

The letter that follows reflects the FDA's response to *Pearson v. Shalala* as it relates to the specific proposed claim for folic acid's relationship to neural tube defects. How seriously is the FDA taking the court's decision?

Letter Regarding Dietary Supplement Health Claim for Folic Acid With Respect to Neural Tube Defects

From Christine J. Lewis, Director, Office of Nutritional Products, Labeling, and Dietary Supplements, Center for Food Safety and Applied Nutrition
To Jonathan W. Emord, Emord & Associates, P.C., Washington, D.C.
October 10, 2000

Dear Mr. Emord:

This letter is in reference to the court decision directing the Food and Drug Administration (FDA) to reconsider whether to authorize use of your proposed claim "0.8 mg of folic acid in a dietary supplement is more effective in reducing the risk of neural tube defects than a lower amount in foods in common form" in dietary supplement labeling (*Pearson v. Shalala*, 164 F.3d 650 (D.C. Cir. 1999))....

I. Procedure and Standard for Evaluating the Claim

In reconsidering your claim and the three other health claims that were the subject of *Pearson*, FDA proceeded as described in the October 6, 2000, Federal Register notice entitled "Food Labeling; Health Claims and Label Statements for Dietary Supplements; Update to Strategy for Implementation of *Pearson* Court Decision." 65 Fed. Reg. 59,855 (2000).... FDA gathered new scientific evidence on the claims by contracting for a literature search and publishing two notices in the Federal Register soliciting comments and data. After reviewing the updated body of evidence on the claims, FDA applied the "significant scientific agreement" standard by which the health claim regulations require the agency to evaluate the scientific validity of claims. Under this standard, FDA may issue a regulation authorizing a health claim only "when it determines, based on the totality of publicly available scientific evidence (including evidence from well-designed studies conducted in a manner which is consistent with generally recognized scientific procedures and principles), that there is significant scientific agreement, among experts qualified by scientific training and experience to evaluate such claims, that the claim is supported by such evidence." 21 C.F.R. §101.14....

II. Summary of Review

. . .

Based on its review of the scientific evidence, FDA finds that (1) the evidence does not show that 800 micrograms (mcg) folic acid per day is more effective in reducing the risk of NTD's than 400 mcg folic acid; (2) the evidence does not show that dietary supplements are more effective in reducing the risk of NTD's than foods in common form; and (3) the available evidence consistently shows that 400 mcg folic acid daily is a highly effective dose. FDA concludes from this review that the totality of publicly available scientific evidence demonstrates the lack of significant scientific agreement with respect to the comparative claim of effectiveness. FDA has also concluded that the weight of the evidence is against the proposed comparative claim....

V. Agency's Consideration of Significant Scientific Agreement

Having reviewed the currently available scientific evidence, including the recent report of the IOM/NAS (1998), FDA concludes that, based on the totality of the scientific evidence, there is not significant scientific agreement among qualified experts that:

> 0.8 mg of folic acid in a dietary supplement is more effective in reducing the risk of neural tube defects than a lower amount in foods in common form.

FDA concludes that a dose/response relationship between folic acid intake and reduced risk of NTD's has not yet been defined. Moreover, FDA concludes that the weight of the scientific evidence does not support the conclusion that 800 mcg folic acid/day is more effective than lower amounts in reducing the risk of NTD's. FDA also concludes that a claim of superior effectiveness of dietary supplements to foods in common form relative to reduced risk of NTD's is not consistent with the available scientific evidence.

The scientific evidence does not support the superiority of 800 mcg folic acid daily over other doses and sources. There is no well designed study to determine this issue. Moreover, comparisons of results across available studies of varying rigor, test doses, and sources show quite different magnitudes of reduced risk of NTD's in different population groups. There are limited studies on the effectiveness of graded intakes of dietary folate. Additionally, a recent population surveillance study showed effectiveness in reducing NTD risk with intakes of 400 mcg or less per day. In their totality, these studies show no dose-related response between 400 mcg and 4,000-5,000 mcg folic acid per day. Most studies do not provide any information on which to evaluate dose-related response below 400 mcg/day. However, the available evidence consistently shows that 400 mcg folic acid/day is a highly effective dose. As with all nutrients, intakes above the effective dose would not be expected to add additional benefit. Therefore, given the lack of evidence of a dose-related response above 400 mcg/day, and the paucity of evidence on the effectiveness of intakes below 400 mcg/day, FDA finds that the comparison that "0.8 mg is more effective than lower amounts" is not supported by the available scientific evidence.

The comparison in your proposed claim implying superiority of dietary supplements over foods as a source of the vitamin folate is also not consistent with the available scientific evidence. Many fortified foods contain the same form of folic acid as in dietary supplements, and in some cases, amounts similar to those found in dietary supplements. Labeling information ensures that consumers are not misled as to the vitamin content of foods and supplements, and also provides information, when applicable, to help consumers minimize losses of the vitamin during home food preparation. Although folic acid and food folate may differ in bioavailability, the impact of these differences can be meaningful only within the context of the total diet. Adequate intakes of bioavailable folate, regardless of source, are effective in reducing risk of NTD's. Inadequate intake of bioavailable folate can be corrected by increased intakes of folic acid from fortified food and/or dietary supplements. Increasing intakes of dietary folate to meet these needs is also likely to be effective, given known mechanisms of vitamin function and metabolism....

VI. Agency's Consideration of a Qualified Claim

As discussed above, your proposed claim states that 0.8 mg folic acid is more effective than a lesser amount of folic acid, which statement is not supported by the weight of the evidence. Your proposed claim also implies that dietary supplements are more effective than foods in common form, which is not supported by the weight of the evidence. FDA is not aware of any statement that could adequately qualify this proposed claim, which is misleading in these two ways.

A qualifying statement such as that suggested by the court in *Pearson*, "The evidence in support of this claim is inconclusive," is inadequate because the weight of the evidence is against both aspects of the proposed claim, as discussed above. The qualifying statement, "The FDA has not evaluated this claim," is false because FDA *has* evaluated the proposed claim. In any case, the qualifying statement does nothing to remedy the claim's basic untruthfulness.

Therefore, FDA has determined that your proposed claim is inherently misleading and cannot be made non-misleading with a disclaimer or other qualifying language. Therefore, use of the proposed claim is prohibited by the Federal Food, Drug, and Cosmetic Act. A dietary supplement that bears the proposed claim will be subject to regulatory action as a misbranded food under 21 U.S.C. §343(a)(1) and (r)(1)(B); as a misbranded drug under 21 U.S.C. §352(a) and (f)(1); and as an unapproved new drug under 21 U.S.C. §355(a).

However, FDA recognizes that the available studies and the recent conclusions of IOM/NAS (1998) support the use of certain statements in conjunction with the currently authorized claim to inform consumers of the nature of the evidence relative to recommended intakes and ways to achieve these intakes. For example, the IOM/NAS (1998) recommendation identifies an intake of 400 mcg/day and also indicates that this amount should be obtained from fortified foods and/or a supplement, in addition to food folate from a varied diet. The IOM/NAS (1998) also states that the scientific evidence that folic acid reduces the risk of NTD's is stronger than the evidence for the effectiveness of food folate.

The agency also concludes that an appropriately qualified claim would not threaten consumer health or safety. Because your proposed claim itself cannot be adequately qualified, as discussed above, the agency is providing examples of appropriately qualified claims....

[T]he agency intends to exercise its enforcement discretion with respect to a dietary supplement that bears such health claims.... Should new data shift the weight of the evidence against this claim, the agency would no longer exercise its enforcement discretion with respect to use of the claim in dietary supplement labeling, and would inform you of that by letter.

For example, the agency intends to exercise its enforcement discretion with respect to use of the following claims in dietary supplement labeling:

Example 1: Healthful diets with adequate folate may reduce a woman's risk of having a child with a brain or spinal cord birth defect. The Institute of Medicine of the National Academy of Sciences recommends that women capable of becoming pregnant consume 400 mcg folate daily from supplements, fortified foods, or both, in addition to consuming food folate from a varied diet.

Example 2: Healthful diets with adequate folate may reduce a woman's risk of having a child with a brain or spinal cord birth defect. The scientific evidence that 400 mcg folic acid daily reduces the risk of such defects is stronger than the evidence for the effectiveness of lower amounts. This is because most such tests have not looked at amounts less than 400 mcg folic acid daily.

Example 3: Healthful diets with adequate folate may reduce a woman's risk of having a child with a brain or spinal cord birth defect. Women capable of becoming pregnant should take 400 mcg folate/day from fortified foods and/or a supplement, in addition to food folate from a varied diet. It is not known whether the same level of protection can be achieved by using only food that is naturally rich in folate. Neither is it known whether lower intakes would be protective or whether there is a threshold below which no protection occurs.

Example 4: Healthful diets with adequate folate may reduce a woman's risk of having a child with a brain or spinal cord birth defect. Women capable of becoming pregnant should take 400 mcg of folate per day from a supplement or fortified foods and consume food folate from a varied diet. It is not known whether the same level of protection can be achieved by using lower amounts....

Note

The FDA describes its allowance of particular claims as an intended exercise of "enforcement discretion." Here is how a district court judge described the distinction between authorizing or permitting claims and exercising enforcement discretion with respect to them (Alliance for Natural Health v. Sebelius, 786 F.Supp.2d 1 (DDC 2011):

> Technically, the FDA does not "authorize" or "permit" qualified claims, but rather "exercises enforcement discretion" to allow qualified claims that are supported by credible evidence and are not misleading. The reason for this technical distinction is that under the NLEA and the FDA's regulations, "the evidence supporting a health claim [must] be presented to FDA for review before the claim may appear in labeling," and the FDA is required to make a finding of "significant scientific agreement" before authorizing a health claim. In other words, the FDA is not permitted by its statutory and regulatory authority to authorize claims that lack significant scientific agreement. Pursuant to *Pearson I*, however, the First Amendment precludes the FDA from prohibiting all claims that lack significant scientific agreement. Accordingly, the FDA exercises "enforcement discretion" to permit qualified claims — i.e., claims that the FDA cannot prohibit under the First Amendment, but that it also cannot technically authorize due to a of lack significant scientific agreement. For simplicity's sake, the Court will use the terms

"allowed" or "permitted" in lieu of "exercise enforcement discretion."

Pearson v. Shalala

130 F.Supp.2d 105 (D.D.C. 2001)

KESSLER, District Judge.

[The *Pearson* case returns to court, with plaintiffs challenging the FDA's latest decision, excerpted above, on their folic acid health claims.]

[It] is clear that the FDA simply failed to comply with the constitutional guidelines outlined in Pearson. Indeed, the agency appears to have at best, misunderstood, and at worst, deliberately ignored, highly relevant portions of the Court of Appeals Opinion. However, given that it is not the Court's institutional role to draft accurate, adequate, and succinct health claim disclaimers, the Court will permit the FDA to draft and submit one or more alternative disclaimers which may be chosen by designers, sellers, and manufacturers of dietary supplements....

Given that the FDA has continually refused to authorize the disclaimers suggested by the Court of Appeals – or any disclaimer, for that matter – it is essential to carefully review its analysis in reaching that decision. First, the FDA divided Plaintiffs' proposed claim (".8 mg of folic acid in a dietary supplement is more effective in reducing the risk of neural tube defects than a lower amount in foods in common form") into essentially two sub-claims: (1) a comparison of the effectiveness of 0.8 mg of folic acid to that of lower amounts, especially 0.4 mg, and (2) a comparison of the effectiveness of folic acid found in dietary supplements to folate found in "foods in common form." Then, the FDA analyzed each sub-claim separately....

1. Whether 0.8 Mg of Folic Acid is Superior to 0.4 Mg

With respect to the first sub-claim (the superiority of 0.8 mg over 0.4 mg), despite the FDA's conclusory assertion to the contrary, the studies that it included in its Folic Acid Decision cannot be accurately described as being "against" the claim that 0.8 mg of folic acid is superior to 0.4 mg of folic acid.

First, it is undisputed that there is ample evidence that 0.4 mg of folic acid is highly effective in reducing the neural tube defect risk.[26] Second, it is true that there is not a scientific consensus which affirmatively supports Plaintiffs' assertion that 0.8 mg of folic acid is superior to 0.4 mg. For these reasons, among others, the sub-claim is undoubtedly "potentially" misleading, because it reasonably implies that 0.8 mg has been proven more effective than 0.4 mg, which is far from true.

However, neither of the two statements described above lead to the conclusion that the "weight" of the scientific evidence is "against" the superiority of 0.8 mg over 0.4 mg – which is what the FDA must show to remove the Folic Acid Claim from First Amendment protection. The mere absence of significant affirmative evidence in support of a particular claim (i.e., the superior effectiveness of 0.8 mg over 0.4 mg of folic acid) does not translate into negative evidence "against" it.[27]

No study has concluded that doses between 0.4 mg and 0.8 mg are harmful, or that 0.8 mg is demonstrably less effective than 0.4 mg of folic acid.[28] More importantly, in the Cziezel Study – a clinical intervention trial involving 2,104 Hungarian women taking multivitamin supplements containing 0.8 mg of folic acid (the results of which were published in the New

---

[26] In examining the effect of 0.4 mg of folic acid, one study cited by the FDA found a 72% reduced risk of NTDs, while other studies found reduced risks of 40%, 60%, 70% and 80%. To the extent that Plaintiffs suggest there is a scientific consensus that 0.4 mg results in a 50% reduction of NTDs, they are incorrect.

[27] In the legal brief filed on its behalf, the FDA seems to now recognize this distinction. It no longer contends that the "weight" of the scientific evidence is "against" the Folic Acid Claim, as it did in the Folic Acid Decision, but instead argues simply that "the scientific evidence does not support a claim that 800 mcg is a necessary, recommended, or more effective dose . . ." Govt's Opp'n at 15, and that "the weight of the scientific evidence does not support the claim that 800 mcg is more effective than 400 mcg or lesser amounts..." Id. at 18.

[28] In October 1993, the FDA "tentatively decided to use 1 mg (1,000 ug)/day of total folate intake as the safe upper limit," admitting that its conclusion was "not without controversy." However, a scientist reporting the findings of a 1997 workshop sponsored by a standing committee of the Food and Nutrition Board, Institute of Medicine, stated that "during this workshop it became apparent that consensus has been reached among the scientific community [that] folate and folic acid are completely without adverse effects in any population or subgroup at intakes up to 5000 ug/d [5 mg per day]." At any rate, the FDA has never contended that a dosage of less than 1 mg is harmful.

England Journal of Medicine in 1992) – 0.8 mg of folic acid yielded a 100% reduction in the incidence of NTDs. When considered in conjunction with other studies of folic acid, the implication of the Cziezel Study is that 0.8 mg of folic acid is more effective than 0.4 mg at reducing the incidence of NTDs.[29]

The FDA tries to discount the significance of the findings of the Czeizel Study because the agency places "lesser weight on the outcome of randomized clinical trials in which the test substance, i.e folic acid, is fed as part of a multivitamin/multimineral supplement." However, the FDA has previously relied on numerous studies involving multivitamin supplements containing folic acid, without questioning the validity of those studies. Further, the FDA does not suggest any other nutrients or vitamins in the multivitamin/multimineral supplements which could be responsible for decreased NTD risk besides folic acid. Indeed, one of the studies the FDA relies on as presenting the "strongest data" associating folic acid and decreased NTD risk examined the effects of both multivitamin supplements and folic acid taken separately, and concluded that it was only the folic acid – not any other substance in the multivitamins – which was responsible for the decreased incidence of NTDs.

When the affirmative findings of the Cziezel Study are taken into account, in conjunction with the lack of evidence that doses in excess of 0.4 mg of folic acid are ineffective or harmful, it is clear that the first sub-claim is only "potentially" misleading. Consequently, the Court concludes that the FDA erred in determining that the sub-claim is inherently misleading.

2. Whether Folic Acid is Superior to Folate Found in "Foods in Common Form"

With respect to the second sub-claim, the FDA similarly concluded in its Folic Acid Decision that the "weight" of the scientific evidence was

---

[29] In the Cziezel Study, women planning a pregnancy were randomly given either a multivitamin supplement containing 0.8 mg of folic acid or a "trace-element supplement" containing no folic acid. Of the women in the first group (taking 0.8 mg of folic acid), none gave birth to infants with NTDs; of the women in the second group, six gave birth to infants with NTDs. The Cziezel Study did not evaluate the effectiveness of 0.4 mg of folic acid, but reputable studies have found its effectiveness to range from 40% to 80%.

against the superiority of folic acid over folate occurring in foods. The FDA relied primarily on the following two criticisms of the sub-claim:

a. whether folic acid is superior to naturally occurring food folate

To begin with, the FDA concedes that "it is well-recognized that the bioavailability of free folic acid, the form included in fortified foods and in dietary supplements, is severalfold higher than that of naturally occurring food folates. Estimates of the increased bioavailability ('potency') of free folic acid relative to food folates range from at least twofold to fourfold or greater." The FDA also acknowledges that, based on the findings of the 1998 IOM/NAS Study, "the available evidence for protective effect from folic acid is much stronger than that for food folate."

Indeed, countless scientific bodies have expressed skepticism that food folate is as effective at reducing NTDs as is folic acid, including the Centers for Disease Control ("CDC"), the Food and Nutritional Board of the Institute of Medicine ("IOM"), and the National Center for Environmental Health ("NCEH").

The FDA does not seriously challenge any of these findings. Instead, it questions whether synthetic folic acid's superior bioavailability necessarily makes it a "more effective delivery vehicle" in reducing NTDs.[30] Again, the FDA misreads the Court of Appeals decision in Pearson. The Court stated:

> The FDA's concern regarding the fourth claim – "0.8 of folic acid in a dietary supplement is more effective in reducing the risk of neural tube defects than a lower amount in foods in common form" – is different from its reservations regarding the first three claims; the agency simply concluded that "the scientific evidence does not support the superiority of any one source [of folic acid] over others." But it appears that credible evidence did support this claim, see, e.g., Diet and Health: Implications for Reducing Chronic Disease Risk 67 (Committee on Diet and Health, Food and Nutrition Board 1989) (concluding that "losses [of folic acid] in cooking and canning [foods] can be very high due to heat destruction"), and we suspect that a clarifying disclaimer could be added to the effect that "the evidence in support of this claim is inconclusive."

---

[30] The FDA isolated two distinct "aspects" of the sub-claim: "a) compositional issues, e.g., dietary supplements contain more of the vitamin or are subject to fewer losses of the vitamin than are foods, and b) issues of physiologic effectiveness, e.g., the folic acid ingredient in dietary supplements is physiologically superior to the naturally occurring folate in foods."

In attacking the Court of Appeals' observation ("it appears that credible evidence did support this claim"), the FDA noted, among other things, that "many foods that are good sources of food folate are minimally processed or eaten raw," and concluded that the putative problem identified by the Court of Appeals – that folic acid may be destroyed when certain foods are cooked – is therefore insignificant. The FDA conceded that "some vitamins, minerals and other nutrients may be lost from some foods during home cooking," but concluded, without any scientific or empirical support, that the cooking labels accompanying such foods (e.g., "To retain vitamins do not rinse before or drain after cooking") would solve that potential problem.

However, as the Pearson opinion strongly suggests, the FDA may not ban the Folic Acid Claim simply because the scientific literature is inconclusive about whether synthetic folic acid is superior to naturally occurring food folate. The question which must be answered under Pearson is whether there is any "credible evidence" that synthetic folic acid is superior to naturally occurring food folate. See id. (observing that "it appears that credible evidence did support" the Folic Acid Claim). There clearly is such evidence, as the FDA itself acknowledged. J.R. at 14 ("IOM/NAS (1998) did note that the available evidence for a protective effect from folic acid is much stronger than that for food folate."). Consequently, the agency erred in concluding otherwise. In short, even if the FDA's criticism of the sub-claim is valid, this criticism does not make the Claim inherently misleading; rather, it suggests the need for a well-drafted disclaimer, which the FDA has steadfastly thus far refused to even consider.

b. whether the term "foods in common form" includes fortified foods

A second complaint the FDA levels against the second sub-claim is that it implies that folic acid in dietary supplements is more effective than the folic acid used to fortify foods. The FDA presently considers foods in "common form" to include fortified foods. It argues that there is no scientific evidence that the folic acid found in dietary supplements is any better than the folic acid found in fortified foods. Accordingly, the FDA contends that Plaintiffs' Folic Acid Claim, by asserting the superiority of folic acid over "foods in common form," is inaccurate and misleading.

While the parties can reasonably disagree about whether fortified foods should be considered "foods in common form," Plaintiffs correctly focus their argument on the only relevant legal question: assuming the inference is to be fairly drawn, and assuming that the claim is misleading, can the Folic

Acid Claim be made non-misleading through a clarifying disclaimer? The FDA patently refused to consider any such disclaimers, including what appears to be a reasonable one recently suggested by Plaintiffs: "Foods fortified with similar amounts of folic acid may be as effective as dietary supplements in reducing the risk of neural tube defects." The Pearson Court clearly ruled that the FDA may not prohibit a health claim unless it first makes a "showing" that the claim's alleged "misleadingness" could not be cured through the use of a disclaimer or other types of disclosure. The FDA has not made such a showing, and its decision to classify the second sub-claim as inherently misleading is therefore erroneous....

IV. Conclusion

...

[B]ecause it is the FDA's, rather than the Court's, institutional role to draft accurate, adequate, and succinct health claim disclaimers, the Court hereby remands this case to the FDA, instructing the agency to draft one or more appropriately short, succinct, and accurate disclaimers.[34] The Court strongly suggests the agency consider the two disclaimers suggested by the Pearson Court ("The evidence in support of this claim is inconclusive" and "The FDA does not approve this claim"), as well as the disclaimer put forth by Plaintiffs ("Foods fortified with similar amounts of folic acid may be as effective as dietary supplements in reducing the risk of neural tube defects").

Note

By now you may be wondering whether the Pearson v. Shalala/folic acid/neural tube defects saga will ever end. Thankfully, it did. In response to the decision above, the FDA determined that the following disclaimer "best meets the criteria specified in the Court's decision":

---

[34] The Court is aware that there are certain constraints on its ability to mandate specific time limits for agency action. Because of those constraints, the Court will not impose an absolute time limit for the drafting of disclaimers. However, there is no question that the agency has acted with less than reasonable speed in this case; for example, it waited for more than 18 months before revoking rules declared unconstitutional by our Court of Appeals. Further, as discussed above, the health risks to the public from neural tube defects, as well as the economic consequences, are very substantial. Consequently, the Court anticipates that the agency will complete its task within 60 days.

> FDA does not endorse this claim. Public health authorities recommend that women consume 0.4 mg folic acid daily from fortified foods or dietary supplements or both to reduce the risk of neural tube defects.

The agency explained that it rejected the court's proposed "does not endorse" disclaimer because it worried that consumers would infer that the agency endorsed no claims regarding folic acid and neural tube defects. The agency also stated that it thought it important to give consumers the reason why the agency did not endorse the claim. The FDA replaced the court's term "approve" with the word "endorse" because the NLEA does not require FDA approval before a health claim can be made.

All is clear now, yes?

Later in this chapter we will return to the FDA's framework for evaluating health claims. For now, let's consider another decision exploring the tension between required disclosures and the first amendment.

International Dairy Foods Association v. Amestoy

92 F.3d 67 (2d Cir. 1996)

ALTIMARI, Circuit Judge:

. . . The [appellant] dairy manufacturers challenged the constitutionality of Vt. Stat. Ann. tit. 6, ' 2754(c), which requires dairy manufacturers to identify products which were, or might have been, derived from dairy cows treated with a synthetic growth hormone used to increase milk production. The dairy manufacturers alleged that the statute violated the United States Constitution's First Amendment and Commerce Clause.

Because we find that the district court abused its discretion in failing to grant preliminary injunctive relief to the dairy manufacturers on First Amendment grounds, we reverse and remand. . . .

In 1993, the federal Food and Drug Administration ("FDA") approved the use of recombinant Bovine Somatotropin ("rBST") (also known as recombinant Bovine Growth Hormone ("rGBH")), a synthetic growth hormone that increases milk production by cows. It is undisputed that the dairy products derived from herds treated with rBST are indistinguishable from products derived from untreated herds; consequently, the FDA declined to require the labeling of products derived from cows receiving the supplemental hormone.

In April 1994, defendant-appellee the State of Vermont ("Vermont") enacted a statute requiring that "if rBST has been used in the production of milk or a milk product for retail sale in this state, the retail milk or milk product shall be labeled as such." Vt. Stat. Ann. tit. 6, ' 2754(c). The State of Vermont's Commissioner of Agriculture ("Commissioner") subsequently promulgated regulations giving those dairy manufacturers who use rBST four labeling options, among them the posting of a sign to the following effect in any store selling dairy products:

> rBST INFORMATION
>
> THE PRODUCTS IN THIS CASE THAT CONTAIN OR MAY CONTAIN MILK FROM rBST-TREATED COWS EITHER (1) STATE ON THE PACKAGE THAT rBST HAS BEEN OR MAY HAVE BEEN USED, OR (2) ARE IDENTIFIED BY A BLUE SHELF LABEL LIKE THIS [BLUE RECTANGLE] OR (3) A BLUE STICKER ON THE PACKAGE LIKE THIS. [BLUE DOT]

The United States Food and Drug Administration has determined that there is no significant difference between milk from treated and untreated cows. It is the law of Vermont that products made from the milk of rBST-treated cows be labeled to help consumers make informed shopping decisions....

Generally, preliminary injunctive relief is appropriate when the movant shows "(a) irreparable harm and (b) either (1) likelihood of success on the merits or (2) sufficiently serious questions going to the merits to make them a fair ground for litigation and a balance of hardships tipping decidedly toward the party requesting the preliminary relief." However, because the injunction at issue stays "government action taken in the public interest pursuant to a statutory . . . scheme," this Court has determined that the movant must satisfy the more rigorous "likelihood of success prong."

1. Irreparable Harm

Focusing principally on the economic impact of the labeling regulation, the district court found that appellants had not demonstrated irreparable harm to any right protected by the First Amendment. We disagree.

Irreparable harm is "injury for which a monetary award cannot be adequate compensation." See Jackson Dairy, Inc., 596 F.2d at 72. It is established that "the loss of First Amendment freedoms, for even minimal periods of time, unquestionably constitutes irreparable injury." Elrod v. Burns, 427 U.S. 347, 373 (1976). . . . Because the statute at issue requires appellants to make an involuntary statement whenever they offer their products for sale, we find that the statute causes the dairy manufacturers irreparable harm. . . .

. . . The wrong done by the labeling law to the dairy manufacturers' constitutional right not to speak is a serious one that was not given proper weight by the district court. See Wooley v. Maynard, 430 U.S. 705, 714 (1977) ("We begin with the proposition that the right of freedom of thought protected by the First Amendment against state action includes both the right to speak freely and the right to refrain from speaking at all."); West Virginia State Bd. of Ed. v. Barnette, 319 U.S. 624, 633 (1943) ("involuntary affirmation could be commanded only on even more immediate and urgent grounds than silence").

The right not to speak inheres in political and commercial speech alike, see Zauderer v. Office of Disciplinary Counsel, 471 U.S. 626, 651 (1985), and extends to statements of fact as well as statements of opinion, see Riley v. National Federation of the Blind, 487 U.S. 781, 797-98 (1988). If, however, as Vermont maintains, its labeling law compels appellants to engage in purely commercial speech, the statute must meet a less rigorous test. See Central Hudson Gas & Elec. Corp. v. Public Serv. Comm'r, 447 U.S. 557, 562-63 (1980) ("The Constitution . . . accords a lesser protection to commercial speech than to other constitutionally guaranteed expression."). The dairy manufacturers insist that the speech is not purely commercial because it compels them "to convey a message regarding the significance of rBST use that is 'expressly contrary to' their views." . . .

. . . [E]ven assuming that the compelled disclosure is purely commercial speech, appellants have amply demonstrated that the First Amendment is sufficiently implicated to cause irreparable harm. The dairy manufacturers have clearly done more than simply "assert" their First Amendment rights: The statute in question indisputably requires them to speak when they would rather not. Because compelled speech "contravenes core First Amendment values," appellants have "satisfied the initial requirement for securing injunctive relief." . . . .

2. Likelihood of Success on the Merits . . .

In *Central Hudson*, the Supreme Court articulated a four-part analysis for determining whether a government restriction on commercial speech is permissible. We need not address the controversy concerning the nature of the speech in question -- commercial or political -- because we find that Vermont fails to meet the less stringent constitutional requirements applicable to compelled commercial speech. . . .

In our view, Vermont has failed to establish the second prong of the *Central Hudson* test, namely that its interest is substantial. . . . Vermont "does not claim that health or safety concerns prompted the passage of the Vermont Labeling Law," but instead defends the statute on the basis of "strong consumer interest and the public's 'right to know' . . . ." These interests are insufficient to justify compromising protected constitutional rights.[9]

Vermont's failure to defend its constitutional intrusion on the ground that it negatively impacts public health is easily understood. After exhaustive studies, the FDA has "concluded that rBST has no appreciable effect on the composition of milk produced by treated cows, and that there are no human safety or health concerns associated with food products derived from cows treated with rBST." Because bovine somatotropin ("BST") appears naturally in cows, and because there are no BST receptors in a cow's mammary glands, only trace amounts of BST can be detected in milk, whether or not the cows received the supplement. Moreover, it is undisputed that neither consumers nor scientists can distinguish rBST-derived milk from milk produced by an untreated cow. Indeed, the already extensive record in this case contains no scientific evidence from which an objective observer could conclude that rBST has any impact at all on dairy products. It is thus plain that Vermont could not justify the statute on the basis of "real" harms..

We do not doubt that Vermont's asserted interest, the demand of its citizenry for such information, is genuine; reluctantly, however, we conclude that it is inadequate. We are aware of no case in which consumer interest alone was sufficient to justify requiring a product's manufacturers to publish the functional equivalent of a warning about a production method that has no discernable impact on a final product. See, e.g., Ibanez [v. Florida Dep't of Business and Professional Regulation, 512 U.S. 136, 146 (1994)] (invalidating state requirement that Certified Financial Planner ("CFP") disclose in advertisement that CFP status was conferred by unofficial private organization despite unsubstantiated claim that public might otherwise be misled by CFP's advertisement).

Although the Court is sympathetic to the Vermont consumers who wish to know which products may derive from rBST-treated herds, their desire is insufficient to permit the State of Vermont to compel the dairy manufacturers to speak against their will. Were consumer interest alone suf-

---

[9]Although the dissent suggests several interests that if adopted by the state of Vermont may have been substantial, the district court opinion makes clear that Vermont adopted no such rationales for its statute. Rather, Vermont's sole expressed interest was, indeed, "consumer curiosity." The district court plainly stated that, "Vermont takes no position on whether rBST is beneficial or detrimental. However," the district court explained, "Vermont has determined that its consumers want to know whether rBST has been used in the production of their milk and milk products." It is clear from the opinion below that the state itself has not adopted the concerns of the consumers; it has only adopted that the consumers are concerned. Unfortunately, mere consumer concern is not, in itself, a substantial interest.

ficient, there is no end to the information that states could require manufacturers to disclose about their production methods. For instance, with respect to cattle, consumers might reasonably evince an interest in knowing which grains herds were fed, with which medicines they were treated, or the age at which they were slaughtered. Absent, however, some indication that this information bears on a reasonable concern for human health or safety or some other sufficiently substantial governmental concern, the manufacturers cannot be compelled to disclose it. Instead, those consumers interested in such information should exercise the power of their purses by buying products from manufacturers who voluntarily reveal it.

Accordingly, we hold that consumer curiosity alone is not a strong enough state interest to sustain the compulsion of even an accurate, factual statement, in a commercial context. See, e.g., United States v. Sullivan, 332 U.S. 689, 693 (1948) (upholding federal law requiring warning labels on "harmful foods, drugs and cosmetics"); see also Zauderer, 471 U.S. at 651 (disclosure requirements are permissible "as long as [they] are reasonably related to the State's interest in preventing deception of consumers."); In re R.M.J., 455 U.S. 191, 201 (1982) ("warnings or disclaimers might be appropriately required . . . in order to dissipate the possibility of consumer confusion or deception."); Bates v. State Bar of Arizona, 433 U.S. 350, 384 (1977) (state bar association could not ban advertising that was neither misleading nor deceptive); Virginia State Bd. of Pharmacy v. Virginia Citizens Consumer Council, Inc., 425 U.S. 748, 771-72 (1975) (regulation aimed at preventing deceptive or misleading commercial speech would be permissible). Because Vermont has demonstrated no cognizable harms, its statute is likely to be held unconstitutional.

Conclusion

Because appellants have demonstrated both irreparable harm and a likelihood of success on the merits, the judgment of the district court is reversed, and the case is remanded for entry of an appropriate injunction.

LEVAL, Circuit Judge, dissenting:

I respectfully dissent. Vermont's regulation requiring disclosure of use of rBST in milk production was based on substantial state interests, including worries about rBST's impact on human and cow health, fears for the survival of small dairy farms, and concerns about the manipulation of nature through biotechnology. The objective of the plaintiff milk producers is to conceal their use of rBST from consumers. The policy of the First Amendment, in its application to commercial speech, is to favor the flow of accurate, relevant information. The majority's invocation of the First Amendment to invalidate a state law requiring disclosure of information consumers reasonably desire stands the Amendment on its ear. In my view, the district court correctly found that plaintiffs were unlikely to succeed in proving Vermont's law unconstitutional. . . .

Recent advances in genetic technologies led to the development of a synthetically isolated metabolic protein hormone known as recombinant bovine somatotropin (rBST), which, when injected into cows, increases their milk production. Monsanto Company, an amicus in this action on the side of the plaintiff milk producers, has developed the only commercially approved form of rBST and markets it under the brand name "Posilac." This is, of course, at the frontiers of bio-science. A 1994 federal government study of rBST describes it as "one of the first major commercial biotechnology products to be used in the U.S. food and agricultural sector and the first to attract significant attention." Executive Branch of the Federal Government, Use of Bovine Somatotropin (BST) in the United States: Its Potential Effects (January 1994) [hereafter "Federal Study"], at 58.

The United States Food and Drug Administration ("FDA") and others have studied rBST extensively. Based on its study, the FDA authorized commercial use of rBST on November 5, 1993, concluding that "milk and meat from [rBST-treated] cows is safe" for human consumption.

The impending use of rBST caused substantial controversy throughout the country. The Federal Study reports, based on numerous surveys, that consumers favor the labeling of milk produced by use of rBST. In Vermont, a state highly attuned to issues affecting the dairy industry, use of rBST was the subject of frequent press commentary and debate, and provoked considerable opposition. In response to public pressure, the state of Vermont enacted a law requiring that "if rBST has been used in the production of milk or a milk product for retail sale in this state, the retail milk or milk product shall be labeled as such." 6 V.S.A. ' 2754(c). . . .

The interests which Vermont sought to advance by its statute and regulations were explained in the Agriculture Department's Economic Impact Statement accompanying its regulations. The Statement reported that consumer interest in disclosure of use of rBST was based on "concerns about FDA determinations about the product as regards health and safety or about recombinant gene technology"; concerns "about the effect of the product on bovine health"; and "concerns about the effect of the product on the existing surplus of milk and in the dairy farm industry's economic status and well-being." This finding was based on "consumer comments to Vermont legislative committees" and to the Department, as well as published reports and letters to the editors published in the press.

The state offered survey evidence which demonstrated similar public concern. Comments by Vermont citizens who had heard or read about rBST were overwhelmingly negative. The most prevalent responses to rBST use included: "Not natural," "More research needs to be done/Long-term effects not clear," "Against additives added to my milk," "Worried about adverse health effects," "Unhealthy for the cow," "Don't need more chemicals," "It's a hormone/Against hormones added to my milk," "Hurts the small dairy farmer," "Producing enough milk already."

On the basis of this evidence the district court found that a majority of Vermonters "do not want to purchase milk products derived from rBST-treated cows," International Dairy Farmers Ass'n v. Amestoy, 898 F. Supp. 246, 250 (D. Vt. 1995) (hereafter "IDFA"), and that the reasons included:

> (1) They consider the use of a genetically-engineered hormone in the production unnatural; (2) they believe that use of the hormone will result in increased milk production and lower milk prices, thereby hurting small dairy farmers; (3) they believe that the use of rBST is harmful to cows and potentially harmful to humans; and, (4) they feel that there is a lack of knowledge regarding the long-term effects of rBST.

The court thus understandably concluded that "Vermont has a substantial interest in informing consumers of the use of rBST in the production of milk and dairy products sold in the state." . . .

In the face of this evidence and these explicit findings by the district court, the majority oddly concludes that Vermont's sole interest in requiring disclosure of rBST use is to gratify "consumer curiosity," and that this alone "is not a strong enough state interest to sustain the compulsion of even an accurate factual statement." The majority seeks to justify its conclusion in three ways.

First, it simply disregards the evidence of Vermont's true interests and the district court's findings recognizing those interests. Nowhere does the majority opinion discuss or even mention the evidence or findings regarding the people of Vermont's concerns about human health, cow health, biotechnology, and the survival of small dairy farms.

Second, the majority distorts the meaning of the district court opinion. It relies substantially on Judge Murtha's statement that Vermont "does not claim that health or safety concerns prompted the passage of the Vermont Labeling Law," but "bases its justification . . . on strong consumer interest and the public's 'right to know'." The majority takes this passage out of context. The district court's opinion went on, as quoted above, to explain the concerns that underlie the interest of Vermont's citizenry. Unquestionably the district court found, and the evidence showed, that the interests of the citizenry that led to the passage of the law include health and safety concerns, among others. In the light of the district judge's further explicit findings, it is clear that his statement could not mean what the majority concludes.[10] More likely, what Judge Murtha meant was that Vermont does not claim to know whether rBST is harmful. And when he asserted that Vermont's rule was passed to vindicate "strong consumer interest and the public's right to know," this could not mean that the public's interest was based on nothing but "curiosity," because the judge expressly found that the consumer interest was based on health, economic, and ethical concerns.

Third, the majority suggests that, because the FDA has not found health risks in this new procedure, health worries could not be considered "real" or "cognizable." I find this proposition alarming and dangerous; at the very least, it is extraordinarily unrealistic. Genetic and biotechnological manipulation of basic food products is new and controversial. Although I have no reason to doubt that the FDA's studies of rBST have been thorough, they could not cover long-term effects of rBST on humans.[11] Furthermore, there are many possible reasons why a government agency might fail to find real health risks, including inadequate time and budget for testing, insufficient advancement of scientific techniques, insufficiently large sampling popula-

---

[10]Indeed had the judge really intended such a finding, it would be unsupportable in view of the evidence that the concerns of the citizenry were communicated to the legislature. When the citizens of a state express concerns to the legislature and the state's lawmaking bodies then pass disclosure requirements in response to those expressed concerns, it seems clear (without need for a statutory declaration of purpose) that the state is acting to vindicate the concerns expressed by its citizens, and not merely to gratify their "curiosity." Vermont need not, furthermore, take the position that rBST is harmful to require its disclosure because of potential health risks. The mere fact that it does not know whether rBST poses hazards is sufficient reason to justify disclosure by reason of the unknown potential for harm.

[11]One of Vermont's experts, a specialist in medical information and the review of scientific literature, stated in an affidavit:

> It is not reasonable to conclude that there is uniform agreement that milk from rBST treated cows is 100% safe for human consumption. . . . Longitudinal studies have been called for to establish the long-term health effects of the use of rBST on cows, and until the results of these studies are published, disagreement on the effects of rBST will likely continue. . . . Milk from rBST treated cows is generally considered safe by the Food and Drug Administration and some scientists, while the General Accounting Office and other scientists feel that more research is needed before a universal agreement can be reached.

Affidavit of Dr. Julie McGowan, at 26-27.

tions, pressures from industry, and simple human error. To suggest that a government agency's failure to find a health risk in a short-term study of a new genetic technology should bar a state from requiring simple disclosure of the use of that technology where its citizens are concerned about such health risks would be unreasonable and dangerous. Although the FDA's conclusions may be reassuring, they do not guarantee the safety of rBST.

Forty years ago, when I (and nearly everyone) smoked, no one told us that we might be endangering our health. Tobacco is but one of many consumer products once considered safe, which were subsequently found to cause health hazards. The limitations of scientific information about new consumer products were well illustrated in a 1990 study produced at the request of Congress by the General Accounting Office. Looking at various prescription drugs available on the market, the study examined the risks associated with the drugs that became known only after they were approved by the FDA, and concluded:

> Even after approval, many additional risks may surface when the general population is exposed to a drug. These risks, which range from relatively minor (such as nausea and headache) to serious (such as hospitalization and death) arise from the fact that preapproval drug testing is inherently limited. . . .
>
> In studying the frequency and seriousness of risks identified after approval, GAO found that of the 198 drugs approved by FDA between 1976 and 1985 for which data were available, 102 (or 51.5 percent) had serious postapproval risks, as evidenced by labeling changes or withdrawal from the market. All but six of these drugs . . . are deemed by FDA to have benefits that outweigh their risks. The serious postapproval risks are adverse reactions that could lead to hospitalization . . . severe or permanent disability, or death.

GAO Report, "FDA Drug Review: Postapproval Risks, 1976-85," April 1990, at 2-3. As startling as its results may seem, this study merely confirms a common sense proposition: namely, that a government agency's conclusion regarding a product's safety, reached after limited study, is not a guarantee and does not invalidate public concern for unknown side effects.

In short, the majority has no valid basis for its conclusion that Vermont's regulation advances no interest other than the gratification of consumer curiosity, and involves neither health concerns nor other substantial interests. . . .

Freedom of speech is not an absolute right, particularly in the commercial context. . . . [G]overnment's power to regulate commercial speech includes the power to compel such speech. Zauderer v. Office of Disciplinary Counsel, 471 U.S. 626, 651 (1985) (upholding state law requiring attorneys who advertised contingent fee services to disclose specific details about how contingent fee would be calculated and to state that certain costs might be borne by the client even in the event of loss).

Except for its conclusion that Vermont had no substantial interest to support its labeling law, the majority finds no fault with the district court's application of these governing standards. Nor do I. Accordingly, the sole issue is whether Vermont had a substantial interest in compelling the disclosure of use of rBST in milk production.

In my view, Vermont's multifaceted interest, outlined above, is altogether substantial. Consumer worries about possible adverse health effects from consumption of rBST, especially over a long term, is unquestionably a substantial interest. As to health risks to cows, the concern is supported by the warning label on Posilac, which states that cows injected with the product are at an increased risk for: various reproductive disorders, "clinical mastitis [udder infections] (visibly abnormal milk)," "digestive disorders such as indigestion, bloat, and diarrhea," "enlarged hocks and lesions," and "swellings" that may be permanent. As to the economic impact of increased milk production, caused by injection of rBST, upon small dairy farmers, the evidence included a U.S. Department of Agriculture economist's written claim that, "if rBST is heavily adopted and milk prices are reduced, at least some of the smaller farmers that do not use rBST might be forced out of the dairy business, because they would not be producing economically sufficient volumes of milk." Public philosophical objection to biotechnological mutation is familiar and widespread.

Any one of these concerns may well suffice to make Vermont's interest substantial; all four, taken together, undoubtedly constitute a substantial governmental justification for Vermont's labeling law.

Indeed, the majority does not contend otherwise. Nowhere does the majority assert that these interests are not substantial. As noted above, the majority justifies its conclusion of absence of a substantial interest by its assertion that Vermont advanced no interest other than consumer curiosity, a conclusion that is contradicted by both the record and the district court's findings. . . .

Notwithstanding their self-righteous references to free expression, the true objective of the milk producers is concealment. They do not wish consumers to know that their milk products were produced by use of rBST because there are consumers who, for various reasons, prefer to avoid rBST. Vermont, on the other hand, has established a labeling requirement whose sole objective (and whose sole effect) is to inform Vermont consumers whether milk products offered for sale were produced with rBST.[12] The dis-

---

[12] I disagree with the majority's contention, that voluntary labeling by producers who do not use rBST can be relied on to effectuate Ver-

pute under the First Amendment is over whether the milk producers' interest in concealing their use of rBST from consumers will prevail over a state law designed to give consumers the information they desire. The question is simply whether the First Amendment prohibits government from requiring disclosure of truthful relevant information to consumers.

In my view, the interest of the milk producers has little entitlement to protection under the First Amendment. The caselaw that has developed under the doctrine of commercial speech has repeatedly emphasized that the primary function of the First Amendment in its application to commercial speech is to advance truthful disclosure -- the very interest that the milk producers seek to undermine....

The application of these principles to the case at bar yields a clear message. The benefit the First Amendment confers in the area of commercial speech is the provision of accurate, non-misleading, relevant information to consumers. Thus, regulations designed to prevent the flow of such information are disfavored; regulations designed to provide such information are not.

The milk producers' invocation of the First Amendment for the purpose of concealing their use of rBST in milk production is entitled to scant recognition. They invoke the Amendment's protection to accomplish exactly what the Amendment opposes. And the majority's ruling deprives Vermont of the right to protect its consumers by requiring truthful disclosure on a subject of legitimate public concern. . . .

Note

To return to health claims and qualified health claims... The first reading below is excerpted from a study by the FDA on the effects on consumer perceptions of disclaimers concerning the strength of the scientific evidence underlying health claims. The results may be surprising – and disquieting. The second reading gives you a sense of the structure of the qualified health

---

mont's purpose. There is evidence that, notwithstanding the FDA's determination to permit such voluntary labeling, certain states, no doubt influenced by the rBST lobby, will "not allow any labeling concerning rBST." Affidavit of Ben Cohen, at 3-4. This effectively prevents multistate distributors from including such labeling on their packaging. Producers complying with Vermont's law do not face the same problem. The blue dot has meaning only in conjunction with the signs posted in Vermont retail establishments. Thus producers can inexpensively affix the blue dot without violating the laws of states that forbid all rBST labeling.

claim apparatus the FDA has had to construct in the wake of *Pearson v. Shalala*.

Effects of Strength of Science Disclaimers on the Communication Impacts of Health Claims (Working Paper No. 1)

Brenda M. Derby & Alan S. Levy
U.S. Food and Drug Administration
Center for Food Safety and Applied Nutrition, Office of Regulations and Policy, Division of Social Sciences
September 2005

The opinions and conclusions expressed in this working paper are solely the views of the authors and do not necessarily reflect those of the Food and Drug Administration.

Abstract

In this paper we investigate the communication impacts of various schemes for conveying information about the certainty of the scientific evidence supporting a health claim that appears on a food product label. Disclaimers about the level of scientific evidence supporting a health claim have been recommended by recent Court decisions as a remedy for otherwise potentially misleading claims. We evaluate four possible schemes for conveying the strength of science supporting a health claim. Two experimental schemes rely on specific wording and word order, and use claim language similar to that used in FDA's interim guidance for qualified health claims. The other two experimental schemes use report card grades to convey strength of science.

For the experiment, we selected four dietary substance/disease relationships (calcium/osteoporosis, omega-3 fatty acids/heart disease, selenium/cancer and lycopene/cancer) to represent a range of scientific certainty. These "health claims" did not necessarily reflect authorized health claims allowed under FDA regulations or qualified health claims already considered by the agency. For each hypothetical health claim, we also identified an everyday food product that contained the identified nutrient and met all or most qualifying and disqualifying criteria for other nutrients (calcium/orange juice, omega-3/tuna, selenium/eggs, and lycopene/spaghetti sauce). Each respondent was randomly assigned to an experimental condition where he/she saw two different products consecutively. One of the products showed a label with one of the four following conditions (No

Claim, Nutrient Content Claim, Unqualified Health Claim stated with "may", Unqualified Health Claim stated without "may"). Some respondents were first briefed about the scientific evidence for one of the health claims and later saw the product label for the Nutrient Content Claim condition for the relevant nutrient ("Full Information" condition). The other product showed a disclaimer from one of the four schemes that convey the strength of science that is appropriate for the level assigned to the hypothetical claim being tested or one level above or below this level. The order and combinations of presented products were counterbalanced to avoid possible bias in the estimation of experimental effects. Respondents answered questions about the perceived certainty of science for the claim and about perceived health benefits for the product.

The results suggest that text sentences using adjectives do not correctly convey to respondents the intended strength of science. The schemes using report card grades did convey the intended strength of science, but report card grade disclaimers had unintended effects on respondents' perceptions of scientific certainty relative to unqualified claims, such that respondents attributed more certainty to claims with disclaimers than those without disclaimers. Finally, there was evidence that respondents' perceptions of product health benefits were not diminished by conveying greater scientific uncertainty for a claim. In some cases conveying more scientific certainty for a claim actually led to more negative perceptions of product health benefits. This overall pattern of results suggests important caveats on the possible effectiveness of strength of science disclaimers....

The intent of the present study is to assess the relative effectiveness of different ways of communicating the strength of science underlying a food label health claim using different possible wordings or graphic presentations of strength of science disclaimers to implement a four-level scheme (i.e., unqualified health claim statement and three-levels of qualified health claim statements).[13]...

There are many possible ways to construct disclaimers to communicate the degree of scientific support for a health claim. The present study looks at

---

[13] Throughout this research report "unqualified health claim" or "health claim" refers to a health claim statement of the form "X may reduce the risk of Y," and "qualified health claim" refers to a health claim statement accompanied by a disclaimer. As used herein, the terms are not intended to encompass the more complex definitions and requirements provided in FDA's regulations.

four possible schemes, two similar to those currently being used by manufacturers under FDA's interim guidance for qualified health claims and two other alternatives. Within each scheme, the top level is an unqualified health claim (i.e., without an SS ["strength of science"] disclaimer), similar to how authorized claims that meet SSA ["significant scientific agreement"] are currently presented on product labels. Each scheme also defines three levels of disclaimers below this top level. Two schemes (Point/Counterpoint and Embedded[14]) rely on text sentences with different grammatical structure and adjectives to communicate the levels of scientific support for the claim. Two schemes use a familiar A-B-C-D report card grade to communicate the level. The Report Card-Text scheme uses text to describe the system and the letter grade assigned ("B", "C" or "D") to the qualified health claim statement. The Report Card-Graphic scheme uses a visual depiction of the report card grading scheme where the claim's grade is indicated by a checkmark next to the B, C or D box....

Discussion

None of the different ways tested to communicate the strength of science supporting a food label health claim performed very satisfactorily. The ways that different disclaimer schemes failed, however, may help us understand why it is so difficult to communicate strength of science to consumers. Text disclaimers that relied on plain English and adjectives (i.e., Point/Counterpoint and Embedded disclaimer schemes) failed the key communication test. They did not reliably convey the intended level of scientific support for a health claim. This suggests a need to better understand the operating assumptions that influence consumers' reactions to health claim statements and the ways consumers' assumptions and knowledge may affect their perceptions in this communication situation.

Even when strength of science disclaimers were easier to comprehend (i.e., with the familiar communication device of report card grade), they did not show the intended effects. Report card grade disclaimer schemes successfully conveyed the intended ordering of scientific certainty, but they failed a compensatory effect test. For example, when respondents saw B and

---

[14] Point/Counterpoint claims are worded with the statement of the relationship first, followed by the disclaimer, e.g., "Selenium may reduce the risk of cancer but the scientific evidence is promising but not conclusive." Embedded claims are stated with the disclaimer first, e.g., "Promising but not conclusive scientific evidence suggests that selenium may reduce the risk of cancer."

C report card grade disclaimers appropriate for the "correct" level of scientific support for the claim, they became more certain about the scientific evidence supporting the claim than when they saw an unqualified ("A" level) health claim. Rather than compensate for the effect of an unqualified claim, such qualified claims led to stronger effects in the same direction. Similarly, strength of science disclaimers did not significantly diminish the impact of health claims on consumer perceptions of product health benefits.

The failure of report card grade disclaimers, which successfully convey the level of scientific support, to reverse the perceived certainty effects of unqualified health claims is especially worrisome. It raises questions, such as how can consumers understand the usual meaning of a report card grade of B or C to imply more certainty than their prior assumptions about the certainty of unqualified health claims? One possible explanation is that consumers may fail to recognize how much better the scientific evidence is for a health claim that meets the significant scientific agreement standard, such as those they currently see on food product labels, than it is for a claim that requires a disclaimer. Or it may be that their perceptions of the meaning of a B or a C letter grade is such that these disclaimers connote more certainty than their prior views about product label health claims in general. This communication failure would follow from consumers' inaccurate prior assumptions about the scientific support for unqualified health claims.

A problem of incorrect prior assumptions may be correctable through education, perhaps by explaining to consumers the implications of a health claim being unqualified or qualified by a SS disclaimer. This would require explaining to consumers the FDA's regulatory approach to health claims. An attempt to update the consumer's prior assumptions at the time of reading the label, however, is functionally equivalent to a disclaimer and would need to be evaluated in the same way. For example, how would a consumer react if a label statement asserts that a health claim is more certain than the consumer previously thought it to be? ...

Another approach to dealing with incorrect prior assumptions might be to include unqualified health claims within the report card grade scheme. By giving unqualified health claims an explicit "A" grade, for example, the correct ordering of scientific certainty for health claims could be communicated for the full range of possible health claims. It should be noted that other health information found on food labels, such as structure-function claims or dietary guidance statements, fall outside this health claim approach.

A recent study by the International Food Information Council (IFIC, 2005) tested the approach of labeling unqualified health claims with an explicit report card grade of "A." IFIC found that although "A" grades conveyed significantly greater scientific certainty, they also produced some significant product preference reversals compared to health claims with lower report card grades (IFIC, 2005).

These findings suggest that consumers' prior beliefs about the certainty of science for a health claim are not easily supplanted by new information in the claim. These prior beliefs apparently play an important role in determining how consumers understand and respond to health claims. When claims seem to convey more scientific certainty than respondents believed to be warranted by their prior beliefs, they reacted by attributing less positive health benefits to the product than they did when the claim conveyed less scientific certainty.

How can conveying more certainty about the science supporting a health claim cause negative effects on product perceptions? One would expect greater scientific certainty to signal more positive product characteristics. One possible explanation is based on the phenomenon of psychological reactance. Reactance is a well known social cognition phenomenon where people react negatively to what they perceive to be an inappropriate or exaggerated attempt to influence them. The crucial perspective applicable here is the idea that the claim/disclaimer on the product label is perceived by consumers as an explicit influence attempt. This suggests that rather than assuming that consumers view health claims/disclaimers on product labels as authoritative and authorless information, it may be that consumers think of health claims as marketing, intended to influence them to buy the product. In this view, when consumers have prior beliefs about either the product or the health claim, they are sensitive to product label claims which seem to be exaggerated or overblown. When the perceived discrepancy is sufficiently large, psychological reactance may result, and normal inferential effects of the claim on perceived product characteristics may be reversed. It may not be enough to convey greater scientific certainty about claims, even if they deserve it, if consumers see that as a basis to doubt the credibility of the claim.

From this perspective, the fundamental communication problem with strength of science disclaimers is not that they are incomprehensible, which they may be, or that consumers have incorrect prior beliefs about the scientific certainty of claims, which they may have, but rather that consumers see health claims and strength of science disclaimers as marketing information which may or may not deserve their trust. Health claims and disclaimers that consumers see on product labels will sometimes provide helpful and useful information about product characteristics and nutrition science, but they also may be misleading. In such a communication context, the first task of the label reader is to judge whether a claim deserves trust. Rather than assume that disclaimers are authoritative (and authorless) information about the science supporting the claim, consumers seem to see disclaimers as one more piece of evidence to help them decide whether the assertions being made about the product are plausible or misleading.

Analyzing health claims and disclaimers as marketing information manufacturers provide to promote their product seems to fit the data. It would explain why consumers are generally skeptical about product label health claims—there is always the possibility that someone is trying to take advantage of your trust. It explains why disclaimers don't reverse the effects of health claims—mild disclaimers may actually increase the perceived plausibility of claims because they seem to regard the disclaimer as a signal that the manufacturer is trying to be balanced and informative. It explains why it is so hard to communicate levels of scientific certainty in a comprehensible way—if consumers don't care that much about scientific certainty of a claim except when it is grossly discrepant from their existing views, they cannot be assumed to read this information with great care or attention. It helps explain why briefing respondents about the state of science for a given health claim before they see a product with a relevant content claim tends to make the content claim equivalent to an unqualified health claim, i.e., being briefed about the level of scientific support makes consumers react to a nutrient content claim as a plausible implied health claim. Finally, it helps explain why health claims have more positive effects when they are less familiar—when a health claim is unfamiliar the consumer has less of a knowledge basis that can serve to trigger a critical response.

A marketing perspective on label health claims also sheds light on the individual difference effects observed in the study. Respondents who are more knowledgeable about specific substance/disease relationships are more likely to be positively influenced by related health claims because these health claims are more likely to seem plausible in light of their prior knowledge. Similarly, respondents who are more educated are less likely to be positively influenced by health claims because more educated people tend to be more skeptical of what they see to be marketing claims.

Guidance for Industry: FDA's Implementation of "Qualified Health Claims": Questions and Answers

U.S. Department of Health and Human Services

Food and Drug Administration
Center for Food Safety and Applied Nutrition (CFSAN)
May 12, 2006

This guidance represents the Food and Drug Administration's (FDA's) current thinking on this topic. It does not create or confer any rights for or on any person and does not operate to bind FDA or the public. You may use an alternative approach if the approach satisfies the requirements of the applicable statutes and regulations. If you want to discuss an alternative approach, please contact the FDA staff responsible for implementing this guidance. If you cannot identify the appropriate FDA staff, call the appropriate number listed on the title page of this guidance.

Background

1. Why is FDA providing for "qualified" health claims?

Through the Better Nutrition Information for Consumer Health Initiative, FDA acknowledged that consumers benefit from more information on food labels concerning diet and health. As part of this initiative, the agency established interim procedures whereby "qualified" health claims can be made not only for dietary supplements but for conventional foods as well. Moreover, past court decisions have clarified the need to provide for health claims based on less science evidence rather than just on the standard of significant scientific agreement (SSA), as long as the claims do not mislead the consumers....

2. What are the similarities and differences between SSA health claims established under the 1993 regulations and the newer "qualified" health claims?

Both types of health claims characterize a relationship between a substance (specific food component or a specific food) and a disease (e.g., lung cancer or heart disease) or health-related condition (e.g., high blood pressure), and are supported by scientific evidence. Health claims generally undergo review by FDA through a petition process. All SSA health claims as provided for by Congress in 1990 must meet the SSA standard. Past court decisions resulting in qualified health claims on dietary supplements focused on whether a manufacturer could make statements about diet/disease relationships when the science supporting the claim did not meet the significant scientific agreement standard, provided that the claim about the relationship was stated or "qualified" in such a way as to not mislead consumers. Thus, qualified health claims differ from SSA health claims in that they must be accompanied by a disclaimer or otherwise qualified....

5. What is a letter of enforcement discretion?

A letter of enforcement discretion is a letter issued by FDA to the petitioner specifying the nature of the qualified health claim for which FDA intends to consider the exercise of its enforcement discretion. If a letter of enforcement discretion has been issued, FDA does not intend to object to the use of the claim specified in the letter, provided that the products that bear the claim are consistent with the stated criteria.

All letters of enforcement discretion will be posted on the FDA website. Once the letter is posted on the website, all manufacturers will have notice about how the agency intends to exercise its enforcement discretion on the use of the qualified health claim.

6. How are health claims different from structure/function claims?

Both SSA and qualified health claims characterize the relationship between a substance and its ability to reduce the risk of a *disease* or health-related condition. Structure/function claims describe the effect that a substance has on the structure or function of the body and do not make reference to a disease. An example of a structure/function claim is "Calcium builds strong bones." Structure/function claims must be truthful and not misleading and are not pre-reviewed or authorized by FDA.

7. How are health claims different from statements about dietary guidance?

Health claims characterize a relationship between a substance (specific food or food component) and a disease or health-related condition. Both elements of 1) a substance and 2) a disease are present in a health claim. Dietary guidance does not contain both elements (and therefore does not constitute a health claim), but may contain one element or another. Typically, dietary guidance statements make reference to a category of foods (i.e., a grouping that is not readily characterized compositionally) and not to a specific substance. The following illustrations may be helpful:

Two examples of an authorized health claim, which by definition must contain the elements of a substance and a disease or health-related condition, are: "Diets low in *sodium* may reduce the risk of high blood pressure, a disease associated with many factors" and "Diets low in saturated fat and cholesterol that include 25 grams of *soy protein* a day may reduce the risk of *heart disease*".

An example of dietary guidance, which does not refer to a specific substance but rather refers to a broad class of foods without an expressed or implied connection to a specific substance that is present the class of foods is: "Diets rich in fruits and vegetables may reduce the risk of some types of *cancer*". One element is present, but not both. It is not a health claim because it cannot reasonably be understood to be about a specific substance.

A dietary guidance statement that refers to a specific food or food component but not a disease or health-related condition is: "*Carrots* are good for your health," or "*Calcium* is good for you." Again, one element is present, but not both....

Procedures for Qualified Health Claims

9. What are the regulatory procedures associated with qualified health claims?

All health claims, whether SSA or qualified, require that a petition be submitted to FDA. The requirements for health claim petitions are specified in 21 CFR 101.70, and the general requirements for health claims are in 21 CFR 101.14. Both types of health claims can be applicable to conventional foods and dietary supplements, must characterize the substance's ability to reduce the risk of disease, and cannot be about mitigating or treating disease. Qualified health claims have differences that relate to scientific support, wording of the claim, use of enforcement discretion, and timelines.

10. How is the science supporting a qualified health claim different from that for an SSA health claim?

SSA health claims require significant scientific agreement based on the totality of publicly available scientific evidence. Qualified health claims are still based on the totality of publicly available evidence but the scientific support does not have to be as strong as that for significant scientific agreement. Under its interim guidance, FDA is tentatively providing for 3 levels of science below the Significant Scientific Agreement standard: *good to moderate level* of scientific agreement, *low level* of scientific agreement, and *very low level* of scientific agreement. The criteria for the scientific review are described in the interim guidance....

11. How do the regulatory procedures for qualified health claims differ from SSA health claims?

Petitions requesting an SSA health claim are evaluated under the Significant Scientific Agreement standard. If FDA decides that standard is met, it authorizes the claim through notice-and-comment rulemaking.

Petitions requesting a qualified health claim are posted on the FDA web page for a 60-day public comment period. Qualified health claims meeting the interim procedures criteria are provided for by letters of enforcement discretion (as described above). The letter of enforcement discretion will be posted on the FDA web page. Petitions for a qualified health claim that have no credible scientific evidence for the claim may be denied. These letters will be posted on FDA's website.

12. What is the procedural timeline for qualified health claims?

Within 15 days of receipt, FDA will acknowledge the petition.

Within 45 days of receipt, FDA will file the petition and a docket number will be assigned. Note: Petitions that do not meet content requirements as specified in 21 CFR 101.70 will not be filed and will be returned to the petitioner.

At the time of filing, FDA will post the petition on the FDA webpage for a 60-day public comment period. During this time, written comments may be submitted to the docket.

On or before 270 days after receipt of the petition, a final decision will be sent to the petitioner in the form of a letter as to whether FDA intends to exercise enforcement discretion with respect to a qualified health claim or deny the petition. The letter will be posted on FDA's website.

Extensions beyond 270 days can be granted upon mutual agreement between the petitioner and the agency.

Submitting a Petition

13. How will FDA know that I wish to have my petition reviewed under the standards for a qualified health claim rather than those for an SSA health claim (i.e., under the Significant Scientific Agreement standard)?

The petitioner may indicate within the petition's cover letter that he/she is waiving the right to a review under the Significant Scientific Agreement standard and request that the petition be reviewed under the interim procedures for a qualified health claim. This request will result in FDA proceeding directly to the qualified health claim procedures and its 270-day timeline. In the absence of such a request, FDA contacts the petitioner to determine if they are petitioning for a SSA or qualified health claim....

Notes

1. We are studying claims that are not compelled but voluntary, and yet they are constrained by law because consumers may find them so tempting that the claims are easily abused. Beyond health claims, two additional kinds of claims that consumers may find particularly alluring are what are known as "nutrient content" and "structure/function" claims. The FDA's online guidance document, "Label Claims for Conventional Foods and Dietary Supplements," describes these claims and the regulatory structure for them:

> II. Nutrient Content Claims
>
> The Nutrition Labeling and Education Act of 1990 (NLEA) permits the use of label claims that characterize the level of a nutrient in a food (i.e., nutrient content claims) if they have been authorized by FDA and are made in accordance with FDA's authorizing regulations. Nutrient content claims describe the level of a nutrient in the product, using terms such as *free, high,* and *low*, or they compare the level of a nutrient in a food to that of another food, using terms such as *more, reduced*, and *lite*. An accurate quantitative statement (e.g., 200 mg of sodium) that does not otherwise "characterize" the nutrient level may be used to describe the amount of a nutrient present. However, a statement such as "only 200 mg of sodium" characterizes the level of sodium by implying that it is low. Therefore, the food would have to meet the nutritional criteria for a "low" nutrient content claim or carry a disclosure statement that it does not qualify for the claim (e.g., "not a low sodium food"). Most nutrient content claim regulations apply only to those nutrients that have an established Daily Value. The requirements that govern the use of nutrient content claims help ensure that descriptive terms, such as *high* or *low*, are used consistently for all types of food products and are thus meaningful to consumers. *Healthy* is an implied nutrient content claim that characterizes a food as having "healthy" levels of total fat, saturated fat, cholesterol and sodium, as defined in the regulation authorizing use of the claim. Percentage claims for dietary supplements are another category of nutrient content claims.

These claims are used to describe the percentage level of a dietary ingredient in a dietary supplement and may refer to dietary ingredients for which there is no established Daily Value, provided that the claim is accompanied by a statement of the amount of the dietary ingredient per serving. Examples include simple percentage statements such as "40% omega-3 fatty acids, 10 mg per capsule," and comparative percentage claims, e.g., "twice the omega-3 fatty acids per capsule (80 mg) as in 100 mg of menhaden oil (40 mg)." (See 21 CFR 101.13(q)(3)(ii))....

III. Structure/Function Claims and Related Dietary Supplement Claims

Structure/function claims have historically appeared on the labels of conventional foods and dietary supplements as well as drugs. The Dietary Supplement Health and Education Act of 1994 (DSHEA) established some special regulatory requirements and procedures for using structure/function claims and two related types of dietary supplement labeling claims, claims of general well-being and claims related to a nutrient deficiency disease. Structure/function claims may describe the role of a nutrient or dietary ingredient intended to affect the normal structure or function of the human body, for example, "calcium builds strong bones." In addition, they may characterize the means by which a nutrient or dietary ingredient acts to maintain such structure or function, for example, "fiber maintains bowel regularity," or "antioxidants maintain cell integrity." General well-being claims describe general well-being from consumption of a nutrient or dietary ingredient. Nutrient deficiency disease claims describe a benefit related to a nutrient deficiency disease (like vitamin C and scurvy), but such claims are allowed only if they also say how widespread the disease is in the United States. These three types of claims are not pre-approved by FDA, but the manufacturer must have substantiation that the claim is truthful and not misleading and must submit a notification with the text of the claim to FDA no later than 30 days after marketing the dietary supplement with the claim. If a dietary supplement label includes such a claim, it must state in a "disclaimer" that FDA has not evaluated the claim. The disclaimer must also state that the dietary supplement product is not intended to "diagnose, treat, cure or prevent any disease," because only a drug can legally make such a claim. Structure/function claims may not explicitly or implicitly link the claimed effect of the nutrient or dietary ingredient to a disease or state of health leading to a disease....

Structure/function claims for conventional foods focus on effects derived from nutritive value, while structure/function claims for dietary supplements may focus on non-nutritive as well as nutritive effects. FDA does not require conventional food manufacturers to notify FDA about their structure/function claims, and disclaimers are not required for claims on conventional foods.

2. By now, you are getting accustomed to intricate regulatory schemes. But the FDA's regulations on nutrient content claims are especially byzantine. We will not be learning the details of these regulations. You might get some sense of their complexity, however, from the following chart, taken from the FDA's online Food Labeling Guide. The chart describes several kinds of allowable nutrient content claims and the conditions attached to them.

Nutrient	Free	Low	Reduced/Less	Comments
Total Fat 21 CFR 101.62(b)	Less than 0.5g RACC ["reference amounts customarily consumed"] and per labeled serving (or for meals and main dishes, less than 0.5g per labeled serving) *(b)(1)* Contains no ingredient that is fat or understood to contain fat...	3g or less per RACC (and per 50g if RACCis small) *(b)(2)* Meals and main dishes: 3gor less per 100gand not morethan 30% of calories from fat *(b)(3)*	Atleast 25% less fat per RACC than an appropriate reference food (or for meals and main dishes, at least 25% less fat per 100 g) *(b)(4) & (5)* Reference food may not be "Low Fat"	"Fat Free": may be used iffood meets the requirements for "Low Fat" *21 CFR 101.62(b)(6)* 100%FatFree: food mustbe "Fat Free" *(b)(6)(iii)* "Light" - see previous calorie comments For dietary supplements: total fat claims cannot be made for productsthat are 40 calories or less perserving *21 CFR 101.62(a)(4)*

Saturated Fat 21 CFR 101.62(c)	Less than 0.5 g saturated fat and less than 0.5g trans fatty acids per RACC and main dishes, less than 0.5 g saturated fat and trans fatty acids per labeled serving) *(c)(1)* Contains no ingredient that is understood to contain saturated fat . . .	1 g or less per RACC and 15% or less of calories from saturated fat *(c)(2)* Meals and main dishes: 1 g or less per 100g and less than 10% of calories from saturated fat *(c)(3)*t	At least 25% less saturated fatpr RACC than an appropriate reference food (or for meals and main dishes, at least 25% less saturated fatper 100 g) *(c)(4) & (5)* Reference food may not be "Low Saturated Fat"	Next to all saturated fat claims, must declare the amount of cholesterol if 2 mg or more per RACC; and the amount of total fat if more than 3g per RACC (or 0.5 g or more of total fat per RACC for "Saturated Fat Free") (or for meals and main dishes, per labeled serving) *21 CFR 101.62(c)* For dietary supplements: saturated fat claims cannot be made for productsthat are 40 calories or less per serving *21 CFR 101.62(a)(4)*

Sugars 21 CFR 101.60(c)	"Sugar Free": Less than 0.5 g sugars per RACC and per labeled serving (or for meals and main dishes, less than 0.5 g per labeled serving) *(c)(1)* Contains no ingredient that is a sugar or generally understood to contain sugars… Disclose calorie profile (e.g., "Low Calorie")	Not Defined. May not be used	At least 25% less sugars per RACC than an appropriate reference food (or for meals and main dishes, at least 25% less sugar per 100g) May not use this claim on dietary supplements of vitamins and minerals *(c)(5) & (6)*	"No Added Sugars" and "Without Added Sugars" are allowed if no sugar or sugar containing ingredient is added during processing. State if food is not "Low" or "Reduced Calorie" *(c)(2)* The terms "Unsweetened" and "No Added Sweeteners" remain as factual statements *(c)(3)* The claim does not refer to sugar alcohols, which may be present. For dietary supplements: "Sugar Free" and "No Added Sugar" may be used for vitamins and minerals intended to be used by infants and children less than 2 years of age. *(c)(4)*

3. Structure/function claims are handled very differently. The FDCA does not regulate structure/functions claims on foods, other than by generally prohibiting false or misleading statements. Here is one domain in which dietary supplements are actually more strictly regulated than conventional foods. Moreover, although the FDA could provide legal guidance on the kinds of factors that would make structure/function claims false or misleading, it has not done so. Does the different treatment of nutrient content and structure/function claims make sense? How about the different treatment of conventional foods and dietary supplements?

4. The FDA has, as we have seen in this chapter, devoted a considerable portion of the resources it has to address food labeling to health claims and qualified claims. Yet as the FDA has done so, the food industry has steadily increased the extent to which it relies on nutrient content and structure/function claims and decreased the extent to which it relies on health or qualified health claims. In fact, the General Accountability Office found in 2011 that even when food products were eligible to use a qualified health

claim, they twice as often used a structure/function claim instead. Moreover, research conducted by the FDA itself, and by other research bodies, has found that consumers have a hard time distinguishing between health claims, qualified health claims, nutrient content claims, and structure/function claims. For consumers, in other words, a structure/function claim virtually unregulated by the FDA may be as appealing a marketing tool as a health claim subject to premarket approval by the agency.

PART III SAFETY

CHAPTER 6 THE VARIETIES OF ADULTERATION

We have been studying the ways in which the Food, Drug, and Cosmetic Act aims, through the prohibition on misbranding, to ensure the credibility and reliability of information consumers receive about the food they buy and eat. Adulteration is the other major prohibited category under the Act. Here we begin to encounter a direct concern with the safety of food. As we will see, however, there are many different varieties of adulteration under the Act (and under similar provisions in other federal statutes), and not all of them have to do with safety. In particular, the concept of "economic" adulteration is concerned with economic protection of consumers rather than safety, and the category of "aesthetic" adulteration has more to do with, for lack of a better term, general grossness than with health risks.

We begin, as usual, with the statutory provisions, defining the categories of adulteration. As you read the provisions below, notice which factors are relevant to placing foods in one category of adulteration or another. How many different kinds of adulteration can you find? How are they different?

Food, Drug, and Cosmetic Act

21 U.S.C. §§342, 321, 348

SEC. 402. ADULTERATED FOOD

A food shall be deemed to be adulterated—

(a) Poisonous, insanitary, etc.,ingredients

(1) If it bears or contains any poisonous or deleterious substance which may render it injurious to health; but in case the substance is not an added substance such food shall not be considered adulterated under this clause if the quantity of such substance in such food does not ordinarily render it injurious to health;

(2)

(A) if it bears or contains any added poisonous or added deleterious substance (other than a substance that is a pesticide chemical residue in or on a raw agricultural commodity or processed food, a food additive, a color additive, or a new animal drug) that is unsafe within the meaning of section 406; or

(B) if it bears or contains a pesticide chemical residue that is unsafe within the meaning of section 408(a); or

(C) if it is or if it bears or contains

(i) any food additive that is unsafe within the meaning of section 409. . .; or

(3) if it consists in whole or in part of any filthy, putrid, or decomposed substance, or if it is otherwise unfit for food; or

(4) if it has been prepared, packed, or held under insanitary conditions whereby it may have become contaminated with filth, or whereby it may have been rendered injurious to health; or

(5) if it is, in whole or in part, the product of a diseased animal or of an animal which has died otherwise than by slaughter; or

(6) if its container is composed, in whole or in part, of any poisonous or deleterious substance which may render the contents injurious to health....

(b) Absence, substitution, or addition of constituents

(1) If any valuable constituent has been in whole or in part omitted or abstracted therefrom; or

(2) if any substance has been substituted wholly or in part therefore; or

(3) if damage or inferiority has been concealed in any manner; or

(4) if any substance has been added thereto or mixed or packed therewith so as to increase its bulk or weight, or reduce its quality or strength, or make it appear better or of greater value than it is....

(c) Color additives. If it is, or it bears or contains, a color additive which is unsafe within the meaning of section 721(a).

Economic Adulteration

Reread section (b), above. Can you think of any food products in the modern food marketplace that might violate this provision? Any products from which a "valuable constituent has been in whole or in part omitted or abstracted"? Any for which "any substance has been substituted wholly or in part"? Any product whose "damage or inferiority has been concealed in any matter"? And so on. You get the idea. It appears that this is a statutory provision with little current legal bite. Why do you suppose that is? What if the FDA started enforcing this provision? How would the food marketplace change?

A close cousin of economic adulteration is the kind of "unfit-for-food" adulteration that turns on the taste, texture, or other, similar characteristics of food. An allegation of this kind of adulteration is at work in the following case.

United States v. 24 Cases, More or Less ["Herring Roe"]

87 F.Supp. 826 (D. Me. 1949)

CLIFFORD, District Judge.

This is a motion by claimant to dismiss a libel in rem in so far as the libel relates to that part of the libelled goods, consisting of twenty-four cases of canned herring roe. The libel was brought by the United States of America under the Federal Food, Drug and Cosmetic Act, for the seizure and condemnation, under section 334 of said Act, of two lots of canned herring roe. These lots contained 181 and 24 cases, respectively, each case containing 24 cans of this product. The libel alleged that both lots were shipped in interstate commerce; that the contents of the 181 case lot were unfit for food, within the meaning of the Act, in that they consisted wholly or in part of a decomposed substance; and that the contents of both lots were unfit for food, within the meaning of the Act, in that they were of a "tough, rubbery consistency."

...[T]he claimant, Riviera Packing Company, filed this motion to dismiss the complaint, so far as it relates to the lot consisting of 24 cases.

The only allegation contained in the complaint against the 24 case lot rests on the claim that the product therein contained was of a "tough, rubbery, consistency." By its motion to dismiss the complaint so far as it relates to the 24 case lot, claimant raises the question whether a food product, not otherwise unfit for food, may ever be condemned as unfit for food merely because it is "of a tough and rubbery consistency."

The motion to dismiss this portion of the libel should not be granted unless it appears to a certainty that the government could not prevail under any state of facts which could be proved in support of the libel....

Section 402(a)(3) of the Act provides as follows: "A food shall be deemed to be adulterated- (a)...(3) if it consists in whole or in part of any filthy, putrid, or decomposed substance, or if it is otherwise unfit for food;...."

The answer to the question raised by the motion at bar is not to be found in any of the cases cited by counsel for the Government or for the claimant.

The claimant's brief, supporting this motion, argues that the man on the street would never interpret or understand the word "adulterated" to include the sense "of a tough and rubbery consistency." The claimant argues that the statutory words "otherwise unfit for food" are intended merely to enlarge the ban of the statute from "filthy, putrid, or decomposed" matter, and to reach only other substances not within that classification but in some other way injurious to health. Finally, claimant urges that toughness is a term peculiarly subject to personal taste and therefore not a proper subject for regulation under the Food, Drug and Cosmetic Act. These points will be considered in order.

In its interpretation of the word "adulterated," this Court must be guided by the definition given in the statute. This definition and its construction clearly extend beyond the dictionary meaning of the word, which is "corruption by the addition of a foreign substance."

The statutory phrase "otherwise unfit for food" is general on its face. The Government's brief lays great stress on the policy of Congress, as expressed in the Food, Drug and Cosmetic Act, to protect the consuming public in the purchase of food products. Counsel for the Government cite several cases where the Act has been applied, in carrying out this policy, to condemn food products which contained no filthy, putrid or decomposed substances, nor any other harmful material, but which were characterized by an abnormal odor, taste or color.

The case of United States v. 184 Barrels Dried Whole Eggs, D.C.E.D.Wis. 1943, 53 F.Supp. 652, from which claimant quotes extensively, rules that the words "filthy, putrid, or decomposed substance"--which had stood alone in an earlier version of the statute and had been construed to apply whether or not the decomposed substance made the product injurious to health--lost none of their force by the addition of the word "or if it is otherwise unfit for food." It is the opinion of this Court that the words "otherwise unfit for food," following as they do the word "or," must be construed as having strengthened and enlarged the intended scope of the coverage of the Act.

Toughness was the issue in a recent case in the United States District Court for the District of Oregon, United States v. 298 Cases, etc., Ski Slide Brand Asparagus. In that case the court considered whether canned center cuts of asparagus were too tough and woody to be fit for food. The case was heard on the merits: the Court himself sampled the product and dismissed the case, ruling that the product was fit for food. Fairly to be understood, but not expressed in his ruling was the assumption that the product could have been so tough as to warrant condemnation as unfit for food.

It is the opinion of this Court that a food product may conceivably be "unfit for food" by reason of an excessively tough or rubbery consistency;

and that a product which is unfit for food for this reason, as for any other, properly falls within the construction of the statute and the policy of the Congress, that such products should be condemned for the protection of the consumer. The issue, whether the product is so tough as to be unfit for food, is solely a factual one, and must be determined by the Court in a trial on the merits.

The question of the standard to be applied in determining the decree of toughness which constitutes an article unfit for food may be somewhat troublesome. As claimant has argued, the question is, in large measure, one of personal taste. Some products are, by their very nature, much tougher to eat than others. The fussy, fastidious, finicky individual might, with disdain, refuse to accept and throw out the product of the claimant, because, to his taste it was too tough and rubbery to eat; yet the case hardened individual who brags he can eat anything, might, with relish, eat and enjoy the product of the claimant. We cannot accept as the standard or test that which might be applied by either one of these two types of individuals.

In the opinion of this Court, in order for a product to be subject to condemnation as unfit for food, on account of its tough and rubbery consistency, the product must be proved to be so tough and rubbery that the average, normal person, under ordinary conditions, would not chew and swallow it....

Note

What is the justification for protecting consumers from this sort of "adulteration"? Why would the government bring a case like this?

Aesthetic Adulteration

United States v. 449 Cases, Containing Tomato Paste

212 F.2d 567 (2d Cir. 1954)

CLARK, Circuit Judge.

This appeal concerns a seizure proceeding under the Federal Food, Drug, and Cosmetic Act involving 449 cases of tomato paste allegedly 'adulterated' within the meaning of §402(a)(3) of that act. The government as libelant has sought -- so far unsuccessfully -- condemnation of the food in question upon a showing that it contained tissues rotted, but not necessarily deleterious to health.

The tomato paste, imported from Portugal, was landed in Brooklyn in the Eastern District on April 9, 1951, the entry being in bond. Representatives of the Federal Security Agency took samples for inspection; and on April 16 claimant, A. Fantis, the importer, received official notice from the Food and Drug Administration that the goods need not be further held. Claimant thereupon paid for the shipment and removed and sold fifty cases from the entire lot. In July, however, a government food inspector, checking the warehouse, noticed that several of the cases had been recoopered; and closer inspection revealed that several cans had been resoldered. This discovery led to a retesting of the shipment, which disclosed the presence of mold in the tomato paste in quantities exceeding administrative tolerances. The instant proceedings ensued.

It is undisputed that mold in tomato products indicates decomposition. It is also undisputed that when, as here, it results from rot in the tomatoes present before processing, it is not visible to the naked eye, but is detectable only by microscopic examination. Libelant at the trial did not offer proof that the paste was deleterious or unfit for food, in any way other than the decomposition, but contended that it was no part of the government's case to go beyond the showing made as to decomposition. Thereafter the district judge filed an opinion holding that the government had not sustained its burden of proof and that the shipment should be released to the claimant. Libelant appeals from the resulting order.

Section 402(a)(3) provides that a food shall be deemed to be "adulterated," and hence subject to condemnation...upon shipment in interstate commerce: "if it consists in whole or in part of any filthy, putrid, or decomposed substance, or if it is otherwise unfit for food." The district court apparently read "unfit for food" as limiting the entire section by virtue of the word "otherwise," and as requiring a showing that the produce was deleterious. It is this construction which presents the issue on appeal. The point is novel in this circuit, though it has been decided by several other courts which have uniformly held that the government need not prove unfitness for food other than filth or decomposition. This unanimity of view is itself impressive; moreover, we think the conclusion it represents is required both by the statutory language and by the history and general pattern of the legislation.

The entire subject matter of this subdivision of the statute is covered by two co-ordinate "if" clauses; and the second "if" indicates plainly that the second clause introduced thereby is co-ordinate and independent, rather than a qualification of the antecedent clause. The first clause expressly bans all products composed in whole or in part of any filthy, putrid, or decomposed substance; and the second clause goes on to add to the ban substances which were unfit for food for any other reason.

Furthermore, the other subdivisions of §402(a) make specific reference to products which are "poisonous," "deleterious," "injurious to health," or "the product of a diseased animal." These provisions cover those cases where danger to health is direct and demonstrable. The specific listed characteristics are clearly essential elements to be proved in actions under those provisions which refer to them. But in the first clause of §402(a)(3) the sweeping ban of products consisting in whole or in part of any decomposed substance without reference to their effect on health is not made to depend on any such additional proper or findings to support the ultimate conclusion, requiring the ban. It may well be that, in the judgment of the legislators, the presence of any substantial amount of rot in any food product was a sign of danger sufficiently pointed to justify and require the exclusion of the product from unrestricted circulation in interstate commerce. Or we may accept an acute suggestion of Judge Maris in United States v. 133 Cases of Tomato Paste, D.C.E.D.Pa., 22 F.Supp. 515, 516, that this section "was designed to protect the aesthetic tastes and sensibilities of the consuming public," and that the presence of such material in food, whether "perceptible by the consumer" or not, would offend both. For present decision it matters not which rationale is preferred, since in either event congressional power is clear and is not now challenged.

It should be noted also that the further class of adulterated foods thus added, i.e., "otherwise unfit for food," is a broad general classification...not limited to either proof of filth or decomposition or to conditions deleterious to health. There is therefore no basis for equating unfitness for food with injury to health, and the assumed logical progression from decomposition to unfitness for food to injury to health as showing identic terms thus doubly fails.

The conclusion..., following the statutory language, that the phrase "unfit for food" is not constrictive, but rather is additional or cumulative, is of controlling importance here. Any attempt to develop a constrictive meaning runs into the difficulty...that there is literally no place to which the argument may lead. As appears, complete identification of this phrase with "injurious to health" is universally excluded. But it is manifestly impossible to work out some tertium quid, of content sufficient to be grasped and acted upon by government inspectors or courts, of matter which is worse than "filthy, putrid, or decomposed," but still less than injurious to health. At most, search for such an intermediate ground can only suggest something by way of a greater degree of filthiness or putridity, perhaps along the line of the government tolerance actually allowed, or, if not this, something hopelessly vague and variable, dependent upon the taste buds or olefactory senses of the inspectors and too shifty a basis to serve as embodiment of congressional intent of drastic prohibition with both civil and criminal sanctions. So it is not surprising that no precedent or authority actually supports such a classification. And so the argument for restrictive interpretation of the statute slips insensibly, although perhaps necessarily, into an identification of food unfitness with health injury....

It is of course true, as is often pointed out, that the power granted is very broad, and "literal application of the statute could lead to unjustified harshness." But Congress has attempted to meet this difficulty by granting a large measure of discretion to the administrator, originally the Secretary of Agriculture, later the Federal Security Administrator, and now the Secretary of Health, Education and Welfare. In addition to provisions not here immediately pertinent for regulations making certain exemptions or granting certain tolerances, 21 U.S.C. §§345, 346, there is a significant provision in the chapter authorizing penalties, injunctions, and seizures that nothing therein "shall be construed as requiring the Secretary to report for prosecution, or for the institution of libel or injunction proceedings, minor violations of this chapter whenever he believes that the public interest will be adequately served by a suitable written notice or warning." 21 U.S.C. §336. Obviously the Congress considered such administrative control a wiser course than the hedging of power by various theoretical restrictions, the negativing of which might be difficult of proof in a particular case. And its wisdom is indicated in this very case, where the product is prepared for and sold in quantity distribution, in cans of "Net Contents 10 Lbs. About" of concentrated paste, thus indicating distribution to restaurants and institutions, where customers and inmates cannot easily, if at all, protest the serving of rotten tomato paste, unlike ordinary retail sales, where housewives do have some possible change of protecting themselves against unwholesome products by buying first-grade articles at top prices....

The order denying condemnation and releasing the goods to the claimant must therefore be reversed....

FRANK, Circuit Judge (dissenting).

Fantis, the owner of this tomato paste, imported it under a contract which provided that he need not pay for it unless it was released from bond on its approval by the Food and Drug Administrator. On April 9, 1951, the Administrator (through a subordinate) having inspected it, gave Fantis the necessary approval. As a consequence, Fantis paid some $ 9,000 to the seller. Some three months later, the Administrator re-inspected the shipment, declared it in violation of the Act, seized it and, by this proceeding, sought a court order confiscating it. The Administrator having won in this court under my colleagues' decision, Fantis will lose his property without any compensation -- i.e., he will be out the $ 9,000.

1. The pertinent section of the Federal Food, Drug, and Cosmetic Act of 1938, is [section 402(a)(3)], which authorizes condemnation (confiscation) of food as adulterated, "if it consists in whole or in part of any filthy, putrid, or decomposed substance, or if it is otherwise unfit for food." The words "filthy or putrid" have no relevance here, for the government does not charge that this tomato paste was either filthy or putrid. The government proved only that it contained some "decomposed substance" -- namely mold. It did not prove, or even try to prove, that this food was either deleterious to health or "unfit for food." Indeed, the government and my colleagues assert that such proof was not necessary. For an understanding of my position, it is desirable to highlight these facts:

(a) The phrase "decomposed matter," as applied here, means simply and solely "mold."

(b) The government admits that no one looking at this tomato paste, or tasting it or smelling it, would have any knowledge that it contained any mold. The government's experts testified, and the government's brief states, that the presence of such mold in tomato paste can be detected only through a microscope and by an expert.

(c) The evidence here discloses that virtually all tomato paste contains some mold.

(d) So the use of the word "rotten" (or of any other pejorative) indicates nothing in any way unpleasant or harmful but merely that the tomato paste contains some utterly harmless mold.

(e) As several kinds of cheese which thousands of our citizens consider delectable -- e.g., Roquefort or Gorgonzola -- contain very substantial quantities of mold, my colleagues' interpretation means that Congress authorized the Pure Food and Drug administrator to condemn such cheese any time the Administrator happens to decide that it should not be sold.

(f) No one (including the government, except my colleagues in their opinion here) has ever so much as intimated that the presence of mold in a can indicates a possible future deterioration of the contents of the can which may later render the contents injurious to health. Indeed, in this very case a government expert witness testified that, in a properly made can, the amount of mold present in the can when it is sealed, will never increase; and there is no proof that the cans here were not properly made and sealed.

(g) This suit is based upon alleged adulteration, under [section 402(a)(3)], not upon "economic adulteration," or misbranding, i.e., not upon any misrepresentation of the contents of the can. The Administrator, to protect consumers, has the power, under [section 401], to issue regulations fixing reasonable standards of identity, quality and fill of containers, and has issued such regulations as to many foods. He might have issued such a regulation relating to canned tomato paste, with specific reference to the percentage of mold. In that event, if the cans here had failed to meet that standard, there would have been misbranding under [section 402(g) or (h)], and confiscation would have been justified. But no such regulation exists. (In its absence, it is difficult to understand just what my colleagues mean when they say that housewives buying canned tomato paste -- as distinguished from consumers of tomato paste, like that here, destined for sale to restaurants or institutions -- "do have some possible chance of protecting themselves against unwholesome products by buying first-grade articles at top prices." For, as above noted, no consumer is able to tell whether, or how much, mold is in a can of such paste.)

2. My colleagues construe "decomposed" as an absolute, i.e., unqualified by the subsequent words "or otherwise unfit for food." [I would construe] 'decomposed' as meaning so decomposed as to be "unfit for food" but not so decomposed as to be deleterious to health. The record discloses not even a soupçon of evidence that this tomato paste, when seized, was unfit for food. Consequently, under my interpretation of [section 402(a)(3)], the district court's order should be affirmed.

3. However, under either interpretation, the Administrator has an amazingly wide and unregulated discretion (since, as my colleagues say, even "unfit for food" has a most latitudinarian meaning). So, according to my colleagues' view, if the Administrator, without any previous publication of a standard, chose to seize tomato paste containing but 5% of mold, the courts would have to enforce the seizure and confiscate the paste. This means the absence of any impediment to unequal treatment in the administration of the statute.

My colleagues, to be sure, point to 21 U.S.C. §336 which reads, "Nothing in this chapter shall be construed as requiring the Secretary to report for prosecution, or for the institution of libel or injunction proceedings, minor violations of this chapter whenever he believes that the public interest will be adequately served by a suitable written notice or warning." But...my colleagues themselves recognize that it does not cut down the Administrator's immense power, even as to most "minor violations," but leaves it entirely in the Administrator's uncontrolled discretion to institute a proceeding to condemn any food containing mold: My colleagues explicitly rule that, once the Administrator has exercised his uncontrolled discretion and begun such a proceeding, the court must order the food condemned, no matter how small the amount or percentage of mold (unless perhaps it is so small as to come within the "de minimis" principle). It follows that §336 does not in any way diminish the vast delegation of discretionary authority to the Administrator or preclude inequality in the exercise of that authority.

4. I am not now prepared to say that such statutory delegation, although (as my colleagues say) coupled with no recognizable standard whatever, is unconstitutional. But our responsibility goes beyond adjudication of the validity of the legislative grant. It includes the duty of scrutinizing the methods employed in the processes of administering the granted power. Unless this power is in some way constrained (as I believe it has been by the Administrative Procedure Act), it permits dangerous administrative arbitrariness: The Administrator may one day confiscate Smither's food product because it contains 10% of mold; the next day confiscate Williams' because it contains 15%; and the day after, Robinson's because it contains 40%.

The fact that the Administrator had in no such case previously announced a standard binding upon him would not (except as I shall note in a moment) invalidate his action. I stress this fact because, in answer to Fantis' complaint that he relied on the Administrator's initial approval, the government says that he had no business thus to rely but, before expending his $9,000, should have obtained the advice of an expert he might have hired. But, absent knowledge of some fixed standard, no expert could have given such advice.

No doubt to avoid this sort of situation, Congress, in the Administrative Procedure Act, required administrative officials to publish their standards. Section 3(a)(3) of that Act provides that "Every agency shall separately state and currently publish in the Federal Register...(3) substantive rules adopted as authorized by law and statements of general policy or interpretations formulated and adopted by the agency for the guidance of the public...." The Administrator's determination that food containing a certain percentage of mold is "decomposed" and therefore subject to condemnation under the Act, is both an interpretation of the Act and a statement of policy as to standards. As such, that determination should be published in the Federal Register in accordance with the provisions of §3(a)(3). The necessity of apprising the public of administrative standards and interpretations was apparent to the drafters of the Administrative Procedure Act for, in a report dealing with §3(a)(3), the House Committee stated: "The section forbids secrecy of rules binding upon or applicable to the public or of delegations of authority. Mimeographed releases of many kinds now common should no longer be necessary since, if they contain really informative matter, they must be published as rules, policies, or interpretations. Substantive rules include the Statement of Standards." H.Rep. 1980 on S. 7 -- 79th Cong. 2nd Sess. May 3, 1946.

The Administrator did not comply with this provision. Indeed, one of the government experts testified in this case that the Administrator, since the seizure here, has changed his standard; but no standard whatever, relative to mold in tomato paste, has ever been published in the Federal Register.

It may be noted that, in the trial court, Fantis' counsel stated that "it has been recognized by President Truman that various departments in our Government, in order to overcome the necessity of increasing tariff laws, or increasing tariff rates and duty rates, have found other ways of discouraging importers from importing merchandise, and it is acknowledged, and a committee was appointed by President Truman, and there have been articles on this in the New York Times, and it is a well known by-word in the trade that various departments of the Government find methods other than duty to restrict importers from importing certain types of merchandise." Fantis offered no proof to support such a conclusion. But, with utterly uncontrolled discretion, restricted by no announced and binding standards, such administrative behavior may occur. Compliance with the Administrative Procedure Act will help to prevent it. Publication of binding standards has another virtue: If a citizen thinks the published standard unreasonably low, he can complain, through his congressional representatives, and Congress may reduce the statutory discretion.

Unhampered discretion of the type conferred by [section 402(a)(3)] is at best, insidious. Possessed of such power, an official may stop the sale of perfectly good food merely because he happens not to like it. (One recalls the tale of the totalitarian agitator who, having promised in a speech that, after the revolution, everybody would eat strawberries, replied to a heckler who loathed that fruit: "Comes the revolution, you'll eat strawberries.") More than a century ago, in 1840, Tocqueville warned that, even in a political democracy there might arise "an immense and tutelary power" which would be "absolute, minute, regular and mild," aiming to keep the citizens "in perpetual childhood." Such a government would seek "to spare them all the care of thinking and all the trouble of living.... It must not be forgotten that it is especially dangerous to enslave men in the minor details of life.... Subjection in minor affairs...does not drive men to resistance, but it crosses them at every turn, till they are ready to surrender the exercise of their own will. Thus their spirit is gradually broken and their character enervated...."

Such a possibility should cause courts like ours, when they can, to insist that administrative officers exercise wide discretionary powers in accordance with any statutory provision which requires that they commit themselves to properly publicized standards. In that way, to some extent at least, can there be reconciled unavoidable delegation of extensive discretion to administrators with needed protection of the individual.

Even assuming, then, the correctness of my colleagues' interpretation of the 1938 statute, I think we should affirm the order of the district court because of the lack of compliance with the Administrative Procedure Act.

Note

Recognizing that some level of filth, decomposition, etc., is unavoidable in food, the FDA set "defect action levels" that indicated the level of filth etc. it would tolerate. Defects above these levels might lead to enforcement action by FDA, but defects below these levels would generally be given a pass. The materials that follow show some of the defect action levels set by the FDA. What do you think of them? Although the action levels initially were kept confidential by the agency, as noted by the dissent in the case we just read, eventually they were made public. What do you think about "secret" action levels?

Food Defect Action Levels: Levels of natural or unavoidable defects in foods that present no health hazards for humans [selected]

U.S. Food and Drug Administration
Center for Food Safety and Applied Nutrition

ASPARAGUS, CANNED OR FROZEN

Defect: Insect filth

Action level: 10%...of spears or pieces are infested with 6 or more attached asparagus beetle eggs and/or sacs

Defect: Insects

Action level: Asparagus contains an average of 40 or more thrips per 100 grams OR insects (whole or equivalent) of 3mm or longer have an aggregate length of 7mm or longer per 100 grams of asparagus

Defect Source: Pre-harvest insect infestation

Significance: Aesthetic

CORNMEAL

Defect: Insects

Action level: Average of 1 or more whole insects or equivalent [a whole insect, separate head or body portions with head attached] per 50 grams

Defect: Insect filth

Action level: Average of 25 or more insect fragments per 25 grams

Defect: Rodent filth

Action level: Average of 1 or more rodent hairs per 25 grams OR average of 1 or more rodent excreta fragments per 50 grams

Defect Source: Insects and insect fragments—pre-harvest and/or post-harvest and/or processing insect infestation; Rodent hair and excreta fragments—post-harvest and/or processing contamination with animal hair or excreta

Significance: Aesthetic

PEPPER, WHOLE (BLACK & WHITE)

Defect: Insect filth and/or insect mold

Action level: Average of 1% or more pieces by weight are infested and/or moldy

Defect: Mammalian excreta

Action level: Average of 1mg or more mammalian excreta per pound

Defect: Foreign matter

Action level: Average of 1% or more pickings and siftings by weight

Defect source: Insect infested—post-harvest and/or processing infestation; Moldy—post-harvest and/or processing infestation; Mammalian excreta—

post-harvest and/or processing animal contamination; Foreign material—post-harvest contamination

Significance: Aesthetic; potential health hazard—mammalian excreta may contain salmonella

RAISINS, GOLDEN

Defect: Insects and insect eggs

Action level: 10 or more whole (or equivalent) insects and 35 Drosophila eggs per 8 oz.

Defect source: Post-harvest and/or processing infestation

Significance: Aesthetic

Added Substances

United States v. Anderson Seafoods, Inc.

622 F.2d 157 (5th Cir. 1980)

WISDOM, Circuit Judge:

This appeal poses the question whether mercury in the tissues of swordfish is an "added substance" within the meaning of the Food, Drug, and Cosmetic Act, 21 U.S.C. § 342(a)(1) [FDCA], and is, therefore, subject to regulation under the relaxed standard appropriate to added substances. Only part of that mercury has been added by man.

In April 1977, the United States sought an injunction against Anderson Seafoods, Inc., and its president, Charles F. Anderson, to prevent them from selling swordfish containing more than 0.5 parts per million (ppm) of mercury, which it considered adulterated under the meaning of section 342(a) of the FDCA. Anderson responded in May 1977 by seeking a declaratory judgment that fish containing 2.0 ppm of mercury or less are not adulterated. Anderson also sought an injunction against the Food and Drug Administration commensurate with the declaratory judgment. Anderson's suit was certified as a class action, and these suits were consolidated for trial.

The district court denied the injunction that the government sought. In Anderson's suit, the court also denied an injunction, but issued a declaratory judgment that swordfish containing more than 1.0 ppm mercury is adulterated under s 342(a)(1). In doing so, the court determined that mercury is an "added substance" under the Act and rejected Anderson's contention that a level of 2.0 ppm is acceptable.... This appeal ... consists of Anderson's challenge to the way the district court parsed the statute and to the sufficiency of the evidence. We affirm.

I.

Section 342(a)(1) of the Act provides:

> A food shall be deemed to be adulterated (a)(1) if it bears or contains any poisonous or deleterious substance which may render it injurious to health; but in case the substance is not an added substance such food shall not be considered adulterated under this clause if the quantity of such substance in such food does not ordinarily render it injurious to health.

The Act does not define "added substance." Whether a substance is added or not is important because of the evidentiary showing that the Food and Drug Administration must make to succeed in an enforcement action. If a substance is deemed "added." then the Agency need show only that it "may render (the food) injurious to health" in order to regulate consumption of the food containing the substance. The "may render" standard has been interpreted to mean that there is a reasonable possibility of injury to the consumer. If, however, a substance is considered "not-added," the Agency must go further, and show that the substance would "ordinarily render (the food) injurious to health," 21 U.S.C. § 342(a)(1), before it can regulate its consumption.

In the trial of this case three theories about the meaning of the term "added" emerged. The Food and Drug Administration sponsored the first theory. It argues that an "added substance" is one that is not "inherent." According to FDA regulations:

> (c) A "naturally occurring poisonous or deleterious substance" is a poisonous or deleterious substance that is an inherent natural constituent of a food and is not the result of environmental, agricultural, industrial, or other contamination.
>
> (d) An "added poisonous or deleterious substance" is a poisonous or deleterious substance that is not a naturally occurring poisonous or deleterious substance. When a naturally occurring poisonous or deleterious substance is increased to abnormal levels through mis-

> handling or other intervening acts, it is an added poisonous or deleterious substance to the extent of such increase.

21 C.F.R. §§ 109.3(c), (d). Under this theory, all the mercury in swordfish is an added substance, because it results not from the creature's bodily processes but from mercury in the environment, whether natural or introduced by man.

Anderson put forward a second theory. A substance, under this theory, is not an added substance unless it is proved to be present as a result of the direct agency of man. Further, only that amount of a substance the lineage of which can be so traced is "added." If some mercury in swordfish occurs naturally, and some is the result of man-made pollution, only that percentage of the mercury in fish proved to result directly from pollution is an added substance.

The district court adopted a third theory. Under the court's theory, if a de minimis amount of the mercury in swordfish is shown to result from industrial pollution, then all of the metal in the fish is treated as an added substance and may be regulated under the statute's "may render injurious" standard. The legislative history and case law, though sparse, persuade us that this is the proper reading of the statute.

The distinction between added and not-added substances comes from the "adulterated food" provisions of the original Food, Drug, and Cosmetic Act of 1906. The legislative history shows that "added" meant attributable to acts of man, and "not-added" meant attributable to events of nature. See H.R. Rep. No. 2118, 59th Cong., 1st Sess. 6, 7, 11 (1906); 40 Cong.Rec. 1133 (Jan. 16, 1906) ("human action") (remarks by Sen. Heyburn). That the distinction was carried through to the present Act is shown by its legislative history. S. Rep. No. 493, 73rd Cong., 2d Sess. 3 (1934) ("added by man or put there by nature . . . introduced by artifice or (occurring) naturally").

The Supreme Court drew the same distinction in United States v. Coca Cola, 241 U.S. 265, 284 (1915). Construing the "added . . . ingredient" provisions of the 1906 Act, the Court said:

> Congress, we think, referred to ingredients artificially introduced; these are described as 'added.' The addition might be made to a natural food product or to a compound . . . we think that it was the intention of Congress that the artificial introduction of ingredients of a poisonous or deleterious character which might render the article injurious to health should cause the prohibition of the statute to attach.

The Food and Drug Administration argues that there need not be any connection between man's acts and the presence of a contaminant for it to be considered an added substance. The Agency points to the rule it recently promulgated interpreting section 342(a)(1), quoted above, which defines an added substance as one which is not "an inherent natural constituent of the food," but is instead the "result of an environmental, agricultural, industrial, or other contamination." 21 C.F.R. §§ 109.3(c), (3). Under the rule, mercury in swordfish tissue deriving from the mercury naturally dissolved in sea water would be an added substance, as would any substance not produced by or essential for the life processes of the food organism. In light of the legislative history and the *Coca Cola* case, however, we agree with the district court that the term "added" as used in section 342(a)(1) means artificially introduced, or attributable in some degree to the acts of man....

Determining that man must appear on the stage before a substance is an added one does not determine the size of the role he must play before it is. The dichotomy in 342(a)(1) is between two clear cases that bracket the present case. The Act considers added things such as lead in coloring agents or caffeine in *Coca Cola*. It considers not-added things like oxalic acid in rhubarb or caffeine in coffee. The Act did not contemplate, however, the perhaps rare problem of a toxin, part of which occurs "naturally," and part of which results from human acts. The section is designed, of course, to insure the scrutiny of toxins introduced by man. As Senator Heyburn said of the 1906 Act:

> Suppose you would say if there is poison in (a food) already it cannot do much harm to put in more. Suppose commercial cupidity should tempt someone to add to the dormant poison that is in a hundred things that we consume everyday, are they to be permitted to do it? This bill says they shall not do it.

40 Cong.Rec. 2758 (1906).

Anderson argues that when a toxin derives in part from man and in part from nature, only that part for which man is responsible may be considered added and so regulated under the "may render injurious" standard. In such a case, however, neither the statute nor FDA regulations suggest that the amount of an added toxic substance be quantified and shown to have a toxic effect of its own if the total amount of the substance in a food is sufficient to render the food potentially hazardous to health. It may be possible as in this case to prove that man introduced some percentage of a toxin into a food organism, but difficult or impossible to prove that percentage.

Since the purpose of the "may render injurious" standard was to facilitate regulation of food adulterated by acts of man, we think that it should apply to all of a toxic substance present in a food when any of that substance is shown to have been introduced by man. Anderson argues that this reading of the statute would result "in the anomalous situation where a substance in a food can be 90 percent natural and 10 percent added if the entire substance is considered as added." There is no anomaly, however, in such a situation. The Act's "may render it injurious to health" standard is to be applied to the food, not to the added substance. The food would not be considered adulterated under our view unless the 10 percent increment creates or increases a potentiality of injury to health. If the increment does create or increase such a potentiality, then, because the increment that triggered the potentiality was introduced by man, the Food and Drug Administration ought to be able to regulate it under the standard designed to apply to adulterations of food caused by man. Anderson's argument proves too much. Anderson would argue that if a swordfish contained 0.99 ppm of natural mercury, and 0.99 ppm of mercury from human sources, the fish could be sold although it contained nearly twice as much mercury as the district court found to be a safe level. Such a reading of the statute hardly accords with its "overriding purpose to protect the public health." United States v. Bacto-Unidisk, 1969, 394 U.S. 784, 798, 89 S.Ct. 1410, 1418, 22 L.Ed.2d 726. The reading we have adopted does accord with this purpose. It may be severe in practice. It may permit the Food and Drug Administration to regulate in some cases where the amount of substance contributed by man which triggers the potentiality of harm is minute. But it is the only alternative that fits into the statutory scheme. Congress should amend the statute if our reading produces impracticable results.

In sum, we hold that where some portion of a toxin present in a food has been introduced by man, the entirety of that substance present in the food will be treated as an added substance and so considered under the "may render injurious to health" standard of the Act.

II.

. . .

There was sufficient evidence to show that some mercury is attributable to the acts of man. There was evidence that mercury is dumped into rivers and washes onto the continental shelf, where some of it is methylated by bacteria and taken up by plankton. It thereby enters the food chain of swordfish, for the plankton is consumed by small organisms and fish, such as copepods, herring, and hake, which are in turn eaten by larger organisms, and eventually by swordfish, a peak predator. This evidence was enough to trigger the Act's "may render injurious to health" standard.

III.

The district court set 1.0 ppm as the health limit for mercury in swordfish. It noted that the decision was:

> based only on the scientific and empirical data accepted into evidence in these cases. It may be that further studies will reveal the decisions here made were based on erroneous or insufficient data.

We noted above that the government withdrew its appeal and cross-appeal. It is apparently considering new evidence to determine whether its present action level should be reaffirmed or changed. Our decision does not engrave the district court's 1.0 ppm level in administrative stone. While the government may not now prevent the sale of swordfish containing 1.0 ppm or less of mercury, the durability of our order is founded on the evidence the district court accepted.

Note

To this day, the FDA's action level for mercury in swordfish remains 1.0 ppm. Average recorded levels of mercury in swordfish are at about this level. Should swordfish be sold in this country, given the FDA's action levels? The FDA and EPA together periodically issue fish consumption advisories, giving information to the public about levels of mercury in fish and telling pregnant women, in particular, which types of fish to avoid or eat sparingly. Are such advisories a sensible substitute for blocking sales of fish that exceed action levels for various contaminants?

Insanitary Conditions and Injuriousness to Health

American Public Health Association v. Butz

511 F.2d 331 (D.C. Cir. 1974)

ROBB, Circuit Judge:

As plaintiffs in the District Court our appellants alleged in their complaint that the Secretary of Agriculture was violating certain provisions of the Wholesome Meat Act, and the Wholesome Poultry Products Act. Specifically, they alleged that the Secretary was wrongfully refusing to affix to meat and poultry products, inspected by the Department of Agriculture, labels containing handling and preparation instructions to protect the consumer against food poisoning caused by salmonellae and other bacteria. The complaint prayed that the Secretary be enjoined 'from affixing the label 'U.S. Passed and Inspected' or 'U.S. Inspected for Wholesomeness' on meat and poultry unless it is accompanied by an adequate explanation to the consumer that the product may contain organisms capable of causing food poisoning or infection which will multiply unless the product is properly handled and cooked, along with proper instructions on how to minimize such risk.' In substance, the plaintiffs claimed that the official inspection labels constituted misbranding. On cross motions for summary judgment the District Court granted the defendants' motion and dismissed the case.

In the Poultry Products Inspection Act, as amended by the Wholesome Poultry Products Act, and the Federal Meat Inspection Act of March 4, 1907, as amended by the Wholesome Meat Act (Dec. 15, 1967), Congress declared its intent to protect the health and welfare of consumers and to prevent and eliminate burdens on commerce by assuring that meat and poultry products are wholesome and properly labeled. To help achieve these ends, Congress required inspections at packing plants for both meat and poultry and their products. In the case of meat, if the item is found to be not adulterated, Congress has further required inspectors appointed by the Secretary of Agriculture to mark, stamp or label the item 'Inspected and passed.' In the case of poultry, if the item is found to be not adulterated, the Secretary is required to affix an official inspection legend on the item or on its container. Under his statutorily delegated authority to promulgate necessary regulations, the Secretary has provided markings for poultry and meat products.

Salmonellae are bacteria found in meats, poultry, eggs and their products. Salmonellosis or 'food poisoning' caused by the ingestion of salmonellae may produce nausea, abdominal cramps, vomiting, high fever, dizziness, headaches, dehydration and diarrhea. Preventive measures against salmonellae are care in cooking and storage of foods, and adequate refrigeration. To prevent cross-contamination from raw material to finished food, utensils, working surfaces and the hands of food preparers should be thoroughly washed. Proper cooking destroys salmonellae.

As alleged in the complaint, and established by the record, 'The inspection procedures now required by the Wholesome Meat Act and the Wholesome Poultry Products Act do not include any investigation to detect the presence of salmonella in meat or poultry, because no such microscopic examination is considered feasible as a routine matter.' The reason for this situation is apparent: a poultry inspector, for example, may conduct post mortem examinations of more than 10,000 birds in one day. Microscopic examination of each bird would obviously be impractical. Recognizing and accepting this fact the appellants do not seek revision of inspection techniques. They argue however that since salmonellae are likely to be present in all meat and poultry the inspection labels used by the Department of Agriculture create a false sense of security in consumers. In terms of the statutes the appellants say the inspection labels are 'false or misleading' so that the meat and poultry to which they are affixed are 'misbranded.' The remedy, according to the appellants, is the inclusion of preparation and handling instructions on each label.

The appellants presented their case to the Secretary of Agriculture in letters and conferences beginning with a letter on June 28, 1971. In this letter the appellants referred to a report issued by the Department of Agriculture on the salmonellae problem, together with other documentation, and urged the Secretary to require the following label or some reasonable equivalent to be affixed to all raw meat and poultry approved for human consumption:

> Caution: Improper handling and inadequate cooking of this product may be hazardous to your health. Despite careful government inspection, some disease-producing organisms may be present. Consult your local health department for information on the safe handling and preparation of this product.

In response the Department by letter of July 21, 1971, expressed its concern with the salmonellae problem and its recognition of the importance of control of salmonellosis. The Department quoted from a report of the National Research Council which stated:

> '... the problem of controlling salmonellosis in man is greatly complicated because of the widespread distribution of the organisms in the environment and the many ways by which they can reach the host.'
>
> 'Recent experience has implicated a variety of processed foods and drugs (e.g., egg products, dry milk, coconut, inactive dry yeast...) in out-breaks of salmonellosis.'

The Department's letter concluded that since 'there are numerous sources of contamination which might contribute to the overall problem' it would be 'unjustified to single out the meat industry and ask that the Department require it to identify its raw products as being hazardous to health. Such an act would have to apply to any and all sources of salmonellae in order to be fairly administered.'

Dissatisfied with the Department's response of July 21 the appellants on July 29, 1971 again wrote to the Secretary requesting that he 'review this situation once again, and in the interests of the consumers' health and safety . . . take prompt action to avoid the continuation of the mislabeling and misbranding as 'U.S. Inspected' and 'U.S. Inspected for Wholesomeness' (of) contaminated raw meats and poultry.' In response the Department on August 18, 1971, wrote:

> ... you appear to disregard the fact that the American consumer knows that raw meat and poultry are not sterile and, if handled improperly, perhaps could cause illness.
>
> The Department's philosophy in this matter is that the salmonella problem can be handled most effectively at the consumer level where all contributing factors converge--where the final preparation of food takes place. The consumer education program which you have advocated would fit in well with this concept and would be instrumental in informing the American public of the proper methods for handling all foods, including meat and poultry, so that any hazard is reduced to a minimal level.

The Department reiterated this position in a letter of October 20, 1971 as follows:

> You will recall that we firmly believed that the salmonella problem could be handled most effectively at the consumer level where final food preparation took place. We maintained then, and wish to reemphasize now, that a soundly designed consumer education program is the best manner in which to approach the entire problem of food-borne disease. Such a program would reduce the incidence of mishandling of foods and thereby reduce potential hazards to a minimum.
>
> The Department is actively supporting a number of consumer education programs which are designed with this goal in mind. We would hope you and your respected organization would join with us in this effort.

On December 7, 1971 the appellants renewed their request and proposed a label to this effect:

> WARNING: This product may contain bacteria which can cause food-poisoning. Refrigeration and adequate cooking will make it safe to eat. To keep bacteria from spreading to other foods: (1) Do not let other foods touch this uncooked product or the surfaces where it has been placed. (2) After handling, carefully wash your hands and all equipment which touched the raw product.

In a meeting on December 21, 1971 between officials of the Department and representatives of the appellants the Department finally rejected the appellants' proposal and took the position that a consumer education program on the proper way to handle and prepare meat and poultry was the answer to the problem. This lawsuit followed.

The Wholesome Poultry Products Act, provides that an article is 'misbranded'

> (1) If its labeling is false or misleading in any particular; ...
>
> (12) If it fails to bear on its containers, ... as the Secretary may by regulations prescribe, the official inspection legend . . . and, unrestricted by any of the foregoing, such other information as the Secretary may require in such regulations to assure that it will not have false or misleading labeling and that the public will be informed of the manner of handling required to maintain the article in a wholesome condition.

Similar provisions appear in the Wholesome Meat Act. The appellants contend that the official inspection legends are false and misleading and therefore constitute misbranding within the meaning of these statutes, since the legends fail to warn against the dangers of salmonellae. The appellants argue further that the Secretary has abused his discretion by refusing to supplement the inspection legends with a warning and instructions for the storage and preparation of meat and poultry. We are not persuaded by the appellants' arguments.

The Wholesome Meat Act providing for inspections, requires that meat 'found to be not adulterated shall be marked, stamped, tagged, or labeled as 'Inspected and passed.". The 'U.S. Inspected and passed' legend therefore conforms to the statute; and unless the presence of salmonellae makes meat 'adulterated' the legend is not false or misleading. The term 'adulterated' is defined by the statute, and we think that the presence of salmonellae in meat does not constitute adulteration within this definition. The definition is directed at poisonous or deleterious additives and filthy, putrid or decomposed substances but not at substances such as salmonellae which may be inherent in the meat. This we think plainly appears from 21 U.S.C. § 601(m)(1) which provides:

> The term 'adulterated' shall apply to any...meat...:
>
> (1) if it bears or contains any poisonous or deleterious substance which may render it injurious to health; but in case the substance is not an added substance, such article shall not be considered adulterated under this clause if the quantity of such substance in or on such article does not ordinarily render it injurious to health.

As the Department said in its letter of August 18, 1971 'the American consumer knows that raw meat and poultry are not sterile and, if handled improperly, perhaps could cause illness.' In other words, American housewives and cooks normally are not ignorant or stupid and their methods of preparing and cooking of food do not ordinarily result in salmonellosis.

The Wholesome Poultry Products Act also refers to inspections and findings that poultry products are 'not adulterated.' The definition of the term 'adulterated' in the Act conforms to that found in the Wholesome Meat Act. The term 'official inspection legend' is defined as 'any symbol prescribed by regulations of the Secretary showing that an article was inspected for wholesomeness in accordance with this chapter.' This differs from the definition of the term 'official inspection legend' found in the Wholesome Meat Act, which is 'any symbol prescribed by regulations of the Secretary showing that an article was inspected and passed in accordance with this chapter.' We think however that the term 'inspected for wholesomeness' as used in the Wholesome Poultry Products Act means 'inspected and found not to be adulterated.' The term is so construed and defined by the Secretary in his regulations, and this construction is confirmed by the House Report on the bill which became the Wholesome Poultry Products Act. This report evidences the intention of Congress to conform the provisions of the Wholesome Poultry Products Act to those of the Federal Meat Inspection Act, as amended. We conclude that the legend 'inspected for wholesomeness' prescribed by the Secretary, conforms to the statute and is not false or misleading because of the possibility that salmonellae may be present in the poultry products inspected.

In construing both the Wholesome Meat Act and the Wholesome Poultry Products Act we are mindful that the presence of salmonellae can be detected only by microscopic examination. No one contends that Congress meant that inspections should include such examinations. We think it follows therefore that Congress did not intend the prescribed official legends to import a finding that meat and poultry products were free from salmonellae.

Both statutes provide that an article is 'misbranded' if it fails to bear on its container or the inspection label 'such other information as the Secretary may require . . . to assure that it will not have false or misleading labeling and that the public will be informed of the manner of handling required to maintain the article in a wholesome condition.' Plainly, these provisions give the Secretary discretion to determine what labeling, if any, will be required in addition to the official inspection stamp. Although the appellants recognize this discretion in the Secretary they say he has abused his discretion in failing to require cautionary labeling. We are unable to accept this conclusion. After carefully considering the appellants' proposals the Secretary concluded that warning labels were not the answer to the problem and that the solution was a consumer education program which the Department proposed to undertake. We cannot say that this conclusion was unreasonable; certainly we may not substitute our judgment for that of the Secretary....

ROBINSON III, Circuit Judge (dissenting):

A majority of the court holds that the official inspection legends challenged herein are not 'false or misleading,' and that therefore the products inspected are not 'misbranded,' because the products are not to be considered 'adulterated' merely by reason of the presence of salmonellae. They further hold that the Secretary did not abuse his discretion when he decided against cautionary labels and instead embarked on a consumer education program. I must dissent because I am unable to conclude that on these branches of the litigation 'there is no genuine issue as to any material fact.'...

Meat or poultry is not 'adulterated' within the meaning of the relevant statutes if the presence of salmonellae 'does not ordinarily render it injurious to health.' The court apparently takes the position that meat and poultry 'ordinarily' pose no threat of salmonellosis, because American consumers are aware of the problem and familiar with the precautions necessary to prevent its occurrence. That, however, is a debatable proposition, and appellants, with substantial backing, seriously dispute it. The record contains facts supporting appellants' assertion that people are not generally aware of the danger of salmonellae, much less of the safeguards required to avoid salmonellosis. Moreover, a study conducted for the Department of Agriculture and the Food and Drug Administration states that 'the vast majority of the public and personnel of various food-associated industries barely know that salmonellae exist. Many of them have suffered from salmonellosis, but they do not know why or how to avoid future incidents. Nor is it any clearer that salmonellae in food do not ordinarily render it injurious to health. Meat, particularly pork, and poultry are likely to contain salmonellae when they reach the kitchens of our homes and restaurants, and each year more than two million people in this country contract salmonellosis.

I am also unable to accept the court's premise that labeling nonadulterated meat 'Inspected and passed' is never false and misleading. An article is 'misbranded' if its label is 'false or misleading in any particular,' and the Secretary is authorized to require informative legends to prevent false and misleading labeling. In Armour & Company v. Freeman, the leading case in this jurisdiction on mislabeling, we held that the question whether a label is false or deceptive is to be determined by the ordinary meaning of the words used. More recently, in Federation of Homemakers v. Butz, we concluded that a label was misleading because of the meaning its words imparted to the ordinary consumer. As appellees concede, 'the proper measure of whether (the labels) are misleading is the ordinary understanding of the consumer,' and that is a matter for proof by the parties, not surmise by the court.

My colleagues try to support their holding by the claim that Congress 'did not intend the prescribed official legends to import a finding that meat and poultry products were free from salmonellae.' That observation, I submit, is wide of the mark. Congressional intent is not helpful in determining whether the labels are misleading; the relevant inquiry is the understanding of consumers. Appellants proffer evidence tending to show that consumers in large numbers understand the challenged labels to mean that the Federal Government has inspected the labeled food products for the presence of salmonellae. That indication is false, for no such inspections are ever made, and labeled products are 'passed' even if they contain salmonellae

Supreme Beef Processors v. U.S. Department of Agriculture

275 F.3d 432 (5th Cir. 2001)

HIGGINBOTHAM, Circuit Judge:

Certain meat inspection regulations promulgated by the Secretary of Agriculture, which deal with the levels of *Salmonella* in raw meat product, were challenged as beyond the statutory authority granted to the Secretary by the Federal Meat Inspection Act. The district court struck down the regulations. We hold that the regulations fall outside of the statutory grant of rulemaking authority and affirm.

I

The Federal Meat Inspection Act authorizes the Secretary of Agriculture to "prescribe the rules and regulations of sanitation" covering

> slaughtering, meat canning, salting, packing, rendering, or similar establishments in which cattle, sheep, swine, goats, horses, mules and other equines are slaughtered and the meat and meat food products thereof are prepared for commerce... [21 U.S.C. §608]

Further, the Secretary is commanded to,

> where the sanitary conditions of any such establishment are such that the meat or meat food products are rendered adulterated, ...refuse to allow said meat or meat food products to be labeled, marked, stamped, or tagged as "inspected and passed." [21 U.S.C. §608]

In sum, the FMIA instructs the Secretary to ensure that no adulterated meat products pass USDA inspection, which they must in order to be legally sold to consumers.

The FMIA contains several definitions of "adulterated," including 21 U.S.C. §601(m)(4), which classifies a meat product as adulterated if "it has been prepared, packed, or held under insanitary conditions whereby it may have become contaminated with filth, or whereby it may have been rendered injurious to health." Thus, the FMIA gives the Secretary the power to create sanitation regulations and commands him to withhold meat approval where the meat is processed under insanitary conditions. The Secretary has delegated the authority under the FMIA to the Food Safety and Inspection Service.

In 1996, FSIS, after informal notice and comment rulemaking, adopted regulations requiring all meat and poultry establishments to adopt preventative controls to assure product safety. These are known as Pathogen Reduction, Hazard Analysis and Critical Control Point Systems or "HACCP." HACCP requires, *inter alia*, that meat and poultry establishments institute a hazard control plan for reducing and controlling harmful bacteria on raw meat and poultry products. In order to enforce HACCP, FSIS performs tests for the presence of *Salmonella* in a plant's finished meat products.

The *Salmonella* performance standards set out a regime under which inspection services will be denied to an establishment if it fails to meet the standard on three consecutive series of tests. The regulations declare that the third failure of the performance standard "constitutes failure to maintain sanitary conditions and failure to maintain an adequate HACCP plan ... for that product, and will cause FSIS to suspend inspection services." The performance standard, or "passing mark," is determined based on FSIS's "calculation of the national prevalence of *Salmonella* on the indicated raw product."

In June, 1998, plaintiff-appellee Supreme Beef Processors, Inc., a meat processor and grinder, implemented an HACCP pathogen control plan, and on November 2, 1998, FSIS began its evaluation of that plan by testing Supreme's finished product for *Salmonella.* After four weeks of testing, FSIS notified Supreme that it would likely fail the *Salmonella* tests. Pursuant to the final test results, which found 47 percent of the samples taken from Supreme contaminated with *Salmonella,*[9] FSIS issued a Noncompliance Report, advising Supreme that it had not met the performance standard. Included in the report was FSIS's warning to Supreme to take "immediate action to meet the performance standards." Supreme responded to FSIS's directive on March 5, 1999, summarizing the measures it had taken to meet the performance standard and requesting that the second round of testing be postponed until mid-April to afford the company sufficient time to evaluate its laboratory data. FSIS agreed to the request and began its second round of tests on April 12, 1999.

On June 2, 1999, FSIS again informed Supreme that it would likely fail the *Salmonella* tests and, on July 20, issued another Noncompliance Report--this time informing Supreme that 20.8 percent of its samples had tested positive for *Salmonella.* Supreme appealed the Noncompliance Report, citing differences between the results obtained by FSIS and Supreme's own tests conducted on "companion parallel samples." Those private tests, Supreme asserted, had produced only a 7.5 percent *Salmonella* infection level, satisfying the performance standard. FSIS denied the appeal; but based on Supreme's commitment to install 180 degree water source on all boning and trimming lines, granted the company's request to postpone the next round of *Salmonella* testing for 60 days. FSIS later withdrew the extension, however, after learning that Supreme was merely considering installation of the water source.

The third set of tests began on August 27, 1999, and after only five weeks, FSIS advised Supreme that it would again fall short of the ground beef performance standard. On October 19, 1999, FSIS issued a Notice of Intended Enforcement Action, which notified Supreme of the agency's intention to suspend inspection activities. The Notice gave Supreme Beef until October 25, 1999 to demonstrate that its HACCP pathogen controls were adequate or to show that it had achieved regulatory compliance. Although Supreme Beef promised to achieve the 7.5 percent performance standard in 180 days, it failed to provide any specific information explaining how it

[9] The performance standard for raw ground beef is 7.5 percent.

would accomplish that goal, and FSIS decided to suspend inspection of Supreme's plant.

On the day FSIS planned to withdraw its inspectors, Supreme brought this suit against FSIS's parent agency, the USDA, alleging that in creating the *Salmonella* tests, FSIS had overstepped the authority given to it by the FMIA. Along with its complaint, Supreme moved to temporarily restrain the USDA from withdrawing its inspectors. The district court granted Supreme's motion and, after a subsequent hearing, also granted Supreme's motion for a preliminary injunction....

[T]he district court granted summary judgment in favor of Supreme, finding that the *Salmonella* performance standard exceeded the USDA's statutory authority and entering a permanent injunction against enforcement of that standard against Supreme. The USDA now appeals....

III

Our analysis in this case is governed by the approach first enunciated by the Supreme Court in *Chevron U.S.A., Inc. v. Natural Resources Defense Council, Inc.* [467 U.S. 837 (1984)] The *Chevron* inquiry proceeds in two steps. First, the court should look to the plain language of the statute and determine whether the agency construction conflicts with the text. Then, "if the agency interpretation is not in conflict with the plain language of the statute, deference is due." [503 U.S. 407, 417 (1992)]...

A

Following *Chevron*, we first repair to the text of the statute that the USDA relies upon for its authority to impose the *Salmonella* performance standard. The USDA directs us to 21 U.S.C. §601(m)(4), which provides that a meat product is adulterated

> if it has been prepared, packed or held under insanitary conditions whereby it may have become contaminated with filth, or whereby it may have been rendered injurious to health.

This statutory definition is broader than that provided in 21 U.S.C. §601(m)(1), which provides that a meat product is adulterated

> if it bears or contains any poisonous or deleterious substance which may render it injurious to health; but in case the substance is not an added substance, such article shall not be considered adulterated under this clause if the quantity of such substance in or on such article does not ordinarily render it injurious to health.

Thus if a meat product is "prepared, packed or held under insanitary conditions" such that it *may* be adulterated for purposes of §601(m)(1), then it is, by definition, adulterated for purposes of §601(m)(4). The USDA is then commanded to refuse to stamp the meat products "inspected and passed." [21 U.S.C. § 608]

The difficulty in this case arises, in part, because *Salmonella,* present in a substantial proportion of meat and poultry products, is not an adulterant *per se,*[21] meaning its presence does not require the USDA to refuse to stamp such meat "inspected and passed." [21 U.S.C. §608] This is because normal cooking practices for meat and poultry destroy the *Salmonella* organism,[23] and therefore the presence of *Salmonella* in meat products does not render them "injurious to health"[24] for purposes of §601(m)(1). *Salmonella*-infected beef is thus routinely labeled "inspected and passed" by USDA inspectors and is legal to sell to the consumer.

Supreme maintains that since *Salmonella*-infected meat is not adulterated under §601(m)(1), the presence or absence of *Salmonella* in a plant cannot, by definition, be "insanitary conditions" such that the product "may have been rendered injurious to health," as required by §601(m)(4). The USDA, however, argues that *Salmonella*'s status as a non-adulterant is not relevant to its power to regulate *Salmonella* levels in end product. This is because the USDA believes that *Salmonella* levels can be a proxy for the presence or absence of means of pathogen[25] controls that are required for sanitary conditions under §601(m)(4). However, as we discuss, and as the USDA admits,

---

[21] *See American Pub. Health Ass'n v. Butz,* 511 F.2d 331, 334 (D.C. Cir. 1974) ("The presence of salmonellae on meat does not constitute adulteration within this definition [of 'adulterated,' provided in 21 U.S.C. §601(m)]."). The USDA agrees in this case that *Salmonella* is not an adulterant *per se,* meaning it is not a §601(m)(1) adulterant.

[23] *Butz,* 511 F.2d at 334 ("American housewives and cooks normally are not ignorant or stupid and their methods of preparing and cooking of food do not ordinarily result in salmonellosis.").

[24] *Cf. Continental Seafoods, Inc. v. Schweiker,* 674 F.2d 38, 41 (D.C. Cir. 1982) (stating that *Salmonella* is a *per se* adulterant in shrimp).

[25] The USDA uses the term "pathogen" to refer to both §601(m)(1) adulterants, such as pathogenic *E. coli,* and non-adulterants, such as *Salmonella*. Thus, under the proxy theory, *Salmonella* control correlates with adulterant-pathogen control.

the *Salmonella* performance standard, whether or not it acts as a proxy, regulates more than just the presence of pathogen controls.

The district court agreed with Supreme and reasoned that "because the USDA's performance standards and *Salmonella* tests do not necessarily evaluate the *conditions* of a meat processor's establishment, they cannot serve as the basis for finding a plant's meat adulterated under §601(m)(4)." The district court therefore held that the examination of a plant's end product is distinct from "conditions" within the plant for purposes of §601(m)(4) because *Salmonella* may have come in [contact] with the raw material.

We must decide two issues in order to determine whether the *Salmonella* performance standard is authorized rulemaking under the FMIA: a) whether the statute allows the USDA to regulate characteristics of raw materials that are "prepared, packed or held" at the plant, such as *Salmonella* infection; and b) whether §601(m)(4)'s "insanitary conditions" such that product "may have been rendered injurious to health" includes the presence of *Salmonella*-infected beef in a plant or the increased likelihood of cross-contamination with *Salmonella* that results from grinding such infected beef. Since we are persuaded that the *Salmonella* performance standard improperly regulates the *Salmonella* levels of incoming meat and that *Salmonella* cross-contamination cannot be an insanitary condition such that product may be rendered "injurious to health," we conclude that the *Salmonella* performance standard falls outside of the ambit of §601(m)(4).

B

1

In order for a product to be adulterated under §601(m)(4), as the USDA relies on it here,[27] it must be "prepared, packed or held under insanitary conditions...whereby it may have been *rendered* injurious to health." [21 U.S.C. §601(m)(4) (emphasis added)] The use of the word "rendered" in the statute indicates that a deleterious change in the product must occur while it is being "prepared, packed or held" owing to insanitary conditions. Thus, a

---

[27] The USDA does not contend that failure of the *Salmonella* performance standard serves as a proxy for contamination with filth, the other prong dealt with by §601(m)(4). Even if the USDA made such an assertion, §601(m)(4) speaks of insanitary conditions such that a product "becomes" contaminated with filth, which has a similar textual meaning as "rendered."

characteristic of the raw materials that exists before the product is "prepared, packed or held"[29] in the grinder's establishment cannot be regulated by the USDA under §601(m)(4).[30] The USDA's interpretation ignores the plain language of the statute, which includes the word "rendered." Were we to adopt this interpretation, we would be ignoring the Court's repeated admonition that, when interpreting a statute, we are to "give effect, if possible, to every clause and word of a statute." [533 U.S. 167 (2001)]

The USDA claims, however, that the *Salmonella* performance standard serves as a proxy for the presence or absence of pathogen controls, such that a high level of *Salmonella* indicates §601(m)(4) adulteration.[32] Supreme oversimplifies its argument by claiming, essentially, that the USDA can never use testing of final product for a non-adulterant, such as *Salmonella*, as a proxy for conditions within a plant.

We find a similar, but distinct, defect in the *Salmonella* performance standard. The USDA admits that the *Salmonella* performance standard provides evidence of: (1) whether or not the grinder has adequate pathogen con-

---

[29] This case does not require us to define precisely when a product begins the process of being "prepared, packed or held." We recognize only that this process cannot begin until the raw materials are brought to the plant. Thus, the condition of the raw materials may not be regulated by §601(m)(4).

[30] However, measures that would alter such a characteristic, such as heating fish to destroy the bacteria that causes botulism, are within the scope of §601(m)(4).

[32] We note that the USDA's assertions on this point are suspect. It is clear that the motivation behind the *Salmonella* performance standard was the regulation of *Salmonella* itself, and the FSIS has admitted as much in the Final Rule, though this admission is absent from the USDA's briefs in this case. *See* Pathogen Reduction; Hazard Analysis and Critical Control Point (HACCP) Systems; Final Rule, 61 Fed. Reg. 38806, 38850 ("Because testing for *E. coli* cannot serve as a surrogate for the presence of *Salmonella*, FSIS's *specific public health objective of reducing nationwide* Salmonella *levels on raw meat and poultry products, including raw ground products,* requires a standard and testing regime that are directed at *that* pathogen." (emphasis added)). The difficulty with this, of course, is that the USDA has no statutory authority to regulate the levels of non-adulterant pathogens.

While we do not question the agency's expertise, we also note that several equivocal statements about the effectiveness of *Salmonella* levels as a proxy for pathogen controls appear in the Final Rule. *See Id.* at 38835 ("And, interventions targeted at reducing *Salmonella may be beneficial* in reducing contamination by other enteric pathogens." (emphasis added)); *Id.* at 38846 ("Intervention strategies aimed at reducing fecal contamination and other sources of *Salmonella* on raw product *should be* effective against other pathogens.").

trols; and (2) whether or not the grinder uses raw materials that are disproportionately infected with *Salmonella*. Supreme has, at all points in this litigation, argued that it failed the performance standard not because of any condition of its facility, but because it purchased beef "trimmings" that had higher levels of *Salmonella* than other cuts of meat. The USDA has not disputed this argument, and has merely argued that this explanation does not exonerate Supreme, because the *Salmonella* levels of incoming meat are fairly regulated under §601(m)(4). Our textual analysis of §601(m)(4) shows that it cannot be used to regulate characteristics of the raw materials that exist before the meat product is "prepared, packed or held." Thus, the regulation fails, but not because it measures *Salmonella* levels and *Salmonella* is a non-adulterant. The performance standard is invalid because it regulates the procurement of raw materials....

3

The USDA and its amicus supporters argue that there is no real distinction between contamination that arrives in raw materials and contamination that arises from other conditions of the plant. This is because *Salmonella* can be transferred from infected meat to non-infected meat through the grinding process. The *Salmonella* performance standard, however, does not purport to measure the differential between incoming and outgoing meat products in terms of the *Salmonella* infection rate. Rather, it measures final meat product for *Salmonella* infection. Thus, the performance standard, of itself, cannot serve as a proxy for cross-contamination because there is no determination of the incoming *Salmonella* baseline.

Moreover, the USDA has not asserted that there is any correlation between the *presence* of *Salmonella* and the *presence* of §601(m)(1) adulterant pathogens. The rationale offered by the USDA for the *Salmonella* performance standard – that "intervention strategies aimed at reducing fecal contamination and other sources of *Salmonella* on raw product should be effective against other pathogens" [61 Fed. Reg. at 38846] – does not imply that the presence of *Salmonella* indicates the presence of these other, presumably §601(m)(1) adulterant, pathogens.[41] Cross-contamination of *Salmonella* alone

---

[41] One might speculate that such a conclusion would create problems for the USDA, because a statement that *Salmonella* was a proxy for, for example, pathogenic *E. coli* could arguably require the determination that the presence of *Salmonella* rendered a product §601(m)(1) adulterated. This would prevent *Salmonella*-infected meat from

cannot form the basis of a determination that a plant's products are §601(m)(4) adulterated, because *Salmonella* itself does not render a product "injurious to health" for purposes of both § § 601(m)(1) and 601(m)(4).

Not once does the USDA assert that *Salmonella* infection indicates infection with §601(m)(1) adulterant pathogens. Instead, the USDA argues that the *Salmonella* infection rate of meat product correlates with the use of pathogen control mechanisms and the quality of the incoming raw materials. The former is within the reach of §601(m)(4), the latter is not....

Agency Response Letter: Salmonella as Adulterants

From Daniel L. Engeljohn, Assistant Administrator, Office of Policy and Program Development, United States Department of Agriculture
To Sarah Klein, Staff Attorney, Food Safety Program & Caroline Smith DeWaal, Food Safety Director, Center for Science in the Public Interest
July 31, 2014

Dear Ms. Klein and Ms. DeWaal:

The Food Safety and Inspection Service (FSIS) has completed its review of the May 25, 2011, petition submitted by you on behalf of the Center for Science in the Public Interest (CSPI) asking that the Agency issue an interpretive rule declaring antibiotic-resistant (ABR) strains of *Salmonella* Hadar, *Salmonella* Heidelberg, *Salmonella* Newport, and *Salmonella* Typhimurium to be adulterants when found in raw ground meat and raw ground poultry. The petition asserts that if FSIS declares these strains of ABR *Salmonella* to be adulterants in raw ground meat or raw ground poultry, the Agency must also take steps to ensure adequate sampling and testing for these pathogens and to remove contaminated ground meat and ground poultry products from the human food supply. To support the requested action, the petition references studies and includes information on recalls and outbreaks associated with ABR *Salmonella.* The petition also references data that show that certain strains of ABR *Salmonella* have been found in the retail setting.

After thoroughly reviewing the available data, FSIS has concluded that the data do not support giving the four strains of ABR *Salmonella* identi-

---

being sold in the United States to consumers.

fied in the petition a different status as an adulterant in raw ground meat and raw ground poultry than *Salmonella* strains that are susceptible to antibiotics. Additional data on the characteristics of ABR *Salmonella* are needed to determine whether certain strains of ABR *Salmonella* could qualify as adulterants under the Federal Meat Inspection Act (FMIA) (21 U.S.C. 601 *et seq.)* and the Poultry Products Inspection Act (PPIA) (21 U.S.C. 453 *et seq.).* Therefore, FSIS is denying yourpetition without prejudice.

Adulteration under 21 U.S.C. 601(m)(l) and 453(g)(l)

Shiga toxin-producing E. coli (STEC)

Most foodborne pathogens, including *Salmonella,* are not considered adulterants of raw meat or poultry products because ordinary cooking and preparation of these products is generally sufficient to destroy the pathogens. [Citing D.C. Circuit's 1974 decision in *Butz.*] However, as noted in your petition, in 1994, FSIS declared *E. coli* 0157:H7 to be an adulterant of raw ground beef, and on January 19, 1999, FSIS issued a policy statement on the status of other non-intact beef products contaminated with *E. coli* 0157:H7.

In September 2011, FSIS determined that six other STEC serogroups (026, 045, 0103, 0111, 0121, and 0145) are also adulterants of raw non-intact beef products and product components used to manufacture these products. Available data show that, like *E. coli* 0157:H7, these six STECs have been associated with serious illnesses and that they have a relatively low infectious dose. Like *E. coli* 0157:H7, all of these strains can cause hemorrhagic colitis, and all except 045 have been shown to cause hemolytic uremic syndrome (HUS), a condition that can result in kidney failure and other serious, life- threatening complications. There is also evidence that these strains have very similar characteristics to *E. coli 0157:H7* strains so that they too can survive in raw, non-intact beef products that many consumers consider to be properly cooked. The FSIS temperature recommendation for consumers to cook ground beef to achieve a safe product is 160 degrees Fahrenheit. FSIS is well aware that some consumers ordinarily or typically do not cook ground beef to 160 degrees Fahrenheit, and that some consumers consider ground beef to be properly cooked rare, medium- rare, or medium. When cooked in such a manner, ground beef contaminated with the STECs identified above may cause serious physical problems, including death. Thus, raw, non-intact beef products and product components that are contaminated with *E. coli* 0157:H7 and pathogenic STEC

026, 045, 0103, 0111, 0121, and 0145 contain a poisonous or deleterious substance and are adulterated within the meaning of 21 U.S.C. 601(m)(1).

Salmonella

As noted in your petition, in the absence of a clear association with human illnesses, FSIS does not consider raw meat and poultry products, including ground meat and ground poultry, to be adulterated when they contain *Salmonella* because ordinary methods of cooking and preparing food kill *Salmonella.* Your petition asserts that ABR *Salmonella* has distinguishing characteristics that support its classification as an adulterant in raw ground meat and raw ground poultry even in the absence of associated illness. We have considered information in the petition and published scientific literature through May 2014 regarding:

- Antimicrobial resistant and antimicrobial susceptible nontyphoidal salmonellosis;
- Phenotypic and genotypic attributes and the ecology of nontyphoidal salmonellae; and
- Effectiveness of thermal inactivation of antimicrobial resistant and antimicrobial susceptible strains of nontyphoidal salmonellae.

We have concluded that more data are needed to determine whether ABR *Salmonella* should have a different status as an adulterant under the FMIA and PPIA than *Salmonella*strains that are susceptible to antibiotics.

<u>1. Legal Distinction – Added Substance</u>

The petition asserts that the crucial legal difference between ABR *Salmonella* and susceptible *Salmonella* strains is that ABR *Salmonella* occurs as the result of human intervention, i.e., the administration of antibiotics to live animals used in the production of meat and poultry. Therefore, according to the petition, to declare ABR *Salmonella* an adulterant, FSIS must only show that it "may render" a ground meat or poultry product injurious to health (21 U.S.C. 601 (m)(1) and 453 (g)(1)). The petition notes that if a substance is not an added substance, FSIS must show that the quantity of such substance would "ordinarily render" a product injurious to health (21 U.S.C 601(m)(1)) and 453 (g)(1)).

At the outset, we note that the petition does not define "antibiotic resistance" or specify the number or types of antibiotics that the *Salmonella* strains identified in the petition would need to be resistant to in order to qualify as adulterants. For example, would a *Salmonella* strain be considered an adulterant if it were resistant to any antibiotic or only those antibiotics used to treat human illnesses? This information is important to our evaluation of your request because the petition asserts that only certain strains of ABR *Salmonella* should be treated differently from other strains of *Salmonella.* Therefore, understanding the characteristics of the strains that significantly increase the risk to human health is essential for developing the appropriate risk management strategies.

As to the role human intervention plays in ABR *Salmonella,* we have reviewed published scientific literature and have found studies that indicate that ABR microorganisms may be present in food animals regardless of whether the animals have had exposure to antibiotics. In fact, studies demonstrate that there can be an exchange of resistance characteristics between microorganisms through horizontal gene transfer of antibiotic resistance genes even when antibiotic pressure is not present in the bacterial environment. We believe that more study is needed to evaluate the extent to which the administration of antibiotics in livestock and poultry production contributes to the presence of ABR *Salmonella* in raw meat and poultry. Accordingly, we have concluded that the available data do not clearly support the legal distinction between *Salmonella* and ABR *Salmonella* under the FMIA and PPIA that is suggested in the petition.

2. Proper Cooking and Lethality

The petition also asserts that ABR *Salmonella* in raw ground meat and raw ground poultry is injurious to health because "proper" cooking often fails to reach the necessary temperature for lethality, and it is difficult to measure internal temperature properly in ground products. As discussed above, FSIS is aware that some consumers consider ground beef to be properly cooked rare, medium- rare, or medium. However, we are not aware of any data to suggest that consumers consider ground poultry, ground pork, or ground lamb to be properly cooked when rare, medium rare, or medium. The petition does not include data on consumer preparation and cooking practices for ground poultry, ground pork, or ground lamb, or consumer views of what is considered to be properly cooked ground poultry, pork or lamb. Furthermore, as discussed below, the available data do not indicate that ABR *Salmonella* strains have a higher resistance to heat than susceptible strains. Thus, from the data presented in the petition, FSIS has no basis to conclude that proper cooking of ground poultry, ground pork, or ground lamb will not destroy *Salmonella,* whether the strain is resistant or susceptible to antibiotics.

With respect to raw, ground beef, the available data do not conclusively demonstrate that certain strains of ABR *Salmonella* should have a different status as an adulterant than susceptible *Salmonella* strains. As discussed above, in 2011, FSIS declared certain STEC strains to be adulterants in non-intact beef products because the available data show that, like *E. coli* 0157:H7, these STECs have a relatively low infectious dose, have been associated with serious illness conditions such as hemorrhagic colitis and HUS, and that these strains have very similar physiology to *E. coli* 0157:H7 strains so that they can survive what many consumers consider to be proper cooking of ground beef products.

Based on the current data, *Salmonella* does not appear to present the same issues as STEC, regardless of whether it is resistant or susceptible to antibiotics.

Infectious Dose. Although the data are limited, there appears to be a range of minimum infectious dose required for *Salmonella,* including ABR *Salmonella,* to cause illness. Studies indicate that the infectious dose for *Salmonella* may be influenced by factors such as the circumstances under which the pathogen is ingested, host factors (such as prior history of taking antibiotics and immune system status), the food matrix and the particular *Salmonella* strain....

Virulence. More data are also needed to determine whether ABR *Salmonella* results in more severe illnesses than susceptible *Salmonella* strains and are thus more likely to render a product injurious to health, as suggested by the petition. We have found that, although some published articles suggest an association of increased severity of illness with ABR Salmonella these studies are limited in their ability to conclusively determine whether the ABR in itself caused the increased severity....

Further, most *Salmonella* species are pathogenic in that they can cause disease. Thus, the issue is whether ABR *Salmonella* strains are more virulent than susceptible strains. The level of virulence of a pathogen may vary, and determining whether a pathogen carries virulence attributes can be objectively determined. Genetic elements such as plasmids may carry combinations of antimicrobial resistance genes and virulence genes and move between strains of bacteria. The genetic composition of strains of the same serotype can vary. Some studies raise concerns about a linkage between antibiotic resistance genes and virulence genes, and there is some evidence of a linkage or co-existence; however, other studies have found no difference between antibiotic-resistant and antibiotic-susceptible *Salmonella* strains in the carriage of virulence factors. We have not found any published scientific studies that support the proposition that antibiotic resistance and virulence genes always occur together for specific serotypes of *Salmonella.*

Heat resistance. The available data also do not suggest that ABR *Salmonella* is more heat resistant than susceptible *Salmonella* strains....

Accordingly, because more data are needed on infectious dose, and because the available data do not definitively demonstrate that ABR *Salmonella* strains are more likely to result in serious illness or are more heat resistant than susceptible strains, or that ABR *Salmonella* strains are otherwise more likely to render injurious to health what many consumers consider to be properly cooked ground meat and ground poultry, we are unable to conclude that ABR *Salmonella* should have a different status as an adulterant in raw ground meat and raw ground poultry under 21 U.S.C. 601 (m)(1) and 453(g)(1) than antibiotic susceptible strains. As noted above, more data on the characteristics of ABR *Salmonella* are needed for FSIS to further evaluate whether certain strains of ABR resistant *Salmonella* could qualify as adulterants under the FMIA and PPIA.

Adulteration under 21 U.S.C. 601(m)(2)(A) and 452(g)(2)(A)

The petition also asserts that a raw ground meat or raw ground poultry product that contains certain ABR *Salmonella* strains is adulterated because "...it bears or contains (by reason of administration of any substance to the live animal or otherwise) any added poisonous or added deleterious substance ...which may, in the judgment of the Secretary make such article unfit for human food" (21 U.S.C. 601(m)(2)(A) and 452(g)(2)(A)).

According to the petition, ABR *Salmonella* qualifies as an adulterant under the first part of this definition because it results from the administration of antibiotics to the live animal and under the second part, i.e., that renders products "unfit for human food," because a person would be unlikely to consume a food if they knew that it had the potential to cause severe illness with a possible risk for an untreatable infection.

As discussed above, the available studies indicate that ABR microorganisms may be present in food animals, regardless of exposure of the animals to an antibiotic. We believe that further study is needed to evaluate the extent to which the administration of antibiotics contributes to the presence of ABR *Salmonella* in raw ground meat and poultry. Although some published articles suggest an association of increased severity of illness with ABR *Salmonella,* these studies are limited in their ability to conclusively establish whether the ABR in itself caused the increased severity.

Therefore, we have no basis to conclude that raw ground meat and raw ground poultry products that contain certain strains of ABR *Salmonella* are unfit for human food within the meaning of 21 U.S.C. 601(m)(2)(A) or 452(g)(2)(A)....

For the reasons discussed above, FSIS is denying your petition. Because our denial is without prejudice, CSPI is not precluded from submitting a revised petition that contains additional information to support the requested action. In accordance with our regulations, we have posted your petition on the FSIS Web site. We intend to post this response as well.

Note

Two months after the USDA denied CSPI's 2011 petition, CSPI refiled its petition, asking for expanded relief in the form of an interpretive rule declaring four strains of antibiotic-resistant salmonella to be adulterants within the meaning of the Federal Meat Inspection Act and Poultry Products Inspection Act. CSPI asked USDA to cover all meat and poultry products with this interpretive rule. CSPI relied on evidence gathered since its initial petition, and documented 19 outbreaks of foodborne illness related to antibiotic-resistant salmonella in meat and poultry, linked to 2,358 illnesses, 424 hospitalizations, and 8 deaths.

Particularly noteworthy for our purposes is the legal basis CSPI asserted for its petition:

> In denying the CSPI 2011 petition, USDA failed to address the key issue of whether ABR *Salmonella* is an "added substance" that may render meat or poultry injurious to health. Instead, the agency focused its response on requesting additional information it would like to consider before rendering a decision on whether ABR *Salmonella* is an adulterant.
>
> Importantly, the agency did not discuss the public health data submitted by CSPI, including the outbreaks linked to ABR *Salmonella*, or reflect on its own direct experience managing outbreaks linked to ABR *Salmonella* in meat and poultry that have occurred since the 2011 petition was originally filed. The evidence that these four *Salmonella* strains are linked to outbreaks demonstrates their public health significance. This evidence is proof-positive that the "substance" ABR *Salmonella* may render meat or poultry injurious to health.

The FMIA and PPIA definitions[20] of adulteration incorporate two independent standards, one addressing added substances and the second applying if the substance occurs naturally.

Depending on how the substance is characterized, the standards for determining harm to consumers change as well: For added substances, the law allows FSIS to act if the substance "may render" the food injurious to health; while for natural substances, the standard covers food that is "ordinarily injurious to health."

While FSIS does not yet classify *Salmonella* in raw meat as an adulterant, it has done so on a case-by-case basis. However, ABR *Salmonella* has unique characteristics that justify stricter and more uniform treatment. The chief characteristic is that the risk of illness to consumers increases as a result of human intervention—namely, the administration of antibiotics in meat and poultry production that increases the presence of ABR *Salmonella* on regulated meat and poultry.... The fact that ABR *Salmonella* infections in patients are less susceptible to existing antibiotics creates a greater risk of injury to human health and lends further support to finding these pathogens to be adulterants.

A. ABR Salmonella is an "Added Substance" that "May Render" Meat or Poultry Injurious to Health

ABR *Salmonella* is an added substance within the meaning of 21 U.S.C. § 601(m)(1) (meat products, as cited below) and 21 U.S.C. § 453(g)(1) (covering poultry products). Therefore, to declare it an adulterant under the law, FSIS must only find that it contains a poisonous or deleterious substance that "<u>may</u> render" the food injurious to health.

ABR *Salmonella* is an added substance in meat and poultry because its increasing prevalence is directly attributable to human actions: i.e. the use of antibiotics in animal production. The use of antibiotics in

---

[20] Both the FMIA and the PPIA definitions, found at 21 U.S.C. §§ 601(m)(1) and 453(g)(1) state in pertinent part that a carcass, part thereof, meat, or meat food product, or poultry product is adulterated "if it bears or contains any poisonous or deleterious substance which may render it injurious to health but in case the substance is not an added substance, such article shall not be considered adulterated under this clause if the quantity of such substance in or on such article does not ordinarily render it injurious to health."

farm animals selects for the genetic varieties of *Salmonella* and other contaminants that are resistant. While some proportion of "wild-type" *Salmonella* may carry resistant genes, the use of the antibiotics distorts the overall population of bacteria, rendering ABR *Salmonella* far more common on meat and poultry products. Further evidence that *Salmonella* is present in retail meat is documented by the National Antimicrobial Resistance Monitoring System (NARMS), which found that the number of *Salmonella* isolates gathered from retail meat that were resistant to one or more antibiotics has steadily risen since 2002.

Where a portion of a substance is derived from "acts of man," courts have interpreted the added substances to cover the entirety of the substance is in the food:

> "Since the 'may render injurious' standard was to facilitate regulation of food adulterated by the acts of man, we think that it should apply to all of a toxic substance present in the food when any of the substance is shown to have been introduced by man."[24]

Thus ABR *Salmonella* is correctly classified as an adulterant under the first part of the adulteration definition that addresses added substances. Since 1916, courts have interpreted the term "added" to mean that a substance is added to food if its presence in the food is due to some action by a person.[25] The definition of added substances has been applied to intentional applications of man-made additives, as well as unintentional applications such as bacteria in oysters that was sourced to sewage, and chemicals in fish linked to human-caused pollution.[26]

To find adulteration, FSIS must only determine if a poisonous or deleterious substance is "artificially introduced or attributable in some degree to the acts of man."[27] Scientists have shown that resistant strains of ABR *Salmonella* increase in prevalence because in industrial agriculture, producers use antibiotics extensively in livestock production to

---

[24] *United States v. Anderson Seafoods, Inc.*, 622 F.2d 157 (5th Cir., 1980).

[25] *United States v. Forty Barrels*, 241 U.S. 265, 283 (1916).

[26] *Forty Barrels*, 241 U.S. at 283; *Merck & Co., Inc. v. Kidd*, 242 F.2d 592, 595 (6th Cir., 1957)(citing *United States v. Sprague*, 208 F. 419 (E.D.N.Y., 1913)); *Anderson Seafoods, Inc.*, 622 F.2d at 157.

[27] *Anderson Seafoods, Inc.*, 622 F.2d at 160.

promote growth and treat or prevent disease. This is comparable to the facts in *United States v. Anderson Seafoods, Inc.*, where the court found the link between mercury dumped with other pollutants into rivers that washed into the ocean — where it was methylated by bacteria, taken up by plankton that were eaten by fish, that were in turn eaten by larger fish, concentrating the mercury to hazardous levels before it entered the human food supply—sufficient to rule that FDA could regulate mercury as an "added" adulterant in seafood.[29] It did not matter that some mercury occurred naturally in the environment because an act of man was responsible for increasing and concentrating the substance in fish used as human food.[30] Similarly, the use of antibiotics in farm animals has been shown to increase the prevalence of antibiotic-resistant bacteria in meat produced from those animals.

B. FSIS 2014 Response to the CSPI 2011 Petition

FSIS largely failed to respond to the legal argument presented to the agency on the point that ABR *Salmonella* is an added substance. The agency said, "At the outset, we note that the petition does not define 'antibiotic resistance' or specify the number or types of antibiotics that the *Salmonella* strains identified in the petition would need to be resistant to in order to qualify as adulterants.... This information is important to our evaluation of your request because the petition asserts that only certain strains of *Salmonella* should be treated differently from other strains of *Salmonella*. Therefore, understanding the characteristics of the strains that significantly increase the risk to human health is essential for developing the appropriate risk management strategies."

CSPI outlined in the factual basis for its 2011 petition the reason for the selection of the specific ABR *Salmonella* strains, specifically that they were associated with disease outbreaks and were present in retail meat products. Thus, the evidence of human illness, which has only grown stronger since 2011, is sufficient to form the basis of an agency determination of adulteration. The history of outbreaks and the presence of ABR *Salmonella* in retail meats provides proof of adulteration, even in the absence of a complete understanding of the number or types of anti-

---

[29] *Anderson Seafoods*, 662 F.2d at 162.

[30] *Anderson Seafoods*, 662 F.2d at 161-162.

biotics or the "characteristics of the strains." The fact that FSIS has also requested recalls of these ABR *Salmonella* strains on numerous occasions provides additional support that the agency is ready treating them as adulterants on a case-by-case basis and CSPI renews its request that FSIS make its policy consistent across the board, in order to protect consumers....

While CSPI provides further evidence in the Appendix as requested by FSIS in its denial, CSPI disputes that more scientific information is essential to the legal determination before the agency. Under the cited case law, it is not relevant that a certain proportion of ABR *Salmonella* is naturally present, if any other part of that substance is present on meat or poultry as a result of human activity, e.g. the use of antibiotics in animal production. *United States v. Anderson Seafoods, Inc.*, 622 F.2d 157 (5th Cir., 1980) supports this reading of the statute in interpreting added substance: "In sum, we hold that where some portion of a toxin present in food has been introduced by man, the entirety of that substance present in the food will be treated as an added substance and so considered under the 'may render injurious to health' standard of the Act."[34]

Although decided under a provision of the Food, Drug, and Cosmetic Act, courts give the same meaning to the definition of added substance in the FMIA and PPIA.

C. ABR Salmonella Meets the "May Render Injurious" Standard

A finding of adulteration is triggered when the added substance "may render [food] injurious to health." Courts have interpreted the term "may render [food] injurious to health" in the statute as meaning there is a reasonable possibility of injury to the consumer.[36] That determination relies on a reasonable consideration of the facts.[37] It also does not mean the substance must cause injury, only that it has the capability of causing injury.[38]

---

[34] *Anderson Seafoods*, 622 F.2d at 161.

[36] *Anderson Seafoods*, 622 F.2d at 159; *Berger v. United States*, 200 F.2d 818, 821 (8th Cir. 1952).

[37] *United States v. Lexington Mill & Elevator Co.*, 232 U.S. 399, 411 (1914).

[38] *Lexington Mill & Elevator*, 232 U.S. 399.

Although the *Anderson Seafoods* holding does not require that the adverse health effect be distinct from other illnesses, ABR *Salmonella* poses an additional risk of injury to consumers because it is more resistant to traditional treatment. Patients stricken with antibiotic-resistant illnesses often suffer longer and more extreme forms of illness, increased likelihood of hospitalizations and serious side effects from alternative drugs needed to treat them. Further proof is provided by the outbreak data cited in this petition. This additional risk meets the statutory definition as increasing the potential of injury to consumers. It also adds urgency to FSIS making a determination that ABR *Salmonella* is an adulterant.

Even in dismissing the CSPI 2011 petition, the agency provided an analysis of existing studies that documented an association of increased severity of illness with ABR *Salmonella*. The agency cited six articles suggesting an association of increased severity of illness with ABR *Salmonella* and identified three more studies supporting the statement that "[p]ublic health officials report increased bloodstream infections and hospitalizations for multi-drug-resistant *Salmonella* Typhimurium."

In the FSIS response to the 2011 petition, the agency said that *Salmonella* is not considered an adulterant of raw meat and poultry products "because ordinary cooking and preparation of these products is generally sufficient to destroy the pathogens." While the increasing number and impact of outbreaks belies this assertion, in any case such evidence is not legally required for the agency to find that ABR *Salmonella* is an "added substance" that "may render" the meat or poultry "injurious to health." Nonetheless, in order to be helpful in advancing the agency's thinking, CSPI has provided an appendix with numerous studies addressing the agency's questions on consumer handling, cooking practices, virulence, infectious dose, and heat resistance.

USDA has not responded to this petition.

CHAPTER 7
THE CHALLENGES OF FOOD ADDITIVES

Food, Drug, and Cosmetic Act

21 U.S.C. §321

SEC. 201. DEFINITIONS

(s) The term "food additive" means any substance the intended use of which results or may reasonably be expected to result, directly or indirectly, in its becoming a component or otherwise affecting the characteristics of any food (including any substance intended for use in producing, manufacturing, packing, processing, preparing, treating, packaging, transporting, or holding food; and including any source of radiation intended for any such use), if such substance is not generally recognized, among experts qualified by scientific training and experience to evaluate its safety, as having been adequately shown through scientific procedures (or, in the case of a substance used in food prior to January 1, 1958, through either scientific procedures or experience based on common use in food) to be safe under the conditions of its intended use, except that such term does not include—

(1) a pesticide chemical residue in or on a raw agricultural commodity or processed food; or
(2) a pesticide chemical; or
(3) a color additive; or
(4) any substance used in accordance with a sanction or approval granted prior to the enactment of this paragraph 4 pursuant to this Act [enacted Sept. 6, 1958], the Poultry Products Inspection Act, or the Meat Inspection Act;
(5) a new animal drug; or
(6) an ingredient described in paragraph (ff) in, or intended for use in, a dietary supplement.

Unlike some of the other substances we encountered in the last class (such as mold, rodent parts, salmonella, etc.), "food additives" as defined under the FDCA are defined according to intent; they are substances "the *intended* use of which results or may reasonably be expected to result ... in its becoming a component or otherwise affecting the characteristics of any food." A substance need not become part of the food in order to be an "additive"; it must merely "affect[] the characteristics" of the food. Thus, so-called "food contact substances" are food additives. Even the *process* of irradiation ("any source of radiation"), approved in many food-based applications by the FDA, is itself an "additive." By the same token, many substances that *are* added to food are not additives within the meaning of the FDCA; pesticide residues and chemicals, color additives, prior-sanctioned substances, new animal drugs, ingredients in dietary supplements, and substances "generally recognized as safe" ("GRAS") are all excluded from the definition of "additive."

Upon surveying this list, one can perhaps understand Professor James O'Reilly's advice to students of the FDCA: "Leave the baggage of colloquial understanding behind you, discard the mathematician's view of the concept of adding, and suspend disbelief about what is 'food,' and you are in the proper mental state for parsing the term 'food additive' under the 1958 amendments to the Food Drug and Cosmetic Act...." (O'Reilly, Food and Drug (2d ed. 2004).)

Pesticides, color additives, new animal drugs, and ingredients in dietary supplements are all regulated, to varying degrees, by other provisions of the FDCA. The provision that follows, section 409, sets out the specific regulatory framework for "food additives" as defined by the FDCA. As you read this provision, consider the following questions: Who has the burden of proving the safety of an additive? What must be shown in order to prove safety? Given the detailed nature of the framework described here, do you think Congress intended for this to be the primary means of ensuring the safety of food additives? (Spoiler: as we will see, the "GRAS" provision of section 201 – not section 409 – has become the predominant legal portal through which additives come into the food marketplace.)

21 U.S.C. §321

SEC. 409. FOOD ADDITIVES

(a) Unsafe food additives; exception for conformity with exemption or regulation

A food additive shall, with respect to any particular use or intended use of such additives, be deemed to be unsafe for the purposes of the application of clause (2)(C) of section 342(a) of this title, unless—

(1) it and its use or intended use conform to the terms of an exemption which is in effect pursuant to subsection (j) of this section;

(2) there is in effect, and it and its use or intended use are in conformity with, a regulation issued under this section prescribing the conditions under which such additive may be safely used; or

(3) in the case of a food additive as defined in this chapter that is a food contact substance, there is—

(A) in effect, and such substance and the use of such substance are in conformity with, a regulation issued under this section prescribing the conditions under which such additive may be safely used...

While such a regulation relating to a food additive ... is in effect, ... a food shall not, by reason of bearing or containing such a food additive in accordance with the regulation..., be considered adulterated under section 342(a)(1) of this title.

(b) Petition for regulation prescribing conditions of safe use; contents; description of production methods and controls; samples; notice of regulation

(1) Any person may, with respect to any intended use of a food additive, file with the Secretary a petition proposing the issuance of a regulation prescribing the conditions under which such additive may be safely used.

(2) Such petition shall, in addition to any explanatory or supporting data, contain—

(A) the name and all pertinent information concerning such food additive, including, where available, its chemical identity and composition;

(B) a statement of the conditions of the proposed use of such additive, including all directions, recommendations, and suggestions proposed for the use of such additive, and including specimens of its proposed labeling;

(C) all relevant data bearing on the physical or other technical effect such additive is intended to produce, and the quantity of such additive required to produce such effect;

(D) a description of practicable methods for determining the quantity of such additive in or on food, and any substance formed in or on food, because of its use; and

(E) full reports of investigations made with respect to the safety for use of such additive, including full information as to the methods and controls used in conducting such investigations.

(3) Upon request of the Secretary, the petitioner shall furnish (or, if the petitioner is not the manufacturer of such additive, the petitioner shall have the manufacturer of such additive furnish, without disclosure to the petitioner) a full description of the methods used in, and the facilities and controls used for, the production of such additive.

(4) Upon request of the Secretary, the petitioner shall furnish samples of the food additive involved, or articles used as components thereof, and of the food in or on which the additive is proposed to be used.

(5) Notice of the regulation proposed by the petitioner shall be published in general terms by the Secretary within thirty days after filing.

(c) Approval or denial of petition; time for issuance of order; evaluation of data; factors

(1) The Secretary shall—

(A) by order establish a regulation (whether or not in accord with that proposed by the petitioner) prescribing, with respect to one or more proposed uses of the food additive involved, the conditions under which such additive may be safely used (including, but not limited to, specifications as to the particular food or classes of food in or in which such additive may be used, the maximum quantity which may be used or permitted to remain in or on such food, the manner in which such additive may be added to or used in or on such food, and any directions or other labeling or packaging requirements for such additive deemed necessary by him to assure the safety of such use), and shall notify the petitioner of such order and the reasons for such action; or

(B) by order deny the petition, and shall notify the petitioner of such or-

> der and of the reasons for such action....
> (3) No such regulation shall issue if a fair evaluation of the data before the Secretary—
> (A) fails to establish that the proposed use of the food additive, under the conditions of use to be specified in the regulation, will be safe: *Provided*, That no additive shall be deemed to be safe if it is found to induce cancer when ingested by man or animal, or if it is found, after tests which are appropriate for the evaluation of the safety of food additives, to induce cancer in man or animal, except that this proviso shall not apply with respect to the use of a substance as an ingredient of feed for animals which are raised for food production, if the Secretary finds (i) that, under the conditions of use and feeding specified in proposed labeling and reasonably certain to be followed in practice, such additive will not adversely affect the animals for which such feed is intended, and (ii) that no residue of the additive will be found (by methods of examination prescribed or approved by the Secretary by regulations, which regulations shall not be subject to subsections (f) and (g) of this section) in any edible portion of such animal after slaughter or in any food yielded by or derived from the living animal; or
> (B) shows that the proposed use of the additive would promote deception of the consumer in violation of this chapter or would otherwise result in adulteration or in misbranding of food within the meaning of this chapter.
> (4) If, in the judgment of the Secretary, based upon a fair evaluation of the data before him, a tolerance limitation is required in order to assure that the proposed use of an additive will be safe, the Secretary—
> (A) shall not fix such tolerance limitation at a level higher than he finds to be reasonably required to accomplish the physical or other technical effect for which such additive is intended; and
> (B) shall not establish a regulation for such proposed use if he finds upon a fair evaluation of the data before him that such data do not establish that such use would accomplish the intended physical or other technical effect.
> (5) In determining, for the purposes of this section, whether a proposed use of a food additive is safe, the Secretary shall consider among other relevant factors—
> (A) the probable consumption of the additive and of any substance formed in or on food because of the use of the additive;
> (B) the cumulative effect of such additive in the diet of man or animals, taking into account any chemically or pharmacologically related substance or substances in such diet; and
> (C) safety factors which in the opinion of experts qualified by scientific training and experience to evaluate the safety of food additives are generally recognized as appropriate for the use of animal experimentation data....

The FDA has, in its regulations on food additives, defined "safe or safety" to mean that there is a "reasonable certainty in the minds of competent scientists that the substance is not harmful under the intended conditions of use." FDA's regulations recognize that it is " impossible in the present state of scientific knowledge to establish with complete certainty the absolute harmlessness of the use of any substance. Safety may be determined by scientific procedures or by general recognition of safety." (21 C.F.R. 170.3(i).)

Notice that, for carcinogens, the statute takes a position of zero tolerance: "no additive shall be deemed to be safe if it is found to induce cancer when ingested by man or animal..." (409(c)(3).) This provision – one of the famous "Delaney clauses," named after the congressional sponsor – has been widely criticized for its rigidity and for its singular focus on carcinogens. Can you think of any reason for such a provision? In the Food Quality Protection Act of 1996, Congress repealed the Delaney clause that had applied to pesticide residues in food, but it retained the Delaney clause of section 409, applied to food additives.

"Added" Ingredients

The following case provides an early example of the challenges of figuring out when a substance is an "added" food substance. As you will see, the challenges are particularly great when the entire food product is made up – that is, there is no obvious, discrete "food" to which a particular substance is "added." Although the relevant statutory provisions have changed since this case was decided, the puzzle of figuring out what is the "food" and what is the "additive" has only grown more pervasive in the modern era of processed foods.

United States v. Forty Barrels and Twenty Kegs of Coca Cola

241 U.S. 265 (1916)

MR. JUSTICE HUGHES delivered the opinion of the Court.

This is a libel for condemnation under the food and drugs act, of a certain quantity of a food product known as 'Coca Cola' transported for sale, from Atlanta, Georgia, to Chattanooga, Tennessee. It was alleged that the product was adulterated.... The allegation of adulteration was, in substance, that the product contained an added poisonous or added deleterious ingredient, caffeine which might render the product injurious to health.... The claimant answered, admitting that the product contained as one of its ingredients 'a small portion of caffeine,' but denying that it was either an 'added' ingredient, or a poisonous or a deleterious ingredient which might make the product injurious....

Jury trial was demanded, and voluminous testimony was taken. The district judge directed a verdict for the claimant, and judgment entered accordingly was affirmed on writ of error by the circuit court of appeals. And the government now prosecutes this writ.

First. As to '*adulteration.*' The claimant, in its summary of the testimony, states that the article in question 'is a syrup manufactured by the claimant . . . and sold and used as a base for soft drinks both at soda fountains and in bottles. The evidence shows that the article contains sugar, water, caffeine, glycerine, lime juice, and other flavoring matters. As used by the consumer, about 1 ounce of this syrup is taken in a glass mixed with about 7 ounces of carbonated water, so that the consumer gets in an 8-ounce glass or bottle of the beverage, about 1.21 grains of caffeine.' It is said that in the year 1886 a pharmacist in Atlanta 'compounded a syrup by a secret formula, which he called 'Coca Cola Syrup and Extract;" that the claimant acquired 'the formula, name, label, and good will for the product' in 1892, and then registered 'a trademark for the syrup consisting of the name Coca Cola,' and has since manufactured and sold then syrup under that name. The proportion of caffeine was slightly diminished in the preparation of the article for bottling purposes.... It is further stated that, in manufacturing in accordance with the formula, 'certain extracts from the leaves of the coca shrub and the nut kernels of the cola tree were used for the purpose of obtaining a flavor,' and that 'the ingredient containing these extracts,' with cocaine eliminated, is designated as 'Merchandise No. 5.' It appears that in the manufacturing process water and sugar are boiled to make a syrup; there are four meltings; in the second or third the caffeine is put in; after the meltings the syrup is conveyed to a cooling tank and then to a mixing tank, where the other ingredients are introduced and the final combination is effected; and from the mixing tank the finished product is drawn off into barrels for shipment.

The questions with respect to the charge of 'adulteration' are (1) whether the caffeine in the article was an added ingredient within the meaning of the act (§ 7, subdiv. 5th), and, if so, (2) whether it was a poisonous or deleterious ingredient which might render the article injurious to health. The decisive ruling in the courts below resulted from a negative answer to the first question. Both the district judge and the circuit court of appeals assumed for the purpose of the decision that as to the second question there was a conflict of evidence which would require its submission to the jury. But it was concluded, as the claimant contended, that the caffeine-even if it could be found by the jury to have the alleged effect-could not be deemed to be an 'added ingredient' for the reason that the article was a compound, known and sold under its own distinctive name, of which the caffeine was a usual and normal constituent. The government challenges this ruling and the construction of the statute upon which it depends....

The term 'food,' as used in the statute, includes 'all articles used for food, drink, confectionery, or condiment ... whether simple, mixed, or compound' (§ 6). An article of 'food' is to be deemed to be 'adulterated' if it contain 'any added poisonous or other added deleterious ingredient which may render such article injurious to health.' (§ 7, subdiv. 5th).[1] ...

In support of the ruling below, emphasis is placed upon the general purpose of the act, which, it is said, was to prevent deception, rather than to protect the public health by prohibiting traffic in articles which might be determined to be deleterious. But a description of the purpose of the statute would be inadequate which failed to take account of the design to protect the public from lurking dangers caused by the introduction of harmful ingredients, or which assumed that this end was sought to be achieved by simply requiring certain disclosures. The statute is entitled, 'An Act for Preventing the Manufacture, Sale, or Transportation of Adulterated or Misbranded or Poisonous or Deleterious Foods, Drugs, Medicines, and Liquors,' etc.... In United States v. Lexington Mill & Elevator Co., 232 U.S. 399, 409, it was said that 'the statute upon its face shows that the primary purpose of Congress was to prevent injury to the public health by the sale and transportation

---

[1] Section 7, with respect to ... 'food' is as follows: 'Sec. 7. That for the purposes of this act an article shall be deemed to be adulterated:...'In the case of food:

'First. If any substance has been mixed and packed with it so as to reduce or lower or injuriously affect its quality or strength.

'Second. If any substance has been substituted wholly or in part for the article.

'Third. If any valuable constituent of the article has been wholly or in part abstracted.

'Fourth. If it be mixed, colored, powdered, coated, or stained in a manner whereby damage or inferiority is concealed.

'Fifth. If it contain any added poisonous or other added deleterious ingredient which may render such article injurious to health: Provided, That when in the preparation of food products for shipment they are preserved by any external application applied in such manner that the preservative is necessarily removed mechanically, or by maceration in water, or otherwise, and directions for the removal of said preservative shall be printed on the covering or the package, the provisions of this act shall be construed as applying only when said products are ready for consumption.

'Sixth. If it consists in whole or in part of a filthy, decomposed, or putrid animal or vegetable substance, or any portion of an animal unfit for food, whether manufactured or not, or if it is the product of a diseased animal, or one that has died otherwise than by slaughter.'

in interstate commerce of misbranded and adulterated foods.... As against adulteration, the statute was intended to protect the public health from possible injury by adding to articles of food consumption poisonous and deleterious substances which might render such articles injurious to the health of consumers.' It is true that in executing these purposes Congress has limited its prohibitions, and has specifically defined what shall constitute adulteration or misbranding; but, in determining the scope of specific provisions, the purpose to protect the public health, as an important aim of the statute, must not be ignored.

Reading the provisions here in question in the light of the context, we observe:

(a) That the term 'adulteration' is used in a special sense. For example, the product of a diseased animal may not be adulterated in the ordinary or strict meaning of the word, but by reason of its being that product the article is adulterated within the meaning of the act. The statute with respect to 'adulteration' and 'misbranding' has its own glossary. We cannot, therefore, assume that simply because a prepared 'food' has its formula and distinctive name, it is not, as such, 'adulterated.'...

(b) The provision in § 7, subdivision 5th, assumes that the substance which renders the article injurious, and the introduction of which causes 'adulteration,' is an ingredient of the article. It must be an 'added' ingredient; but it is still an ingredient. Component parts, or constituents, of the article which is the subject of the described traffic, are thus not excluded, but are included in the definition. The article referred to in subdivision 5th is the article sought to be made an article of commerce, -the article which 'contains' the ingredient.

(c) 'Adulteration' is not to be confused with 'misbranding.' The fact that the provisions as to the latter require a statement of certain substances if contained in an article of food, in order to avoid 'misbranding,' does not limit the explicit provisions of § 7 as to adulteration. Both provisions are operative. Had it been the intention of Congress to confine its definition of adulteration to the introduction of the particular substances specified in the section as to misbranding, it cannot be doubted that this would have been stated, but Congress gave a broader description of ingredients in defining 'adulteration.' It is 'any' added poisonous or 'other added deleterious ingredient,' provided it 'may render such article injurious to health.'...

Having these considerations in mind we deem it to be clear that, whatever difficulties there may be in construing the provision, the claimant's argument proves far too much. We are not now dealing with the question whether the caffeine did, or might, render the article in question injurious; that is a separate inquiry. The fundamental contention of the claimant, as we have seen, is that a constituent of a food product having a distinctive name cannot be an 'added' ingredient. In such case, the standard is said to be the food product itself which the name designates. It must be, it is urged, this 'finished product' that is 'adulterated.' In that view, there would seem to be no escape from the conclusion that, however poisonous or deleterious the introduced ingredient might be, and however injurious its effect, if it be made a constituent of a product having its own distinctive name it is not within the provision. If this were so, the statute would be reduced to an absurdity. Manufacturers would be free, for example, to put arsenic or strychnine or other poisonous or deleterious ingredients with an unquestioned injurious effect into compound articles of food, provided the compound were made according to formula and sold under some fanciful name which would be distinctive. When challenged upon the ground that the poison was an 'added' ingredient, the answer would be that without it the so-called food product would not be the product described by the name. Further, if an article purporting to be an ordinary food product, sold under its ordinary name, were condemned because of some added deleterious ingredient, it would be difficult to see why the same result could not be attained with impunity by composing a formula and giving a distinctive name to the article with the criticized substance as a component part. We think that an analysis of the statute shows such a construction of the provision to be inadmissible....

It is apparent, however, that Congress, in using the word 'added,' had some distinction in view. In the Senate bill (for which the measure as adopted was a substitute) there was a separate clause relating to 'liquors,' providing that the article should be deemed to be adulterated if it contained 'any added ingredient of a poisonous or deleterious character;' while in the case of food (which was defined as excluding liquors) the article was to be deemed to be 'adulterated' if it contained 'any added poisonous or other ingredient which may render such article injurious to human health.' Cong. Rec., 59th Cong., 1st Sess. vol. 40, p. 897. In explaining the provision as to 'liquors,' Senator Heyburn, the chairman of the Senate committee having the bill in charge, stated to the Senate (Id., p. 2647): 'The word 'added,' after very mature consideration by your committee, was adopted because of the fact that there is to be found in nature's products as she produces them, poisonous substances to be determined by analysis. Nature has so combined them that they are not a danger or an evil,-that is, so long as they are left in the chemical connection in which nature has organized them; but when they are extracted by the artificial processes of chemistry they become a poison. You can extract poison from grain or its products and when it is extracted it is a deadly poison; but if you leave that poison as nature embodied it in the original substances, it is not a dangerous poison or an active agency of poison at all. So, in order to avoid the threat that those who produce a perfectly legitimate article from a natural product might be held liable because the product contained nature's poison, it was thought sufficient to provide against the adding of any new substance that was in itself a poison, and thus emphasizing the evils of existing conditions in nature's product. That is the reason the word 'added' is in the bill. Fusel oil is a poison. If you extract it, it becomes a single active agency of destruction, but allow it to remain in the combination where nature has placed it, and, while it is nominally a poison, it is a harmless one, or comparatively so.'...

This statement throws light upon the intention of Congress.... It is urged that whatever may be said of natural food products, or simple food products, to which some addition is made, a 'proprietary food' must necessarily be 'something else than the simple or natural article;' that it is an 'artificial preparation.' It is insisted that every ingredient in such a compound cannot be deemed to be an 'added' ingredient. But this argument, and the others that are advanced, do not compel the adoption of the asserted alternative as to the saving efficacy of the formula....

Congress, we think, referred to ingredients artificially introduced; these it described as 'added.' The addition might be made to a natural food product or to a compound. If the ingredient thus introduced was of the character and had the effect described, it was to make no difference whether the resulting mixture or combination was or was not called by a new name or did or did not constitute a proprietary food. It is said that the preparation might be 'entirely new.' But Congress might well suppose that novelty would probably be sought by the use of such ingredients, and that this would constitute a means of deception and a menace to health from which the public should be protected. It may also have been supposed that, ordinarily, familiar food bases would be used for this purpose. But, however the compound purporting to be an article of food might be made up, we think that it was the intention of Congress that the artificial introduction of ingredients of a poisonous or deleterious character which might render the article injurious to health should cause the prohibition of the statute to attach.

In the present case, the article belongs to a familiar group; it is a syrup. It was originally called 'Coco-Cola Syrup and Extract.' It is produced by melting sugar,-the analysis showing that 52.64 per cent of the product is sugar and 42.63 per cent is water. Into the syrup thus formed by boiling the sugar, there are introduced coloring, flavoring, and other ingredients, in order to give the syrup a distinctive character. The caffeine, as has been said, is introduced in the second or third 'melting.' We see no escape from the conclusion that it is an 'added' ingredient within the meaning of the statute.

Upon the remaining question whether the caffeine was a poisonous or deleterious ingredient which might render the article injurious to health, there was a decided conflict of competent evidence. The government's experts gave testimony to the effect that it was, and the claimant introduced evidence to show the contrary. It is sufficient to say that the question was plainly one of fact which was for the consideration of the jury...

"Generally Recognized as Safe"

Recall from section 201(s) of the FDCA, reproduced at the beginning of this chapter, that a food substance is not a "food additive" within the meaning of the statute if it is "generally recognized, among experts qualified by scientific training and experience to evaluate its safety, as having been adequately shown through scientific procedures (or, in the case of a substance used in food prior to January 1, 1958, through either scientific procedures or experience based on common use in food) to be safe under the conditions of its intended use." This seemingly innocuous exception has, as the materials below describe, become *the* mechanism for introducing food additives into the food supply.

Generally Recognized As Safe?: Analyzing Flaws in the FDA's Approach to GRAS Additives

Laurie J. Beyranevand
37 Vt. L. Rev. 887 (2013)

Introduction

As consumer demand for natural food products with fewer ingredients grows, so does curiosity and concern about the many food additives approved for use in the United States. In the broadest sense, an additive is any substance that "may reasonably be expected to result, directly or indirectly, in its becoming a component or otherwise affecting the characteristics of any food," and not all of them are worthy of concern. While additives have long held an important place in the food supply, due largely to their preservative and other beneficial functions, the legitimate concerns of advocates and consumers regarding the Food and Drug Administration's (FDA) safety assessment and treatment of additives appear to be falling on deaf ears.

As consumer demand for natural food products with fewer ingredients grows, so does curiosity and concern about the many food additives approved for use in the United States. In the broadest sense, an additive is any substance that "may reasonably be expected to result, directly or indirectly, in its becoming a component or otherwise affecting the characteristics of any food," and not all of them are worthy of concern. While additives have long held an important place in the food supply, due largely to their preservative and other beneficial functions, the legitimate concerns of advocates and consumers regarding the Food and Drug Administration's (FDA) safety assessment and treatment of additives appear to be falling on deaf ears.

Currently, there are more than 3,000 substances that fall under the FDA's designation of "Everything Added to Food in the United States" (EAFUS), which includes all "ingredients added directly to food that FDA has either approved as food additives or listed or affirmed as GRAS [[(generally recognized as safe)]." However, this list has been criticized for its failure to include more than "half of all substances allowed by FDA and less than 10% of the substances allowed by the Agency in the past 10 y[ears]." Given the amount of substances permitted for use in food, it should come as no surprise that the average person in the United States consumes approximately 150 pounds of additives per year. Many of these added substances are seemingly innocuous, such as common cooking spices. However, a great number of approved additives that are frequently used in American foods, including aspartame and partially hydrogenated oils (trans fats), raise serious health and safety concerns. From a safety perspective, two of the most commonly added substances – salt and sugar – present perhaps the most challenging issues for the FDA. Although both substances have been consumed for decades in safe quantities, they nevertheless present a host of health problems that the Agency appears either ill-equipped or yet unwilling to address.

The American public has been concerned about the number of additives in our food supply since the passage of the Food, Drug, and Cosmetic Act in 1938. While it took almost two decades for Congress to enact legislation giving the FDA authority to regulate food additives, it finally passed the Food Additives Amendment of 1958. Under this amendment, all additives are presumed unsafe and must receive pre-market approval by the Agency unless they are exempted as prior approved or GRAS substances. For a substance to be considered GRAS, and thereby excluded from regulation as a food additive, it must be "recognized, among experts qualified by scientific training and experience to evaluate its safety, as having been adequately shown through scientific procedures . . . to be safe under the conditions of its intended use." General recognition of safety can be established through either "scientific procedures" or, for those substances used prior to the passage of the Food Additives Amendment in 1958, "experience based on common use in food." Practically speaking, these standards have not prevented many substances from being either affirmed as GRAS or delisted due to evolving science.

Many of the substances considered GRAS by the Agency may not be considered unsafe per se because they have been used for generations and are not unhealthy in the sense that they are not toxic and do not cause cancer. Yet, the statutory and regulatory provisions addressing the safety of these substances are incredibly broad. To determine a product's safety, the Agency is required to consider whether "there is a reasonable certainty in the minds of competent scientists that the substance is not harmful under the intended conditions of use." There is no corresponding definition of what may be considered "harmful." Arguably, Congress included this broad statutory language to provide the FDA with discretion to remove substances considered harmful in any manner from the marketplace. However, because these substances are largely unregulated by the Agency, they have been included in large quantities in many food products, such that they could become harmful or unsafe due to the unhealthy conditions that result from their consumption. Both sugar and salt are examples of GRAS substances that can be included in limitless quantities in any food product. However, both substances have been shown to increase risks of certain chronic diseases and other conditions when consumed in larger than recommended amounts. Despite the overwhelming evidence to demonstrate the relative harm of these substances, the FDA has taken no steps toward significant regulation of either of them....

II. GRAS Substances and the Standard of Safety

A. History of the GRAS Exemption

Specifically exempt from the definition of "food additive" under section 321(s) of the FFDCA, GRAS substances are defined as "generally recognized, among experts qualified by scientific training and experience to evaluate [their] safety . . . to be safe under the conditions of [their] intended use."

Because these substances are excluded from the definition of "food additive," they are also exempted from the statutory requirements that apply to new food additive petitions. Largely, the GRAS exemption applies to what were commonly considered "safe additives" used before passage of the FAA – for example, salt, sugar, and other substances that had been used in foods without evidence of harm. Following passage of the FAA, the FDA created a "list of food substances that, when used for the purposes indicated and in accordance with current good manufacturing practice, are GRAS." Once listed, a GRAS substance could effectively be used without restriction subject only to "good manufacturing practices," which address the quantity of the substance used in and its effects on the food, as well as the grade and quality.

Following its creation, the FDA updated the original GRAS list over the years. While the list was relatively broad, many substances that manufacturers considered GRAS did not make their way onto the list. As discussed, the FAA did not require pre-market approval of GRAS substances. Yet, as a matter of practice, manufacturers often sought informal review by the Agency in the form of an "opinion letter" before placing their products into the market. These opinion letters were not binding on the Agency, and ultimately the process was formally revoked in 1970 in favor of a more formal set of procedures. The opinion letter process was also voluntary, meaning that the FDA learned of a manufacturer's GRAS determination only if the manufacturer notified the Agency. Soon thereafter, the Agency published notice in the Federal Register to announce the FDA's comprehensive review of the individual substances included on the GRAS list. This announcement came in direct response to President Nixon's directive to the Agency to reconsider the safety of GRAS substances after a group of cyclamate salts had been found to cause bladder tumors in rodents.

The stated purpose of the Agency's comprehensive study was to evaluate each substance on the GRAS list using what were then "contemporary standards" and "to issue each item in a new (i.e., affirmed) GRAS list, a food additive regulation, or in an interim food additive regulation pending completion of additional [toxicity] studies." Many in industry hoped the comprehensive review would answer the remaining questions regarding the convoluted GRAS process. The review generated a tremendous amount of information through the use of surveys, which encouraged the National Academy of Sciences to develop data providing an estimate of the individual daily intake of GRAS substances. To conduct this review, the Agency worked with the Federation of American Societies for Experimental Biology, an independent scientific organization, and asked it to recommend restrictions for any of the reviewed substances.

From 1972 to 1982, the committee reviewed 422 substances that were directly added to food, finding issues with thirty-five of those. For thirty of those substances, the committee anticipated revocation of GRAS status unless the FDA was provided with additional evidence demonstrating the substance's safety. "For the remaining [five] substances," the committee determined the substances were not harmful at the current levels of consumption, but did question the safety of the substances. One of these substances was sodium chloride, or salt, for which the committee suggested that the FDA draft guidelines to limit its use in processed foods. As of 2009, the FDA had affirmed the GRAS status of seventeen of these substances and issued regulations to that effect, while taking no action on the remaining eighteen substances. After engaging in its comprehensive review and requesting assistance and guidance from an independent scientific organization, the Agency essentially ignored all of the recommendations without explaining its reasons for doing so.

In addition, the Agency's 1970 notice proposed revising the existing regulations regarding safety to state that "'[s]afe' must be understood to connote that the Food and Drug Administration, after reviewing all available evidence, can conclude there is no significant risk of harm from using the substance as intended." For substances that the FDA had not included on the GRAS list, GRAS affirmation could be sought by submitting the relevant data and information to the Agency. With regard to substances whose status might change as a result of the promulgation of new regulations, the FDA made clear that, although new testing establishing harm could not be considered definitive proof of potential harm, it would establish that the substance should be removed from the GRAS list.

Following the Agency's 1970 notice, the FDA revised its regulations "to establish the general administrative plan for classifying substances as GRAS," which some argue demonstrated the Agency's determination that certain GRAS substances were "more GRAS than others." Specifically, the Agency singled out a small group of substances that would be considered GRAS without any further evidence or studies. These substances were of "natural biological origin that [have] been widely consumed for [their] nutrient properties in the United States prior to January 1, 1958, without detrimental effect when used under reasonably anticipated patterns of consumption." This exemption also included substances that fell under this category but had been modified through conventional processing techniques prior to January 1, 1958. For all other GRAS substances, the Agency sought advice from experts regarding their safety through notice and comment in the Federal Register.

Because the Agency's review did not encompass every GRAS substance – namely, those that had been marketed after a manufacturer's independent determination of GRAS status – the FDA developed a process by which individuals could petition the Agency to consider the GRAS status of substances not included in its review. The Agency's decisions regarding these issues were highly criticized, as they provided no definition or guidance regarding what specific factors should go into the consideration of general recognition of safety, except to say that certain substances would be excluded and no longer considered GRAS. According to critics, the Agency was making it incredibly difficult for new substances to receive GRAS affirmation, while simultaneously making it increasingly challenging for those already affirmed by the Agency to remain on the list. In other words, it appeared that the FDA determined that the only substances that would be affirmed as GRAS-excluding those of "natural biological origin" that were consumed for their nutritional properties prior to January 1, 1958-were the substances that had not yet been affirmed as GRAS, but would be subsequently listed. Any substances that did not fall into this category, regardless of their prior GRAS status, would be removed from the list. Because neither the FFDCA nor the FAA explicitly granted the FDA the authority to make final GRAS determinations, many saw this decision as within the province of the courts, which was also problematic given the degree of uncertainty. Unlike the provisions for new food additive petitions-where the Agency clearly had the final say regarding the petition's status-in the realm of GRAS substances, it was unclear whether the Agency's decisions in this regard were final and authoritative.

Finally, in 1974, the Agency attempted to specify the criteria for GRAS status, explain the difference between GRAS status and food additive petitions, and provide some guidance regarding the procedures used in the review of GRAS substances. For a substance to be considered GRAS, "general recognition of safety" must be demonstrated in one of two ways. First, safety can be established through scientific procedures. Second, safety can be established through experience based on common use in food prior to January 1, 1958. Prior to the FDA's issuance of its 1974 notice in the Federal Register, there was a fair amount of confusion over what the Agency intended to require when affirming a GRAS substance through scientific procedures. In 1974, the Agency clearly expressed its interpretation of the Act, stating that "Congress intended the phrase 'scientific procedures' as used in section 201(s) of the act to have the same dimensions as the full reports of investigations required to prove the safety of a food additive under section 409 of the act."

In other words, the FDA determined that "scientific procedures" would "require the same quantity and quality of scientific evidence as is required to obtain approval of a food additive regulation for the ingredient." The Agency based this interpretation on two Supreme Court decisions – Weinberger v. Hynson, Westcott & Dunning, Inc. and Weinberger v. Bentex Pharmaceuticals, Inc. – that addressed GRAS affirmation in the context of drugs and required the same standard of scientific evidence for GRAS drugs as for new drug applications. Comparing the provisions addressing drugs to those addressing food in the Act, the Agency determined that Congress must have also intended for the same degree of scientific evidence to apply for GRAS substances as for new additive petitions. With this notice, the FDA completely changed the landscape for affirmation of GRAS substances. The issue was no longer simply whether experts recognized the GRAS substance as safe; rather, the issue was now whether the substance met the criteria required for a food additive.

The FDA also stated that the scientific procedures relied upon "shall ordinarily be based upon published studies which may be corroborated by unpublished studies and other data and information." This decision was also based on the Bentex case, which held that "whether a particular drug is a 'new drug' depends in part on the expert knowledge and experience of scientists based on controlled clinical experimentation and backed by 'substantial support in scientific literature.'" Equating the legal issues involving drugs to the issues regarding GRAS substances and food additives, the Agency determined that the scientific evidence required for GRAS status must be "widely disseminated" such that it becomes "common knowledge among such scientists." Critics of this provision noted that the evidentiary requirements were above and beyond what the statute seemed to require. Moreover, they claimed that requiring the evidence be not only published, but also common knowledge, was impractical because it meant scientists had to take the extra step of considering and absorbing the literature.

The Agency noted that, unlike applications for new drugs, substances could be GRAS based on common use in food so long as it was marketed prior to January 1, 1958. For these substances, there was no requirement that scientific procedures establish the safety for GRAS status. The FDA defined "[c]ommon use in food" as requiring a substantial history of consumption of a substance by a significant number of consumers in the United States. Arguably, the Agency developed a rigid standard for GRAS substances marketed and developed after 1958 that did not exist for those marketed prior to 1958. While justifying the need to "grandfather" in certain substances that most people would consider safe based on their long history of use as reasonable, the Agency created a seemingly objective standard for some substances, which have ill effects in the quantities in which they are now being consumed. Consequently, even though the same requirements for a food additive petition need not necessarily be included for GRAS affirmation, when attempting to establish "general recognition of safety" through scientific procedures, it is clear that the same requirements should be considered. To address substances that might be considered safe now – but might not be later upon new information – the Agency developed a de-GRAS provision, which allowed for the removal of GRAS status upon reevaluation. These regulations constituted the FDA's final set of regulations on the matter, and have remained relatively unchanged.

In 1997, the FDA proposed a GRAS notification program to replace the petition process developed in 1972. The Agency's rationale for the proposed change was based on its belief that the petition process was simply too onerous and, despite being voluntary, it worked to discourage individuals from requesting the FDA's affirmation of their self-determined GRAS status. Specifically, the petition process formerly used by the Agency required notice and comment rulemaking – meaning that the Agency was required to publish notice in the Federal Register; review and respond to public comments on the petition; evaluate the information submitted with the petition, as well as any data received through the public comment process to determine whether the evidence establishes the substance's GRAS status; draft a detailed response to the petition explaining the rationale behind the Agency's determination that the substance is GRAS; and publish notice of that determination in the Federal Register. Ironically, the burdens cited by the Agency that would prevent an individual from filing a petition fell largely on the Agency. The data and information submitted with the petition needed to be collected for an independent determination of GRAS status regardless of whether the information was submitted to the FDA. Put simply, the only part of this "resource-intensive process" that placed a burden on industry was the actual filing of the petition.

For a more streamlined process, and to receive more information about independent GRAS determinations from industry, the FDA proposed a notification program whereby a person simply notifies the Agency of its GRAS determination. Like the petition process, the notification procedure was also completely voluntary. Each notification had to include "a succinct description of the 'notified substance' (i.e., the substance that is the subject of the notice), the applicable conditions of use, and the basis for the GRAS determination (i.e., through scientific procedures or through experience based on common use in food)," as well as the notifier's signature and date.

Upon receipt of the notification, the Agency evaluates the information and responds by letter in one of three ways. First, the Agency can determine that it has no issue with the basis for the GRAS determination. Second, the Agency may conclude the notification does not provide a sufficient basis for determining GRAS status because it either fails to include the appropriate data or the data raises questions about the safety of the substance. Finally, the Agency can respond by informing the notifier that it has ceased its review upon the notifier's request.

While the "FDA did not formally terminate the petition . . . process," it has stated that it no longer devotes resources to the reviews of individually submitted petitions. The FDA has never promulgated a final rule regarding the procedures for the notification program and the procedure remains voluntary. Not surprisingly, from 1998 to 2008, companies submitted just 274 GRAS determination notifications to the FDA. For all other GRAS determinations, the Agency usually does not possess information about these substances as companies are not required to comply with the notification procedure. Once the substance becomes marketed, the FDA would be hard-pressed to determine that it presents a food safety problem since the Agency is typically unaware of the GRAS determination....

[D]espite recognizing that the status of a GRAS substance may change over time – as additional information is discovered about the substance's safety – the FDA has not comprehensively reconsidered the safety of GRAS substances since 1982. The Agency justifies its failure based on a database called the "Priority Based Assessment of Food Additives," which it suggests helps prioritize substances for reassessment using "administrative, chemical, and toxicological information." Relying on this database to demonstrate measures that it is taking to reevaluate the safety of existing GRAS substances, the Agency has yet to provide an example of reconsideration made pursuant to the information generated from the database.

The Agency also cites media reports, individual complaints from the public, citizen petitions, or reports published by groups the Agency considers "authoritative" as sources of information to help prioritize reassessments. Yet, even after receiving eleven citizen petitions from both individuals and consumer groups, the Agency has, for the most part, failed to respond meaningfully to these concerns. Indeed, the Agency has neither revoked the GRAS status of any substances that have been affirmed since 1972, nor retracted its "no questions" position for any substance about which it received a notification letter since 1997. In addition to cyclamate salts, the FDA has completely prohibited the use of only one other GRAS substance – cinnamyl anthranilate, a flavoring agent known to cause cancer in mice. The Agency also prohibited the use of sulfites on raw fruits and vegetables due to severe allergic reactions in a portion of the population. This limited agency action – tantamount to inaction – fails to address the myriad of concerns regarding many GRAS substances presently on the market. While the Agency cites either limited resources as the reason it has yet failed to respond or the need for additional information and studies before revoking or amending the substance's GRAS status, the time has come for the FDA to respond....

Note

In June 2015, the FDA issued a final determination that most trans fats in food are not GRAS. The agency gave food companies three years to remove these substances from their products or to petition the agency for a case-specific determination that a particular usage is safe. The procedural vehicle for the agency's determination was a "declaratory order," provided for under section 554(e) of the Administrative Procedure Act. Section 554(e) allows an agency, "in its sound discretion," to "issue a declaratory order to terminate a controversy or remove uncertainty." On the substance of its determination on the GRAS status of trans fats, the FDA had this to say:

> [T]he GRAS status of a specific use of a particular substance in food may change as knowledge changes. For example, as new scientific data and information develop about a substance or the understanding of the consequences of consumption of a substance evolves, expert opinion regarding the safety of a substance for a particular use may change such that there is no longer a consensus that the specific use is safe. The fact that the status of the use of a substance under section 201(s) of the FD&C Act may evolve over time is the underlying basis for FDA's regulation at § 170.38, which provides, in part, that we may, on our own initiative, propose to determine that a substance is not GRAS. Further, ... history of the safe use of a substance in food prior to 1958 is not sufficient to support continued GRAS status if new evidence demonstrates that there is no longer expert consensus that an ingredient is safe (§ 170.30(l))....
>
> ... FDA need not demonstrate that PHOs are unsafe to determine that they are not GRAS, only that there is a lack of consensus among qualified experts regarding their safety. In addition, our consideration of PHOs as a class is justified because the available, relevant scientific evidence demonstrates an increased risk of coronary heart disease (CHD) attributable to trans fat; PHOs are the primary dietary source of IP-TFA; and there is a lack of consensus among qualified experts that PHOs are safe for use in food at any level.
>
> ... FDA disagrees with the argument that FDA must address health risks related to PHOs through food labeling requirements rather than through the food additive provisions of the FD&C Act. The NLEA amended the FD&C Act to provide, among other things, for certain nutrients and food components to be included in nutrition labeling. Section 403(q)(2)(A) and (q)(2)(B) (21 U.S.C. 343(q)(2)(A) and (q)(2)(B)) of the FD&C Act state that the Secretary of Health and Human Services (the

Secretary) (and, by delegation, FDA) can, by regulation, add or delete nutrients included in the food label or labeling if he or she finds such action necessary to assist consumers in maintaining healthy dietary practices. We have used this authority to require labeling of trans fat content (68 FR 41434 (July 11, 2003); see also § 101.9(c)(2)(ii) and § 101.36(b)(2)(i)) (21 CFR 101.36(b)(2)(i)). Although we may further address trans fat through labeling requirements in the future, labeling is not the only method by which we may address health risks related to trans fats, and more specifically health risks related to PHOs, the primary dietary source of IP-TFA. Nothing in the NLEA suggested that its passage limited the preexisting food additive provisions in the FD&C Act, or that the food additive provisions did not apply to nutrients and chronic multifactorial disease under appropriate circumstances. On the contrary, ... the NLEA contained a clause stating that "[t]he amendments made by this Act shall not be construed to alter the authority of the Secretary of Health and Human Services ... under the [FD&C Act]" (NLEA section 9).

The FD&C Act's nutrition labeling and food additive provisions are two different kinds of authority, with different standards, and we may choose among available approaches to a public health problem when the FD&C Act provides multiple options. See, e.g., Chevron U.S.A. Inc. v. Natural Resources Defense Council, 467 U.S. 837, 865-6 (1984) ("While agencies are not directly accountable to the people, the Chief Executive is, and it is entirely appropriate for this political branch of the Government to make such policy choices—resolving the competing interests which Congress itself either inadvertently did not resolve, or intentionally left to be resolved by the agency charged with the administration of the statute in light of everyday realities"); United States v. Mead Corp., 533 U.S. 218, 227 (2001) ("agencies charged with applying a statute necessarily make all sorts of interpretive choices"). There is no "conflict" between the FD&C Act's nutrition labeling provisions and food additive provisions.... It is also worth noting that we have previously determined that a use of a substance is not GRAS while rejecting a labeling-based approach to the health risks presented by that use (51 FR 25021 (July 9, 1986) (final rule revoking GRAS status of sulfiting agents on fruits and vegetables intended to be served or sold raw to consumers); and 50 FR 32830 (August 14, 1985) (proposal to revoke GRAS status of sulfiting agents on fruits and vegetables intended to be served or sold raw to consumers))....

Generally Recognized as Secret: Chemicals Added to Food in the United States

Tom Neltner and Maricel Maffini
Natural Resources Defense Council
April 2014

When President Eisenhower signed the Food Additives Amendment of 1958, he established a regulatory program intended to restore public confidence that chemicals added to foods are safe. In the intervening 56 years, the basic structure of the law has changed little. However, the regulatory programs the U.S. Food and Drug Administration (FDA) established to implement the law have fallen behind over time as the agency strived to keep up with the explosion in the number and variety of chemicals in food, and to manage its huge workload with limited resources.

The 1958 law exempted from the formal, extended FDA approval process common food ingredients like vinegar and vegetable oil that are "generally recognized as safe" (GRAS). It may have appeared reasonable at the time, but that exemption has been stretched into a loophole that has swallowed the law. The exemption allows manufacturers to make safety determinations that the uses of their newest chemicals in food are safe without notifying the FDA.

The agency's attempts to limit these undisclosed GRAS determinations by asking industry to voluntarily inform the FDA about their chemicals are insufficient to ensure the safety of our food in today's global marketplace with a complex food supply. Furthermore, no other developed country in the world has a system like GRAS to provide oversight of food ingredients.

Because of the apparent frequency with which companies make GRAS safety determinations without telling the FDA, NRDC undertook a study to better understand companies' rationale for not participating in the agency's voluntary notification program. First, we built a list of companies and the chemicals they market. Then we reviewed public records, company websites, and trade journals to identify additives that appear to be marketed in the U.S. pursuant to an undisclosed GRAS determination, i.e. without notification to the FDA.

All told, we were able to identify 275 chemicals[a] from 56 companies that appear to be marketed for use in food based on undisclosed GRAS safety determinations. This is likely the tip of the iceberg—we previously published in an industry journal an estimate that there have been 1,000 such secret GRAS determinations. For each chemical we identified in this study, we did not find evidence that FDA had cleared them.

In addition, using the Freedom of Information Act (FOIA), we obtained from the FDA copies of communications between the agency and companies who voluntarily sought agency review of their GRAS determinations. We found this glimpse into the review process shows that often the agency has had serious concerns about the safety of certain chemicals, and that companies sometimes make safety decisions with little understanding of the law or the science. As discussed later, companies found their chemicals safe for use in food despite potentially serious allergic reactions, interactions with common drugs, or proposed uses much greater than company-established safe doses.

On those occasions when the FDA is asked to review a GRAS determination, the agency rejects or triggers withdrawal of about one in five notices. Moreover, the public has even less information about the many substances with GRAS determinations that are never submitted to the agency in the first place—and which may pose a much greater danger. It is often virtually impossible for the public to find out about the safety—or in many cases even the existence— of these chemicals in our food.

NRDC believes that "Generally Recognized as SECRET" rather than "Generally Recognized as SAFE" is a better name for the GRAS loophole. A chemical additive cannot be "generally recognized as safe" if its identity, chemical composition, and safety determination are not publicly disclosed. If the FDA does not know the identity of these chemicals and does not have documentation showing that they are safe to use in food, it cannot do its job. In an increasingly global marketplace where many additives and foods are imported into the United States, this loophole presents an unsettling situation that undermines public confidence in the safety of food and calls into question whether the FDA is performing its duty to protect public health.

---

[a] We use the term "chemicals" to apply to the products sold by additive manufacturers. They may be individual substances or mixtures of substances. They are sometimes referred to as substances, additives, or ingredients, which, in reality, are all chemicals or mixtures of them. They may be extracted from natural products or synthesized from other chemicals.

The problem is rooted in a law adopted in 1958 when Dwight Eisenhower was president and Elvis was drafted. It is time for the FDA and Congress to fix the problems. In the meantime, consumers need to demand that their grocery stores and their favorite brands sell only those food products with ingredients that the FDA has found to be safe.

GRAS: How the Loophole Swallowed the Law

Over the last five years, there have been many news stories about unsafe foods that have sickened people. There have been a few reports of acute health problems related to chemicals added to foods, such as energy drinks containing a mixture of caffeine and alcohol, or rice with excessive amounts of the vitamin niacin. But chemicals added to food are more likely to be associated with health problems that may appear after years of frequent food and beverage consumption. These problems are often chronic in nature. The FDA is unlikely to detect an adverse health effect (short of immediate serious injury).

That is why Congress required that a chemical's intentional use in food be determined to be safe prior to its entering the marketplace. In 1958 President Eisenhower signed the Food Additives Amendment to the Federal Food Drug and Cosmetic Act to address these concerns. The law presumed that a chemical intentionally added to food was potentially unsafe and required that no chemical be used without a "reasonable certainty in the minds of competent scientists that the substance is not harmful under the intended conditions of use." Congress required food companies to file a "food additive petition" as the primary means by which to get an FDA approval of a chemical's use in food. If the agency did propose to approve the chemical, it would inform the public and request comments before adopting a regulation allowing the use. The system was designed at a time when an estimated 800 chemical additives were in use, far fewer than the more than 10,000 allowed today.

Determining that a chemical's use in food is and remains safe typically involves significant professional judgment. Rarely are these decisions clear cut; there is no bright line. So who decides is critical. Congress concluded that the FDA would make all safety decisions, except in the most obvious situations in which a chemical's use in food was "generally recognized as safe." This is known as the GRAS exemption. Examples include such common food ingredients as oil and vinegar. When a chemical's use was determined to be GRAS, the FDA did not need to adopt a regulation specifically allowing its use, and the formal public notice and comment rulemaking process was not required. In other words, the chemical didn't need premarket approval by the agency, and manufacturers could use it without delay. To qualify as GRAS, a chemical's safety had to be generally recognized by knowledgeable scientists, as borne out by published safety studies unless commonly and safely used before 1958.

However, the FDA and the food industry interpreted the law as allowing manufacturers to determine that a chemical's use in food was safe without notifying the agency. As a result, the identity of the chemical and the foods in which it was being used could be unknown to the public and the agency. Since 1958, an estimated 1,000 chemicals have been determined as GRAS by manufacturers and have been used in food without any approval or review by the FDA. The exemption has become a loophole that has swallowed the law.

The FDA's Attempts to Limit Undisclosed Industry Safety Decisions

Recognizing the problem of undisclosed safety decisions, the FDA adopted regulations in 1972 inviting manufacturers to voluntarily submit "GRAS affirmation petitions" in a rulemaking process that was similar to the one for food additive petitions, but without statutory deadlines for action. Companies sought FDA's approval, it appears, because their product would be more widely accepted by food manufacturers.

By the early 1990s, confronted with limited resources and an increasingly complicated and time-consuming formal rulemaking process, the FDA faced an overwhelming backlog of unresolved reviews. In response, the agency proposed a rule in 1997 to replace the 1972 GRAS petition process with a less formal review process that did not involve adopting regulations for specific chemicals. The next year, the FDA began accepting voluntary notifications from the companies that summarized the safety evidence and issuing decision letters. In some cases, these decision letters are often cited by the companies as evidence of FDA clearance, although the agency maintains that the letters are informal and do not constitute approval. This process, however, largely cuts the public and outside experts out of meaningful participation in decision making. The proposed rule has never been finalized despite its wide use by industry and the FDA. Since 2000, almost all new chemicals have passed through the loophole rather than being subjected to the food additive petition process established by Congress in 1958.

In 2010, the Government Accountability Office (GAO), the nonpartisan investigative arm of Congress, scrutinized the agency's GRAS program and found serious shortcomings. It concluded that "FDA's oversight process does not help ensure the safety of all new GRAS determinations" and that "FDA is not systematically ensuring the continued safety of current GRAS substances."

Given these concerns, NRDC sought to identify examples of chemicals marketed pursuant to undisclosed GRAS safety determinations, procure such safety determinations from companies, and examine why companies choose to forgo even the voluntary FDA notification process.

Claiming General Recognition While Avoiding Disclosure

As mentioned above, some 1,000 chemicals have been determined by manufacturers to be safe for use in food without FDA review or approval. Some of them, like artificial *trans* fat, were self-certified by industry as safe ingredients decades ago and are well known.

NRDC's investigation focused on newer, less known chemicals marketed as GRAS for use in food in the United States since 1997. We looked at situations in which:

- the manufacturer opted to rely on an undisclosed GRAS determination, without using the FDA's voluntary notification process;
- the manufacturer notified the FDA, and the agency subsequently rejected the company's GRAS notice;
- the manufacturer notified the FDA but subsequently withdrew its notice from FDA review. (We will discuss the problems with withdrawal of notices later.)

Our investigation began with a list of companies and chemicals from three sources:

- the little-known (outside of the food additives industry) web-based "GRAS Self-Determination Inventory Database," compiled by a consulting firm that makes GRAS safety determinations for industry;
- consultants who provided company names based on their experience at food industry trade shows;
- withdrawn or rejected notices in FDA's GRAS Notice Inventory.

Overall, we identified 398 chemicals marketed by 163 companies that appear to be marketed in the U.S. based on GRAS determinations not reviewed by FDA.

For each chemical, we sought a copy of the written documentation of the GRAS safety determination required by FDA's regulations (21 CFR §170.), which companies must have completed before marketing a product as GRAS. This documentation must provide the chemical composition of the substance, describe how it is made, estimate how much people are likely to consume (exposure), and describe what is known about the chemical's potential hazards. Unless a chemical was commonly and safely used before 1958, the key studies evaluating the hazards ordinarily must be published, preferably in a peer review journal but the FDA does not exclude publication on a company's website. While identifying a key study is helpful, it is not a substitute for providing the full safety determination.

Where a company appeared to be marketing a chemical for use in the United States as GRAS without final FDA review, NRDC contacted the company to request a copy of the undisclosed safety determination. If the company declined or did not respond to our request, we classified the GRAS determination as "undisclosed". Also, if the company did not provide us with a revised GRAS determination that addressed the FDA's concerns after the agency rejected the company's notice, or if the company withdrew its notice before the agency made a final decision, we considered the GRAS determination to be undisclosed.

"Generally Recognized as Secret"

All told, 56 companies appear to rely on undisclosed GRAS safety determinations for 275 chemicals:

- 35 companies selling 57 chemicals responded to our inquiries, but did not provide their GRAS safety determination.
- 21 companies selling 218 chemicals did not respond to our repeated inquiries.

The 35 companies that responded but did not provide us with their GRAS determinations fit into the following four categories:

- 13 companies provided us only with assurances that their chemicals were safe and complied with the law.
- 4 companies were willing to share the documentation only if NRDC signed a confidentiality agreement, which we declined to do.
- 7 companies declined to provide the GRAS determination but identified a published toxicology study that supported their analysis without providing the additional information such as exposure calculations and product composition needed to evaluate the safety.

- 11 companies acknowledged the inquiry but did not follow through.

The remaining 107 companies selling 123 chemicals fell into three general categories:

- 50 companies did not appear to market their chemicals for use in food in the United States.
- 54 companies that withdrew notices to the FDA later submitted revised notices and received a final review by the agency confirming product safety.
- 3 companies provided NRDC with a copy of their GRAS determination without requiring confidentiality.

...Of the 163 companies we reviewed, 56, or 34 percent, appear to rely on undisclosed GRAS determinations....

Why Did Companies Forgo FDA Review?

About 20 companies provided explanations for why they decided not to submit a voluntary notification to the FDA. These can be distilled into the following categories:

- **Concerns about too much FDA transparency.** The most common concern was the FDA's routine posting of GRAS safety determinations to its website. These companies said they were worried that easy access to information about product composition and the manufacturing process would enable competitors to develop identical or similar chemicals and would simplify the competition's own GRAS determinations.
- **Concerns about FDA delays.** Several companies claimed they did not want to wait for the FDA to make a decision, even though the agency explicitly allows the use and marketing of a chemical while a review is under way.
- **Desire to keep investment low.** Submitting a GRAS determination to FDA typically means additional work whether by company employees or a consultant doing the analysis. The agency asks many questions that must be answered. Often there are meetings with the agency. We found that almost all of the chemicals NRDC reviewed were also ingredients in dietary supplements and served no essential purpose in food other than to attract consumers' attention. Several companies indicated that a GRAS determination sometimes is done

in connection with a test of the food market for a chemical previously used only as a dietary supplement ingredient, thus minimizing the investment in an unproven market by opting out of the FDA review process.

- **Wish to avoid new dietary ingredient review.** The Dietary Supplement Health and Education Act of 1994 (DSHEA) requires manufacturers to notify FDA about dietary ingredients that either were not on the market before 1994 or whose use in food is not GRAS. Several dietary supplement manufacturers appear to be making a GRAS determination to avoid having to notify the FDA under both DSHEA and the Food Additives Amendment of 1958.
- **Misunderstanding of the law.** Some companies apparently did not understand the requirements for a GRAS determination. It appears that they did not realize that the determination must be written, that safety information must be drawn from published scientific studies, or that "generally recognized as safe" means more than obtaining the opinion an employee or consultant. Others apparently believed that an independent panel of experts was required even though the FDA states that no panel is needed. Finally, some companies appeared not to understand the difference between an efficacy study, which determines whether a chemical is effective in addressing a health problem, and a toxicology study, which evaluates whether a chemical may cause harm. The scope of most efficacy studies falls far short of an adequate toxicology study.

FDA Reviews of Notices Revealed Troubling Risks

As described earlier, companies may voluntarily submit GRAS notices (which contain the GRAS safety determination) to FDA seeking the agency's agreement with their safety determination, and when they do, the agency posts these notices on its website. We reviewed the quality of the industry's notices and identified three, still under review by the FDA as of September 2013 (listed as "pending" on the FDA site), that appeared to be poorly done. They were GRN No. 466 for polyglycerol polyricinoleic acid by McCormick and Co., GRN No. 471 for annatto seed extract by DeltaGold, and GRN No. 474 for Bioperine by Sabinsa Corp. All three had the same weaknesses: limited toxicology data, poor or inadequate exposure assessment, and lack of consideration of children's exposures. For each we submitted to the FDA detailed comments on the shortcomings of the safety determinations. See www.nrdc.org/food/safety-loophole- for-chemicals-in-food.asp.

If the FDA rejects a GRAS notice, it explains its safety concerns in a letter to the company and publishes the letter on the agency's website. But when a company withdraws a notice and asks FDA to stop further review, the agency issues a letter confirming the withdrawal without publicly explaining any of the concerns that could have prompted the withdrawal. The withdrawal does not prevent the company from continuing to market the product for use in food.

Between 1998 and the end of February 2014, the FDA rejected 17 out of 466 notices submitted to the agency; another 32 are still pending. During that time, 80 notices were withdrawn by the companies. For notices no longer pending, one out of five were either withdrawn or rejected.

After analyzing the poor quality of notices and the number of withdrawn notices, NRDC filed a FOIA request for communications between the FDA and manufacturers for 20 GRAS notifications. We chose notices for chemicals whose use in food we were able to document through a commercial database that provides product information for more than 200,000 food products; and the notices were submitted throughout the length of the program, starting in 1998. Sixteen of these notices were withdrawn, several of them multiple times. Although interested primarily in understanding what concerns raised by FDA prompted manufacturers to ask the agency to stop reviewing the notices, we also included two notices that the agency rejected and two that FDA accepted as sufficient, issuing what is known as a "no questions" letter. To see the FDA's FOIA response, go to www.nrdc.org/food/safety-loophole-for- chemicals-in-food.asp.

The FOIA documents reveal that the FDA does carefully review the notifications and asks tough questions. The agency's reviews often raise serious safety concerns or reveal that the company's scientific analysis is flawed or inconsistent with the law. Often the FDA tells the company that it will reject a notice if it is not voluntarily withdrawn. If rejected, food manufacturers would be more reluctant to buy the product since FDA posts its rejection letter and its reasoning on its website.

The following are examples of four withdrawn GRAS notices and our summary of the back-and-forth communications between the FDA and manufacturers. Despite the safety concerns, these chemicals have been listed as an ingredient in some food products:

Epigallocatechin-3-gallate (EGcG):

A Japanese company declared this chemical to be GRAS for use in beverages including teas, sport drinks, and juices, despite evidence it may cause leukemia in fetuses based on studies using newborn and adult human cells grown on a dish. Moreover, the company did not address a short-term study on rats showing it affected the thyroid, testis, spleen, pituitary, liver, and gastrointestinal tract. The notice did not explain potentially dangerous interactions with sodium nitrite, a common preservative, or with acetaminophen (the active ingredient in Tylenol® and many other over the counter pain-killers). The company withdrew the notice, resubmitted it, but withdrew that one as well. In response to our inquiries, the company assured us it was not marketing the product in the United States. However, two other companies, DSM and Kemin, appear to market chemicals high in EGCG in the United States pursuant to undisclosed GRAS determinations. We identified more than 25 food products with EGCG as a named ingredient.

Gamma-amino butyric acid (GAbA):

A Japanese company declared this neurotransmitter to be GRAS for use in beverages, chewing gum, coffee, tea, and candy. It did so despite having estimated exposure well in excess of what the company considered safe, relying on unpublished safety studies, providing the specifications in Japanese, and failing to consider existing exposures. The company told NRDC that it withdrew the notice "from a business perspective" and was selling the product in the United States only as an ingredient in a dietary supplement. It also indicated that it would not use the chemical in food without an FDA final review. We identified five food products with GABA as a named ingredient. These products included bottled tea and nutrition bars.

Sweet lupin protein, fiber, and flour:

An Australian firm declared these chemicals to be GRAS for use in baked goods, dairy products, gelatin, meats, and candy, despite concerns that the chemicals would cause allergic reactions in those with peanut allergies. The FDA noted that a warning label for sweet lupin would be insufficient to alert consumers who suffered from peanut allergies. The company did not respond to our inquiries and we could not find evidence that the company was marketing the product in the U.S. However, sweet lupin was a listed ingredient in more than 20 food products, none of which appear to bear any warning to those allergic to peanuts.

Theobromine:

A U.S. firm declared it to be GRAS for use in bread, cereal, beverages, chewing gum, tea, soy milk, gelatin, candy, and yogurt and fruit smoothies, despite having an estimated consumption rate more than five times the safe consumption level reported by the company's consultant. In addition, the manufacturer did not provide convincing explanations for the testicular degeneration in rats and rabbits and delayed bone formation in rats that were seen in animal studies of theobromine. The FDA was especially concerned that the product would be used in baby food. The company did not respond to our inquiries. Although we don't know the provider, theobromine was a named ingredient in more than 20 food products, including isotonic waters, nutrition bars, and diet foods. Fortunately, from what we could tell, none appeared in baby food.

The evidence from these FOIA responses makes it clear: the FDA's review adds value, and many companies' GRAS safety determinations are seriously flawed. The agency should make its concerns publicly available when companies withdraw their notices. Chemicals that, at least in some instances, prompted the FDA to raise safety concerns are used as ingredients in our food supply, and consumers are unprotected from their health effects....

Many GRAS Chemicals Began as Dietary Supplement Ingredients

Most of the GRAS chemicals NRDC examined were primarily marketed as "active" ingredients in dietary supplements. The availability of the GRAS loophole allows for the expansion of the market for such into conventional foods with claims that they made food "better for you." The chemicals were often extracts of plants or highly purified or synthetic versions of the biologically active chemicals in those extracts, such as antioxidants, which were purported to have possible health benefits.

Since the Dietary Supplement Health and Education Act of 1994, when Congress created separate, less rigorous safety standards for dietary supplements under DSHEA, there has been an explosion of these products. Ingredients allowed in dietary supplements are not necessarily safe when used in conventional food.

A product may be a natural extract or a highly purified version of one, but that does not necessarily mean it is safe. In 2014, the FDA recognized the safety threat when it issued guidance regarding substances added to foods, including beverages and dietary supplements. The agency stated:

> We have seen a growth in the marketplace of beverages and other conventional foods that contain novel substances, such as added botanical ingredients or their extracts. Some of these substances have not previously been used in conventional foods and may be unapproved food additives. Other substances that have been present in the food supply for many years are now being added to beverages and other conventional foods at levels in excess of their traditional use levels, or in new beverages or other conventional foods. This trend raises questions regarding whether these new uses are unapproved food additive uses.

It is likely that had the FDA reviewed the undisclosed GRAS determinations, it would have found some to be unapproved food additives.

The System Is Broken and Plagued with Conflicts of Interest

When the FDA reviewed GRAS determinations made by manufacturers, the agency found flaws with one in five, based on the number of notices rejected or withdrawn prior to a final decision. These notices presumably were those in which the manufacturer's had the most confidence, since the manufacturers voluntarily submitted them for agency scrutiny.

Food manufacturers are ultimately responsible for the safety of the food they make. However, in today's highly competitive global marketplace, there are strong economic incentives to minimize expenditures, which may lead to insufficiently-justified decisions. Our understanding of the health effects of many of the more than 10,000 chemicals allowed in food is far from complete, and as the number grows over time, concerns grow as well.

For example, some manufacturers still consider *trans* fats to be GRAS despite the FDA's concluding that it causes eight deaths a day in the United States and that if it were banned from food, our country would realize more than $117 billion in health benefits including reduced healthcare costs over 20 years.

Here is another issue of serious concern. For years, companies have used their own employees or hired consultants to evaluate their chemicals' safety and then relied on such undisclosed safety determinations to market their products for use in food. This raises serious conflict- of-interest concerns because a company's financial benefit from selling a particular product can bias its employees' or contractors' judgment. The lack of independent review in GRAS determinations compromises the integrity of the process and calls into question whether it can effectively ensure the safety of the food supply.

The FDA has acknowledged that a company's potential legal liability and its interest in protecting its brand are insufficient to ensure that food is safe. In 2013 the agency said, "Because the demand for many manufactured or processed foods may not be sufficiently affected by safety considerations, incentives to invest in safety measures from farm to fork is diminished. Consequently, the market may not provide the incentives necessary for optimal food safety."

"Even in cases where consumers are aware that their illness was contracted from a specific food," the FDA explained, "it is often difficult to determine who is ultimately responsible for their illness, since the particular source of contamination is not known in many circumstances." It concluded that "it is unlikely that the existence of brands in the food sector creates the optimal level of safety for society."

As the Institute of Medicine explained in the context of medical safety, conflicts of interest can result in bad decisions. Similarly, undisclosed safety determinations affecting the food that Americans eat may be undermining public health. Without FDA and public scrutiny—as Congress intended that there be—we cannot be confident in the safety of chemicals added to food.

Conclusions

A chemical additive cannot be "generally recognized as safe" if its identity, chemical composition, and safety determination are not publicly disclosed. Congress never intended that almost all new food chemicals would pass through the GRAS loophole without formal agency review and approval. The law places responsibility on FDA to ensure that food additive petitions are submitted for additives without general recognition of safety and to ensure that manufacturers' GRAS determinations are properly made. If the FDA does not know the identity of these chemicals and does not have documentation showing that their uses in food are safe, it cannot not do its job.

In an increasingly global marketplace where many additives and foods are imported into the United States, this loophole presents an unsettling situation that undermines public confidence in the safety of food and calls into question whether the FDA is performing its duty to protect public health. Until conflicts of interest are minimized and safety decisions are subject to mandatory FDA review, the safety of chemicals in food will depend largely on the integrity and competence of food manufacturers. That is not in the public's best interest, because manufacturers have a financial incentive that may bias their judgment about an additive's safety.

When consumers buy dietary supplements, they make a choice to consume chemicals that the FDA has not reviewed for safety. Indeed, under the law, consumers must be told that FDA has not reviewed the health claims made for ingredients in dietary supplements. As a result, dietary supplements carry labels disclosing that they have not been reviewed for safety by the FDA. However, when buying food, consumers can't make informed choices because they don't know which ones contain reviewed chemicals or which contain substances not reviewed by the FDA for safety. There are no warning labels. There is no disclosure. As a consequence, they may unknowingly be putting their health at risk. The current processes allowing this to occur should be addressed and changed to better protect the health of the American public....

Note

In August 2016, after pondering the issue for many years, the FDA issued a final rule "amending and clarifying" its regulations on establishing a substance's GRAS status. The preamble to the final rule is provided on Canvas. It is 97 pages long, and these are Federal Register pages, so the document is heavy going. Please look over the preamble, and consider the following questions: How is the FDA changing the process for determining GRAS status? How is it dealing with the problems identified by previous commentators? What do you think of the regulatory structure the FDA is embracing? Returning to the statutory provisions provided at the beginning of these readings, could the FDA have chosen a different legal course in addressing the GRAS issue? In skimming the Federal Register explanation for answers to these questions, you will likely find it helpful first to consult the table of contents. Keyword searches will probably also be useful. The work you will do here is not only an exercise in learning the latest on the legal parameters of the GRAS program, but also an exercise in learning to absorb the gist of a complex regulatory document rather quickly. Good luck!

CHAPTER 8
MODERNIZING FOOD SAFETY

The Food Safety Modernization Act (FSMA), passed by Congress in December 2010 and signed into law by President Obama in January 2011, is the most sweeping revision to our federal food safety laws in over 70 years. The law aims, as the FDA has put it, to bring food safety into the 21st century. It gives the agency the authority to issue mandatory recalls of unsafe foods – not just to recommend voluntary recalls. It requires more frequent inspections, targeting the riskiest facilities. It attempts to ensure the safety of imported food – which represents about 15 percent of the U.S. food supply – by requiring food importers to verify that their foreign suppliers have adequate safety controls in place, and it allows the FDA to accredit third-party auditors to conduct food safety audits and issue certification of foreign facilities and their food products, for certain purposes. FSMA's approach is intended to be science- and risk-based, and preventive rather than merely reactive. Thus, for example, food producers must have plans in place to address the likely points in the food supply chain where safety problems might emerge, and must also have plans in place to fix any problems that do arise. In short, it is fair to say that FSMA tries to bring U.S. the food safety system more in line with the reality of a global, interconnected, industrial food system.

FSMA does not, however, bring food safety under one regulatory roof. Responsibilities remain split between the FDA and other agencies, particularly the U.S. Department of Agriculture (USDA). USDA remains responsible for ensuring the safety of meat, poultry, and egg products (and catfish!). FSMA encourages better coordination between the FDA and USDA, but they retain separate legal authority. FSMA exempts "very small businesses" from preventive controls. There are also perennial worries about whether the FDA will be given sufficient resources to do the job well.

Many of FSMA's provisions required implementing regulations from the FDA. In fact, the statute directed the FDA to produce more than 50 rules, guidance documents, reports, and studies, on tight time frames. The FDA missed many of the deadlines, in part due to delays in the regulatory review process run by the Office of Management and Budget within the White House. Several important rules languished at OMB for over a year. To give you a sense of the complex task the FDA faced in implementing

FSMA, the next page reproduces a chart showing the FDA's "implementation management structure" for this law. In looking at the chart, bear in mind that each separate task represents a significant undertaking and that many of these tasks are related to and even dependent on decisions made with respect to other tasks. Ask yourself what purposes might be served by drawing up a chart like this, with discrete tasks and names of team leaders.

For these reasons, although the large trends of the law are clear, much of FSMA is a work in progress. We will focus our discussion on several potential problems with the law as written and on several discrete issues that have emerged as the FDA tries to implement the law. But first, a chart from the FDA showing the tasks it faces.

Implementation Management Structure for Food Safety Modernization Act

http://www.fda.gov/Food/GuidanceRegulation/FSMA/ucm247556.htm

Implementation Executive Committee	**Strategic Communications & Outreach Team**
Mike Taylor, Deputy Commissioner for Foods (Chair) Mike Landa, Bernadette Dunham, Mel Plaiser, Elizabeth Dickinson & Leslie Kux	Sharon Natanblut (Team Leader)

Prevention Standards Don Kraemer & Dan McChesney (Team Leaders)	**Inspections & Compliance** Barbara Cassens (Team Leader)	**Imports** Roberta Wagner, Camille Brewer & Leslie Kux (Team Leaders)
Produce safety regulation	Mandatory recall and recall communications	Importer verification & VQIP
Produce safety guidelines	Administrative enforcement tools	Import certification
Preventive controls regulation	Registration	Accredited third-party certification
Preventive controls guidance	Frequency of inspections	Lab accreditation & integrated consortium/FERN
Safe food transport	Manner of inspection/food safety plan review	International capacity building
Food defense	Tracing	Comparability
Contaminants	RFR improvement	Task A: prior notice
Federal/State Integration Tracey Forfa (Team Leader)	**Fees** Roxanne Schweitzer & Bob Miller (Team Leaders)	**Reports & Studies** Cathy Beck & Chad Nelson (Team Leaders)
Operational partnership	Inspection & auditor fees	Reports to Congress/studies
Capacity building		
Training		

Note

The following paper provides a nice summary of the Food Safety Modernization Act and offers a broad-brush critique of some of the law's basic provisions.

The Food Safety Modernization Act of 2011: Too Little, Too Broad, Too Bad

Nicholas Obolensky
17 Roger Williams U. L. Rev. 887 (2012)

I. Introduction

...

Over the course of the 20th century, as the nation transitioned from the predominately agricultural society of the 19th century to an industrial nation with an urbanized population, there was a dramatic shift in the method of food production. In response to the growing demand of the newly urbanized population, food production shifted away from local production and processing, and toward more industrial processing and national marketing. Food manufacturers met this growing demand by adopting similar techniques to those utilized by the industrial sector. Various technologies and chemicals were developed to sustain this new, streamlined, mega-farm, assembly-line method of food production. The evils inherent in this new food production system first became publicly apparent with respect to the "appalling and grossly unsanitary working conditions in meat packing factories" when Upton Sinclair published his book The Jungle. Following this shocking revelation, the legislature responded by enacting the Pure Food and Drug Act (PFDA) and the Meat Inspection Act (MIA) in 1906, thus establishing the initial U.S. food safety statutory framework.

A few decades later, upon recognizing a need to further develop the food safety regulatory framework and provide for direct government oversight, Congress passed the Federal Food, Drug and Cosmetic Act (FD&C) in 1938. The FD&C expanded the Food and Drug Administration's (FDA) power to regulate food safety by authorizing inspections, adding authority for injunctions, setting tolerance levels for dangerous substances, and requiring labeling standards. Since its inception, the FD&C has been amended over thirty times, each addition either providing more detailed food production and marketing requirements or granting more authority to federal agencies for implementing safety standards.

Recently, several Jungle-like revelations have once again shocked the nation. For example, a 2006 E. coli H7 outbreak first recognized by a scientist in Wisconsin and characterized as "one of the largest and deadliest in the country," caused 3 deaths, 204 illnesses, and 104 hospitalizations in 26 states. A salmonella outbreak in 2008, initially associated with certain types of tomatoes, cost the tomato industry an estimated $200 million, although jalapeno peppers were later discovered to have been the contaminated source. Shortly after, a much more severe salmonella outbreak, causing 9 deaths and 660 illnesses, was traced back to two processing plants owned by the Peanut Corporation of America (PCA) in Georgia and Texas. The most shocking aspect of the peanut-related salmonella outbreak was not that it cost the industry over one billion dollars, but that the PCA plant in Georgia had been inspected nine times between 2006 and 2008 by state officials under agreement with the FDA, and no action was taken to remedy the abysmal conditions and safety violations they noted. In response to this peanut scandal, as well as growing public concern about imported food safety due to melamine tainted pet foods from China, Congress decided to put food safety at the top of its legislative agenda.

The result, the FDA Food Safety Modernization Act (FSMA), passed by Congress on December 21, 2010, and signed into law by President Obama on January 4, 2011, is the focus of this article. While there is clearly a societal need for enhanced food safety, the FSMA is an inadequate response because it does too little to minimize safety risks posed by large-scale food production facilities and it does too much by imposing excessive regulatory burdens on small and mid-sized farms and facilities. The comprehensive scheme of the FSMA essentially imposes one-size-fits-all, across-the-board regulations with little regard to the scale of the individual operations, even though "[a]ll of the well-publicized incidents of contamination in recent years...occurred in industrialized food supply chains that span national and even international boundaries." Small and mid-sized farms and food production facilities do not pose the same risks because of the inherent transparency and accountability accompanying a closer proximal relationship to consumers' food supply.

Conscious of this apparent discrepancy in scale, legislators sought to mitigate potential harms by providing an exemption for small food facilities in the Tester-Hagan Amendment. This highly controversial amendment, ultimately adopted in the final form of the FSMA, does indeed contemplate the discrepancy, but is, unfortunately, too limited in scope, and is undermined by too much agency discretion. The FSMA falls short of achieving its goal for improved food safety because its application to large food production facilities, the primary sources of food-borne illnesses, barely improves the status quo and the requirements imposed on smaller farms and facilities that do not qualify for an exemption under the Tester-Hagan Amendment are a significant impediment to the viability of their operations.

In discussing how and why the FSMA misses its target, this article proceeds as follows. Part II will first examine the key provisions of the FD&C that have been amended by the FMSA, and will then focus on the provisions included by the adoption of the Tester-Hagan Amendment. Part III will provide an in depth analysis of (1) the shortcomings of the FSMA with respect to large food production facilities, (2) the disproportionate effect it will have on smaller farms and food production facilities, and (3) the large role agency discretion plays in its implementation and effect on food safety. Part IV will conclude by explaining and suggesting the need for a shift in the role that government plays with respect to food safety, health, and nutrition.

II. The FDA Food Safety Modernization Act

Foodborne illness is a significant problem in the United States as demonstrated by the 2011 Center for Disease Control (CDC) findings that estimate "that each year roughly 1 in 6 Americans (or 48 million people) get sick, 128,000 are hospitalized, and 3,000 die of foodborne diseases." In an effort to remedy this "largely preventable" public health problem, Congress passed the FSMA to provide the FDA with wider latitude in combating the issue. The major elements of the FSMA can be divided into the following five categories: Preventive Controls, Inspection and Compliance, Imported Food Safety, Response, and Enhanced Partnerships.

A. Key Provisions Established by the FSMA

1. Preventative Controls

One of the key elements of the FSMA is the requirement that food production facilities develop preventative controls similar to the Hazard Analysis and Critical Control Point (HACCP) plans already required of seafood producers, juice producers, and the meat and poultry industry. Section 103 of the FSMA, "Hazard Analysis and Risk-Based Preventive Controls" adds a new section 418 to the FD&C, which generally requires facilities to evaluate potential hazards, identify and implement preventative controls to prevent the potential hazards, monitor the performance of the controls, and maintain records of the monitoring. The potential hazards requiring analysis, implementation of controls, and maintenance of records include: biological, chemical, physical, and radiological hazards, natural toxins, pesticides, drug residues, decomposition, parasites, allergens, unapproved food and color additives, and any naturally occurring or unintentionally introduced hazards.

This new requirement for developing hazard analysis and risk-based control plans (HARCP) basically requires facilities to identify points in their processing system that could become potentially dangerous and then develop controls to prevent that from occurring. It also requires facilities to maintain a written plan and documentation of their HARCP, monitor its effectiveness, take any necessary corrective actions, and verify that the HARCP is adequate to prevent the hazards identified. The plan must be made available to the FDA during inspections and must be reevaluated every three years or "whenever a significant change is made in the activities conducted at [the] facility." Section 418(l) is where the Tester-Hagan Amendment was added to "modif[y] requirements for qualified facilities," or to exempt certain facilities from the HARCP requirements if they meet certain criteria, which will be discussed more fully below. Within eighteen months of the enactment of the FSMA, the FDA is required to promulgate science-based minimum standards for the section, define the terms "small business" and "very small business," and "provide sufficient flexibility to be practicable for all sizes and types of facilities."

Produce safety is addressed in Section 105, which adds section 419 to the FD&C, and requires the Secretary of Health and Human Services to establish "science-based minimum standards" for fruit and vegetables in conjunction with the Secretaries of Agriculture and Homeland Security, and with consideration given to existing standards established under the Organic Foods Production Act of 1990. Special priority is established for raw fruits and vegetables that have known risks. The standards must consider naturally occurring hazards, as well as those that may be introduced either unintentionally or intentionally, and must address materials added to the soil (e.g., compost), hygiene, packaging, temperature controls, animals in the growing area, and water.

2. Inspection and Compliance

To ensure compliance with the preventative control standards established to improve food safety and to enable the FDA to respond effectively to food safety problems that may arise, the FSMA provides for increased mandatory inspection frequency, access to records, and testing by accredited laboratories. Section 201 of the FSMA, adding new section 421 to the

FD&C, establishes more frequent mandatory inspections of food facilities based on the Secretary's assessment and classification of the level of risk posed by individual facilities. The risk profile of a facility is determined by the known safety risks of the food produced at the facility, the compliance history of the facility, the facility's hazard analysis and risk-based preventative controls, whether the food produced at the facility meets the criteria for priority under section 801(h)(1), whether the facility has been third-party certified under new sections 801(q) and 806, and in light of any other criteria "deemed necessary and appropriate by the Secretary." Domestic high-risk facilities must be inspected at least once during the first five-year period following the enactment of the FSMA, and again at least once every three years thereafter. Domestic non-high-risk facilities must be inspected at least once during the first seven-year period following the enactment of the FSMA, and then at least once every five years thereafter. Additionally, at least 600 foreign facilities must be inspected within the first year following the enactment of the FSMA and the number of foreign facilities inspected must be doubled every subsequent year for the five years thereafter. To carry out these tasks, as well as other duties required by the FSMA, section 401 authorizes the appropriation of FDA funds for field activities and to increase the number of FDA field staff.

Section 101 of the FSMA amends section 414(a) of the FD&C (21 U.S.C. 350c(a)) by authorizing the Secretary to have access to all records relating to an article of food "the Secretary reasonably believes" will cause "serious adverse health consequences or death to humans or animals," or that might be "likely to be affected in a similar manner."

Section 202 of the FSMA, adding new section 422 to the FD&C, directs the FDA to establish a program for the testing of food by accredited laboratories and establishes a system for laboratory accreditation.

Section 402, adding new section 1012 to the FD&C, establishes whistleblower protections for employees of entities involved in the manufacturing, processing, packing, transportation, distribution, reception, holding, or importation of food, who provide information relating to a violation of food safety laws.

3. Imported Food Safety

A significant portion of the U.S. food supply is imported and in order to ensure that imported foods are safe and meet U.S. safety standards, the FSMA provides the FDA with "unprecedented authority" to regulate imported food, and imposes preventative duties on the industry. Title III of the FSMA includes sections amending the FD&C to improve importer accountability, provide programs for third-party certification, create requirements for certification of high-risk foods, establish voluntary qualified importer programs, and grant authority to deny admission of foreign food products.

4. Response

Another key provision of the FSMA is the improved capacity it provides the FDA for responding to food safety problems. Mandatory recall authority is the most significant and novel authority provided to the FDA by the FSMA but additional authorities granted by the FSMA include: expanded administrative detention, suspension of registration, enhanced product tracing abilities, and additional recordkeeping for high-risk foods. Section 206, adding new section 423 to the FD&C, authorizes the FDA to issue a cease distribution order to any producer and/or distributor of food that the FDA determines there is a reasonable probability of its adulteration or misbranding (under FD&C sections 402 and 403(w) respectively), which will cause "serious adverse health consequences or death to humans or animals," after first providing the producer the opportunity to voluntarily cease distribution and recall the food product in question. Civil fines are imposed on any person not complying with a recall order.

Section 207 of the FSMA enhances the FDA's power to order administrative detentions of food products that may be in violation of food safety requirements. By changing the language of FD&C section 304(h)(1)(A) from "credible evidence or information indicating" to "reason to believe," this section of the FSMA is essentially lowering the standards for an administrative detention and expanding the circumstances in which a detention may be ordered. Additionally, the standard for which food product is in violation of the food safety requirements is further diminished by changing the language from "presents a threat of serious adverse health consequences or death to humans or animals" to "is adulterated or misbranded."

Registration of food production facilities with the FDA is required under section 350d(a) of the FD&C, and section 102 of the FSMA, amending section 415 of the FD&C, allows the FDA to suspend a facility's registration if it determines that the registrant was responsible for, or knew or should have known that there was a reasonable probability that its food product posed a risk of "causing serious adverse health consequences or death to humans or animals." Section 102 includes the right for a registrant to obtain an informal hearing on an FDA determination to suspend its registration and requires the FDA to vacate the suspension if the FDA determines there are inadequate grounds to continue the suspension. Otherwise, a facility under a suspension order is prohibited from introducing food into interstate or intrastate commerce in the United States. This section also includes a requirement that the FDA promulgate a small entity compliance guide within 180 days of the enactment of the FSMA to assist small entities in complying with registration requirements compelled by section 102, and clarifies the definition of "retail food establishments."

The FDA is directed by section 204 of the FSMA to establish a system to enhance its ability to track and trace both domestic and imported foods. The FDA must create pilot projects "to explore and evaluate methods to rapidly and effectively identify recipients of food to prevent or mitigate a foodborne illness outbreak and to address credible threats" of serious harm resulting from adulterated food. Lastly, the FDA is directed to publish a notice of proposed rulemaking establishing recordkeeping requirements for facilities it designates as producing high-risk foods.

5. Enhanced Partnerships

Throughout the FSMA there are numerous sections that require the FDA to consult with other agencies, such as the Department of Health and Human Services and the Department of Homeland Security, as well as foreign government agencies, recognizing the need for interagency cooperation in order to achieve public health goals through an integrated system. For example, it is up to the Secretary of Health and Human Services to issue guidelines with respect to "activities that constitute on-farm packing or holding of food that is not grown, raised, or consumed" on that farm and rulemaking for produce standards must be done in coordination with the Secretary of Agriculture, representatives of state departments of agriculture, and the Secretary of Homeland Security. With respect to imported food, the FSMA directs the FDA to "develop a comprehensive plan to expand the capacity of foreign governments and their industries. One component of the plan is to address training of foreign governments and food producers on U.S. food safety requirements." The small farm exemption, provided by the Tester-Hagan Amendment (addressed below), includes a reliance on state and local agencies to address the safety measures used by these exempt facilities.

B. Tester-Hagan Amendment

... Recognizing that all of the well-publicized incidents of contamination in recent years occurred in industrialized food supply chains, Senators Jon Tester and Kay Hagan sponsored this amendment to remove small, local food growers and processors from federal oversight, leaving them to the existing regulatory framework of states and localities....

It is first important to note that the Tester-Hagan Amendment pertains only to Title I of the FSMA and particularly to the HARCP requirements of the FSMA, and does not extend to other provisions of the FSMA. In section 102 of the FSMA (registration of food facilities), the Tester-Hagan Amendment clarifies the definition of "retail food establishment" in response to the 2002 Bioterrorism Act, which required all food facilities to register with the FDA but exempted "retail food establishments." The amendment required the "FDA to clarify that 'direct sales' of food to consumers includes sales that occur other than where the food was manufactured, such as at a roadside stand or farmers' market." Therefore, in section 102(c) of the FSMA, the Secretary is directed to amend the previously narrow definition of "retail food establishment" to specifically include the sale of food products or food directly to the consumer at a roadside stand or farmer's market, even if the stand or market is not located where the food is manufactured or processed, as well as to include the sale and distribution of food through a community supported agriculture program (CSA) and any other direct food sales platform as determined by the Secretary.

The main thrust of the Tester-Hagan Amendment is contained in section 103 of the FSMA, the HARCP section, adding new FD&C section "418(l) Modified Requirements for Qualified Facilities." Here, food facilities may qualify for an exemption from the HARCP requirements if they meet the following conditions: (1) the facility is a "very small business" (as defined by a study that the FDA is required to conduct within 18 months of the enactment of the FSMA; or (2) the average annual monetary value of all food sold by the facility during the previous three-year period was less than $500,000 (adjusted for inflation), and during that three-year period the majority of the food sold by the facility was to "qualified end-users." Section 103(a) (FD&C section 418(l)(4)(B)) defines a qualified end user as a direct consumer (which is not a business), restaurant, or retail food establishment (e.g., a grocery store) that was either in the same state of the facility or within 275 miles of the facility.

Qualified facilities that are exempted from the HARCP requirements must still submit documentation to the FDA proving their status as qualified exempted facilities and demonstrating either that (1) they have identified potential hazards associated with their food production, are implementing preventative controls to address the hazards, and are monitoring the controls to ensure their efficacy, or (2) their facility is in compliance with state, local, county, or other applicable non-Federal food safety law. If the facility chooses the second option (compliance with non-Federal food safety law), it must prominently and conspicuously provide the name and address of the facility that produced the food on a packaging label, or display the same information at the point of purchase.

Small-scale, direct-marketing farms may also qualify for an exemption from the separate produce safety standards in section 105 of the FSMA, in which the FDA regulates growing and harvesting practices, provided that they meet the same requirements for exempted facilities under section 103(a).

Additionally, the Tester-Hagan Amendment requires the FDA to conduct a study (mentioned above) of the food-processing sector to determine the definitions of the terms "small business" and "very small business." The study will focus on the distribution of food by type and size of operation, including the monetary value of food sold; the proportion of food produced by each type and size of operation; the number and types of food facilities co-located on farms; the incidence of foodborne illnesses originating from each size and type of operation (as well as which types have no reported or known hazards); and the effect on foodborne illness risk with respect to the scale of operation. The definition of the terms required by section 103(a) of the FSMA requires the FDA to consider such factors as harvestable acres, income, number of employees, and the volume of food harvested.

The exemption provided for qualified facilities in section 103(a) of the FSMA (amending section 418(l) of the FD&C) may be withdrawn at the FDA's discretion if the Secretary determines that it is necessary to protect the public health. Section 103(a), which amends FD&C section 418(l)(3), provides such discretion in the event of an active investigation of a foodborne illness outbreak that is directly linked to an exempted facility, or if the FDA finds it "necessary to protect the public health and prevent or mitigate a foodborne illness outbreak based on conduct or conditions associated with a qualified facility that are material to the safety of the food" at that facility.

The FDA is required to provide, within 180 days of promulgating new regulations under FD&C section 418(n), a small entity compliance policy guide to assist small entities that meet the definition of "small business" and "very small business" (to be determined by the study), explaining the FSMA's hazard analysis compliance requirements in "plain language." Furthermore, the regulations must "provide sufficient flexibility to be practicable for all sizes and types of facilities, including small businesses," in establishing science-based minimum standards for HARCP under section 103 and for establishing science-based minimum standards for produce safety under section 105.

III. Too Little, Too Broad, Too Bad

While the amendments and key provisions detailed in Part II provide the FDA with more authority and establish preventative measures to minimize the potential of foodborne illness outbreaks, the legislation is insufficient for tackling the problems posed by large-scale, industrialized food production, and unnecessarily burdens small and mid-sized facilities and farms that do not pose the same threats as larger operations. Additionally, many of the improvements established by the FSMA are dependent on agency discretion for their implementation and enforcement, and therefore the potential impact the law will have for food safety and its burden on small farms and facilities is dependent on the character and policies of the FDA.

Before analyzing the drawbacks of the FSMA it is important to briefly discuss the assertion that large-scale, industrialized food production operations pose a greater threat to food safety than do smaller, local food production operations. Large-scale industrial food production, often referred to as agribusiness, "relies upon heavy pesticide use, radiation, and other harsher interventions to kill germs in food grown in assembly line fashion." Large-scale food production involves "highly mechanized, monocultural, chemical-intensive methods" that transport raw materials to centralized processing facilities where they are mixed with production from other farms, and then packaged and shipped throughout the country. The rate of foodborne illness incidents has increased in tandem with the growth of this industrial food system, and most cases of contaminated food "are the result of unsanitary conditions in the large-scale facilities that mass produce and process foods."

Conversely, small and mid-sized farming practices, and notably organic farming practices, focus on the health of the soil, plant, and food, and are typically more accountable to consumers because of their proximity to the end-user. Local, sustainable food producers "use a systems approach that achieves greater safety and quality than any industrial producer using [Hazard Analysis and Critical Control Points] or [good agricultural practices], and are held accountable by the direct-to-consumer relationship, which creates greater transparency than any government regulation." Animals raised on small-scale, diverse farms, particularly organic, free-range farms, do not contribute the harmful pathogens that end up in other agricultural products because their varied diet, exercise, and exposure to good bacteria help them build resistance to the harmful pathogens.

A. Too little: The FSMA does not adequately address the problems and health risks posed by large-scale, industrial food production operations.

The key provisions of the FSMA amending the FD&C to enhance food safety are the preventative measures established by the HARCP, the increased rate of inspections, the mandatory recall authority, and the whistleblower protections. On their face these additions to the FD&C appear to be improvements, but will not likely have the significant effect intended by the proponents of the legislation. This sub-section will discuss how the FSMA requires too little of large-scale food production operations.

1. Hazard Analysis and Risk-Based Preventative Control Plans

The HARCP requirement (for which small farms and facilities may be exempted) is analogous to the HACCP programs, which were first developed within the food industry and later imposed through regulations, and "require companies to examine their production streams, identify points where pathogens or other hazards may enter the system, and take steps to make those processes safer." This systematic method of identifying foodborne hazards, assessing their criticality, and controlling weak points provides food production operations with a flexible approach capable of adapting to changing conditions rather than a specific mandate for the use of specific controls. The meat, poultry, juice, and seafood industries are already required to have HACCP programs. While some critics acknowledge that HACCP has made modest safety improvements within these industries, it has received a mixed response from the food industry and consumers. Because "HACCP requires relatively sophisticated administration and management," it tends to work well for large companies that already have complicated "industrial engineering management practices," but "[a]s implemented by regulators...HACCP tends to smother [smaller companies] in paperwork and impose rigid, costly, and out-of-date practices that simply have not kept up with changes in the food industry." Thus, the requirements discourage innovation of new safety mechanisms, and compliance with HACCP is very expensive. The HACCP requirements imposed by section 103 of the FSMA will do little to improve safety at large-scale food production facilities primarily because these facilities already have voluntary HACCP programs in place.

2. Increased Inspections

The mandatory inspections provided for in section 201 of the FSMA, which are to increase in frequency depending on a facility's risk-profile, do little to improve food safety in three reasons: (1) inspections are marginally useful for detecting harmful microbial pathogens that cause foodborne illness outbreaks; (2) increasing the frequency of inspections requires funding, which is not provided by the FSMA; and (3) the modest increase in frequency is not likely to make a significant difference. Inspections generally include visual observations of the premises and production, examination of records and safety plans, and written reports of the inspector's findings after considering the many factors detailed in the FDA's "Investigations Operations Manual." The FDA's lofty goals for inspections are laudable, but the quality of an inspection is only as good as the inspector and is limited by what the inspector focuses on. For example, even if a facility appears clean and is not listed as "high-risk," it may still harbor harmful pathogens, while another facility that appears dirty and disorganized may indeed be sterile. It is impractical for an inspector to visually determine whether or not a facility poses a safety risk, which is "the main reason why meat and poultry account for about half of all the food-borne illness outbreaks even though slaughterhouses may not legally operate without USDA inspectors on the premises at all times."

Furthermore, the costs associated with increasing the frequency of inspections are staggering, and doubling the current inspection rates would "account for most of the [FSMA's] $1.4 billion four-year cost." Section 401 authorizes the appropriation of funds from the FDA budget to increase the number of field staff; however, it remains to be seen whether Congress will make the necessary appropriations to fully fund the provisions of the FSMA. The FSMA is an authorizing bill and appropriations for it must still come from future Congressional legislation. Even Deputy Commissioner of the FDA's Office of Foods, Michael Taylor, publicly recognized the funding limitation of the FSMA when he noted that, "fulfilling the Congressional vision embedded in the new law...will require new resources and investment."

It is also difficult to contemplate how doubling the rate of inspections to once every three or five years (depending on the facility's risk-profile) will seriously improve food safety. The salmonella outbreak originating from the PCA plant in Georgia (mentioned in the introduction) occurred even though the facility was inspected nine times within a three-year period. The PCA example is also indicative of the ineffectiveness of random sampling, as the sample of processed peanuts tested by inspectors there came up negative for salmonella. However, the FSMA does incorporate a lesson learned from the PCA scandal. Section 307 incorporates a system for accrediting third-party auditors and includes a sub-section specifically addressing conflicts of interest as well as proscribing announced inspections by third-party auditors (both problematic in the PCA context where the third-party inspector of the

Georgia plant was paid by PCA and not its customer Kellogg, and had pre-arranged a date for inspection with plant personnel).

3. Mandatory Recall Authority

The mandatory recall authority provided by the FSMA has been characterized as "a solution in search of a problem." Previous recalls were strictly voluntary and the FDA relied on "the cooperation of food manufacturers, processors, wholesalers, and retailers to accomplish the arduous and expensive job of extracting contaminated food from commerce." Companies are usually willing to voluntarily recall tainted food. While a voluntary system makes obvious sense in that companies have a vested interest in maintaining the public's goodwill toward their products, a case can be made post-PCA scandal for greater government power to address "laz[y] or malfeasan [t]" manufacturers like PCA. Nevertheless, this added authority is a mere formality because in reality it would be difficult "to identify a single case in which producers refused to honor a recall request based on evidence that a product was actually or likely to be tainted." Additionally, it is a power begging to be abused in the face of public and media pressure over foodborne illness outbreaks. However, section 206(a) of the FSMA does contemplate this to some extent by first providing a company with the opportunity to issue a voluntary recall before proceeding to section 206(a), whereby the FDA has the authority to require a cease distribution order. Unfortunately, the mandatory recall authority does little to improve food safety overall because the real food safety threat occurs prior to the knowledge of that threat, which makes the recall essentially a last resort that rarely resolves the problem.

4. Whistleblower Protections

The employee protections provided by section 402 of the FSMA are an important aspect of the legislation intended to assist the FDA in preventing food safety issues. Like much of the FSMA, it is a noble addition to the FD&C, but one with few teeth in its practical application. Employees in the food industry, particularly those working for large-scale, industrial food operations, are not necessarily equipped with the knowledge and experience to recognize potential food safety risks. For example, like inspectors who cannot see the microbial pathogens through visual observation, employees are similarly situated in that they cannot with their eyes perceive potential threats that are likely microscopic. Furthermore, as with other similar legislation, the employees capable of "whistleblowing" (i.e. not management) are not likely to be aware of the protection afforded them by this legislation nor are they likely to have the confidence to take on their employers while already working at presumably low wage jobs. However, this component of the FSMA could prove quite effective for enhancing food safety with respect to a specific sub-set of employees, those involved in quality control, because they are acutely aware of health-risks and are privy to lab reports and other data that may reveal food safety hazards. Section 402 of the FSMA would allow them to report violations even when pressured by management to be complicit in misrepresenting data, or risk losing their jobs.

5. Missing from the FSMA

Several elements missing from the FSMA would have provided consumers with enhanced food safety with respect to large-scale industrial food operations: limitations on the use of chemical pesticides and fertilizers, a ban on sub-therapeutic antibiotics, and criminal penalties for knowingly violating and selling contaminated food. Section 105 of the FSMA purports to provide "science-based minimum standards" for produce safety and good agricultural practices for the "safe production and harvesting" of fruits and vegetables that are "raw agricultural commodities," but noticeably absent from the section is any reference to the use of chemical pesticides in growing these raw agricultural commodities. In the letter opening its 2008-2009 Annual Report, the President's Cancer Panel "urge[d]" the President to "use the power of [his] office to remove the carcinogens and other toxins from our food, water, and air that needlessly increase health care costs, cripple our Nation's productivity, and devastate American lives." The report advised that individuals could avoid "[e]xposure to pesticides" by choosing "food grown without pesticides or chemical fertilizers." The report was not conducted by "fringe" elements of the scientific community but by "the mission control of mainstream scientific and medical thinking," thus suggesting that the hazards and risks posed by chemical pesticides and fertilizers are apparent to the scientific community and should seriously be considered in determining "science-based minimum standards for the safe production and harvesting" of produce as well as for the publication of what constitute "good agricultural practices" under section 105 of the FSMA.

Furthermore, section 104's, "performance standards," direct the FDA to "review and evaluate the relevant health data and other relevant information, including that from toxicological and epidemiological studies and analyses" in determining the most significant foodborne contaminants. That the President's Cancer Panel report was available to both Congress and the FDA prior to the final proposal of this legislation is indicative of its failure to adequately address serious health concerns posed by the dominant form of agricultural food production in the U.S. (i.e. the large-scale, centralized industrial food production operations).

Additionally, the report warned individuals against "exposure to antibiotics, growth hormones, and toxic run-off from livestock feed lots," advising them to choose "free-range meat raised without these medications." Although meat and poultry products are beyond the purview of the FDA, the antibiotics and hormones used in factory farming is within its power to regulate, and should have been addressed in the FSMA by withdrawing approval for animal drug use. The movement from small, local, family farms to large, industrial factory farms mentioned supra Part I includes a similar transition within context of livestock farming.

The only way for the modern system of industrialized, concentrated animal farms to be viable is through the use of antibiotics to prevent dangers of disease and death prevalent when animals are confined in the cramped quarters of concentrated animal feed operations (CAFOs). "American farm policies and meat processing industries have sacrificed human health for the economic efficiency of industrialized livestock production." Sub-therapeutic doses of antibiotics ("low levels of antibiotics that are insufficient to kill an invading bacterial infection, but are effective in preventing bacterial infection from occurring") are particularly dangerous because they are responsible for creating strains of antibiotic-resistant bacteria that are "transferred to humans through the animal product, through human contact with livestock, and through environmental channels such as a contaminated water supply." Relevant to the FSMA and its goal of preventing foodborne illness outbreaks, the rise of drug resistant bacteria like salmonella and E. coli (the usual suspects in foodborne illness outbreaks), is largely a result of the use of antibiotics in raising livestock. These drug resistant bacteria enter the agricultural food supply - and those fruits and vegetables regulated under produce safety standards section 105 of the FSMA - when manure from CAFOs is used as fertilizer in agricultural fields, and when it enters the groundwater used for irrigation in agricultural fields. Given "the plethora of available data on the impact of the use of animal antibiotics to human health," the absence of this obvious food safety concern from the FSMA is remarkable and deplorable.

Finally, the absence of severe criminal sanctions for violators that knowingly and intentionally put contaminated food into the stream of commerce, is another example of the failure of the FSMA to adequately address the hazards posed by large-scale food production operations. Criminal penalties would provide a serious deterrent to reckless behavior endangering the health and lives of Americans. Under the current system, egregious violators like PCA chief executive officer Stewart Parnell, whose "[p]lant operators knowingly shipped peanut products" after they had tested positive for salmonella, would merely receive misdemeanors, with little to no jail time and small fines. As mentioned supra Part III.A.3, recalls are only minimally effective for protecting consumers, and thus, a deterrence mechanism beyond fines (that have relatively little impact on large businesses), is critical for enhancing food safety and was unfortunately left out of the FSMA.

B. Too Broad: The FSMA unnecessarily burdens small and mid-sized facilities and farms that do not pose the same threat as large-scale operations.

While many of the reforms enhanced the authority of the FDA, and heightened restrictions in the FSMA will have only a minimal effect on large food production operations, the one-size-fits-all legislation of the FSMA, which is barely discerning in its scope, may have a disproportionate and disastrous effect on small and midsized farms that do not fit within the exemption provided by the Tester-Hagan Amendment. This section will discuss how the FSMA overburdens small food production operations that do not qualify for an exemption from the preventative measures of section 103 as well as the positive and negative aspects of the Tester-Hagan Amendment as enacted.

1. The Regulatory Burden of the FSMA on Small and Mid-Sized Farms

The extent of the regulatory burden of the FSMA is relative to the size and nature of the operation being regulated. For the most part, those facilities and farms selling a majority of their products directly, and grossing less than $500,000 annually, will not be subject to the preventative measures, or HARCP, of section 103, and will not be subject to the produce safety standards and good agricultural practices of section 105. Additionally, those businesses deemed "very small" following the study prescribed by section 103 will also be exempt from the regulatory burdens of sections 103 and 105. While the discretionary aspects of this study's determination will be addressed more fully below, it is noteworthy here that many small and mid-sized farms and facilities will not fall within the exemption and will thus be subject to these sections' requirements. At the outset it is also important to point out that all businesses are subject to the remainder of the requirements and authority of the FDA provided by the FSMA. Finally, it should be noted that the definition of a small business, specifically with respect to farms, is relative to the geographic region where it is located. "[O]ne of the main tenets of local foods is [the recognition] that every area is different, based on its ecology and the community."

The first and most obvious burden on small and mid-sized facilities is the HARCP requirements in section 103. While they may not be overly burdensome on large facilities that have "capital-intensive, compliance department-managed, standardized, large-scale operations" (and likely already have voluntary HACCP programs in place), the reality for "low-input, owner-manned and -operated, diversified, small-scale operations" is distinctly different. These smaller facilities would have to analyze the potential hazards of their operation, "identify and implement preventative controls" to mitigate the identified hazards, "monitor the performance of those controls," and "maintain records of the monitoring as a matter of routine practice." As much of the HARCP requirements are highly technical and must be "science-based," in reality, this likely involves hiring third-parties to assist in the initial analysis, specialists to assist in developing and implementing controls, and employees to handle the administrative task of monitoring and record-keeping.

Although the regulations imposed by the FDA under this section are supposed to "provide sufficient flexibility to be practicable for all sizes and types of facilities," and the FDA is required to provide "a small entity compliance guide setting forth in plain language the requirements," it is unclear whether such protective measures would actually minimize the costs for smaller facilities. For example, a recently published FDA guidance document for processing cut leafy greens, which many small and mid-sized farms that prepare salad mixes would be potentially subject to, "estimates that it would take a trained corporate team 100 hours to develop an appropriate safety plan, not to mention the cost of tests that such a plan would have to require." Simply reading guidance documents issued by the FDA is time-consuming and requires a level of sophistication beyond the "plain language" requirements.

HACCP, and here HARCP, compliance is "hugely expensive," and forcing small and mid-sized facilities to absorb these costs could potentially drive them out of business. Evidence of this effect can be found by looking at what the mandatory HACCP plans did to small and mid-sized slaughterhouses. After USDA regulations requiring HACCP plans for slaughterhouses were promulgated in 1996, many slaughterhouses went out of business because of the high costs involved in implementing the programs. It has been argued that small slaughterhouses were already in decline, but small, local farms are actually becoming more prevalent, and it cannot be argued that hiring safety consultants, identifying, implementing, monitoring controls, maintaining records, and training employees does not add expenses. In fact, an analysis conducted by a farm operator at Rivendelle Farm in North Carolina estimated that "a typical small farm doing on-farm processing would need 150 hours to create, implement and monitor the [HARCP] plan, and [would] spend $9,500 per year on consulting and testing costs. If the farm hired a consultant to create the plan, the first year costs zoo[m] to $20,000." This analysis is "consistent with the concerns of local and organic farming advocates across the country" as evidenced by the findings of a small California farm that estimated that "it would cost their operation 100 hours to develop and implement a HARPC plan, plus two hours per day to maintain it, and $15,000 in annual testing fees."

The second disadvantage to small and mid-sized facilities is that the provision disincentives growth by making profitability a potential liability. Setting the qualification for exemption at $500,000 constrains small and mid-sized farms and facilities that may be close to that threshold. Considering that it is a gross revenue threshold or "value of all food sold by such facility," not accounting for expenses and overhead, a farm or facility may not be turning a profit, yet would still have to comply with the expensive HARCP requirements. One farmer interviewed by Mike Adams, Natural News Editor, said "that's so un-American to say hey, you're going to stay in this box, and you can never grow your business bigger than that. $500,000 [in revenue] is your cap." He told Mr. Adams that his farm was actually halting plans for expansion as a result of the FSMA "because we don't want to get too successful."

An example of a small, local food facility (packer and distributor) that has gross revenues just above $500,000 is the Appalachian Harvest Network, which brings local farms together under a common brand and into a distribution system with major retailers and grocers in the region. With total revenue at $515,000, and over half of its sales to wholesalers and distributors, Appalachian Harvest Network does not fall within the Tester-Hagan Amendment's exemption but is "operat[ing] on a tight budget with slim margins, leaving them especially vulnerable to periods of economic downturn," or to burdensome regulations that would require allocating time, money, and energy to paperwork, equipment upgrades, and creating HARCP plans. It is unfortunate that an enterprise that has created a system to assist small, local farmers while providing good, healthy food in an environmentally sustainable manner will be threatened by the over-burdensome requirements of the FSMA.

2. Tester-Hagan Pros & Cons

The Tester-Hagan Amendment adopted in the final legislation of the FSMA, as detailed in Part II.B, is an important protection for small-scale food producers. It insulates qualifying facilities and farms from the HARCP requirements and produce safety standards, but does not go far enough to mitigate the effects of legislation that otherwise does not differentiate in regard to scale. The significant achievements of the Tester-Hagan Amendment are that it provides an exemption for small facilities and farms; it clarifies the definition of "retail food establishments," specifically stating that "direct sales" include roadside stands, farmer's markets, and CSAs; it includes flexibility and guidance for small entities; and it requires the FDA to "conduct a study of the food processing sector" by evaluating food production and health risks in relation to size, type, product value, and scale and to use the results of that study to ultimately define the terms "small business" and "very small business." The drawbacks of the Tester-Hagan Amendment are its limited threshold for qualification; the discretionary nature of the withdrawal provision; and its failure to address geographical differences in scale.

Once ubiquitous in American society, small farms serving local needs are having a renaissance in American culture that the Tester-Hagan Amendment protects. "The growing trend toward healthy, fresh, locally sourced vegetables, fruit, dairy, and value-added products improves food safety by providing the opportunity for consumers to know their farmers and processors, to choose products on the basis of that relationship, and to readily trace any problems should they occur." Consumers choosing local food often buy it directly from the farm, at roadside stands, at farmer's markets, or participate in CSA programs. Local and state authorities (not to mention existing federal laws) already regulate these local methods of supplying consumers with food. Sparing them from further federal oversight and regulations, which translates into higher costs, not only protects their financial viability but allows them to be more responsive to local and community needs, which can differ from region to region. The study of the food processing sector that the FDA is mandated to conduct and report is a unique achievement because it will "foster the development of multiple climate-, scale- and market-appropriate models for promoting safe and healthy food in a sector of the farm economy largely ignored heretofore by research institutions." Researchers conducting the study will have an opportunity to closely examine the "unique conditions of small and diversified farming operations" while enabling the FDA to define the terms "small business" and "very small business." It is hoped that the government will recognize the impact and safety aspects of small, local farms provided it has the opportunity and funding to conduct a meaningful study.

Unfortunately the Tester-Hagan Amendment did not go far enough. The $500,000 threshold leaves out many farms and facilities that would consider themselves "small" and does not recognize offsetting factors such as expenditures and types of commodities. While it appears Congress recognized the need to add the words "adjusted for inflation," it did not add wording that considered offsetting factors that may belie the size of a farm or facility with sales over $500,000. Ideally this shortcoming will be resolved after the FDA conducts the required study. Even though qualifying facilities are theoretically exempt from the HARCP requirements, they must still prove to the FDA, with documentation, that they have identified hazards associated with their food production, are implementing controls to address the hazards, and are monitoring the controls. This additional requirement to establish exemptions seems contradictory because it essentially requires them to have an informal HARCP system. While they may opt out of this requirement by submitting documentation proving compliance with non-federal food safety laws, both options nonetheless impose requirements that could be burdensome for very small operations, and the second option leaves some discretion to the FDA as to which evidence of compliance will be acceptable. As with the $500,000 threshold, this hurdle might also be minimized after the FDA defines the terms "small business" and "very small business."

The discretionary withdrawal provision that allows the FDA to withdraw an exemption in the event of an active investigation directly linked to the exempted facility or a determination by the FDA that it is necessary to protect the public health leaves quite a bit of room for the FDA to choose to withdraw an exemption if its analysis of the type of operation leads it to consider the facility a threat to public health. Therefore, as discussed further infra Part III.C, a small facility otherwise meeting the qualifications for exemption may still not be exempted if it is not in accord with FDA policies for food safety.

Finally, the Tester-Hagan Amendment does not accommodate differences in scale related to geography and market availability. "[A] small farm in California is a massive farm in New England, and $200,000 worth of cabbage comes from a much different-sized operation than $200,000 of artisanal cheese." Additionally, a small facility located in a remote region may have little opportunity for direct sales and have to sell more than half of its products through a third-party or at a distance greater than 275 miles, thus curtailing its opportunity for exemption under section 103. Both sections 103 and 105 do direct the FDA to provide "flexibility" for "small businesses," but the long list of "highly prescriptive and specific requirements...contradict the 'flexibility.'"

Overall, the Tester-Hagan Amendment is a positive addition to the FSMA and much of its practical application for preserving small farms will depend on the outcome of the mandated study.

C. Too Bad: Agency Discretion

The notion of agency discretion has been alluded to throughout this article and is a subject for further analysis because the realities of this new legislation have not yet been realized, and the inherent speculation of its impact on food safety is largely dependent on one's perspective of government decision-making. However, as this section further explores, after considering the FDA's history of persecution of alternative food producers, skewed priorities, revolving-door hiring policy, and lack of understanding of the specific needs of small farmers, it is apparent that the FSMA grants too much discretion to an unreliable and untrustworthy agency. This section will focus on the discretionary aspects of the FSMA, a brief history of the FDA's use of its discretion, and the policies and goals the FDA intends to pursue.

Throughout the FSMA there are numerous provisions that leave key decisions to the discretion of the FDA. Part of the trouble with analyzing the legislation, as well as the controversy surrounding its passage through Congress, is that much of the language is vague, many of its effects depend on its interpretation and implementation, and many of the standards have yet to be defined or promulgated. Citizen concern over agency discretion is not without merit. Because federal agency's decisions are given great deference and reviewed using the Chevron standard, there is little recourse for challenging a decision so long as it was based in reason. For the purposes of this article, this section will briefly discuss several instances of vague, discretionary language within the FSMA to illustrate the wide latitude granted to the FDA that may disproportionally impact small and mid-sized farms.

The ultimate determination of the definition of the terms "small business" and "very small business" rests with the FDA after it receives the results of the study described in section 103(a), creating section 418(l)(5)(A). While the FDA is constrained by the language requiring it to consider "harvestable acres, income, the number of employees, and the volume of food harvested," the weight given to each factor, and whether to consider other factors when actually defining those terms, is left to the FDA. This is a significant power because this determines which facilities must comply with the

HARCP requirements and which ones may qualify for an exemption without having to meet the threshold standards in section 103(a).

The change to section 207 is an example of intentionally providing the FDA with additional discretionary authority for the administrative detention of food by replacing a stricter standard for quarantine of "credible evidence" with a looser one: "reason to believe." The FDA may now impound food based on a hunch that it may be dangerous. This relaxed standard may be helpful in situations where food was intentionally poisoned but could easily be abused for reasons other than food safety. Similarly, the potential for abuse is inherent in the articulated standard for the mandatory recall authority of section 206, which allows the FDA to offer the responsible party an "opportunity to cease distribution and recall such article" based on a "reasonable probability that an article of food...is adulterated...or misbranded...and the use of or exposure to such article will cause serious adverse health consequences or death to humans or animals." Relatively benign labeling issues, like the one that prompted kombucha producers to voluntarily recall their beverages from stores nationwide during the summer of 2010 because of potential disparities in the actual alcohol content and that labeled, may now be strictly enforced by the FDA.

Another example of FDA discretion embedded in the FSMA is the "sufficient flexibility to be practicable for all sizes and types of facilities, including small businesses" that the FDA is required to provide in promulgating "science-based minimum standards for conducting [the] hazard analysis, documenting hazards, implementing preventative controls, and documenting the implementation of the preventative controls" in section 103. Further factors that shape this rulemaking are contained in section 103(a), such as acknowledging differences in risk, minimizing the separate standards applied to separate foods, and not forcing companies to hire consultants, but again, these rules will ultimately be determined by the FDA with few enforceable limitations. There is, as with most agency rulemaking, a public comment period, but an agency is not required, unless specifically required by statute, to change its regulations or adopt any portion of the public's comments. For example, the "FDA has repeatedly approved genetically modified foods without labeling despite significant public opposition."

In fact, as the FSMA provides the FDA with quite a bit of expanded authority to inspect records upon a "reasonable belie[f]" of a "reasonable probability" of serious risk under section 101 and to establish science-based minimum produce safety standards and good agricultural practices based under section 105, the remaining questions are, who is the FDA and what food safety goals does it wish to pursue?

The FDA is a federal agency within the executive branch of the U.S. government. The commissioner, Dr. Margaret Hamburg, was nominated by President Obama and confirmed by the Senate on May 18, 2009. "[S]he is an experienced medical doctor, scientist, and public health executive." More relevant is the Deputy Commissioner for Foods, Michael R. Taylor, who Dr. Hamburg appointed to a new position that she created in August 2009 to "develop and carry out a prevention-based strategy for food safety" and "plan for new food safety legislation":

> The new Office of Foods is responsible, on behalf of the Commissioner, for providing all elements of FDA's Foods Program leadership, guidance, and support to achieve the Agency's public health goals. The Office is also the focal point for planning implementation of the recommendations of the President's Food Safety Working Group and the new food safety authorities being considered by Congress.

Therefore, Mr. Taylor, former vice president for public policy of Monsanto, former administrator of USDA's Food Safety and Inspection Service and acting under secretary for food safety at USDA, former partner at King & Spalding law firm, and former staff attorney at the FDA, is the authority whose discretion matters. The point of highlighting Mr. Taylor's career is to illustrate the inherent industry bias of this top official tasked with the final determination of discretionary agency decisions. Although some of the discretionary decisions highlighted below were pursued by the FDA prior to his appointment, Mr. Taylor nevertheless represents the agency's adherence to the current mainstream, one-size-fits-all, industrial approach to food production, and therefore its approach to food safety.

An examination of some recent instances in which the FDA has exercised its authority reveals its preferences and policies for controlling food safety. The current trend of enforcement by the FDA against farmstead dairies is an ominous indicator of where the FDA wants to go. For example, on April 20, 2010, two FDA agents, two federal marshals, and one state trooper went to the Rainbow Acres farm in Pennsylvania at 5 a.m. "to execute an administrative search warrant," ultimately fining the farm-owner for violating a law against selling raw milk. The FDA has targeted twenty different buying clubs in Chicago suspected of obtaining raw milk from out-of-state sources and "has a similar strategy for the states, with the plan being to pressure one state at a time to ban raw milk sales." Morningland Dairy, a farmstead raw milk cheese operation in Missouri, has been involved in litigation for over a year, and has had approximately 29,000 pounds of its cheese impounded since August 26, 2010, even though there have been no reported illnesses from consumption of its products throughout the thirty years it has been in business. The list of recalls, suspensions, and enforcement actions against raw milk products goes on and on even though there is not yet a federal prohibition of raw milk. The zero tolerance policy on Listeria monocytogenes, a foodborne pathogen that can sometimes be virulent, threatens to eliminate raw milk artisanal cheese production, and thus cut out a significant high-value niche for small and mid-sized farming operations.

Even seemingly innocuous products, like walnuts and cherries, are not immune from being targeted by the FDA for making "false" health claims. In 2006, the FDA demanded that twenty-nine cherry producers stop making claims that their products were healthy, and in 2010, the FDA threatened an attack against a large walnut producer to remove health claims on their website and marketing materials. Even though both claims were backed up by scientific evidence, the FDA does not allow health claims about treating or preventing disease without its prior approval, because such claims would categorize the product as a "drug." However, health claims made on Frito-Lay's website have not received the same, if any, attention from the FDA.

Furthermore, the FDA has not banned chemical pesticides and fertilizers known to cause cancer, nor did the FSMA include regulations on the use of bisphenol-A (commonly used in plastic beverage containers and known as BPA), a well-known health risk that Senator Diane Feinstein pushed to be banned. The priorities of the FDA seem to be askew. When the President's Cancer Panel advises changing the paradigm from presuming chemicals are safe until strong evidence emerges to the contrary, to presuming they are dangerous until proven safe, the FDA, charged with protecting food safety and setting agricultural standards, ought to pay attention. It is especially irresponsible and indicative of the heavy influence of big industry that the President's Cancer Panel report was released nine months before the enactment of the FSMA. Thus, it is reasonable to be afraid of the discretionary authority afforded to the FDA by the FSMA. When the FDA states in a legal brief on public record that "there is no generalized right to bodily and physical health" and "there is no absolute right to consume or feed children any particular food," its food safety and health policies become highly suspicious.

Congress was correct to recognize that U.S. food safety regulations were in dire need of a massive overhaul. However, both Congress and the President missed the mark by enlisting personnel like Michael R. Taylor, who represent the very industry creating the greatest risks and in need of the most stringent regulations, to set forth the guidelines and criteria for a revised food-safety regime. Instead of writing legislation with a one-size-fits-all approach, Congress ought to have focused its efforts on the large agribusinesses creating the risks and left small and mid-sized operations to state regulations.

IV. Conclusion

We are what we eat, and our health and nutrition depend on the consumption of nutritious, high-vitamin foods. Food is human sustenance and is the fundamental prerequisite to life. Its production must be transparent and its producers held accountable. What is truly needed is a paradigm shift from our dependence on industrialized food to an increased reliance on local and sustainably grown food rather than further government regulation. Local food can be defined by the proximal relationship between production and consumption but is better understood by examining the "producer's and consumer's motivations for buying and selling local food: '1) a sense of connection, 2) quality, 3) environmental impact, and 4) political and social support for a particular type of agriculture."' Local food may be safer because it is sold fresh and therefore does not require preservatives, or storage and transportation. "[I]t is usually sold unprocessed [and] has come in contact with fewer hands and mechanization." The local producer is directly accountable to its local consumer because the local consumer knows exactly where and when he purchased a particular product from the local producer, and can easily express any dissatisfaction directly to the producer or to the surrounding community.

It is not coincidental that the rise in food-related illnesses has accompanied the "rise of industrial agriculture and food production," and the current rate of outbreaks reflects our over-dependence on an increasingly concentrated food production system. The resulting concern for food safety has led us to adopting "'clean farming' practices, which ironically run directly counter to farming practices developed by sustainable farmers with human health and the larger healthy functioning of the food production system in mind." Our definition of what is a health risk must be re-examined. For example, raw milk cheese may pose a serious health risk if produced by a large, industrial facility, while it may be nutritionally advantageous and perfectly safe if it is produced by a small, local facility.

Congress must recognize that broad, sweeping legislation like the FSMA does not account for the different risks posed by varying sized food production facilities - namely that it does too little to be effective in mitigating risks posed by larger facilities, it is too broad to accommodate the needs of smaller facilities, and in reality, it does little to actually protect consumers. Consumers would be better served by more stringent regulations of large business, defined by market share, and government funded compliance for those businesses that occupy only a minor share of the market. The government's role with respect to food safety, health, and nutrition should be to regulate large-scale food production operations while leaving consumers the choice to determine for themselves what is healthy and safe when buying from their local farm.

Note

The foregoing critiques of FSMA – and of much of the law as it relates to food – put one in mind of a famous essay by Wendell Berry, "Solving for Pattern," which begins:

> Our dilemma in agriculture now is that the industrial methods that have so spectacularly solved some of the problems of food production have been accompanied by "side effects" so damaging as to threaten the survival of farming. Perhaps the best clue to the nature and gravity of this dilemma is that it is not limited to agriculture. My immediate concern here is with the irony of agricultural methods that destroy, first, the health of the soil and, finally, the health of human communities. But I could just as easily be talking about sanitation systems that pollute, school systems that graduate illiterate students, medical cures that cause disease, or nuclear armaments that explode in the midst of the people they are meant to protect. This is a kind of surprise that is characteristic of our time: the cure proves incurable; security results in the evacuation of a neighborhood or a town. It is only when it is understood that our agricultural dilemma is characteristic not of our agriculture but of our time that we can begin to understand why these surprises happen, and to work out standards of judgment that may prevent them.

Please read this essay for class; it is available at: http://www.streetsense.org/storage/Berry_Solving_for_Pattern.pdf.

CHAPTER 9
GENETICALLY ENGINEERED FOOD

One of the most contentious disputes in food law today concerns foods produced using genetically engineered or edited organisms. Critics worry that such foods are not safe, or at least have not been adequately tested, that they are not environmentally sustainable, that they increase corporate dominance over agriculture, and they believe that these foods should at least be labeled to indicate their provenance. Supporters believe the concerns are overblown, even hysterical, and that genetically modified foods hold promise for addressing world hunger and malnutrition and for reducing dependence on pesticides and herbicides. They worry that labeling these foods will only encourage consumers irrationally to reject them.

Many of these concerns surfaced several years ago in a high-profile battle over California's Proposition 37, which would have required labeling on food made from plants or animals that were genetically engineered and would have prohibited the labeling or advertising of such food as "natural." Opponents reportedly spent some $46 million to defeat the measure; proponents spent $5.5 million to try to pass it. A couple of years later, in the spring of 2014, Vermont became the first state in the nation to pass a stand-alone law requiring labeling of foods containing genetically engineered ingredients. (Connecticut and Maine had earlier passed laws requiring such labeling but only if other states did so as well.) The Vermont law also forbade a food producer to use the term "natural" or other "words of similar import" in labeling and advertising a food product containing bioengineered ingredients. The law was embroiled in litigation within a month of being passed.

In part in response to state laws on labeling food containing bioengineered ingredients, in 2016 Congress passed a law requiring the labeling of bioengineered food. We will discuss this law later in this class.

As you read the materials for this week, consider the charge that opponents of genetic engineering are giving in to irrational fears. Is it possible to describe their concerns more charitably? In this regard, consider pioneering work on risk perception done by the psychologist Paul Slovic, summarized ably as follows by Sara Gorman for The Pump Handle:

> In the 1960s, a rapid rise in nuclear technologies aroused unexpected panic in the public. Despite repeated affirmations from the scientific community that these technologies were indeed safe, the public feared both long-term dangers to the environment as well as

immediate radioactive disasters. The disjunction between the scientific evidence about and public perception of these risks prompted scientists and social scientists to begin research on a crucial question: how do people formulate and respond to notions of risk?

Early research on risk perception assumed that people assess risk in a rational manner, weighing information before making a decision. This approach assumes that providing people with more information will alter their perceptions of risk. Subsequent research has demonstrated that providing more information alone will not assuage people's irrational fears and sometimes outlandish ideas about what is truly risky. The psychological approach to risk perception theory, championed by psychologist Paul Slovic, examines the particular heuristics and biases people invent to interpret the amount of risk in their environment.

In a classic review article published in *Science* in 1987, Slovic summarized various social and cultural factors that lead to inconsistent evaluations of risk in the general public. Slovic emphasizes the essential way in which experts' and laypeople's views of risk differ. Experts judge risk in terms of quantitative assessments of morbidity and mortality. Yet most people's perception of risk is far more complex, involving numerous psychological and cognitive processes. Slovic's review demonstrates the complexity of the general public's assessment of risk through its cogent appraisal of decades of research on risk perception theory....

Slovic masterfully summarizes the key qualitative characteristics that result in judgments that a certain activity is risky or not. People tend to be intolerant of risks that they perceive as being uncontrollable, having catastrophic potential, having fatal consequences, or bearing an inequitable distribution of risks and benefits. Slovic notes that nuclear weapons and nuclear power score high on all of these characteristics. Also unbearable in the public view are risks that are unknown, new, and delayed in their manifestation of harm. These factors tend to be characteristic of chemical technologies in public opinion. The higher a hazard scores on these factors, the higher its perceived risk and the more people want to see the risk reduced, leading to calls for stricter regulation. Slovic ends his review with a nod toward sociological and anthropological studies of risk, noting that anxiety about risk may in some cases be a proxy for other social concerns. Many perceptions of risk are, of course, also socially and culturally informed....

> The goal of this research is a vital one: to aid policy-makers by improving interaction with the public, by better directing educational efforts, and by predicting public responses to new technologies. In the end, Slovic argues that risk management is a two-way street: just as the public should take experts' assessments of risk into account, so should experts respect the various factors, from cultural to emotional, that result in the public's perception of risk.

Might this work on risk perception help to explain the public's reaction to genetic engineering? Does it justify a cautious approach to this technology – or not?

The later days of the Obama administration saw a flurry of activity on the legal implications of the genetic manipulation of plants and animals. The Obama administration updated the federal government's "Coordinated Framework" for products of genetic engineering, emphasizing the importance of interagency coordination, reliance on sound science, and promotion of innovation and growth within the biotechnology industry. The Coordinated Framework, first published in 1986, was notable in its embrace of the idea that existing laws – enacted before the introduction of modern genetic techniques – were adequate for products developed through new techniques for genetic manipulaction.

In its last days in office, the Obama administration also proposed a rule concerning the regulation of genetically engineered organisms as "plant pests," opened a docket for comments on FDA's approach to regulating (or not regulating) the use of genome editing techniques to produce new plant varieties that are used for human or animal food, and issued draft guidance on the regulation of intentionally altered genomic DNA in animals.

The Trump administration's approach to these technologies is not yet clear.

The legal issues surrounding the genetic manipulation of plants and animals for purposes of food production are, in other words, in flux. In this session, we will focus on two sets of issues. One is the treatment of genetically engineered food products as food additives within the meaning of the FDCA. Another is the labeling of food products containing genetically engineered components. Before getting to these legal issues, however, it may be helpful to have a better (even if basic) understanding of the underlying technology. The following discussions, drawn from FDA's website, provide basic information about techniques for genetic engineering, and gives early hints about FDA's general regulatory approach to products made using these techniques.

Food and Drug Administration
Consumer Info About Food From Genetically Engineered Plants

FDA regulates the safety of food for humans and animals, including foods produced from genetically engineered (GE) plants. **Foods from GE plants must meet the same food safety requirements as foods derived from traditionally bred plants**.

While genetic engineering is sometimes referred to as "genetic modification" producing "genetically modified organisms (GMOs)," FDA considers "genetic engineering" to be the more precise term.
Crop improvement happens all the time, and genetic engineering is just one form of it. We use the term "genetic engineering" to refer to genetic modification practices that utilize modern biotechnology. In this process, scientists make targeted changes to a plant's genetic makeup to give the plant a new desirable trait. For example, two new apple varieties have been genetically engineered to resist browning associated with cuts and bruises by reducing levels of enzymes that can cause browning.

Humans have been modifying crops for thousands of years through selective breeding. Early farmers developed cross breeding methods to grow numerous corn varieties with a range of colors, sizes, and uses. For example, the garden strawberries that consumers buy today resulted from a cross between a strawberry species native to North America and a strawberry species native to South America.

Why genetically engineer plants?

Developers genetically engineer plants for many of the same reasons that traditional breeding is used. They may want to create plants with better flavor, higher crop yield (output), greater resistance to insect damage, and immunity to plant diseases.

Traditional breeding involves repeatedly cross-pollinating plants until the breeder identifies offspring with the desired combination of traits. The breeding process introduces a number of genes into the plant. These genes may include the gene responsible for the desired trait, as well as genes responsible for unwanted characteristics.

Genetic engineering isolates the gene for the desired trait, adds it to a single plant cell in a laboratory, and generates a new plant from that cell. By narrowing the introduction to only one desired gene from the donor organism, scientists can eliminate unwanted characteristics from the donor's other genes.

Genetic engineering is often used in conjunction with traditional breeding to produce the genetically engineered plant varieties on the market today.

Am I eating food from genetically engineered plants?

Foods from GE plants were introduced into our food supply in the 1990s. Cotton, corn and soybeans are the most common GE crops grown in the U.S. In 2012, GE soybeans accounted for 93 percent of all soybeans planted, and GE corn accounted for 88 percent of corn planted.

The majority of GE plants are used to make ingredients that are then used in other food products. Such ingredients include:

- Corn starch in soups and sauces
- Corn syrup used as a sweetener
- Corn oil, canola oil and soybean oil in mayonnaise, salad dressings, breads, and snack foods
- Sugar from sugar beets in various foods
-

Other major crops with GE varieties include potatoes, squash, apples, and papayas.

Are foods from GE plants safe to eat?

Yes. Credible evidence has demonstrated that foods from the GE plant varieties marketed to date are as safe as comparable, non-GE foods.

Are Foods from GE plants regulated?

Yes. FDA regulates foods from GE crops in conjunction with the U.S. Department of Agriculture (USDA) and the Environmental Protection Agency (EPA).

FDA enforces the U.S. food safety laws that prohibit unsafe food. GE plants must meet the same legal requirements that apply to all food. To help ensure that firms are meeting their obligation to market only safe and lawful foods, FDA encourages developers of GE plants to consult with the agency before marketing their products.

The mission of USDA's Animal and Plant Health Inspection Service (APHIS) is to safeguard the health, welfare and value of American agriculture and natural resources, including regulating the introduction of certain genetically engineered organisms that may pose a risk to plant health.

EPA regulates pesticides, including those genetically engineered into food crops, to make sure that pesticides are safe for human and animal consumption and won't harm the environment.

How Does FDA Evaluate the Safety of GE Plants?

During the FDA consultation process, the food developer conducts a safety assessment. This safety assessment identifies the distinguishing attributes of the new traits in the plant and assesses whether any new material in food made from the GE plant is safe when eaten by humans or animals. As part of this assessment, the developer compares the levels of nutrients and other components in the food to those in food from traditionally bred plants or other comparable foods.

The developer submits a summary of its safety assessment to FDA for FDA's evaluation. When the safety assessment is received by FDA, our scientists carefully evaluate the data and information. FDA considers the consultation to be complete only when its team of scientists is satisfied that the developer's safety assessment has adequately addressed all safety and other regulatory issues.

Questions & Answers on Food from Genetically Engineered Plants

1. What is genetic engineering?

Genetic engineering is the name for certain methods that scientists use to introduce new traits or characteristics to an organism. For example, plants may be genetically engineered to produce characteristics to enhance the growth or nutritional profile of food crops. While these technique are sometimes referred to as "genetic modification," FDA considers "genetic engineering" to be the more precise term. Food and food ingredients from genetically engineered plants were introduced into our food supply in the 1990s.

2. Are foods from genetically engineered plants regulated by FDA?

Yes. FDA regulates the safety of foods and food products from plant sources including food from genetically engineered plants. This includes animal feed, as under the Federal Food, Drug, and Cosmetic Act, food is defined in relevant part as food for man and other animals. FDA has set up a voluntary consultation process to engage with the developers of genetically engineered plants to help ensure the safety of food from these products.

FDA regulates genetically engineered animals in a different way.

3. Are foods from genetically engineered plants safe?

Foods from genetically engineered plants must meet the same requirements, including safety requirements, as foods from traditionally bred plants. FDA has a consultation process that encourages developers of genetically engineered plants to consult with FDA before marketing their products. This process helps developers determine the necessary steps to ensure their food products are safe and lawful. The goal of the consultation process is to ensure that any safety or other regulatory issues related to a food product are resolved before commercial distribution. Foods from genetically engineered plants intended to be grown in the United States that have been evaluated by FDA through the consultation process have not gone on the market until the FDA's questions about the safety of such products have been resolved.

4. How is the safety of food from a genetically engineered plant evaluated?

Evaluating the safety of food from a genetically engineered plant is a comprehensive process that includes several steps. Generally, the developer identifies the distinguishing attributes of new genetic traits and assesses whether any new material that a person consumed in food made from the genetically engineered plants could be toxic or allergenic. The developer also compares the levels of nutrients in the new genetically engineered plant to traditionally bred plants. This typically includes such nutrients as fiber, protein, fat, vitamins, and minerals. The developer includes this information in a safety assessment, which FDA's Biotechnology Evaluation Team then evaluates for safety and compliance with the law.

FDA teams of scientists knowledgeable in genetic engineering, toxicology, chemistry, nutrition, and other scientific areas as needed carefully evaluate the safety assessments taking into account relevant data and information.

FDA considers a consultation to be complete only when its team of scientists are satisfied with the developer's safety assessment and have no further questions regarding safety or regulatory issues.

5. Why do developers genetically engineer plants and which has FDA evaluated for safety?

Developers genetically engineer plants for many of the same reasons that traditional breeding is used, such as resistance to insect damage, hardiness or enhanced nutrition. As of December 2012, the FDA has completed 95 consultations, most of them on corn. The chart below shows the number of consultations completed as of April 1, 2013 for each of the genetically engineered plants FDA has reviewed. There were 30 submissions on corn, 15 on cotton, 12 each on canola and soybean, and 24 on all other crops including alfalfa, canteloupe, creeping bentgrass, flax, papaya, plum, potato, raddichio, squash, sugar beet, tomato, and wheat.

Figure 1. Numbers of Consultations on Genetically Engineered Crops

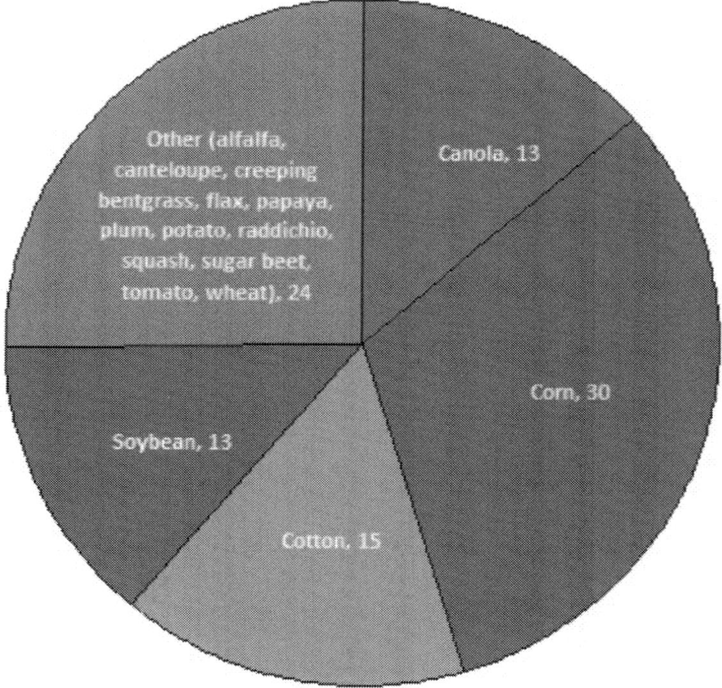

6. Which foods are made from genetically engineered plants?

The majority of genetically engineered plants - corn, canola, soybean, and cotton - are typically used to make ingredients that are then used in other food products. Such ingredients include cornstarch in soups and sauces, corn syrup as a general purpose sweetener, and cottonseed oil, canola oil, and soybean oil in mayonnaise, salad dressings, cereals, breads, and snack foods.

7. Are foods from genetically engineered plants less nutritious than comparable foods?

Nutritional assessments for foods from genetically engineered plants that have been evaluated by FDA through the consultation process have shown that such foods are generally as nutritious as foods from comparable traditionally bred plants.

8. Are foods from genetically engineered plants more likely to (1) cause an allergic reaction or (2) be toxic?

The foods we have evaluated through the consultation process have not been more likely to cause an allergic or toxic reaction than foods from traditionally bred plants. When new genetic traits are introduced into plants, the developer evaluates whether any new material could be (1) allergenic or (2) toxic if consumed in foods made from the genetically engineered plants or from ingredients derived from these plants.

9. Why doesn't FDA require labeling for foods from genetically engineered plants?
FDA recognizes that many consumers are interested in whether food ingredients are derived from genetically engineered plants, and has issued guidance for manufacturers who wish to voluntarily label their foods as containing or not containing such ingredients.

10. Are there long-term health effects of foods from genetically engineered plants?
When evaluating the safety of food from genetically engineered plants, scientists with experience in assessing the long-term safety of food and food ingredients consider several factors, such as information about the long-term safety of the food from traditionally bred crops in combination with information on the food safety of the newly introduced traits. Foods from genetically engineered plants that have been evaluated by FDA through the consultation process have not gone on the market until the FDA's questions about the safety of such products have been resolved.

Note

In thinking through several legal issues relating to biotechnology and food, it will be helpful to recall the FDCA provisions on food additives and misbranding. Is the genetic material that is inserted into bioengineered foods a "food additive"? Are genetically engineered foods that are not labeled as such misbranded?

The document following the FDCA provisions is an FDA policy statement from 1992. It is fair to say that this document helped to usher in the use of genetic engineering in our food system. So pay attention to it!

Food, Drug, and Cosmetic Act

21 U.S.C. §§ 321, 348

SEC. 201. DEFINITIONS

(s) The term "food additive" means any substance the intended use of which results or may reasonably be expected to result, directly or indirectly, in its becoming a component or otherwise affecting the characteristics of any food (including any substance intended for use in producing, manufacturing, packing, processing, preparing, treating, packaging, transporting, or holding food; and including any source of radiation intended for any such use), if such substance is not generally recognized, among experts qualified by scientific training and experience to evaluate its safety, as having been adequately shown through scientific procedures (or, in the case of a substance used in food prior to January 1, 1958, through either scientific procedures or experience based on common use in food) to be safe under the conditions of its intended use...

(n) If an article is alleged to be misbranded because the labeling or advertising is misleading, then in determining whether the labeling or advertising is misleading there shall be taken into account (among other things) not only representations made or suggested by statement, word, design, device, or any combination thereof, but also the extent to which the labeling or advertising fails to reveal facts material in the light of such representations or material with respect to consequences which may result from the use of the article to which the labeling or advertising relates under the conditions of use prescribed in the labeling or advertising thereof or under such conditions of use as are customary or usual.

SEC. 409. FOOD ADDITIVES

(a) A food additive shall, with respect to any particular use or intended use of such additives, be deemed to be unsafe for the purposes of the application of clause (2)(C) of section 402(a), unless—

(1) it and its use or intended use conform to the terms of an exemption which is in effect pursuant to subsection (j) of this section;

(2) there is in effect, and it and its use or intended use are in conformity with, a regulation issued under this section prescribing the conditions under which such additive may be safely used....

Policy Statement: Foods Derived From New Plant Varieties

U.S. Department of Health and Human Services
Food and Drug Administration
57 Fed. Reg. 22984
May 29, 1992

I. Background and Overview of Policy

New methods of genetically modifying plants are being used to develop new varieties that will be sources of foods. These methods, including recombinant DNA techniques and cell fusion techniques, enable developers to make genetic modifications in plants, including some modifications that would not be possible with traditional plant breeding methods. This policy discusses the safety and regulatory status of foods derived from new plant varieties, including plants developed by the newer methods of genetic modification.

FDA has received numerous inquiries from industry, government agencies, academia, and the public requesting clarification of the regulatory status of foods, such as fruits, vegetables, grains and their byproducts, derived from new plant varieties developed using recombinant DNA techniques. The questions that FDA has received center on issues such as whether the agency will conduct premarket review of these new foods, whether such foods introduced into interstate commerce would be challenged by FDA on legal grounds, which new plant varieties might come under the jurisdiction of FDA, what scientific information may be necessary to satisfy FDA that such foods are safe and comply with the law, whether petitions would be required by the agency, and whether special labeling would be required.

Representatives of the food biotechnology industry have expressed to FDA the need for strong but appropriate oversight by Federal agencies to ensure public confidence in foods produced by the new techniques. FDA has received several specific comments and suggestions from the industry and from the public concerning Federal oversight of foods developed through new methods of genetically modifying plants. The agency has considered these and other documents, including scientific research papers, in developing this notice, and is setting forth this policy statement to clarify its interpretation of the act with respect to human foods...derived from new plant varieties, including but not limited to plants developed by new methods of genetic modification.[3]

---

[3] "Genetic modification" means the alteration of the genotype of a plant using any

Under this policy, foods, such as fruits, vegetables, grains, and their by-products, derived from plant varieties developed by the new methods of genetic modification are regulated within the existing framework of the act, FDA's implementing regulations, and current practice, utilizing an approach identical in principle to that applied to foods developed by traditional plant breeding. The regulatory status of a food, irrespective of the method by which it is developed, is dependent upon objective characteristics of the food and the intended use of the food (or its components). The method by which food is produced or developed may in some cases help to understand the safety or nutritional characteristics of the finished food. However, the key factors in reviewing safety concerns should be the characteristics of the food product, rather than the fact that the new methods are used.

The safety of a food is regulated primarily under FDA's postmarket authority of section 402(a)(1) of the act. Unintended occurrences of unsafe levels of toxicants in food are regulated under this section. Substances that are expected to become components of food as result of genetic modification of a plant and whose composition is such or has been altered such that the substance is not generally recognized as safe (GRAS) or otherwise exempt are subject to regulation as "food additives" under section 409 of the act. Under the act, substances that are food additives may be used in food only in accordance with an authorizing regulation.

In most cases, the substances expected to become components of food as a result of genetic modification of a plant will be the same as or substantially similar to substances commonly found in food, such as proteins, fats and oils, and carbohydrates. As discussed in more detail in section V.C., FDA has determined that such substances should be subject to regulation under section 409 of the act in those cases when the objective characteristics of the substance raise questions of safety sufficient to warrant formal premarket review and approval by FDA. The objective characteristics that will trigger regulation of substances as food additives are described in the guidance section of this notice (section VII).

---

technique, new or traditional. "Modification" is used in a broad context to mean the alteration in the composition of food that results from adding, deleting, or changing hereditary traits, irrespective of the method. Modifications may be minor, such as a single mutation that affects one gene, or major alterations of genetic material that affect many genes. Most, if not all, cultivated food crops have been genetically modified.

The guidance section also describes scientific considerations that are important in evaluating the safety and nutritional value of foods for consumption by humans or animals, regardless of whether the food is regulated under section 402(a)(1) or section 409 of the act. The guidance section outlines a "decision tree" approach to safety assessment of foods derived from new plant varieties that FDA believes is compatible with current practice among scientists knowledgeable in this area. The guidance section also identifies certain scientific questions that may raise sufficient safety concern to warrant consultation with FDA....

II. Responsibility for Food Safety

FDA is the primary Federal agency responsible for ensuring the safety of commerical food and food additives, except meat and poultry products. FDA works closely on food safety matters with the U.S. Department of Agriculture (USDA), which regulates meat and poultry products, and with the U.S. Environmental Protection Agency (EPA), which regulates pesticides and sets tolerances for pesticide residues in food. FDA's authority is under the act, the Public Health Service Act, and FDA's implementing regulations codified in title 21 of the CFR. The act gives FDA broad authority to initiate legal action against a food that is adulterated or misbranded within the meaning of the act.

Producers of new foods have an obligation under the act to ensure that the foods they offer consumers are safe and in compliance with applicable legal requirements. Because in some cases the regulatory jurisdiction of a new food product including those produced using innovative methods may not be clear, producers can informally consult with FDA prior to marketing new foods to ensure that the safety and regulatory status of a new food is properly resolved.

Elsewhere in this issue of the Federal Register, FDA announces the filing of the first request by a producer for consultation with FDA concerning a new plant variety developed by recombinant DNA techniques. The request submitted by Calgene, Inc., (Calgene) concerns the FLAVR SAVR TM tomato, a new variety claimed to exhibit improved fruit ripening and other properties. Because Calgene made this request prior to the finalization of this policy statement, FDA advised the firm to submit the information about the tomato initially as a request for advisory opinion under §10.85 (21 CFR 10.85) to permit the agency to consider the status of the new variety, and to utilize an evaluation process that is open to public comment and permits the agency to make its decision known to the public. Future requests for FDA consultation should be made consistent with the principles outlined in this notice. Thus, FDA does not anticipate that future requests of this nature will be filed under §10.85.

III. Scope of This Document

This notice discusses scientific and regulatory considerations for foods derived from new plant varieties. This notice does not address foods and food ingredients regulated by FDA that have been derived from algae, microorganisms, and other nonplant organisms, including: (1) Foods produced by fermentation, where microorganisms are essential components of the food (e.g., yogurt and single cell protein); (2) food ingredients produced by fermentation, such as many enzymes, flavors, amino acids, sweeteners, thickeners, antioxidants, preservatives, colors, and other substances; (3) substances produced by new plant varieties whose purpose is to color food, and (4) foods derived from animals that are subject to FDA's authority, including seafood. FDA is considering whether to address these issues in future Federal Register notices....

IV. Scientific Issues Relevant to Public Health

Plant breeding is the science of combining desirable genetic traits into a variety that can be used in agriculture. The desired traits can be broadly divided into two classes: Those that affect agronomic characteristics of the plant, and those that affect quality characteristics of the food. Agronomic characteristics include those affecting yield; resistance to diseases, insects, and herbicides; and ability to thrive under various adverse environmental conditions. Quality characteristics include those affecting processing, preservation, nutrition, and flavor.

The genetic modification techniques used to develop new plant varieties constitute a continuum. Traditional breeding typically consists of hybridization between varieties of the same species and screening for progeny with desired characteristics. Such hybridizations only can introduce traits found in close relatives. Breeders have developed or adopted a number of techniques to expand the range of genetic variation available to them. These techniques introduce variation either by using mutagenesis to alter the genome or by introducing or modifying DNA segments, including DNA segments derived from other organisms....

Regardless of the particular combination of techniques used, the development of a new plant variety typically will require many site-years (number of sites x number of years of plant testing) of performance trials before introduction into agricultural practice. These range from as few as 10 to 20 site-years for some plants to 75 to 100 site-years for others (some 5 to 10 years). The time of evaluation and the size and number of sites will vary as necessary to confirm performance; to reveal vulnerabilities to pests, diseases, or other production hazards; to evaluate stability of the phenotype; to evaluate characteristics of the food; to evaluate environmental effects; and to produce the required amount of seed before the new plant variety can be grown commercially by farmers. In the course of this intensive assessment, individual plants exhibiting undesirable traits are eliminated.

Recombinant DNA techniques are used to achieve the same types of goals as traditional techniques: The development of new plant varieties with enhanced agronomic and quality characteristics. Currently, over 30 different agricultural crops developed using recombinant DNA techniques are in field trials. Food crops have been developed using these techniques to exhibit improved resistance to pests and disease and to chemical herbicides. For example, a plant's ability to resist insect infestation reportedly has been improved by transferring bacterial genetic material that encodes proteins toxic to certain insects (e.g., *Bacillus thuringiensis delta* endotoxin). Other plants have been given viral coat-protein genes that confer cross-protection to viral pathogens.

Other new plant varieties have been developed that exhibit traits for improved food processing, improved nutritional content, or enhanced protection against adverse weather conditions. For example, genetic modifications of plant enzymes involved in fruit ripening may yield tomatoes with improved ripening characteristics, texture, and flavor. Scientists have used recombinant DNA techniques to transfer genetic material for the production of seed storage protein conferring improvements in nutritional balance of important amino acids in the new plant varieties. Scientists have also identified genes in certain fish that encode proteins that confer increased resistance to cold. Copies of these genes have been introduced into agricultural crops with the goal of producing new plant varieties that show improved tolerance to cold weather conditions.

These examples illustrate only a few of the many improved agronomic and food processing traits currently being introduced into plants using recombinant DNA techniques. Any genetic modification technique has the potential to alter the composition of food in a manner relevant to food safety, although, based on experience, the likelihood of a safety hazard is typically very low. The following paragraphs describe some potential changes in composition that may require evaluation to assure food safety.

A. Unexpected Effects

Virtually all breeding techniques have potential to create unexpected (including pleiotropic[5] effects. For example, mutations unrelated to the desired modification may be induced; undesirable traits may be introduced along with the desired traits; newly introduced DNA may physically insert into a transcriptionally active site on the chromosome, and may thereby inactivate a host gene or alter control of its expression; the introduced gene product or a metabolic product affected by the genetic change may interact with other cellular products to produce a deleterious effect. Plant breeders using well established practices have successfully identified and eliminated plants that exhibit unexpected, adverse traits prior to commercial use.

B. Known Toxicants

Plants are known to produce naturally a number of toxicants and antinutritional factors, such as protease inhibitors, hemolytic agents, and neurotoxins, which often serve the plant as natural defense compounds against pests or pathogens. For example, most cereals contain protease inhibitors, which can diminish the nutritive value of proteins. Many legumes contain relatively high levels of lectins and cyanogenic glycosides. Lectins, if not destroyed by cooking or removed by soaking, can cause severe nausea, vomiting, and diarrhea. Cyanogenic glycosides can be hydrolyzed by specific enzymes in the plant to release cyanide if food from the plant is improperly prepared. The levels of cyanogenic glycosides in cassava and some legumes can lead to death or chronic neurological disease if these foods are eaten uncooked. Cruciferae contain glucosinolates which may impair thyroid function. Squash and cucumber contain cucurbiticin, an acute toxicant. Chickpeas contain lathyrogens, which are neurotoxins.

Many of these toxicants are present in today's foods at levels that do not cause acute toxicity. Others, such as in cassava and some legumes, are high enough to cause severe illness or death if the foods are not properly prepared. FDA seek to assure that new plant varieties do not have significantly higher levels of toxicants than present in other edible varieties of the same species.

Plants, like other organisms, have metabolic pathways that no longer function due to mutations that occurred during evolution. Products or intermediates of some such pathways may include toxicants. In rare cases,

---

[5] Pleiotropic effects refer to multiple effects resulting from a single genetic change.

such silent pathways may be activated by mutations, chromosomal rearrangements, or new regulatory regions introduced during breeding, and toxicants hitherto not associated with a plant species may thereby be produced. Similarly, toxicants ordinarily produced at low levels in a plant may be produced at high levels in a new variety as a result of such occurrences. The likelihood of activation of quiescent pathways or increased expression from active pathways is considered extremely low in food plants with a long history of use that have never exhibited production of unknown or unexpected toxins, since the genetic changes that can lead to such events occur during growth and are induced with traditional breeding manipulations. In the few cases where toxicants have been raised to unsafe levels in a commercial plant variety, the toxicants were known to occur in significant levels in one of the parent species. Except in rare cases, plant breeders using well established practices have successfully identified and eliminated plants that express unacceptably high levels of toxicants prior to commercial use.

C. Nutrients

Another unintended consequence of genetic modification of the plant may be a significant alteration in levels of important nutrients. In addition, changes in bioavailability of a nutrient due to changes in form of the nutrient or the presence of increased levels of other constituents that affect absorption or metabolism of nutrients must be considered for potential nutritional impact.

D. New Substances

Because plant breeders using the new techniques are able to introduce essentially any trait or substance whose molecular genetic identity is known into virtually any plant, it is possible to introduce a protein that differs significantly in structure or function, or to modify a carbohydrate, fat or oil, such that it differs significantly in composition from such substances currently found in food.

E. Allergenicity

All food allergens are proteins. However, only a small fraction of the thousands of proteins in the diet have been found to be food allergens. FDA's principal concern regarding allergencity is that proteins transferred from one food source to another, as is possible with recombinant DNA and protoplast fusion techniques, might confer on food from the host plant the allergenic properties of food from the donor plant. Thus, for example, the introduction of a gene that encodes a peanut allergen into corn might make that variety of corn newly allergenic to people ordinarily allergic to peanuts.

Examples of foods that commonly cause an allergenic response are milk, eggs, fish, crustacea, molluscs, tree nuts, wheat, and legumes (particularly peanuts and soybeans). The sensitive population is ordinarily able to identify and avoid the offending food. However, if the allergen were moved into a variety of a plant species that never before produced that allergen, the susceptible population would not know to avoid food from that variety.

In some foods that commonly cause an allergic response, the particular protein(s) responsible for allergenicity is known, and therefore the producer may know whether the transferred protein is the allergen. However, in other cases, the protein responsible for a food's allergenicity is not known, and FDA considers it prudent practice for the producer initially to assume that the transferred protein is the allergen. Appropriate in vitro or in vivo allergenicity testing may reveal whether food from the new variety elicits an allergenic response in the potentially sensitive population (i.e., people sensitive to the food in which the protein is ordinarily found). Producers of such foods should discuss allergenicity testing protocol requirements with the agency. Labeling of foods newly containing a known or suspect allergen may be needed to inform consumers of such potential.

A separate issue is whether any new protein in food has the potential to be allergenic to a segment of the population. At this time, FDA is unaware of any practical method of predict or assess the potential for new proteins in food to induce allergenicity and requests comments on this issue.

F. Antibiotic Resistance Selectable Markers

In gene transfer experiments, only a small percentage of the recipient plant cells will actually take up the introduced genes, and many desirable traits (i.e., those that specify the intended technical effect) are not easy to detect before the plant has fully developed. Scientists, therefore, enhance their ability to isolate plant cells that have taken up and stably incorporated the desired genes by physically linking the desired gene to a selectable marker gene, such as a gene that specifies the production of a substance that inactivates antibiotics.

The kanamycin resistance gene is one of the most widely used selectable marker genes. The kanamycin resistance gene specifies the information for the production of the enzyme, aminoglycoside 3'-phosphotransferase II. The common name for this enzyme is kanamycin (or neomycin) phosphotransferase II. The kanamycin phosphotransferase II enzyme modifies aminoglycoside antibiotics, including kanamycin, neomycin, and geneticin (G418), chemically inactivating the antibiotic and rendering the cells that produce the kanamycin resistance gene product refractory or resistant to the antibiotic. Plant cells that have received and stably express the kanamycin resistance gene survive and replicate on laboratory media in the presence of the antibiotic, kanamycin. Plant cells that did not take up and express the introduced kanamycin resistance gene will be killed by the antibiotic. By linking the selectable marker gene to another gene that specifies a desired trait, scientists can identify and select plants that have taken up and express the desired genes.

The kanamycin resistance gene has been used as a selectable marker in more than 30 crops to develop varieties that exhibit improved nutritional and processing properties, resistance to pests and diseases, tolerance to chemical herbicides, and other agronomic properties. Once the desired plant variety has been selected, the kanamycin resistance gene serves no further useful purpose, although it continues to produce the kanamycin phosphotransferase II enzyme in the plant tissues. Thus, while the kanamycin resistance gene is a research tool that is important for developing new plant varieties through the current recombinant DNA techniques of gene transfer, both the kanamycin resistance gene and its product, the kanamycin phosphotransferase II enzyme protein, are expected to be present in foods derived from such plants, unless removed through recently developed techniques.

Selectable marker genes that produce enzymes that inactivate clinically useful antibiotics theoretically may reduce the therapeutic efficacy of the antibiotic when taken orally if the enzyme in the food inactives the antibiotic. FDA believes that it will be important to evaluate such concerns with respect to commercial use of antibiotic resistance marker genes in food, especially those that will be widely used. FDA is now evaluating this and other issues with respect to the use of the kanamycin resistance marker in food.

G. Plants Developed to Make Specialty Nonfood Substances

New genetic modification techniques may develop plants that produce nonfood chemicals, such as polymers and pharmaceuticals. In many cases, the plant will not subsequently be used for food. In such cases, the developer must ensure that food-use varieties of the crop do not cross with or become mixed with the nonfood-use varieties. This is not a new issue for breeders and growers. For example, some varieties of rapeseed oil are grown for industrial oil use, and have high levels of toxicants, such as erucic acid and glucosinylates, while other varieties are grown for food use and have low levels of these substances. Similarly, potatoes grown for industrial uses can have higher levels of solanine than those grown for retail food use. The producer of the oil or potato must ensure that the edible plant variety is not adulterated within the meaning of the act. Developers of crops designed to produce specialty nonfood substances have a comparable obligation.

If plants (or materials derived from plants) used to make nonfood chemicals are also intended to be used for food, producers should consult with FDA to determine whether the nonfood chemical would be a food additive requiring an authorizing regulation prior to marketing for food use....

V. Regulatory Status of Foods Derived From New Plant Varieties

A. The Statutory Framework for New Foods and Food Ingredients

The United States today has a food supply that is as safe as any in the world. Most foods derived from plants predate the establishment of national food laws, and the safety of these foods has been accepted based on extensive use and experience over many years (or even centuries). Foods derived from new plant varieties are not routinely subjected to scientific tests for safety, although there are exceptions. For example, potatoes are generally tested for the glycoalkaloid, solanine. The established practices that plant breeders employ in selecting and developing new varieties of plants, such as chemical analyses, taste testing, and visual analyses, rely primarily on observations of quality, wholesomeness, and agronomic characteristics. Historically, these practices have proven to be reliable for ensuring food safety. The knowledge from this past experience coupled with safe practices in plant breeding has contributed to continuous improvements in the quality, variety, nutritional value, and safety of foods derived from plants modified by a range of traditional and increasingly sophisticated techniques (Ref. 1 at xvi). Based on this record of safe development of new varieties of plants, FDA has not found it necessary to conduct, prior to marketing, routine safety reviews of whole foods derived from plants.

Nevertheless, FDA has ample authority under the act's food safety provisions to regulate and ensure the safety of foods derived from new plant varieties, including plants developed by new techniques. This includes authority to require, where necessary, a premarket safety review by FDA prior to marketing of the food. Under section 402(a)(1) of the act, a food is deemed adulterated and thus unlawful if it bears or contains an added poisonous or deleterious substance that may render the food injurious to health or a naturally occurring substance that is ordinarily injurious. Section 402(a)(1) of the act imposes a legal duty on those who introduce food into the market place, including food derived from new crop varieties, to ensure that the food satisfies the applicable safety standard. Foods that are adulterated under section 402(a)(1) of the act are subject to the full range of enforcement measures under the act, including seizure, injunction, and criminal prosecution of those who fail to meet their statutory duty.

FDA has relied almost exclusively on section 402(a)(1) of the act to ensure the safety of whole foods. Toxins that occur naturally in food and that render the food ordinarily injurious to health (such as poisons in certain mushrooms), and thus adulterated, rarely required FDA regulatory action because such cases are typically well known and carefully avoided by food producers.

FDA regards any substance that is not an inherent constituent of food or whose level in food has been increased by human intervention to be "added" within the meaning of section 402(a)(1) of the act. See United States v. Anderson Seafoods, Inc., 622 F. 2d 157 (5th Cir. 1980). Added substances are subject to the more stringent "may render [the food] injurious" safety standard. Under this standard, the food is adulterated if, by virtue of the presence of the added substance, there is a "reasonable possibility" that consumption of the food will be injurious to health. United States v. Lexington Mill & Elevator Co., 232 U.S. 399 (1914). The "may render injurious" standard would apply to a naturally occurring toxin in food if the level of the toxin in a new plant variety were increased through traditional plant breeding or some other human intervention. Section 402(a)(1) of the act would have been the legal basis under which FDA could have blocked marketing in the 1970's of a new variety of potato that had been found during its development to contain elevated and potentially harmful levels of solanine as a result of a cross with an inedible wild potato.

Section 402(a)(1) of the act is most frequently used by FDA to regulate the presence in food of unavoidable environmental contaminants such as lead, mercury, dioxin, and aflatoxin. FDA regularly establishes action levels and takes enforcement action to prevent the sale of foods that contain unacceptable levels of such unintended and undesired contaminants.

Section 402(a)(1) of the act was signed into law in 1938 and has its origins in a similar provision in the Federal Food and Drugs Act of 1906. Until 1958, this authority was the principal tool relied upon by FDA to regulate the safety of food and food ingredients. In 1958, in response to public concern about the increased use of chemicals in foods and food processing and with the support of the food industry, Congress enacted the Food Additives Amendment (the amendment) to the act. Among other provisions, the amendment established a premarket approval requirement for "food additives." The basic thrust of the amendment was to require that, before a new chemical additive (such as a preservative, antioxidant, emulsifier, or artificial flavor) could be used in food processing, its producer must demonstrate the safety of the additive to FDA. Congress recognized under this new scheme that the safety of an additive could not be established with absolute certainty or under all conditions of use. Congress thus provided for a science-based safety standard that requires producers of food additives to demonstrate to a reasonable certainty that no harm will result from the intended use of the additive. See 21 CFR 170.3(i). If FDA finds an additive to be safe, based ordinarily on data submitted by the producer to the agency in a food additive petition, the agency promulgates a regulation specifying the conditions under which the additive may be safely used. Food additives that are not the subject of such a regulation are deemed unsafe as a matter of law, and the foods containing them are adulterated under section 402(a)(2)(C) of the act and are thus unlawful.

In enacting the amendment, Congress recognized that many substances intentionally added to food do not require a formal premarket review by FDA to assure their safety, either because their safety had been established by a long history of use in food or because the nature of the substance and the information generally available to scientists about the substance are such that the substance simply does not raise a safety concern worthy of premarket review by FDA. Congress thus adopted a two-step definition of "food additive." The first step broadly includes any substance the intended use of which results in its becoming a component of food. The second step, however, excludes from the definition of food additive substances that are GRAS. It is on the basis of the GRAS exception of the "food additive" definition that many ingredients derived from natural sources (such as salt, pepper, vinegar, vegetable oil, and thousands of spices and natural flavors), as well as a host of chemical additives (including some sweeteners, preservatives, and artificial flavors), are able to be lawfully marketed today without having been formally reviewed by FDA and without being the subject of a food additive regulation. The judgment of Congress was that subjecting every intentional additive to FDA premarket review was not necessary to protect public health and would impose an insurmountable burden on FDA and the food industry.

Congress' approach to defining food additives means, however, that companies developing new ingredients, new versions of established ingredients, or new processes for producing a food or food ingredient must make a judgment about whether the resulting food substance is a food additive requiring premarket approval by FDA. In many cases, the answer is obvious, such as when the ingredient is a man made chemical having no widely recognized history of safe use in food. Such an ingredient must be approved prior to its use by the issuance of a food additive regulation, based on information submitted to FDA in a food additive petition.

In other cases, the answer is less obvious, such as when an established ingredient derived from nature is modified in some minor way or produced by a new process. In such cases, the manufacturer must determine whether the resulting ingredient still falls within the scope of any existing food additive regulation applicable to the original ingredient or whether the ingredient is exempt from regulation as a food additive because it is GRAS. The GRAS status of some substances is recognized in FDA's regulations (21 CFR parts 182, 184, 186, 582, and 584), but FDA has not attempted to include all GRAS substances in its regulations.

FDA has traditionally encouraged producers of new food ingredients to consult with FDA when there is a question about an ingredient's regulatory status, and firms routinely do so, even though such consultation is not legally required. If the producer begins to market the ingredient based on the producer's independent determination that the substance is GRAS and FDA subsequently concludes the substance is not GRAS, the agency can and will take enforcement action to stop distribution of the ingredient and foods containing it on the ground that such foods are or contain an unlawful food additive.

FDA considers the existing statutory authority under sections 402(a)(1) and 409 of the act, and the practical regulatory regime that flows from it, to be fully adequate to ensure the safety of new food ingredients and foods derived from new varieties of plants, regardless of the process by which such foods and ingredients are produced. The existing tools provide this assurance because they impose a clear legal duty on producers to assure the safety of foods they offer to consumers; this legal duty is backed up by strong enforcement powers; and FDA has authority to require premarket review and approval in cases where such review is required to protect public health.

In the Federal Register of June 26, 1986 (51 FR 23302) (the June 1986 notice), FDA, in conjunction with the Office of Science and Technology Policy in the Executive Office of the President, described FDA's current food safety authorities and stated the agency's intention to regulate foods produced by new methods, such as recombinant DNA techniques, within the existing statutory and regulatory framework. This notice reaffirms that intention. The following paragraphs explain briefly how the current framework will apply specifically to foods derived from new plant varieties, including plants developed by recombinant DNA techniques.

B. The Application of Section 402(a)(1) of the Act

Section 402(a)(1) of the act will continue to be FDA's primary legal tool for regulating the safety of whole foods, including foods derived from plants genetically modified by the new techniques. Section 402(a)(1) of the act will be applied to any substance that occurs unexpectedly in the food at a level that may be injurious to health. This includes a naturally occurring toxicant whose level is unintentionally increased by the genetic modification, as well as an unexpected toxicant that first appears in the food as a result of pleiotropic effects. Such substances are regarded by FDA as added substances whose presence adulterates the food if present at a level that "may render" the food injurious to health.

It is the responsibility of the producer of a new food to evaluate the safety of the food and assure that the safety requirement of section 402(a)(1) of the act is met. In section VII., FDA provides guidance to the industry regarding prudent, scientific approaches to evaluating the safety of foods derived from new plant varieties, including the safety of the added substances that are subject to section 402(a)(1) of the act. FDA encourages informal consultation between producers and FDA scientists to ensure that safety concerns are resolved. However, producers remain legally responsible for satisfying section 402(a)(1) of the act, and they will continue to be held accountable by FDA through application of the agency's enforcement powers.

C. The Application of Section 409 of the Act

When Congress enacted the amendment in 1958, it did not explicitly address the possible application of the food additive approval process to foods derived from new plant varieties. As previously discussed, such foods have historically been regulated successfully under section 402(a)(1) of the act. The new methods of genetic modification have focused attention, however, on the possibility that intended changes in the composition of food resulting from genetic modification might be of a nature sufficient as a legal and public health matter to trigger regulation of a component of the food under section 409 of the act.

As discussed above, the food additive definition broadly encompasses any substance that has an intended use in food, unless the substance is GRAS. It was on this basis that the June 1986 notice indicated that, in some cases, whole foods derived from new plant varieties, including plants developed by new genetic modification techniques, might fall within the scope of FDA's food additive authority. Indeed, FDA's regulations have long recognized that it might be appropriate in some circumstances to review the

GRAS (and implicitly food additive) status of foods or substances of natural biological origin that have a history of safe use but which subsequently have had "significant alteration by breeding and selection." (See 21 CFR 170.30(f).) As already discussed, however, FDA has rarely had occasion to review the GRAS status of foods derived from new plant varieties because these foods have been widely recognized and accepted as safe.

FDA has reviewed its position on the applicability of the food additive definition and section 409 of the act to foods derived from new plant varieties in light of the intended changes in the composition of foods that might result from the newer techniques of genetic modification. The statutory definition of "food additive" makes clear that it is the intended or expected introduction of a substance into food that makes the substance potentially subject to food additive regulation. Thus, in the case of foods derived from new plant varieties, it is the transferred genetic material and the intended expression product or products that could be subject to food additive regulation, if such material or expression products are not GRAS.

In regulating foods and their byproducts derived from new plant varieties, FDA intends to use its food additive authority to the extent necessary to protect public health. Specifically, consistent with the statutory definition of "food additive" and the overall design of FDA's current food safety regulatory program, FDA will use section 409 of the act to require food additive petitions in cases where safety questions exist sufficient to warrant formal premarket review by FDA to ensure public health protection.

With respect to transferred genetic material (nucleic acids), generally FDA does not anticipate that transferred genetic material would itself be subject to food additive regulation. Nucleic acids are present in the cells of every living organism, including every plant and animal used for food by humans or animals, and do not raise a safety concern as a component of food. In regulatory terms, such material is presumed to be GRAS. Although the guidance provided in section VII calls for a good understanding of the identity of the genetic material being transferred through genetic modification techniques, FDA does not expect that there will be any serious question about the GRAS status of transferred genetic material.

FDA expects that the intended expression product or products present in foods derived from new plant varieties will typically be proteins or substances produced by the action of protein enzymes, such as carbohydrates, and fats and oils. When the substance present in the food is one that is already present at generally comparable or greater levels in currently consumed foods, there is unlikely to be a safety question sufficient to call into question the presumed GRAS status of such naturally occurring substances and thus warrant formal premarket review and approval by FDA. Likewise, minor variations in molecular structure that do not affect safety would not ordinarily affect the GRAS status of the substances and, thus, would not ordinarily require regulation of the substance as a food additive.

It is possible, however, that the intended expression product in a food could be a protein, carbohydrate, fat or oil, or other substance that differs significantly in structure, function, or composition from substances found currently in food. Such substances may not be GRAS and may require regulation as a food additive. For example, if a food derived from a new plant variety contains a novel protein sweetener as a result of the genetic modification of the plant, that sweetener would likely require submission of a food additive petition and approval by FDA prior to marketing. FDA invites comments on substances, in addition to proteins, carbohydrates, and fats and oils, that in the future may be introduced into foods by genetic modification.

Section VII of this notice provides guidance to producers of new foods for conducting safety evaluations. This guidance is intended to assist producers in evaluating the safety of the food that they market, regardless of whether the food requires premarket approval by FDA. This guidance also includes criteria and analytical steps that producers can follow in determining whether their product is a candidate for food additive regulation and whether consultation with FDA should be pursued to determine the regulatory status of the product. Ultimately, it is the food producer who is responsible for assuring safety.

FDA has long regarded it to be a prudent practice for producers of foods using new technologies to work cooperatively with the agency to ensure that the new products are safe and comply with applicable legal requirements. It has been the general practice of the food industry to seek informal consultation and cooperation, and this practice should continue with respect to foods produced using the newer techniques of genetic modification.

VI. Labeling

FDA has received several inquiries concerning labeling requirements for foods derived from new plant varieties developed by recombinant DNA techniques. Section 403(i) of the act (21 U.S.C. 343(i)) requires that a producer of a food product describe the product by its common or usual name or in the absence thereof, an appropriately descriptive term (21 U.S.C. part 101.3) and reveal all facts that are material in light of representations made or suggested by labeling or with respect to consequences which may result from use (21 U.S.C. 343(a); 21 U.S.C. 321(n)). Thus, consumers must be informed, by appropriate labeling, if a food derived from a new plant variety differs from its traditional counterpart such that the common or usual name no longer applies to the new food, or if a safety or usage issue exists to which consumers must be alerted.

For example, if a tomato has had a peanut protein introduced into it and there is insufficient information to demonstrate that the introduced protein could not cause an allergic reaction in a susceptible population, a label declaration would be required to alert consumers who are allergic to peanuts so they could avoid that tomato, even if its basic taste and texture remained unchanged. Such information would be a material fact whose omission may make the label of the tomato misleading under section 403(a) of the act (21 U.S.C. 343(a)).

FDA has also been asked whether foods developed using techniques such as recombinant DNA techniques would be required to bear special labeling to reveal that fact to consumers. To date, FDA has not considered the methods used in the development of a new plant variety (such as hybridization, chemical or radiation-induced mutagenesis, protoplast fusion, embryo rescue, somaclonal variation, or any other method) to be material information within the meaning of section 201(n) of the act. As discussed above, FDA believes that the new techniques are extensions at the molecular level of traditional methods and will be used to achieve the same goals as pursued with traditional plant breeding. The agency is not aware of any information showing that foods derived by these new methods differ from other foods in any meaningful or uniform way, or that, as a class, foods developed by the new techniques present any different or greater safety concern than foods developed by traditional plant breeding. For this reason, the agency does not believe that the method of development of a new plant variety (including the use of new techniques including recombinant DNA techniques) is normally material information within the meaning of 21 U.S.C. 321(n) and would not usually be required to be disclosed in labeling for the food....

VII. Guidance to Industry for Foods Derived From New Plant Varieties

A. Introduction

This guidance section describes many of the scientific considerations for evaluating the safety and nutritional aspects of food from new plant varieties derived by traditional methods (such as hybridization or mutagenesis), tissue culture methods (such as somaclonal variation and protoplast fusion), and recombinant DNA methods. Although some of the safety considerations are specific to individual technologies, many safety considerations are similar regardless of the technology used. This guidance section does not attempt to delineate acceptable practices for each specific technology. FDA expects plant breeders to adhere to currently accepted scientific standards of practice within each technology. This guidance section is based on existing practices followed by the traditional plant breeders to assess the safety and nutritional value of new plant varieties and is not intended to alter these long-established practices, or to create new regulatory obligations for them.

This guidance section describes food safety and nutritional concerns, rather than performance characteristics for which the new plant varieties may have been developed. However, this guidance section cannot identify all safety and nutritional questions that could arise in a given situation and, while comprehensive, should not be viewed as exhaustive. In some cases, additional factors may need to be considered, while in other situations, some of the factors may not apply. Therefore, this guidance section also describes situations in which producers should consult with FDA on scientific issues, the design of appropriate test protocols, requirements for labeling, and whether a food additive petition may be required.

Genetic modifications of plants can have unintended or unexpected effects on the phenotype of the plant, such as poor growth or reduced tolerance to conditions of environmental stress, that are readily apparent and can be effectively managed by appropriate selection procedures. However, effects such as an alteration in the concentration of important nutrients, increases in the level of natural toxicants, or the transfer of allergens from one species to another may not be readily detected without specific test procedures. FDA believes that a scientific basis should exist to establish that new plant varieties do not exhibit unacceptable effects with respect to toxicants, nutritional value, or allergens. In cases where the host plant has little or no history of safe use, the assessment of new plant varieties should include evidence that unknown toxicants are not present in the new plant variety at levels that would be injurious to health.

In addition, by using recombinant DNA techniques, plant breeders are now capable theoretically of introducing essentially any trait (and thus substance) whose molecular genetic identity is known into virtually any plant due to the increased power and precision of recombinant DNA techniques. This guidance section, however, discusses only proteins, carbohydrates, and fats and oils, in the belief that these are the principal substances that are currently being intentionally modified or introduced into new plant varieties. Using the new techniques, it is possible to introduce a gene that encodes a protein that differs significantly in structure or function, or to modify a carbohydrate, or fat or oil, such that it differs significantly in composition from such substances currently found in food. FDA believes that plant breeders must carefully evaluate the potential for adverse effects that could result from the presence of these substances in new plant varieties.

Theoretically, genetic modifications have the potential to activate cryptic pathways synthesizing unknown or unexpected toxicants, or to increase expression from active pathways that ordinarily produce low or undetectable levels of toxicants. However, this potential has been effectively managed in the past by sound agricultural practices. The agency believes that the use of host plants with a history of safe use, coupled with a continuation of sound agricultural practice, will minimize the potential for adverse public health consequences that may arise from increased levels of unknown or unexpected toxicants.

This guidance section provides a basis for determining whether new plant varieties are as safe and nutritious as their parental varieties. The assessment scheme focuses on characteristics of the new plant variety, based on characteristics of the host and donor species, the nature of the genetic change, the identity and function of newly introduced substances, and unexpected or unintended effects that accompany the genetic change. The assessment focuses on the following considerations:

1. Toxicants known to be characteristic of the host and donor species;
2. The potential that food allergens will be transferred from one food source to another;
3. The concentration and bioavailability of important nutrients for which a food crop is ordinarily consumed;
4. The safety and nutritional value of newly introduced proteins; and
5. The identity, composition and nutritional value of modified carbohydrates, or fats and oils.

The scientific concepts described in this guidance section are consistent with the concepts of substantial equivalence of new foods discussed in a document under development by the Group of National Experts on Safety in Biotechnology of the Organization for Economic Cooperation and Development (OECD). This guidance section is also consistent with the principles for food safety assessment discussed in the Report of a Joint Food and Agriculture Organization/World Health Organization Consultation....

Alliance for Bio-Integrity v. Shalala

116 F. Supp. 2d 166 (D.D.C. 2000)

KOLLAR-KOTELLY, District Judge.

Technological advances have dramatically increased our ability to manipulate our environment, including the foods we consume. One of these advances, recombinant deoxyribonucleic acid (rDNA) technology, has enabled scientists to alter the genetic composition of organisms by mixing genes on the cellular and molecular level in order to create new breeds of plants for human and animal consumption. These new breeds may be designed to repel pests, retain their freshness for a longer period of time, or contain more intense flavor and/or nutritional value. Much controversy has attended such developments in biotechnology, and in particular the production, sale, and trade of genetically modified organisms and foods. The above-captioned lawsuit represents one articulation of this controversy.

Among Plaintiffs, some fear that these new breeds of genetically modified food could contain unexpected toxins or allergens, and others believe that their religion forbids consumption of foods produced through rDNA technology. Plaintiffs, a coalition of groups and individuals including scientists and religious leaders concerned about genetically altered foods, have brought this action to protest the Food and Drug Administration's ("FDA") policy on such foods in general, and in particular on various genetically modified foods that already have entered the marketplace. The parties have filed cross-motions for summary judgment on plaintiffs' multiple claims. Upon careful consideration of the parties' briefs and the entire record, the Court shall grant Defendants' motion as to all counts of Plaintiffs' Complaint.

I. BACKGROUND

On May 29, 1992, the FDA published a "Statement of Policy: Foods Derived From New Plant Varieties" (Statement of Policy). See 57 Fed. Reg. 22,984. In the Statement of Policy, FDA announced that the agency would presume that foods produced through the rDNA process were "generally recognized as safe" (GRAS) under the Federal Food, Drug and Cosmetic Act ("FDCA"), 21 U.S.C. §321(s), and therefore not subject to regulation as food additives. While FDA recommended that food producers consult with it before marketing rDNA-produced foods, the agency did not mandate such consultation. In addition, FDA reserved the right to regulate any particular rDNA-developed food that FDA believed was unsafe on a case-by-case basis, just as FDA would regulate unsafe foods produced through conventional means.

The Statement of Policy also indicated that rDNA modification was not a "material fact" under the FDCA, 21 U.S.C. §321(n), and that therefore labeling of rDNA-produced foods was not necessarily required. FDA did not engage in a formal notice-and-comment process on the Statement of Policy, nor did it prepare an Environmental Impact Statement or Environmental Assessment. At least thirty-six foods, genetically altered through rDNA technology, have been marketed since the Statement of Policy was issued.

Plaintiffs filed a Complaint in this Court challenging the FDA's policy on six different grounds: (1) the Statement was not properly subjected to notice-and-comment procedures; ... (3) the FDA's presumption that rDNA-developed foods are GRAS and therefore do not require food additive petitions under 21 U.S.C. §321(s) is arbitrary and capricious; [and] (4) the FDA's decision not to require labeling for rDNA-developed foods is arbitrary and capricious.... Plaintiffs have also challenged on the third and fourth grounds each of FDA's specific decisions not to regulate 36 individual rDNA-produced products. The parties have filed cross-motions for summary judgment on all of Plaintiff's claims....

B. Notice and Comment

Plaintiffs argue that the Statement of Policy should be set aside because it was not subjected to notice and comment proceedings, as required under the Administrative Procedure Act ("APA"), 5 U.S.C. §553. While conceding that the Statement of Policy did not undergo a formal notice and comment process, Defendants maintain that the Statement of Policy is a policy statement...not subject to notice and comment requirements. See...5 U.S.C. §553(b)(3)(A) (1994) (exempting from notice and comment...general statements of policy). Plaintiffs contend instead that the Statement of Policy is a substantive rule, and that therefore it was improperly exempted from a formal notice and comment process.

A substantive rule, which must undergo a formal notice-and-comment process, is a rule that "implement[s]" a statute and has "the force and effect of law." Chrysler Corp. v. Brown, 441 U.S. 281, 302 n.31 (1979). Policy statements, on the other hand, are "statements issued by an agency to advise the public prospectively of the manner in which the agency proposes to exercise a discretionary power." Id. Although the distinction between these categories is not entirely clear, in American Bus. Ass'n v. United States, 627 F.2d 525 (D.C. Cir. 1980), the Court of Appeals articulated a two-part test for determining when an agency action is a policy statement. Policy statements (1) must not impose any new rights or obligations, and (2) must "genuinely leave the agency and its decision-makers free to exercise discretion." 627 F.2d at 529. In weighing these criteria, "the ultimate issue is the agency's intent to be bound." Public Citizen v. United States Nuclear Regulatory Comm'n, 940 F.2d 679, 682 (D.C. Cir. 1991). An agency's own characterization of its statement deserves some weight, but it is not dispositive. Rather, courts will look to the actual language of the statement.

By its very name, the Statement of Policy announces itself as a policy statement. More importantly, the plain language of the Statement suggests that it does not have a binding effect. For example, the Statement does not declare that transferred genetic material will be considered GRAS; rather, it announces that "such material is *presumed* to be GRAS." 57 Fed. Reg. 22989 (emphasis added). This presumption of safety is rebuttable, because FDA will "require food additive petitions in cases where safety questions exist sufficient to warrant formal premarket review by FDA to ensure public health protection." Id. at 22990. Rebuttable presumptions leave an agency free to exercise its discretion and may therefore properly be announced in policy statements.

In response to the argument that the Policy Statement vests broad discretion with the agency, Plaintiffs contend that the FDA's application of the Statement has given it a "practical effect" that has effectively bound the agency's discretion, as evidenced by the thirty-six genetically engineered foods that are currently on the market and not regulated by the FDA. Although courts will look to the "agency's actual applications" to determine the nature of an agency statement, such an inquiry occurs "where the language and context of a statement are inconclusive." Public Citizen, 940 F.2d at 682. Here, the plain language of the Statement clearly indicates that it is a policy statement that merely creates a presumption and does not ultimately bind the agency's discretion. Given this unambiguous language, this Court need not consider the agency's application of the Statement to determine the Statement's meaning.[3]

---

[3] Moreover, were the Court to consider the agency's application, Plaintiff has not shown that the agency has treated the Statement as binding. The FDA has used a food additive petition process to declare one genetically engineered food to be safe, and it has labeled two others to account for their differences from traditionally engineered foods. See 21 C.F.R. §§173.170, 573.130 (recognizing as safe the food additive aminoglycoside 3'-phospotransferase II, the additive used to genetically modify the Flavr Savr tomato); AR at 37832-33; 37836; 39947-48. Plaintiffs argue that the food additive petition for aminoglycoside 3' -phototransferase II is irrelevant because

Even if, as Plaintiffs argue, FDA has previously used notice-and-comment procedures to determine GRAS status, in the instant case FDA has not determined GRAS status but has rather announced a GRAS presumption. The Statement of Policy creates a rebuttable presumption of GRAS that does not constrain the FDA's ability to exercise its discretion. Because the Statement is a policy statement merely announcing a GRAS presumption, the omission of formal notice-and-comment procedures does not violate the Administrative Procedure Act....

D. GRAS Presumption

In their challenge to the FDA's Statement of Policy, Plaintiffs further claim that the Statement of Policy's presumption that rDNA-engineered foods are GRAS violates the GRAS requirements of the Federal Food, Drug, and Cosmetic Act ("FDCA"), 21 U.S.C. §321(s), and is therefore arbitrary and capricious. The FDCA provides that any substance which may "become a component or otherwise affect[] the characteristics of any food" shall be deemed a food additive. See 21 U.S.C. §321(s). A producer of a food additive must submit a food additive petition to FDA for approval unless FDA determines that the additive is "generally recognized [by qualified experts] . . . as having been adequately shown through scientific procedures . . . to be safe under the conditions of its intended use."[6] Id.

---

the FDA acted on the petition before the publication of the 1992 Statement of Policy. Final action on this food additive petition, however, took place in 1994, nearly two years after publication of the Statement. FDA proceeded with the food additive petition process even after issuing the Statement of Policy, indicating that FDA did not believe the Statement constrained its authority to consider regulations on specific genetically engineered foods.

[6] This section provides more extensively that:

> The term 'food additive' means any substance the intended use of which results or may result, directly or indirectly, in its becoming a component or otherwise affecting the characteristics of any food (including any substance intended for use in producing, manufacturing, packing, processing, preparing, treating, packaging, transporting, or holding food; and including any source of radiation intended for any such use), if such substance is not generally recognized, among experts qualified by scientific training and experience to evaluate its safety, as having been adequately shown through scientific procedures (or, in the case as a substance used in food prior to January 1, 1958, through either scientific procedures or experience based on common use in food) to be safe under the conditions of its intended use....

In the Statement of Policy, FDA indicated that, under §321(s),

> it is the intended or expected introduction of a substance into food that makes the substance potentially subject to food additive regulation. Thus, in the case of foods derived from new plant varieties, it is the transferred genetic material and the intended expression product or products that could be subject to food additive regulation, if such material or expression products are not GRAS.

57 Fed. Reg. at 22,990. Accordingly, FDA reasoned that the only substances added to rDNA engineered foods are nucleic acid proteins, generally recognized as not only safe but also necessary for survival. See id. ("Nucleic acids are present in the cells of every living organism, including every plant and animal used for food by humans or animals, and do not raise a safety concern as a component of food"). Therefore, FDA concluded that rDNA engineered foods should be presumed to be GRAS unless evidence arises to the contrary. See id. at 22,991 ("Ultimately, it is the food producer who is responsible for assuring safety."). The Statement of Policy does acknowledge, however, that certain genetically modified substances might trigger application of the food additives petitioning process. In that vein, FDA recognized that "the intended expression product in a food could be a protein, carbohydrate, fat or oil, or other substance that differs significantly in structure, function, or composition from substances found currently in food. Such substances may not be GRAS and may require regulation as a food additive." Id. at 22,990....

When Congress passed the Food Additives Amendment in 1958, it obviously could not account for the late twentieth-century technologies that would permit the genetic modification of food. The "object and policy" of the food additive amendments, Mova Pharm. Corp. v. Shalala, 140 F.3d 1060, 1067 (D.C. Cir. 1998), is to "require the processor who wants to add a new and unproven additive to accept the responsibility...of first proving it to be safe for ingestion by human beings." S. Rep. No. 85-2422, at 2 (1958). The plain language of §321(s) fosters a broad reading of "food additive" and includes "any substance intended for use in producing, manufacturing, packing, processing, preparing, treating, packaging, transporting, or holding food; and...any source of radiation intended for any such use." §321(s).

Nonetheless, the statute exempts from regulation as additives substances that are "generally recognized...to be safe under the conditions of its intended use...." §321(s). Plaintiffs have not disputed FDA's claim that nucleic acid proteins are generally recognized to be safe. Plaintiffs have argued, however, that significant disagreement exists among scientific experts as to whether or not nucleic acid proteins are generally recognized to be safe when they are used to alter organisms genetically. Having examined the record in this case, the Court cannot say that FDA's decision to accord genetically modified foods a presumption of GRAS status is arbitrary and capricious. "The rationale for deference is particularly strong when the [agency] is evaluating scientific data within its technical expertise." International Fabricare Institute v. U.S.E.P.A., 972 F.2d 384, 389 (D.C. Cir. 1992). "In an area characterized by scientific and technological uncertainty[,]...this court must proceed with particular caution, avoiding all temptation to direct the agency in a choice between rational alternatives." Environmental Defense Fund, Inc. v. Costle, 578 F.2d 337, 339 (D.C.Cir. 1978).

To be generally recognized as safe, a substance must meet two criteria: (1) it must have technical evidence of safety, usually in published scientific studies, and (2) this technical evidence must be generally known and accepted in the scientific community. See 21 C.F.R. §170.30(a-b); 62 Fed. Reg. 18940. Although unanimity among scientists is not required, "a severe conflict among experts...precludes a finding of general recognition." 62 Fed. Reg. at 18939. Plaintiffs have produced several documents showing significant disagreements among scientific experts.[7] However, this Court's review is confined to the record before the agency at the time it made its decision. Therefore, the affidavits submitted by Plaintiffs that are not part of the administrative record will not be considered.

Nonetheless, Plaintiffs, pointing to the critical comments of lower-level FDA officials insist that even the administrative record reveals a lack of general recognition of safety among qualified experts. However, lower-level comments on a regulation "do[] not invalidate the agency's subsequent application and interpretation of its own regulation." San Luis Obispo Mothers for Peace v. U.S. Nuclear Regulatory Comm'n, 789 F.2d 26, 33 (D.C. Cir. 1986). Moreover, pointing to a 44,000 page record, the FDA notes that

---

[7] *See* Pls.' Mot. Ex. 2 (Plaintiff scientist affidavit describing dangers of rDNA technology), Ex. 3 (Scientist affidavit describing rDNA technology as "inherently risky", Ex. 4 (Scientist affidavit describing risks of rDNA technology); Pls.' Reply Ex. 12 (Administrative Record at 18,952-53 [hereinafter AR]) (FDA scientist comments on the Statement of Policy, noting difference between genetic engineering and cross-breeding); Ex. 13 (AR at 19,179) (FDA scientist criticizing scientific basis of Statement of Policy); Ex. 15 (FDA scientists arguing that pre-market review of genetically engineered foods is necessary); AR at 18,130 (FDA scientist arguing that Food Additives Amendment should be applied to rDNA engineered foods); AR at 18,572 (FDA toxicology group head warning that genetically modified plants could have high levels of toxins).

Plaintiffs have chosen to highlight a selected few comments of FDA employees, which were ultimately addressed in the agency's final Policy Statement. As a result, Plaintiffs have failed to convince the Court that the GRAS presumption is inconsistent with the statutory requirements.

E. Labeling

Plaintiffs have also challenged the Statement of Policy's failure to require labeling for genetically engineered foods, for which FDA relied on the presumption that most genetically modified food ingredients would be GRAS. Plaintiffs claim that FDA should have considered the widespread consumer interest in having genetically engineered foods labeled, as well as the special concerns of religious groups and persons with allergies in having these foods labeled.

The FDCA, 21 U.S.C. §321(n), grants the FDA limited authority to require labeling. In general, foods shall be deemed misbranded if their labeling "fails to reveal facts...material with respect to consequences which may result from the use of the article to which the labeling...relates under the conditions of use prescribed in the labeling...or under such conditions of use as are customary or usual." 21 U.S.C. §321(n). Plaintiffs challenge the FDA's interpretation of the term "material." Thus, the question is again one of statutory interpretation. As is apparent from the statutory language, Congress has not squarely addressed whether materiality pertains only to safety concerns or whether it also includes consumer interest. Accordingly, interpretation of the §321(n)'s broad language is left to the agency.

Because Congress has not spoken directly to the issue, this Court must determine whether the agency's interpretation of the statute is reasonable. Agency interpretations receive substantial deference, particularly when the agency is interpreting a statute that it is charged with administering....

The FDA takes the position that no "material change," under §321(n), has occurred in the rDNA derived foods at issue here. Absent unique risks to consumer health[8] or uniform changes to food derived through rDNA tech-

---

[8] In other contexts, the FDA has identified that the presence of an increased risk to consumer safety constitutes a "material change." See e.g., 49 Fed. Reg. 13679 (pertaining to FDA requirement in 21 C.F.R. § 101.17(d)(1) that a special warning statement appear on the label of protein products intended for use in weight reduction due to health risks associated with very low calorie diets). Likewise, should a material consequence exist for a particular rDNA-derived food, the FDA has and

nology, the FDA does not read §321(n) to authorize an agency imposed food labeling requirement. More specifically irksome to the Plaintiffs, the FDA does not read §321(n) to authorize labeling requirements solely because of consumer demand. The FDA's exclusion of consumer interest from the factors which determine whether a change is "material" constitutes a reasonable interpretation of the statute. Moreover, it is doubtful whether the FDA would even have the power under the FDCA to require labeling in a situation where the sole justification for such a requirement is consumer demand. See Stauber v. Shalala, 895 F. Supp. 1178, 1193 (W.D.Wis. 1995) ("In the absence of evidence of a material difference between [milk from cows treated with a synthetic hormone] and ordinary milk, the use of consumer demand as the rationale for labeling would violate the Food, Drug, and Cosmetic Act.").

Plaintiffs fail to understand the limitation on the FDA's power to consider consumer demand when making labeling decisions because they fail to recognize that the determination that a product differs materially from the type of product it purports to be is a factual predicate to the requirement of labeling. Only once materiality has been established may the FDA consider consumer opinion to determine whether a label is required to disclose a material fact. Thus, "if there is a [material] difference, and consumers would likely want to know about the difference, then labeling is appropriate. If, however, the product does not differ in any significant way from what it purports to be, then it would be misbranding to label the product as different, even if consumers misperceived the product as different." Id. The FDA has already determined that, in general, rDNA modification does not "materially" alter foods, and ... this determination is entitled to deference. Given these facts, the FDA lacks a basis upon which it can legally mandate labeling, regardless of the level of consumer demand.

Plaintiffs also contend that the *process*[10] of genetic modification is a "material fact" under §321(n) which mandates special labeling, implying that

---

will require special labeling. See Fed. Reg. 22991; AR at 37782-843, 39849-963 (discussing the requirement that laureate canola and high-oleic acid soybean oil have special labeling because they differ in composition and use from the traditional canola and soybean oil.). However, the Policy Statement at issue here provides only a very general rule regarding the entire class of rDNA derived foods. Thus, without a determination that, *as a class,* rDNA derived food pose inherent risks or safety consequences to consumers, or differ in some material way from their traditional counterparts, the FDA is without authority to mandate labeling.

[10] Disclosure of the conditions or methods of manufacture has long been deemed unnecessary under the law. The Supreme Court reasoned in 1924, "When considered

there are new risks posed to the consumer. However, the FDA has determined that foods produced through rDNA techniques do not "present any different or greater safety concern than foods developed by traditional plant breeding," and concluded that labeling was not warranted. 57 Fed. Reg. at 22991. That determination, unless irrational, is entitled to deference. Accordingly, there is little basis upon which this Court could find that the FDA's interpretation of §321(n) is arbitrary and capricious.

Note

The letter that follows provides an example of the FDA's response to companies that voluntarily consult with the FDA before marketing products made using genetic engineering techniques. The response is reproduced here in full.

Agency Response Letter: Biotechnology Consultation

From Laura M. Tarantino, Director, Office of Food Safety, Center for Food Safety and Applied Nutrition
To J. Austin Burns, Monsanto Co., St. Louis, Mo.
March 7, 2005

Dear Dr. Burns:

This is in regard to Monsanto Company's (Monsanto) consultation with the Food and Drug Administration (FDA) (Center for Veterinary Medicine and Center for Food Safety and Applied Nutrition) on its genetically engineered cotton MON 88913. According to Monsanto, this new event is engineered to express one new protein, CP4 5-enolpyruvylshikimate-3-phosphate synthase (CP4 EPSPS). The CP4 EPSPS protein confers tolerance to glyphosate herbicide. All materials relevant to this notification have been placed in a file designated BNF 0098. This file will be maintained in the Office of Food Additive Safety.

---

independently of the product, the method of manufacture is not material. The act requires no disclosure concerning it." U.S. v. Ninety-Five Barrels (More or Less) Alleged Apple Cider Vinegar, 265 U.S. 438, 445 (1924) (referring to the Food and Drug Act of June 30, 1906, precursor to the FDCA).

As part of bringing the consultation regarding this product to closure, Monsanto submitted on May 27, 2004, a summary of its safety and nutritional assessment of the genetically engineered cotton. Monsanto provided additional information in submissions dated November 8, and December 10, 2004. These communications informed the FDA of the steps taken by Monsanto to ensure that this product complies with the legal and regulatory requirements that fall within FDA's jurisdiction. Based on the safety and nutritional assessment Monsanto has conducted, it is our understanding that Monsanto has concluded that cottonseed, cottonseed meal and cottonseed oil from the new variety are not materially different in composition, safety, and other relevant parameters from cottonseed, cottonseed meal and cottonseed oil currently on the market, and that the genetically engineered cotton does not raise issues that would require premarket review or approval by FDA.

It is Monsanto's responsibility to obtain all appropriate clearances, including those from the Environmental Protection Agency and the United States Department of Agriculture, before marketing food or feed derived from cotton MON 88913.

Based on the information Monsanto has presented to FDA, we have no further questions concerning cottonseed, cottonseed meal and cottonseed oil from cotton MON 88913 at this time. However, as you are aware, it is Monsanto's continued responsibility to ensure that foods marketed by the firms are safe, wholesome, and in compliance with all applicable legal and regulatory requirements.

Note

Before Congress passed legislation last summer, requiring labeling of foods made with genetically engineered components, the FDA's guidance on labeling such foods was the predominant federal statement about such labeling. Excerpts from this guidance follow.

Guidance for Industry: Voluntary Labeling Indicating Whether Foods Have or Have Not Been Developed Using Bioengineering

U.S. Food and Drug Administration
Center for Food Safety and Applied Nutrition
Draft Guidance, released for comment
January 2001

This draft guidance represents FDA's current thinking on voluntary labeling of foods indicating whether foods have or have not been developed using bioengineering. It does not create or confer any rights for or on any person and does not operate to bind FDA or the public. An alternative approach may be used if such an approach satisfies the requirements of applicable statutes and regulations. The draft guidance is being distributed for comment purposes in accordance with FDA's Good Guidance Practices (65 FR 56468, September 19, 2000)....

In determining whether a food is misbranded, FDA would review label statements about the use of bioengineering to develop a food or its ingredients under sections 403(a) and 201(n) of the act. Under section 403(a) of the act, a food is misbranded if statements on its label or in its labeling are false or misleading in any particular. Under section 201(n), both the presence and the absence of information are relevant to whether labeling is misleading. That is, labeling may be misleading if it fails to disclose facts that are material in light of representations made about a product or facts that are material with respect to the consequences that may result from use of the product. In determining whether a statement that a food is or is not genetically engineered is misleading under sections 201(n) and 403(a) of the act, the agency will take into account the entire label and labeling.

Statements about foods developed using bioengineering

FDA recognizes that some manufacturers may want to use informative statements on labels and in labeling of bioengineered foods or foods that contain ingredients produced from bioengineered foods. The following are examples of some statements that might be used. The discussion accompanying each example is intended to provide guidance as to how similar statements can be made without being misleading.

• "Genetically engineered" or "This product contains cornmeal that was produced using biotechnology."

The information that the food was bioengineered is optional and this kind of simple statement is not likely to be misleading. However, focus group data indicate that consumers would prefer label statements that disclose and explain the goal of the technology (why it was used or what it does for/to the food) (Ref. 1). Consumers also expressed some preference for the term "biotechnology" over such terms as "genetic modification" and "genetic engineering" (Ref. 1).

• "This product contains high oleic acid soybean oil from soybeans developed using biotechnology to decrease the amount of saturated fat."

This example includes both required and optional information. As discussed above in the background section, when a food differs from its traditional counterpart such that the common or usual name no longer adequately describes the new food, the name must be changed to describe the difference. Because this soybean oil contains more oleic acid than traditional soybean oil, the term "soybean oil" no longer adequately describes the nature of the food. Under section 403(i) of the act, a phrase like "high oleic acid" would be required to appear as part of the name of the food to describe its basic nature. The statement that the soybeans were developed using biotechnology is optional. So is the statement that the reason for the change in the soybeans was to reduce saturated fat.

• "These tomatoes were genetically engineered to improve texture."

In this example, the change in texture is a difference that may have to be described on the label. If the texture improvement makes a significant difference in the finished product, sections 201(n) and 403(a)(1) of the act would require disclosure of the difference for the consumer. However, the statement must not be misleading. The phrase "to improve texture" could be misleading if the texture difference is not noticeable to the consumer. For example, if a manufacturer wanted to describe a difference in a food that the consumer would not notice when purchasing or consuming the product, the manufacturer should phrase the statements so that the consumer can understand the significance of the difference. If the change in the tomatoes was intended to facilitate processing but did not make a noticeable difference in the processed consumer product, a phrase like "to improve texture for processing" rather than "to improve texture" should be used to ensure that the consumer is not misled. The statement that the tomatoes were genetically engineered is optional.

• "Some of our growers plant tomato seeds that were developed through biotechnology to increase crop yield."

The entire statement in this example is optional information. The fact that there was increased yield does not affect the characteristics of the food and is therefore not necessary on the label to adequately describe the food for the consumer. A phrase like "to increase yield" should only be included where there is substantiation that there is in fact the stated difference.

Where a benefit from a bioengineered ingredient in a multi-ingredient food is described, the statement should be worded so that it addresses the ingredient and not the food as a whole; for example, "This product contains high oleic acid soybean oil from soybeans produced through biotechnology to decrease the level of saturated fat." In addition, the amount of the bioengineered ingredient in the food may be relevant to whether the statement is misleading. This would apply especially where the bioengineered difference is a nutritional improvement. For example, it would likely be misleading to make a statement about a nutritionally improved ingredient on a food that contains only a small amount of the ingredient, such that the food's overall nutritional quality would not be significantly improved.

FDA reminds manufacturers that the optional terms that describe an ingredient of a multi-ingredient food as bioengineered should not be used in the ingredient list of the multi-ingredient food. Section 403(i)(2) of the act requires each ingredient to be declared in the ingredient statement by its common or usual name. Thus, any terms not part of the name of the ingredient are not permitted in the ingredient statement. In addition, 21 CFR 101.2(e) requires that the ingredient list and certain other mandatory information appear in one place without other intervening material. FDA has long interpreted any optional description of ingredients in the ingredient statement to be intervening material that violates this regulation.

Statements about foods that are not bioengineered or that do not contain ingredients produced from bioengineered foods

Terms that are frequently mentioned in discussions about labeling foods with respect to bioengineering include "GMO free" and "GM free." "GMO" is an acronym for "genetically modified organism" and "GM" means "genetically modified." Consumer focus group data indicate that consumers do not understand the acronyms "GMO" and " GM" and prefer label statements with spelled out words that mean bioengineering (Ref. 1).

Terms like "not genetically modified" and "GMO free," that include the word "modified" are not technically accurate unless they are clearly in a context that refers to bioengineering technology. "Genetic modification" means the alteration of the genotype of a plant using any technique, new or traditional. "Modification" has a broad context that means the alteration in the composition of food that results from adding, deleting, or changing hereditary traits, irrespective of the method. Modifications may be minor, such as a single mutation that affects one gene, or major alterations of genetic material that affect many genes. Most, if not all, cultivated food crops have been genetically modified. Data indicate that consumers do not have a good understanding that essentially all food crops have been genetically modified and that bioengineering technology is only one of a number of technologies used to genetically modify crops. Thus, while it is accurate to say that a bioengineered food was "genetically modified," it likely would be inaccurate to state that a food that had not been produced using biotechnology was "not genetically modified" without clearly providing a context so that the consumer can understand that the statement applies to bioengineering.

The term "GMO free" may be misleading on most foods, because most foods do not contain organisms (seeds and foods like yogurt that contain microorganisms are exceptions). It would likely be misleading to suggest that a food that ordinarily would not contain entire "organisms" is "organism free."

There is potential for the term "free" in a claim for absence of bioengineering to be inaccurate. Consumers assume that "free" of bioengineered material means that "zero" bioengineered material is present. Because of the potential for adventitious presence of bioengineered material, it may be necessary to conclude that the accuracy of the term "free" can only be ensured when there is a definition or threshold above which the term could not be used. FDA does not have information with which to establish a threshold level of bioengineered constituents or ingredients in foods for the statement "free of bioengineered material." FDA recognizes that there are analytical methods capable of detecting low levels of some bioengineered materials in some foods, but a threshold would require methods to test for a wide range of genetic changes at very low levels in a wide variety of foods. Such test methods are not available at this time. The agency suggests that the term "free" either not be used in bioengineering label statements or that it be in a context that makes clear that a zero level of bioengineered material is not implied. However, statements that the food or its ingredients, as appropriate, was not developed using bioengineering would avoid or minimize such implications. For example,

- **"We do not use ingredients that were produced using biotechnology;"**
- **"This oil is made from soybeans that were not genetically engineered;" or**
- **"Our tomato growers do not plant seeds developed using biotechnology."**

A statement that a food was not bioengineered or does not contain bioengineered ingredients may be misleading if it implies that the labeled food is superior to foods that are not so labeled. FDA has concluded that the use or absence of use of bioengineering in the production of a food or ingredient does not, in and of itself, mean that there is a material difference in the food. Therefore, a label statement that expresses or implies that a food is superior (e.g., safer or of higher quality) because it is not bioengineered would be misleading. The agency will evaluate the entire label and labeling in determining whether a label statement is in a context that implies that the food is superior.

In addition, a statement that an ingredient was not bioengineered could be misleading if there is another ingredient in the food that was bioengineered. The claim must not misrepresent the absence of bioengineered material. For example, on a product made largely of bioengineered corn flour and a small amount of soybean oil, a claim that the product "does not include genetically engineered soybean oil" could be misleading. Even if the statement is true, it is likely to be misleading if consumers believe that the entire product or a larger portion of it than is actually the case is free of bioengineered material. It may be necessary to carefully qualify the statement in order to ensure that consumers understand its significance.

Further, a statement may be misleading if it suggests that a food or ingredient itself is not bioengineered, when there are no marketed bioengineered varieties of that category of foods or ingredients. For example, it would be misleading to state "not produced through biotechnology" on the label of green beans, when there are no marketed bioengineered green beans. To not be misleading, the claim should be in a context that applies to the food type instead of the individual manufacturer's product. For example, the statement "green beans are not produced using biotechnology" would not imply that this manufacturer's product is different from other green beans....

Note

Please read the 2016 legislation requiring labeling of bioengineered food. The legislation is available here: **http://www.agriculture.senate.gov/imo/media/doc/Mandatory%20Labeling%20Bill.pdf**. What does the legislation require in terms of labeling? How much discretion does it leave to the government in implementing it?

Part IV
Food Security

Chapter 10
Food Assistance Programs

Food security exists when all people, at all times, have physical and economic access to sufficient safe and nutritious food that meets their dietary needs and food preferences for an active and healthy life.

- World Food Summit, 1996

Convened in Rome in 1996 by the Food and Agriculture Organization (FAO) of the United Nations, the World Food Summit brought representatives of 185 countries together to work toward the goal of eradicating hunger. Building on the declaration in 1974 by the World Food Conference that "every man, woman and child has the inalienable right to be free from hunger and malnutrition in order to develop their physical and mental faculties," the World Food Summit developed the influential definition of food security, quoted above, to guide the work of the participating countries and organizations.

In the United States, the federal government has responded to the problem of household food insecurity primarily by creating government programs that provide access to food for households that have an income below a certain level. Thirteen major federal programs, listed in the chart below, aim to address food insecurity by providing food or food assistance directly to eligible people or to the institutions that assist them. Although States are responsible for the day-to-day operations of these programs, the programs are overseen by the Food and Nutrition Service (FNS) within the Department of Agriculture (USDA). The nutrition assistance programs represent the overwhelming majority of the USDA's overall budget: 73 percent in fiscal year 2016.

Name	Acronym	Description
Child and Adult Care Food Program	CACFP	Provides meals and snacks to children and adults in designated child and adult care centers.
Commodity Supplemental Food Program	CSFP	Provides food assistance for low-income seniors with a monthly package of USDA commodities.
Farmers' Market Nutrition Program	FMNP	Awards cash grants to state agencies to provide WIC recipients with coupons that can be exchanged for eligible foods at pre-approved farmers markets.
Food Distribution Program on Indian Reservations	FDPIR	Provides commodity foods to low-income households living on Indian reservations and to Native American families residing in designated areas near reservations.
Fresh Fruit and Vegetable Program	FFVP	Provides free fresh fruits and vegetables in select low-income elementary schools nationwide.
National School Lunch Program	NSLP	Provides lunch to qualified children each school day.
School Breakfast Program	SBP	Provides breakfast to qualified children each school day.
Senior Farmers' Market Nutrition Program	SFMNP	Awards grants to state agencies to provide low-income seniors with

		coupons that can be exchanged for eligible foods such as fresh fruits and vegetables at pre-approved farmers' markets.
Summer Food Service Program	SFSP	Provides free meals and snacks to low-income children during the summer months.
Special Milk Program	SMP	Participating non-profit schools and institutions receive reimbursement from the USDA for each half pint of milk served. Federal reimbursement must be used to reduce the selling price of milk to all children.
Supplemental Nutrition Assistance Program	SNAP	Provides assistance to low-income Americans to buy groceries. (Works through block grant program in American territories.)
The Emergency Food Assistance Program	TEFAP	Provides USDA commodities to families in need of short-term hunger relief through emergency food providers like food banks.
Special Supplemental Nutrition Program for Women, Infants, and Children	WIC	Provides foods and nutrition education for low-income, at risk women, infants.

Supplemental Nutrition Assistance Program (SNAP)

Of these thirteen federal programs, the Supplemental Nutrition Assistance Program (SNAP) is the largest both in terms of budget and in terms of number of people served. The budget for SNAP for fiscal year 2015 was $84 billion (a decrease from previous years due to provisions of the latest Farm Bill), and the number of people served in the same time frame was almost 47 million.

SNAP is the contemporary incarnation of the Food Stamp Act, part of President Johnson's "War on Poverty," which itself revitalized an earlier New Deal program. In the original programs, participants bought food coupons (stamps) in an amount equal to their normal expenditures on food, and received extra stamps, for free, that could be used to purchase surplus foods. Congress eventually eliminated the purchase requirement, and then replaced altogether the food stamps with an electronic payment system. Today, the program provides benefits to households based on income, with income limits pegged to the federal poverty threshold. SNAP benefits are pegged to the USDA's "Thrifty Food Plan," which is a "market basket" of foods that reflects a nutritious diet at minimal cost. A household's income determines how much of the cost of the Thrifty Food Plan they receive in SNAP benefits.

The "food" available under SNAP is defined very broadly, as follows: "'Food' is 1) any food or food product for home consumption except alcoholic beverages, tobacco, and hot foods or hot food products ready for immediate consumption ... [and] (2) seeds and plants for use in gardens to produce food for the personal consumption of the eligible household." 7 U.S.C. § 2012(k). A recurring question in the legislative debates over SNAP has been whether there should be any limit on the foods participants may purchase with SNAP benefits. Even in the 1970s, for example, Congress debated whether "junk foods" should be included as eligible foods. Worries about imposing administrative burdens on retailers and the difficulty of identifying ineligible foods led Congress to reject such limits. But the debate did not disappear. It has figured in two different kinds of legal disputes, examined below. The first category includes disputes over whether a particular food retailer should be eligible to participate in the program. The second category includes disputes over whether a state or local government that oversees the administration of SNAP within its jurisdiction may experiment with declaring some foods ineligible for SNAP benefits.

Kentucky Fried Chicken of Cleveland v. United States

449 F.2d 255 (5th Cir. 1971)

CLARK, Circuit Judge.

The single question presented by this appeal is whether the Secretary of Agriculture acted beyond the scope of his authority under the Food Stamp Act of 1964 in denying the application to participate as a "retail food store" in the Food Stamp Program filed by Kentucky Fried Chicken of Cleveland, Inc. (Kentucky Fried). If approved as a participant, Kentucky Fried would be authorized to receive stamps issued by the United States in exchange for its prepared foods, which stamps the government would redeem for cash. The court below held that the Secretary's action was unauthorized, and invalidated the denial of the application. We reverse.

The district judge's decision was based on the following findings of law and fact. First, the ready-to-eat food items Kentucky Fried sells fall within the Act's definition of "food," its business within the Act's definition of "retail food store" and the persons to whom it proposes to sell within the Act's definition of "household." Second, the legislative history negates the idea that so-called "luxury" food items are excluded from the program; in fact, foods similar to those Kentucky Fried sells may now be purchased with food stamps at certain supermarkets which are now approved as retail food stores by the Secretary. Finally, though the purposes of the Secretary's action here were commendable, the judge found those purposes could only be pursued in the Congress rather than the courts.

Our reversal turns on other "rules," "authority," and "discretion" which were given to the Secretary by the Act. For beyond its purely definitional aspects, the Act also provides:

> § 2011. It is hereby declared to be the policy of Congress * * * that the Nation's abundance of food * * * be utilized * * * to the maximum extent practicable to safeguard the health and well-being of the Nation's population and raise levels of nutrition among low-income households.
>
> § 2013 (a) The Secretary is authorized to formulate and administer a food stamp program under which * * * eligible households * * * shall be provided with an opportunity more nearly to obtain a nutritionally adequate diet. * * *
>
> (c) The Secretary shall issue such regulations, not inconsistent with this chapter, as he deems necessary or appropriate for the effective and effi-

cient administration of the food stamp program.

§ 2014 (a) Participation in the food stamp program shall be limited to those households whose income is determined to be a substantial limiting factor in the attainment of a nutritionally adequate diet.

§ 2016 (a) The face value of the coupon allotment which State agencies shall be authorized to issue to households certified as eligible to participate in the food stamp program shall be in such amount as will provide such households with an opportunity more nearly to obtain a low-cost nutritionally adequate diet.

§ 2017 (a) Regulations issued pursuant to this chapter shall provide for the submission of applications for approval by retail food stores * * * which desire to be authorized to accept and redeem coupons * * * and for the approval of those applicants whose participation will effectuate the purposes of the food stamp program. In determining the qualifications of applicants there shall be considered among such other factors as may be appropriate, the following: (1) the nature and extent of the retail or wholesale food business conducted by the applicant; (2) the volume of coupon business which may reasonably be expected to be conducted by the applicant * * *; (3) the business integrity and reputation of the applicant.

§ 2019 (a) All practicable efforts shall be made in the administration of the food stamp program to insure that participants used their increased food purchasing power to obtain those staple foods most needed in their diets * * * *

Thus, it is not enough that an applicant for the program merely be a "retail food store" selling "food" to "households," as those words are defined. The Act makes it plain that all such definitionally qualified stores are not ipso facto admitted to the program. If that were so, the criteria for approval of applicants, as stated in § 2017 above, would be a needless appendage to the Act.

Though it is true the legislative history of the Act indicates the Congress dismissed as impractical the idea of designating *which foods* could be purchased with the stamps, it does not follow that the Secretary has no authority to designate *which stores* should be authorized to receive the stamps. Since the Act provides that an eligible household is to receive only that amount of stamps "as will provide such household with an opportunity more nearly to obtain a low-cost nutritionally adequate diet," it is not unreasonable that the Secretary, in order to "effectuate the purposes of the food stamp program," looking to the "nature and extent" of Kentucky Fried's business, and considering other "factors" he deemed "appropriate," decided not to approve an applicant who sold only a limited variety of high-cost prepared foods.

The record indicates that the Secretary has exercised his discretion to approve only grocery establishments which stock a large number of low-cost staples hoping thereby to encourage among low-income groups the most economical use of their food stamp purchasing power. Given the congressional directive and the prerogative vested in him, this is a reasonable choice on the Secretary's part, well within the scope of the executive powers reposed in him. That some of such approved establishments also stock high-cost prepared items similar to those Kentucky Fried sells is no more than an incidental, albeit an undesirable, circumstance. It does not create a claim of disparate treatment which would invalidate his actions. Approved "retail food stores" are only *indirect beneficiaries* of this program. The Secretary has determined that stamp recipients will have that "opportunity more nearly to obtain a lowcost nutritionally adequate diet," which the Act was designed to afford them, if they buy from those establishments that stock a variety of low-cost staple items, than if they buy from those that stock none. Since we have decided that he was authorized to make that decision, we will not thwart the effectuation of his judgment merely to allow Kentucky Fried to share in the proceeds of those occasions when food stamps are used to purchase high-cost items.

Notes

1. Do you agree with the broad definition of "food" under SNAP? Does it make sense to allow SNAP benefits recipients to buy almost any kind of food under the program? Why do you suppose "hot foods or hot food products ready for immediate consumption" are not included in the program?

2. The following materials relate to New York City's effort to obtain USDA approval for a pilot program excluding sugar-sweetened beverages from eligibility under SNAP. The first document is New York City's request for approval to create such a pilot program. The second document is the USDA's rejection of New York City's request.

A Proposal to Create a Demonstration Project in New York City to Modify Allowable Purchases Under the Federal Supplemental Nutrition Assistance Program

Introduction

Since its introduction in the Federal Food Stamp Act of 1964, the Food Stamp Program's intent has always been to "provide for improved levels of nutrition among low-income households". The Food and Nutrition Act of 2008 reinforced this aim, declaring it a policy of Congress "in order to promote the general welfare, to safeguard the health and well-being of the Nation's population by raising levels of nutrition among low-income households."

However, despite the clearly stated intentions of the Food Stamp Program, now called the Supplemental Nutrition Assistance Program (SNAP), a large proportion of expenditures under the SNAP support the purchase of food items defined by the United States Department of Agriculture (USDA) to be of little or no nutritional value, including soda and other sugar-sweetened beverages ["sweetened beverages"]. According to a 1999 USDA survey, 20% of the total caloric intake of SNAP households was from fats, oils, sweets, and soda – with soda accounting for almost 6% of total caloric intake.

The use of SNAP benefits to purchase foods of little or no nutritional value not only contradicts the intent of the program, it also effectively subsidizes a serious public health epidemic. Sweetened beverages are a major contributor to obesity, and although federal food assistance policy increasingly has emphasized improved nutrition, the twin crises of obesity and diabetes continue to worsen across America. Estimates from 2007-2008 suggest that 34% of American adults and 17% of children were obese, which means adult obesity has doubled and child obesity has tripled since 1980. Faced with these alarming trends, the White House Task Force on Childhood Obesity issued a report in 2010 that included recommendations calling for the nation's food assistance programs to be part of the solution by encouraging access to nutritious foods and offering incentives and eliminating disincentives to unhealthy eating habits.

In addition to being inconsistent with the program's stated goal of improving nutrition among low-income households, allowing the purchase of sweetened beverages directly competes with the USDA's nutrition education programming at the federal and local level. An estimated $75 to $135 million dollars of SNAP funds were spent on sweetened beverages in New York City (NYC) alone in 2009. This use of federal funds to purchase a group of products that are leading contributors to the diabetes and obesity epidemics (and whose extensive consumption contradicts the USDA's own recommended dietary guidelines) far outstrips current federal funding for prevention of these health problems. Especially in this extremely challenging economic and fiscal climate, federal nutrition programs and policy should be coordinated to support the goals of nutrition education and the fight against the epidemic of obesity, not to contradict them.

As such, the following proposes a demonstration project to be operated in New York City to modify the list of allowable purchases under the SNAP to exclude the purchase of sweetened beverages with SNAP benefits. The proposed demonstration project will support the stated goal of the SNAP to improve the nutrition of low-income households, while allowing an opportunity to evaluate whether such a restriction can reduce consumption of these beverages.

Proposal

The New York State Office of Temporary and Disability Assistance (OTDA) is proposing that it be granted permission to modify the list of allowable food items to be purchased with SNAP benefits in NYC as a demonstration project. Specifically, the demonstration project would add to the list of exclusions in the definition of "Food" under Section 3 [7 U.S.C. 2012(k)] of the Food and Nutrition Act of 2008:

- Sweetened beverages containing more than 10 calories per cup (exempting fruit juice without added sugar, milk products, and milk substitutes).

Authorized SNAP retailers in NYC will be required to modify the list of allowable purchases by re-programming their point-of-sale (POS) systems using a list of restricted beverages provided by the NYC Department of Health and Mental Hygiene (DOHMH). Currently, these retailers program their systems to accommodate other SNAP exclusions (e.g., alcohol, tobacco, prepared foods, nutrition supplements, etc.) and the proposed change will minimally impact their operations. Retailers who rely on a manual process to identify allowable purchases will be required to update their list of exclusions to include the beverages identified on the DOHMH list and implement as appropriate for their operation. The NYC Human Resources Administration (HRA) will be responsible for engaging retailers and retailer trade associations prior to implementation to gain buy-in and explain the new restrictions. In addition, informational materials will be distributed to retailers prior to implementation so that they are fully informed of the new restrictions. HRA will be available and responsive to retailer concerns and implementation issues.

Similar proposals to eliminate foods of minimal nutritional value from allowable SNAP purchases have been submitted to USDA by other state and local entities, including the Minnesota Department of Human Services in 2004. We believe this proposal effectively addresses the reasons cited by USDA for denial of these other waiver requests. We believe that this proposal will be significantly less complicated to implement, both from policy and logistical perspectives. In addition, we propose a comprehensive and rigorous evaluation of the demonstration project to test whether the restriction is effective in reducing the consumption of sweetened beverages among SNAP participants.

Justification for Request

- **The proposed modification supports the stated nutritional goal of the Supplemental Nutrition Assistance Program.**

Federal food policy has a long history of working to improve nutrition among the nation's poor, which was continued in the Food and Nutrition Act of 2008. The emphasis on nutrition education as part of the program began as early as the 1980s, with the Food Security Act of 1985, which required state agencies to encourage recipients to participate in nutrition education programs. In 1990, Food Stamp Program funding was dedicated to projects aimed at improving nutrition education activities and for fiscal year 2009 over $341 million in federal funding was approved for SNAP nutrition education programming, covering half of the total amount spent by states. There has also been an increasing emphasis on finding innovative ways to improve nutrition among America's poor. Welfare reform in 1996 permitted the USDA to waive program requirements to conduct pilot projects to improve nutrition among needy families and the Food and Nutrition Act of 2008 allowed the same. Allowing the purchase of foods with minimal nutritional value under the current program is a direct contradiction of these efforts and the stated federal policy to improve nutrition among the nation's poor.

- **Obesity is a significant and growing problem across the country and in NYC.**

The significance of the obesity problem is clear and the costs are staggering. In NYC, 22.6% of adults were obese in 2008, compared to 12.3% just over a decade ago. Furthermore, being overweight is a condition that affects the majority of NYC adults, with 57.9% either overweight or obese in 2008. There are also large disparities in obesity rates by income level. In 2008, 27.4% of NYC adults in poverty were obese, compared to 15.2% of adults with incomes greater than 500% of poverty. These high levels of obesity have led to other health problems, including diabetes, the prevalence of which is 12.5% and rising in NYC.

The higher incidence of obesity translates into significant health-related costs at the federal and local levels. In 2000, the total cost of obesity in the United States was estimated to be $117 billion. Nearly half of all medical spending related to adult obesity is financed by the public sector, through Medicaid and Medicare. The proposed modification of allowable purchases under the SNAP is one component of the City of New York's (City) coordinated strategy to combat obesity and diabetes by increasing access to healthy foods, decreasing access to unhealthy foods, and getting New Yorkers engaged in physical activity.

- **Obesity and diabetes have been linked to increased consumption of sweetened beverages.**

Many studies have attributed rising rates of obesity and diabetes to increased calorie consumption, much of which comes from sweetened beverages. The USDA Economic Research Service recognized this in a July 2010 report and acknowledged the use of economic incentives to decrease consumption of sweetened beverages as a strategy for reducing obesity. Americans consume 200 to 300 more calories per day than 30 years ago, with the largest single increase due to sweetened beverages. In addition, nearly half of the sugar consumed by Americans comes from sweetened beverages. Among children, more than 10% of daily caloric intake has been attributed to sweetened beverages, and it is even higher in adolescents. In fact, each additional sweetened beverage per day increases a child's risk of obesity by 60%. Randomized controlled trials have shown that substituting sweetened beverages with low calorie drinks decreases body mass index in overweight children. Another study found the risk of developing diabetes was 83% higher among women who consumed one or more sweetened beverages a day. While restricting the purchase of sweetened beverages under the SNAP alone will not solve the problems identified above, it is an important component in a comprehensive effort to reduce consumption of these products among all NYC residents.

- **Low-income populations are more likely to consume low-cost foods that contribute to obesity and diabetes, including sweetened beverages.**

Research shows that soda, sugary snacks, and fast food are readily available in low-income neighborhoods and have replaced more nutritious foods like milk. A 2008 study found that consumption of non-sugar-free sodas was higher in SNAP participants and income-eligible non-participants than higher-income non-participants. In addition, numerous studies have found that poorer children are more likely to be overweight, and the link between obesity and socioeconomic status has become stronger in the past two decades. The disparity is also true with diabetes. In NYC's poorest households, 16.3% of adults have diabetes, which is quadruple the 4% rate seen in the wealthiest households. Given the increasingly recognized and documented health consequences from frequent and routine consumption of sweetened beverages -- consequences which have been most devastating to NYC's poorest households, it is inappropriate for the City's nutrition assistance program to support this consumption.

- **Significant federal and local funding has been dedicated to nutrition education and the proposed modification would support rather than contradict these efforts.**

The growing problem of obesity in the United States has led to increased spending for prevention and nutrition education programs at both the federal and local levels. In fiscal year 2004, the federal government spent approximately $530 million on nutrition education. In the 2009 federal budget, the Centers for Disease Control and Prevention (CDC) alone included $947 million for health promotion, of which $41 million was earmarked for efforts to improve nutrition, increase physical activity, and reduce obesity levels. In addition to these efforts, the USDA was allocated over $341 million in federal funding for nutrition education in Fiscal Year 2009, funding that was matched by states. Given the significant public investment in healthy eating and obesity prevention, the SNAP should support rather than contradict these efforts.

- **The proposed change complements, and is supported by, the USDA's and the City's strategies to improve nutrition among low- income populations.**

This demonstration project would support the goals of USDA's recently issued Strategic Plan, which specifically calls for "evaluating nutrition promotion interventions to implement and sustain evidence based strategies in communities across the Nation" and which also proposes a focus on areas where the USDA's unique strengths and capabilities can have the greatest impact. The proposed revisions to the US Dietary Guidelines recently issued for public comment also recommend reduction of high-calorie, non-nutritious foods, including sweetened beverages.

Locally, the City has implemented a number of programs and services, designed to educate and improve access to nutritious food, that have laid the groundwork for and can work synergistically with the proposed pilot. Significant public funds have been invested to improve access to healthy foods in underserved neighborhoods, provide healthy school lunches and snacks, and increase physical activity among school-aged children. In fact, in 2007, the City established the first Office of Food Policy Coordination to better coordinate the City's efforts and to highlight the commitment towards nutrition and health at the local level. Through a number of efforts by the Office of Food Policy Coordination and the NYC DOHMH (along with other City agencies), low-income neighborhoods have increased access to nutritious foods and beverages that will serve as appropriate substitutes for sweetened beverages. This means that even with the proposed restriction on using SNAP benefits for the purchase of sweetened beverages participants will have many other more nutritious options available.

Examples of City initiatives that will support the proposed pilot program include the following:

- The NYC DOHMH's Healthy Bodegas Initiative has worked directly and successfully with over 1,000 retail food establishments in low income areas to increase their inventory and promotion of healthier drinks, which would serve as alternatives to sweetened beverages for SNAP participants. The initiative has also worked with approximately 120 stores to promote a variety of healthier foods, including healthier beverages like low fat milk, water, and other low to no calorie drinks. Stores have agreed to increase inventory of these items and promote them throughout the store using shelf talkers, point of selection advertisements, and product placement. Specifically, through this initiative, 21% of bodegas started carrying low-fat milk for the first time and 45% of retailers reported an increase in sales of low fat milk. Low fat milk sales increased from 16% to 53% of all milk purchases. The number of stores placing refrigerated water at eye level increased from 35% to 64% and the number purchasing at least one bottle of water increased from 6% to 12%.
- Green markets in New York City now accept SNAP benefits, which increase clients' access to fresh fruits and vegetables, and the "Health Bucks" program provides vouchers for the purchase of additional

fruits and vegetables to consumers who use SNAP benefits at green markets. These programs provide SNAP participants with healthier alternatives to sweetened beverages.

- The Department of City Planning and the State have worked together to launch the FRESH initiative, to provide incentives to supermarkets to locate in areas with poor access to healthy foods. This would provide another venue to use SNAP benefits for the purchase of healthier alternatives to sweetened beverages.
- The CDC has funded the City's attempt to reduce obesity through policy, systems, and environmental changes that make healthy eating decisions easier. Interventions that affect the price of goods, as well as those that address the consumption of sweetened beverages specifically, have been encouraged by the CDC. Assessing the feasibility of policies to modify the price and accessibility of sweetened beverages was part of the City's successful proposal to the federal government.
- The DOHMH, as well as other City agencies, has imposed nutritional standards for school and other meals that are more stringent than currently required by the USDA and exclude the sale of certain items, such as sodas.
- The DOHMH has trained thousands of daycare staff, parents, and children in physical activity and nutrition, implemented nutrition education curricula in schools, developed School Wellness Councils, and launched various public information and media campaigns, including on sweetened beverages. DOHMH also has successfully restricted trans fats in restaurants and has instituted calorie labeling in chain restaurants.
- The City's SNAP, administered by HRA, provides nutrition education to program participants. HRA participates in the New York State Eat Smart New York (ESNY) Program and educates up to 20,000 adults and over 50,000 children each year on healthy eating habits. The ESNY program curriculum focuses on educating consumers on eating recommended allowances of healthy foods and reducing consumption of sugars. The pilot program will complement these efforts by encouraging SNAP participants to purchase more nutritious foods rather than sweetened beverages.

- **Tax exemptions for food purchased under the SNAP serve as an additional incentive to purchase sweetened beverages.**

SNAP does not allow States to collect sales tax on items purchased with SNAP benefits. This means that program participants can purchase taxable food items, such as soda in New York State, at a lower cost if they use their SNAP benefits than if they used cash. The message being sent is clear - items such as soda are less costly under the SNAP. A recent USDA report supports the evidence that taxing sweetened beverages reduces consumption. Permitting SNAP benefits to be used for purchase of sweetened beverages tax-free promotes greater consumption of these empty calories.

- **Given that a USDA precedent for defining sweetened beverages as a non-nutritious food already exists, the demonstration project will make SNAP rules more consistent with those of other programs.**

The USDA already has set a precedent for defining sweetened beverages as a food with "minimal nutritional value" in their National School Lunch guidelines. The National School Lunch Program/School Breakfast Program excludes "foods of minimal nutritional value (FMNV)." The purchase of such foods with the "nonprofit school food service account (SFSA)" is prohibited, as is the serving of FMNV "during a meal service period(s) in the area(s) where reimbursable meals are served and/or eaten." (See USDA Guidance on this subject dated January 16, 2001.) The Guidance pointedly and specifically cites as an example of FMNV "a carbonated beverage."

Accordingly, this demonstration project would "allow greater conformity with the rules of other programs." In addition, a USDA denial of this project would be in contradiction to its own explicitly stated and implemented policy in the School Lunch and Breakfast Programs as detailed in the 2001 Guidance, as well as a contradiction to the recently issued USDA Strategic Plan.

- **Implementation of food restrictions would not increase program complexity and costs.**

Currently, all retailers who accept SNAP benefits in New York State use the Electronic Benefit Transfer (EBT) system. Based on a file provided by the USDA, large retailers already program their integrated register and point-of-sale (POS) systems to automatically determine whether scanned purchases are allowable under SNAP guidelines. Many small retailers use manual registers and EBT-only POS terminals that require the merchant to enter the SNAP-eligible food purchases into the system, and therefore, rely on employee knowledge to determine allowable purchases. For the purposes of this demonstration, large retailers would need to re-program their register and POS systems to restrict sweetened beverages from purchase with SNAP benefits. Small retailers would be required to train their staff based on a list of restricted items provided by the City DOHMH. In both situations, adding sweetened beverages to the list of exclusions would not significantly increase program complexity or costs, because both of these activities (i.e., re-programming and staff training) already happen on a regular basis as staff turnover occurs and as products change.

- **Participant and retailer confusion related to the proposed changes would be minimal.**

Restrictions on food benefit purchases have been a component of the SNAP since its inception, and consumers and retailers are already accustomed to purchase restrictions. Therefore, concerns about confusing the consumer or increasing the stigma if purchases are rejected seem misplaced. Nevertheless, efforts to ensure that consumers are properly notified and that retailers are not adversely affected will be an important component of the implementation plan for the demonstration project.

A public information campaign will accompany the changes, and retailers will be informed in advance and given time to upgrade their systems and/or procedures. Specifically, the City DOHMH and HRA will meet with representatives from supermarket chains and trade associations that represent the full spectrum of the grocery industry (e.g., the Food Industry Alliance of New York State, Inc.) to discuss the changes, as well as to discuss ways to implement the changes in a manner that works for the retailers. Information will be shared with the food industry representatives to highlight the City's comprehensive efforts to promote the purchase of healthier foods and beverages (e.g., Healthy Bodegas, Health Bucks, FRESH initiative, etc.), which should lead to increased sales of such products and relieve concerns about lost revenue from the sale of sweetened beverages.

In addition to the public information campaign, HRA will obtain the names, addresses and email addresses, if available, of all SNAP retailers in NYC and notify them via mail or email of the new restrictions on SNAP purchases. Specific instructions on how to implement the change will be included in the letter, as well as a list of restricted beverages or the kind of beverages which qualify under the new guidelines. In addition, user-friendly pamphlets, posters and decals will be distributed to retailers to assist in the training of staff. These materials will inform the retailers of the new restrictions, educate them on the benefits of the demonstration project and enlist their cooperation in its successful outcome.

SNAP participants in NYC will be notified of the new restrictions through a mass mailing. This mailing will include both cash assistance/SNAP and non-cash assistance/SNAP households and also will educate SNAP participants on the health benefits of decreasing sweetened beverage consumption. In addition, posters will be placed in all HRA Job Centers and SNAP Offices throughout the City to inform participants of the new restrictions and educate them on the health benefits. Finally, posters explaining the new restrictions to participants will be sent to all SNAP retailers, who can display them in prominent areas of their establishments.

- **Reasons for refusal of similar but non-identical waiver requests are either addressed by this proposal or require further substantiation.**

OTDA believes that the several arguments that were made in USDA's denial of similar proposals, including one made by the Minnesota Department of Human Services in 2004, can be countered as follows:

1) Interoperability – Given the USDA-grant funded Healthy Incentive Pilot project -- a much more complicated project in terms of its impact on EBT and interoperability, this issue should no longer be an obstacle to approval of a purchase restriction program. The restriction on purchases proposed in this demonstration is far simpler than the HIP. It would be comprehensive rather than selective within the project area, would be transparent to the consumer and would not require modification to the State's EBT system.
2) Stigma – The argument that a demonstration project modifying the list of prohibited items would stigmatize SNAP households has been made in the past. However, there are already certain items that cannot be purchased with SNAP benefits, such as alcoholic beverages and hot food and hot food products prepared for immediate consumption. A stigma, if there is any, would already attach to SNAP benefits because of the above listed limitations. The extension of the list of prohibited items will not create any stigma that does not already exist.
3) Monitoring Retail Compliance – Monitoring the compliance with the demonstration project exclusions will be no more onerous or complicated than the present compliance monitoring regime once retailers, participants, and compliance personnel are informed of the new exclusions.

- **The demonstration presents a unique opportunity to evaluate whether SNAP restrictions impact the purchase and consumption of sweetened beverages among low-income populations.**

The demonstration would offer the opportunity to test whether restrictions on SNAP purchases would be effective in changing purchasing and consumption behavior. While nutrition education programs are clearly an important component in addressing the obesity epidemic, given the extent and increasing severity of the problem, additional efforts are needed. As recommended by the White House Task Force on Childhood Obesity, offering incentives and eliminating disincentives to unhealthy eating habits are important. Restricting sweetened beverages from being purchased with federally-funded SNAP benefits is one effort that is worth testing. As such, an evaluation is proposed as part of the demonstration project. The evaluation will evaluate the implementation process, retailer compliance with the new guidelines, and the impact on the purchase and consumption of sweetened beverages among SNAP participants. Research linking consumption of sweetened beverages and obesity leads to the conclusion that reducing consumption is consistent with the SNAP program goal of improving the nutrition of low-income populations.

Evaluation Plan

An evaluation of the demonstration project is planned in order to assess the implementation process of the proposed restrictions and whether it has the intended effect. The evaluation will utilize multiple data sources and will evaluate both the process and the impact of the demonstration project.

To examine the implementation process, the process evaluation will address the following questions:

- How were the restrictions implemented in NYC and what were the implementation impacts on food retailers?
- Are retailers compliant with the new restrictions?

To evaluate the implementation process, key informant interviews of state and local officials will be used. The interviews will investigate the efforts to notify retailers and the public, as well as the technical and system-related processes necessary to implement the restrictions. Key informant interviews will also be conducted with a sample of NYC large and small food retailers to better understand the process they used to implement the restriction and their perspective on the impact that the change had on their operations.

The process evaluation will also include a compliance component, which will measure the extent to which sweetened beverages are purchased with SNAP benefits after the restrictions are in place. Data will be collected with "secret shopper" visits by the evaluation team. A random selection of small retailers (i.e., retailers that utilize EBT-only terminals) will be visited and evaluators will attempt to purchase sweetened beverages and other non-eligible items with SNAP benefits. The level of compliance will be documented and shared with HRA, who will provide additional training to those retailers who were not compliant. Follow-up visits by the evaluation team will be scheduled for all non-compliant retailers to assess whether further education efforts were effective. The results of the initial and follow-up visits will be analyzed and included in the evaluation report. Since large retailers program their EBT systems to accommodate the restrictions, compliance will be less of an issue. The number of retailers included in the sample and the selection methods will be developed in consultation with the external evaluators and included in the final evaluation plan.

Because compliance with other restrictions on SNAP purchases in New York State is monitored by the USDA, HRA is open to suggestions from the USDA on other ways to monitor compliance with the new restrictions. In addition, HRA and the DOHMH will work with the USDA to determine the appropriate response to non-compliant retailers.

To examine the impact of the demonstration project, the evaluation will address the following question:

- Does the SNAP restriction on sweetened beverages impact the overall purchase and consumption of these items among SNAP participants?

Specifically, the impact evaluation will explore whether self-reported purchase and consumption of sweetened beverages by SNAP participants was reduced as a result of the restriction or whether consumption remained the same because participants purchased these items with cash. SNAP participants will be compared to two groups unaffected by the demonstration project, including (1) non-SNAP participants in NYC and (2) SNAP participants in neighboring counties (if possible).

The data sources that will be used for the impact evaluation include:

A population-based telephone survey: The City is planning a telephone survey on consumption of sweetened beverages. The baseline will take place in September, 2010 with a follow-up study in late 2011. This survey tracks changes in public opinion regarding acceptability and access to sweetened beverages, in addition to self-reported consumption of sweetened beverages. Additional questions will be added to assess whether respondents receive SNAP benefits and an estimate of the amount of sweetened beverages purchased with SNAP benefits and with cash. This will allow a baseline assessment of sweetened beverages purchases and consumption among SNAP participants and non-participants, as well as an evaluation of changes in self-reported purchases and consumption from before to after pilot implementation. The final evaluation plan will include details on how the sample size was determined, the sampling strategy, and estimates of sampling error rate and confidence intervals based on the sample size.

Retail store cash register data. The City is currently exploring collaborations with a grocery store supplier of over 1,000 stores in NYC and neighboring areas that would provide electronic data on beverages purchased using SNAP benefits and cash among SNAP participants. The supplier is able to provide an aggregate list of their products purchased by SNAP participants in a given timeframe across stores in a specific zip code – this list includes items purchased during a transaction where EBT was used, including items that may have been bought with cash. This information will permit an analysis of the change in purchases of sweetened and healthy beverages from before to after pilot implementation by SNAP participants who shop at those stores. It may also be possible to compare the purchasing behavior of affected SNAP participants to SNAP participants in neighboring areas. In addition, it would also provide data on other food purchases by SNAP participants to determine whether more nutritious foods were purchased before and after the pilot implementation.

Customer exit and receipt surveys. Another option is to conduct customer exit surveys at a representative sample of retail establishments in NYC to determine the amount of sweetened beverages purchased with SNAP benefits and with cash. Although this method would require significant resources, it would provide information on both beverage purchases and on the individuals purchasing them. Information is available on the amount of SNAP-related sales by retailers in NYC, which could be used to identify the sample of retail establishments.

In addition, to the above data, the City has purchased data on supermarkets beverages sales for 2008-09 from Nielsen. Since SNAP participants make up 20% of individuals in NYC, this demonstration project, in combination with other City initiatives, has the potential to impact beverages sales citywide. The dataset will be analyzed with future Nielsen data to assess trends in the sales of sweetened beverages and alternative healthier beverages.

Evaluation Partners. External evaluators will conduct the evaluation under contract with DOHMH and/or HRA. The external evaluator will be selected by DOHMH and HRA with the assistance of New York State OTDA and the New York State Department of Health. The external evaluator will be responsible for developing a final evaluation plan under the oversight of DOHMH and HRA based on the broad framework presented in this proposal.

The total cost of the evaluation will depend on the availability of existing data and the need for primary data collection. The City is examining internal funding sources, as well as grant funding to cover the cost of evaluation.

Conclusion

This proposal offers a valuable opportunity to make the SNAP even more effective in achieving its stated policy goal of improving nutrition for low-income families. It also eliminates an explicit conflict between the goals of the SNAP and its day-to-day implementation in recipient households. It is inspired in large part by USDA's own guidelines for defining what is and is not nutritious, and reflects a relatively simple and cost-effective means of reconciling those guidelines with the longstanding intentions of the nation's largest food assistance program.

In addition, the proposed demonstration project recognizes the growing nationwide consensus that consumption of sweetened beverages must be reduced in order to improve the health of Americans. National organizations that have supported measures in this direction include the American Academy of Pediatrics, American Heart Association, American Cancer Society, Save the Children, and the National Association of County and City Health Officials. In New York, 200 organizations recently supported proposals to tax sweetened beverages to reduce consumption, including the New York Academy of Medicine, Greater New York Hospital Association, Medical Society of the State of New York, New York State Public Health Association, numerous faith-based organizations, and a major union. By reducing access to sweetened beverages, this demonstration project is consistent with the City of New York's comprehensive efforts to improve the nutrition of all New Yorkers, including low-income households.

Letter

From Jessica Shahin, Associate Administrator, United States Department of Agriculture

To Elizabeth Berlin, Executive Deputy Commissioner, New York State Office of Temporary and Disability Assistance
August 19, 2011

Dear Ms. Berlin:

Thank you for your request of October 6, 2010, that the Department of Agriculture (USDA) waive Supplemental Nutrition Assistance Program (SNAP) rules to permit a demonstration project restricting the purchase of sugar-sweetened beverages with SNAP benefits in New York City (NYC).

While we share in the underlying goal of the waiver to reduce obesity, several aspects of the proposal raise concerns about its potential viability and effectiveness:

- We are concerned that the scale and scope of the proposed demonstration is too large and complex. The proposal would restrict purchases of sugar-sweetened beverages for hundreds of thousands of SNAP households throughout New York City. A change of this significance should be tested on the smallest scale appropriate to minimize any unintended negative effects.
- There are a number of unresolved operational challenges and complexities, including several that could substantially impact the operations of food retailers that accept SNAP benefits. The proposal offers little evidence that the city's retailer community is well-positioned to implement the proposed restrictions. Without the active commitment and participation of all authorized retailers, the chances of operationalsuccess are limited.
- The proposal lacks a clear and practical means to determine product eligibility, which is essential to avoid retailer confusion at point-of-sale and stigma for affected clients. It also lacks a process for disseminating product information to participating retailers, a communications and coordination plan for retailer compliance activities, and clear evidence that small businesses would not be disproportionately affected by the prohibition.
- The proposed evaluation design is not adequate to provide sufficient assurance of credible, meaningful results with respect to the demonstration's effect on obesity and health. It falls short on incorporating strong measures of sugar-sweetened beverage purchases and consumption, and total calorie intake. The proposed

study does not have a strong counterfactual to show what would have happened in the absence of the restriction. It also does not have the capacity to isolate the effect of the SNAP purchase restrictions from the proposed public information campaign that is intended to educate SNAP participants about the consequences of consuming sugar-sweetened beverages.

While it is possible that some of these concerns could potentially be addressed through additional consultation, after carefully and extensively considering your original proposal and your response to our questions, we have decided to deny the waiver request. USDA has a longstanding tradition of supporting and promoting incentive-based solutions to the obesity epidemic, especially among SNAP recipients. In fact, USDA is currently partnering with the State of Massachusetts in implementing the Healthy Incentives Pilot, which increases SNAP benefits when fruits and vegetables are purchased. This pilot also includes a significant and rigorous evaluation component to measure success in consumer behavioral changes and health outcomes. We feel it would be imprudent to reverse policy at this time while the evaluation component of the Healthy Incentives Pilot is ongoing.

We appreciate New York's interest and unparalleled leadership in pursuing innovative approaches to promote healthful diets and healthy weight, and would like to work with you in this area to achieve the goal of reduced obesity rates more effectively and efficiently. We would like to look to potential alternative collaborations such as a private-public partnership to design, implement, and evaluate an anti-obesity intervention targeting consumption and associated behaviors while encouraging healthy choices. As part of this proposed project, USDA could evaluate the intervention's efficacy and cost- effectiveness in promoting healthy choices and reducing overweight/obesity.

I regret that we were unable to reach agreement on your waiver request. However, it is clear that no single approach will reverse the trends in overweight and obesity, and our ultimate success will depend on all of us, parents, nutrition and health care providers, government officials, and other like-minded partners. USDA stands ready to work with New York City on ways to address the problem of obesity and promote good nutrition and health for all Americans.

Notes

1. Do the reasons given for rejecting New York City's proposal make

sense? If USDA had to defend its response under the arbitrary-and-capricious standard of review for agency action, would it be able to do so?

2. The USDA's rejection of New York City's proposal has prompted much academic debate. Here are excerpts from two critiques of the USDA's decision:

> Nine states have now requested permission from Congress or the USDA for tighter controls on the use of SNAP benefits, as policy makers seek novel ways to reduce the burden of obesity-related medical costs on taxpayers. Restructuring programs like SNAP provides attractive opportunities to align government spending with the long-term public health and economic interests of the nation....
>
> The government purchases millions of servings of sugar-sweetened beverages for SNAP participants each day. This practice arguably erodes diet quality and promotes chronic illness among individuals who are at increased risk of obesity-related disease because of limited financial resources. Moreover, the costs of treating chronic illness associated with increased sugar-sweetened beverage consumption in this population will fall primarily to taxpayers. To inform policy change in the public interest, elected leaders require objective data about the consequences of maintaining SNAP benefits for the purchase of sugar-sweetened beverages amid the obesity epidemic. If the USDA denies existing pilot studies by states, the agency should fund research to generate the needed data to inform policy decisions. (Kelly D. Brownell & David S. Ludwig, *The Supplemental Nutrition Assistance Program, Soda, and USDA Policy*, 306 JAMA 1370 (2011).)

> [T]here are two senses in which these policies might be considered inequitable: they are unfair, and so violate distributive equality, or they are disrespectful and so violate social equality. However, neither of these concerns offers decisive ethical objections to these policies. Distributive equality does not require maximal consumer choice, and there are reasons why the government might prioritize citizens' interests in promoting their health over their interests in consuming sugar-sweetened beverages when designing food assistance programs. The concern that these policies send demeaning message about SNAP participants, and so violate social equality, is more pressing. However, we argue that policies can be interpreted as sending various messages, and what a policy is interpreted as saying is complex and negotiated by the various inter-

ests and perspectives in a society. It is not a foregone conclusion that the policy would be widely interpreted as sending negative messages about SNAP participants rather than messages about the nutritional value of sugar-sweetened beverages. Nevertheless, when there is a possibility of negative messaging, lawmakers and others in government have an obligation to participate in the public dialogue to ensure that the policy promotes everyone's equality. (Anne Barnhill & Katherine F. King, *Evaluating Equity Critiques in Food Policy: The Case of Sugar-Sweetened Beverages*, 41 J.L Med. & Ethics 301 (2013).)

School-based Food Assistance Programs

The National School Lunch Program (NSLP) has existed in some form since 1945. Additions to school-based food assistance programs since that time have included the National School Breakfast Program and the Special Milk Program. All of these programs key benefits to income.

As with SNAP, a key challenge under the school-based assistance programs has been to deliver healthy and nutritious foods within a limited budget. This challenge has been made even more difficult by the introduction of "competitive foods" in the school environment – foods that compete with the foods provided through the federal assistance programs. An early case, National Soft Drink Association v. Block, 721 F.2d 1348 (D.C. Cir. 1983), dealt a blow to the USDA's effort to limit competitive foods by banning the sale of soda, chewing gum, and certain candies on school premises until the last lunch period had ended. The D.C. Circuit held that the statutory provision giving the USDA the authority to regulate competitive foods "in food service facilities or areas during the time of service" did not give the agency the authority to limit sales of competitive foods outside the specific areas and times when foods were being served.

The Healthy Hunger-Free Kids Act (HHFKA) of 2010 overturned National Soft Drink Associations v. Block, making national nutrition standards applicable to all foods sold on school premises. The HHFKA also directed the USDA Secretary to

- (i) establish standards that are consistent with the most recent Dietary Guidelines for Americans published under section 5341 of Title 7, including the food groups to encourage and nutrients of concern identified in the Dietary Guidelines; and
- (ii) consider—
    - (I) authoritative scientific recommendations for nutrition standards;

- (II) existing school nutrition standards, including voluntary standards for beverages and snack foods and State and local standards;
- (III) the practical application of the nutrition standards; and
- (IV) special exemptions for school-sponsored fundraisers (other than fundraising through vending machines, school stores, snack bars, a la carte sales, and any other exclusions determined by the Secretary), if the fundraisers are approved by the school and are infrequent within the school.

The USDA's final rule implementing the HHFKA required more fruits and vegetables, whole grains, and low-fat dairy products, while aiming to ensure that snack foods provided by schools were lower in fat, sugar, and sodium. Perhaps it goes without saying that the new requirements generated controversy.

In May 2017, the Trump administration issued an interim rule suspending the sodium limits and whole-grain requirements and allowing 1 percent flavored milk back on the school lunch menu.

Chapter 11 The Environmental Dimension of Food Security

Students of food systems have long drawn a connection between a healthy environment and food security. The representatives of the 185 countries represented at the World Food Summit in 1996, for example, observed the links between food insecurity and environmental problems such as the loss of biodiversity, desertification, overfishing, degradation of land, forests, water, and watersheds, and ecological changes brought on by global warming. A substantial impetus behind the contemporary food movement is the worry that our food system, and the security of the food supply it creates, is only as stable as the environment from which it comes.

Even the Pope is onto the intimate connection between food security and the environment: Pope Francis's 2015 encyclical on the environment and poverty, *Laudato Si'*, emphasizes the importance of a healthy environment to a secure food system. (Paras. 31, 32, 40)

Recall, from Chapter 9, that Wendell Berry has put the point thus:

> [I]f we understand the farm as an organism, we see that it is impossible to sacrifice the health of the soil to improve the health of plants, or to sacrifice the health of plants to improve the health of animals, or to sacrifice the health of animals to improve the health of people. In a biological pattern – as in the pattern of a community – the exploitive means and motives of industrial economics are immediately destructive and ultimately suicidal.... What is good for the water is good for the ground, what is good for the ground is good for the plants, what is good for the plants is good for animals, what is good for animals is good for people, what is good for people is good for the air, what is good for the air is good for the water. And vice versa. (Wendell Berry, Solving for Pattern, in The Gift of Good Land: Further Essay Cultural & Agricultural (North Point Press 1981).)

Given this broader context, perhaps it should not come as a surprise that federal agencies in the United States have increasingly been urged to recognize the relationship between a healthy environment and secure food. In 2015, a scientific advisory committee to the Department of Agriculture (USDA) and the Department of Health and Human Services (HHS) recommended that these agencies revise the Dietary Guidelines for Americans to take into account the environmental consequences of environmental agriculture and their implications for future food security. The recommendation met swift resistance in important quarters, with the Secretary of Agriculture himself describing the scientific advisors' recommendation as "coloring outside the lines."

USDA and HHS rejected this recommendation. Nevertheless, given the persistence of the relevant issues, it is worth considering whether the scientific advice that was presented to these agencies in 2015 was consistent with the underlying statute (or, in the Secretary of Agriculture's words, whether it "colored outside the lines") and whether including environmental consequences in dietary advice would be a useful tool in helping to ensure food security.

The statutory basis for the Dietary Guidelines for Americans is the National Nutrition Monitoring and Related Research Act of 1990. The Nutrition Monitoring Act requires the Secretaries of Agriculture and Health and Human Services to "publish a report entitled 'Dietary Guidelines for Americans.'" The following passages provide the sum total of the statutory requirements for the report containing the Dietary Guidelines:*

301. Establishment of Dietary Guidelines.

(a) Report

(1) In general

At least every five years the Secretaries shall publish a report entitled 'Dietary Guidelines for Americans.' Each such report shall contain nutritional and dietary information and guidelines for the general public, and shall be promoted by each Federal agency in carrying out any Federal food, nutrition, or health program.

(2) Basis of guidelines

---

* Another provision of the Act, section 5341(b), which we will encounter later in this Chapter, lays out requirements for agencies seeking to provide their own dietary guidance for the general population or identified subgroups.

> The information and guidelines contained in each report required under paragraph (1) shall be based on the preponderance of the scientific and medical knowledge which is current at the time the report is prepared.
>
> (3) Pregnant women and young children
>
> Not later than the 2020 report and in each report thereafter, the Secretaries shall include national nutritional and dietary information and guidelines for pregnant women and children from birth until the age of 2.

The Dietary Guidelines for Americans are, as USDA and HHS have described them, "intended to be used in developing educational materials and aiding policymakers in designing and carrying out nutrition-related programs, including Federal nutrition assistance and education programs," and they "also serve as the basis for nutrition messages and consumer materials developed by nutrition educators and health professionals for the general public and specific audiences, such as children." (2010 Dietary Guidelines for Americans, cover note.) Previous iterations of the Dietary Guidelines for Americans have contained recommendations on intake of fat, sodium, alcoholic beverages, and more. The influence of the Guidelines on food assistance programs and educational programs has long made them a focal point for political and scientific controversy.

The following are excerpts from the 2015 recommendations of the scientific advisory committee. These excerpts first give a sense of the overall thrust of the recommendations and then provide the committee's discussion relating to the incorporation of environmental considerations into the dietary guidelines. As you read the report, consider whether the Nutrition Monitoring Act limits the ability of the Secretaries of Agriculture and Health and Human Services to include environmental concerns in the Dietary Guidelines. Recalling the language of the Act, is advice about environmental sustainability appropriately considered "nutritional and dietary information and guidelines"? Is advice about environmental sustainability part of "the scientific and medical knowledge which is current" at this time? Even if environmental sustainability can be fit into the broad language of the Nutrition Monitoring Act, is there any argument that the Secretaries *must* do so if the scientific advisory committee recommends it?

Scientific Report of the 2015 Dietary Guidelines Advisory Committee: Advisory Report to the Security of Health and Human Services and the Secretary of Agriculture

February 2015

Executive Summary

The 2015 Dietary Guidelines Advisory Committee (DGAC) was established jointly by the Secretaries of the U.S. Department of Health and Human Services (HHS) and the U.S. Department of Agriculture (USDA). The Committee was charged with examining the *Dietary Guidelines for Americans,* 2010 to determine topics for which new scientific evidence was likely to be available with the potential to inform the next edition of the Guidelines and to place its primary emphasis on the development of food-based recommendations that are of public health importance for Americans ages 2 years and older published since the last DGAC deliberations.

The 2015 DGAC's work was guided by two fundamental realities. First, about half of all American adults—117 million individuals—have one or more preventable, chronic diseases, and about two-thirds of U.S. adults—nearly 155 million individuals—are overweight or obese. These conditions have been highly prevalent for more than two decades. Poor dietary patterns, overconsumption of calories, and physical inactivity directly contribute to these disorders. Second, individual nutrition and physical activity behaviors and other health-related lifestyle behaviors are strongly influenced by personal, social, organizational, and environmental contexts and systems. Positive changes in individual diet and physical activity behaviors, and in the environmental contexts and systems that affect them, could substantially improve health outcomes.

Recognizing these realities, the Committee developed a conceptual model based on socio-ecological frameworks to guide its work and organized its evidence review to examine current status and trends in food and nutrient intakes, dietary patterns and health outcomes, individual lifestyle behavior change, food and physical activity environments and settings, and food sustainability and safety....

Food and Nutrient Intakes, and Health: Current Status and Trends

The DGAC conducted data analyses to address a series of questions related to the current status and trends in the Nation's dietary intake. The questions focused on: intake of specific nutrients and food groups; food categories (i.e., foods as consumed) that contribute to intake; eating behaviors; and the composition of various dietary patterns shown to have health benefits....

The DGAC found that several nutrients are underconsumed relative to the Estimated Average Requirement or Adequate Intake levels set by the

Institute of Medicine (IOM) and the Committee characterized these as shortfall nutrients: vitamin A, vitamin D, vitamin E, vitamin C, folate, calcium, magnesium, fiber, and potassium. For adolescent and premenopausal females, iron also is a shortfall nutrient.... The DGAC also found that two nutrients—sodium and saturated fat—are overconsumed by the U.S. population relative to the Tolerable Upper Intake Level set by the IOM or other maximal standard and that the overconsumption poses health risks.

In comparison to recommended amounts in the USDA Food Patterns, the majority of the U.S. population has low intakes of key food groups that are important sources of the shortfall nutrients, including vegetables, fruits, whole grains, and dairy. Furthermore, population intake is too high for refined grains and added sugars. The data suggest cautious optimism about dietary intake of the youngest members of the U.S. population because many young children ages 2 to 5 years consume recommended amounts of fruit and dairy. However, a better understanding is needed on how to maintain and encourage good habits that are started early in life. Analysis of data on food categories, such as burgers, sandwiches, mixed dishes, desserts, and beverages, shows that the composition of many of these items could be improved so as to increase population intake of vegetables, whole grains, and other underconsumed food groups and to lower population intake of the nutrients sodium and saturated fat, and the food component refined grains. Improved beverage selections that limit or remove sugar-sweetened beverages and place limits on sweets and desserts would help lower intakes of the food component, added sugars....

The DGAC had enough descriptive information from existing research and data to model three dietary patterns and to examine their nutritional adequacy. These patterns are the Healthy U.S.-style Pattern, the Healthy Mediterranean-style Pattern, and the Healthy Vegetarian Pattern. These patterns include the components of a dietary pattern associated with health benefits.

Dietary Patterns, Foods and Nutrients, and Health Outcomes

A major goal of the DGAC was to describe the common characteristics of healthy diets, and the Committee focused on research examining dietary patterns because the totality of diet—the combinations and quantities in which foods and nutrients are consumed—may have synergistic and cumulative effects on health and disease. The Committee focused on providing a qualitative description of healthy dietary patterns based on scientific evidence for several health outcomes....

The overall body of evidence examined by the 2015 DGAC identifies that a healthy dietary pattern is higher in vegetables, fruits, whole grains, low- or non-fat dairy, seafood, legumes, and nuts; moderate in alcohol (among adults); lower in red and processed meat; and low in sugar-sweetened foods and drinks and refined grains. Vegetables and fruit are the only characteristics of the diet that were consistently identified in every conclusion statement across the health outcomes. Whole grains were identified slightly less consistently compared to vegetables and fruits, but were identified in every conclusion with moderate to strong evidence. For studies with limited evidence, grains were not as consistently defined and/or they were not identified as a key characteristic. Low- or non-fat dairy, seafood, legumes, nuts, and alcohol were identified as beneficial characteristics of the diet for some, but not all, outcomes. For conclusions with moderate to strong evidence, higher intake of red and processed meats was identified as detrimental compared to lower intake. Higher consumption of sugar-sweetened foods and beverages as well as refined grains was identified as detrimental in almost all conclusion statements with moderate to strong evidence....

Following a dietary pattern associated with reduced risk of CVD, overweight, and obesity also will have positive health benefits beyond these categories of health outcomes. Thus, the U.S. population should be encouraged and guided to consume dietary patterns that are rich in vegetables, fruit, whole grains, seafood, legumes, and nuts; moderate in low- and non-fat dairy products and alcohol (among adults); lower in red and processed meat; and low in sugar-sweetened foods and beverages and refined grains. These dietary patterns can be achieved in many ways and should be tailored to the individual's biological and medical needs as well as socio-cultural preferences....

Individual Diet and Physical Activity Behavior Change

The individual is at the innermost core of the social-ecological model. In order for policy recommendations such as the *Dietary Guidelines for Americans* to be fully implemented, motivating and facilitating behavioral change at the individual level is required. This chapter suggests a number of promising behavior change strategies that can be used to favorably affect a range of health-related outcomes and to enhance the effectiveness of interventions. These include reducing screen time, reducing the frequency of eating out at fast food restaurants, increasing frequency of family shared meals, and self-monitoring of diet and body weight as well as effective food labeling to target healthy food choices. These strategies complement comprehensive lifestyle interventions and nutrition counseling by qualified nutrition professionals....

Food Environment and Settings

Environmental and policy approaches are needed to complement individual-based efforts to improve diet and reduce obesity and other diet-related chronic diseases. These approaches have the potential for broad and sustained impact at the population level because they can become incorporated into organizational structures and systems and lead to alterations in sociocultural and societal norms. Both policy and environmental changes also can help reduce disparities by improving access to and availability of healthy food in underserved neighborhoods and communities. Federal nutrition assistance programs, in particular, play a vital role in achieving this objective through access to affordable foods that help millions of Americans meet Dietary Guidelines recommendations.

The DGAC focused on physical environments (settings) in which food is available. Its aim was to better understand the impact of the food environment to promote or hinder healthy eating in these settings and to identify the most effective evidence-based diet-related approaches and policies to improve diet and weight status. The DGAC focused on four settings—community food access, child care, schools, and worksites—and their relationships to dietary intake and quality and weight status.

The DGAC found moderate and promising evidence that multi-component obesity prevention approaches implemented in child care settings, schools, and worksites improve weight-related outcomes; strong to moderate evidence that school and worksite policies are associated with improved dietary intake; and moderate evidence that multi-component school-based and worksite approaches increase vegetable and fruit consumption. For the questions on community food access addressing the relationship between food retail settings and dietary intake and quality and weight status, the evidence was too limited or insufficient to assign grades. To reduce the disparity gaps that currently exist in low resource and underserved communities, more solution-oriented strategies need to be implemented and evaluated on ways to increase access to and procurement of healthy affordable foods and beverages, and also to reduce access to energy-dense, nutrient-poor foods and beverages....

Food Sustainability and Safety

Access to sufficient, nutritious, and safe food is an essential element of food security for the U.S. population. A sustainable diet ensures this access for both the current population and future generations.

The major findings regarding sustainable diets were that a diet higher in plant-based foods, such as vegetables, fruits, whole grains, legumes, nuts, and seeds, and lower in calories and animal-based foods is more health promoting and is associated with less environmental impact than is the current U.S. diet. This pattern of eating can be achieved through a variety of dietary patterns, including the Healthy U.S.-style Pattern, the Healthy Mediterranean-style Pattern, and the Healthy Vegetarian Pattern. All of these dietary patterns are aligned with lower environmental impacts and provide options that can be adopted by the U.S. population. Current evidence shows that the average U.S. diet has a larger environmental impact in terms of increased greenhouse gas emissions, land use, water use, and energy use, compared to the above dietary patterns. This is because the current U.S. population intake of animal-based foods is higher and plant-based foods are lower, than proposed in these three dietary patterns. Of note is that no food groups need to be eliminated completely to improve sustainability outcomes over the current status.

A moderate amount of seafood is an important component of two of three of these dietary patterns, and has demonstrated health benefits. The seafood industry is in the midst of rapid expansion to meet worldwide demand. The collapse of some fisheries due to overfishing in the past decades has raised concern about the ability to produce a safe and affordable supply. In addition, concern has been raised about the safety and nutrient content of farm-raised versus wild-caught seafood. To supply enough seafood to support meeting dietary recommendations, both farm-raised and wild caught seafood will be needed. The review of the evidence demonstrated, in the species evaluated, that farm-raised seafood has as much or more EPA and DHA per serving as wild caught. It should be noted that low-trophic seafood, such as catfish and crawfish, regardless of whether wild caught or farm-raised seafood, have less EPA and DHA per serving than high-trophic seafood, such as salmon and trout.

Regarding contaminants, for the majority of wild caught and farmed species, neither the risks of mercury nor organic pollutants outweigh the health benefits of seafood consumption. Consistent evidence demonstrated that wild caught fisheries that have been managed sustainably have remained stable over the past several decades; however, wild caught fisheries are fully exploited and their continuing productivity will require careful management nationally and internationally to avoid long-term collapse. Expanded supply of seafood nationally and internationally will depend upon the increase of farm-raised seafood worldwide.

The impact of food production, processing, and consumption on environmental sustainability is an area of research that is rapidly evolving. As further research is conducted and best practices are evaluated, additional evidence will inform both supply-side participants and consumers on how best to shift behaviors locally, nationally, and globally to support sustainable diets. Linking health, dietary guidance, and the environment will promote human health and the sustainability of natural resources and ensure current and long-term food security....

Individual behaviors along with sound government policies and responsible private sector practices are all needed to reduce foodborne illnesses. To that end, the DGAC updated the established recommendations for handling foods at home.

Cross-cutting Topics of Public Health Importance

The *2010 Dietary Guidelines* included guidance on sodium, saturated fat, and added sugars, and the 2015 DGAC determined that a reexamination of the evidence on these topics was necessary to determine whether revisions to the guidance were warranted. These topics were considered to be of public health importance because each has been associated with negative health outcomes when overconsumed. Additionally, the Committee acknowledged that a potential unintended consequence of a recommendation on added sugars might be that consumers and manufacturers replace added sugars with low-calorie sweeteners. As a result, the Committee also examined evidence on low-calorie sweeteners to inform statements on this topic.

The DGAC encourages the consumption of healthy dietary patterns that are low in saturated fat, added sugars, and sodium. The goals for the general population are: less than 2,300 mg dietary sodium per day (or age-appropriate Dietary Reference Intake amount), less than 10 percent of total calories from saturated fat per day, and a maximum of 10 percent of total calories from added sugars per day.

Sodium, saturated fat, and added sugars are not intended to be reduced in isolation, but as a part of a healthy dietary pattern that is balanced, as appropriate, in calories. Rather than focusing purely on reduction, emphasis should also be placed on replacement and shifts in food intake and eating patterns. Sources of saturated fat should be replaced with unsaturated fat, particularly polyunsaturated fatty acids. Similarly, added sugars should be reduced in the diet and not replaced with low-calorie sweeteners, but rather with healthy options, such as water in place of sugar-sweetened beverages. For sodium, emphasis should be placed on expanding industry efforts to reduce the sodium content of foods and helping consumers understand how to flavor unsalted foods with spices and herbs.

Reducing sodium, saturated fat, and added sugars can be accomplished and is more attainable by eating a healthy dietary pattern. For all three of these components of the diet, policies and programs at local, state, and national levels in both the private and public sector are necessary to support reduction efforts. Similarly, the Committee supports efforts in labeling and other campaigns to increase consumer awareness and understanding of sodium, saturated fats, and added sugars in foods and beverages. The Committee encourages the food industry to continue reformulating and making changes to certain foods to improve their nutrition profile. Examples of such actions include lowering sodium and added sugars content, achieving better saturated fat to polyunsaturated fat ratio, and reducing portion sizes in retail settings (restaurants, food outlets, and public venues, such as professional sports stadiums and arenas). The Committee also encourages the food industry to market these improved products to consumers.

Physical Activity

This chapter provides strong evidence supporting the importance of regular physical activity for health promotion and disease prevention in the U.S. population. Physical activity is important for all people—children, adolescents, adults, older adults, women during pregnancy and the postpartum period, and individuals with disabilities. The findings further provide guidance on the dose of physical activity needed across the lifecycle to realize these significant health benefits....

Integrating the Evidence

The research base reviewed by the 2015 DGAC provides clear evidence that persistent, prevalent, preventable health problems, notably overweight and obesity, cardiovascular disease, type 2 diabetes, and certain cancers, have adversely affected the health of the U.S. public for decades and raise the urgency for immediate attention and bold action. Evidence points to specific areas of current food and nutrient concerns and it pinpoints the characteristics of healthy dietary and physical activity patterns that can reduce chronic disease risk, promote healthy weight status, and foster good health across the lifespan. In addition, research evidence is converging to show that healthy dietary patterns also are more sustainable and associated with more favorable health as well as environmental outcomes....

It will take concerted, bold actions on the part of individuals, families, communities, industry, and government to achieve and maintain the healthy diet patterns and the levels of physical activity needed to promote the health of the U.S. population. These actions will require a paradigm shift to an environment in which population health is a national priority and where individuals and organizations, private business, and communities work together to achieve a population-wide "culture of health" in which healthy lifestyle choices are easy, accessible, affordable, and normative—both at home and away from home. In such a culture, health care and public health professionals also would embrace a new leadership role in prevention, convey the importance of lifestyle behavior change to their patients/clients, set standards for prevention in their own facilities, and help patients/clients in accessing evidence-based and effective nutrition and comprehensive lifestyle services and programs....

Chapter 5: Food Sustainability and Safety

Introduction

In this chapter, the DGAC addresses food and nutrition issues that will inform public health action and policies to promote the health of the population through sustainable diets and food safety. An important reason for addressing sustainable diets, a new area for the DGAC, is to have alignment and consistency in dietary guidance that promotes both health and sustainability. This also recognizes the significant impact of food and beverages on environmental outcomes, from farm to plate to waste disposal, and, therefore, the need for dietary guidance to include the wider issue of sustainability. Addressing this complex challenge is essential to ensure a healthy food supply will be available for future generations. The availability and acceptability of healthy and sustainable food choices will be necessary to attain food security for the U.S. population over time. Integral to this issue is how dietary guidance and individual food choices influence the nation's capacity to meet the nutritional needs of the U.S. population. Food sustainability and food safety are also interrelated in generating a secure food supply. This chapter focuses on both sustainable diets and food safety.

Food Sustainability

Two definitions are relevant to the material presented in this chapter. These terms were slightly modified from the Food and Agriculture Organization (FAO) definitions to operationalize them for the Committee's work.

Sustainable diets: Sustainable diets are a pattern of eating that promotes health and well-being and provides food security for the present population while sustaining human and natural resources for future generations.

Food security: Food security exists when all people now, and in the future, have access to sufficient, safe, and nutritious food to main tain a healthy and active life.

The topic of *current* food security was addressed in Chapter 3 and to some extent in Chapter 4, where federal food programs were discussed. The topic of *long-term* food security was addressed within this chapter through examination of the evidence on sustainable diets.

The environmental impact of food production is considerable and if natural resources such as land, water and energy are not conserved and managed optimally, they will be strained and potentially lost. The global production of food is responsible for 80 percent of deforestation, more than 70 percent of fresh water use, and up to 30 percent of human-generated greenhouse gas (GHG) emissions. It also is the largest cause of species biodiversity loss. The capacity to produce adequate food in the future is constrained by land use, declining soil fertility, unsustainable water use, and over-fishing of the marine environment. Climate change, shifts in population dietary patterns and demand for food products, energy costs, and population growth will continue to put additional pressures on available natural resources. Meeting current and future food needs will depend on two concurrent approaches: altering individual and population dietary choices and patterns and developing agricultural and production practices that reduce environmental impacts and conserve resources, while still meeting food and nutrition needs. In this chapter, the Committee focuses primarily on the former, examining the effect of population- level dietary choices on sustainability.

Foods vary widely in the type and amount of resources required for production, so as population-level consumer demand impacts food production (and imports) it will also indirectly influence how and to what extent resources are used. As the focus of the dietary guidelines is to shift consumer eating habits toward healthier alternatives, it is imperative that, in this context, the shift also involve movement toward less resource-intensive diets. Individual and population-level adoption of more sustainable diets can change consumer demand away from more resource-intensive foods to foods that have a lower environmental impact.

In this chapter, the DGAC has used an evidence-based approach to evaluate the foods and food components that improve the sustainability of dietary patterns as a step toward this desirable goal. The approach used was to determine dietary patterns that are nutritionally adequate and promote health, while at the same time are more protective of natural resources. This type of comprehensive strategy also has been used by intergovernmental organizations. For example, the FAO has identified the Mediterranean diet as an example of a sustainable diet due to its emphasis on biodiversity and smaller meat portions, and the European Commission has developed a "2020 Live Well Diet" to reduce GHG emissions through diet change.

It should be noted that research in the area of dietary patterns and sustainability is rapidly evolving and the methodologies for determining dietary patterns in populations and Life Cycle Analysis of foods/food components and environmental outcomes have made significant advances in recent years....

Figure D5.1 outlines the interconnected elements that the DGAC believes are necessary based on current evidence to develop sustainable diets. Sustainable diets are realized by developing a food system that embraces a core set of values illustrated in the figure. These values need to be implemented through robust private and public sector partnerships, practices and policies across the supply chain, extending from farms to distribution and consumption. New well-coordinated policies that include, but are not limited to, agriculture, economics, transportation, energy, water use, and dietary guidance need to be developed. Behaviors of all participants in the food system are central to creating and supporting sustainable diets.

Figure D5.1: Elements needed for sustainable diets

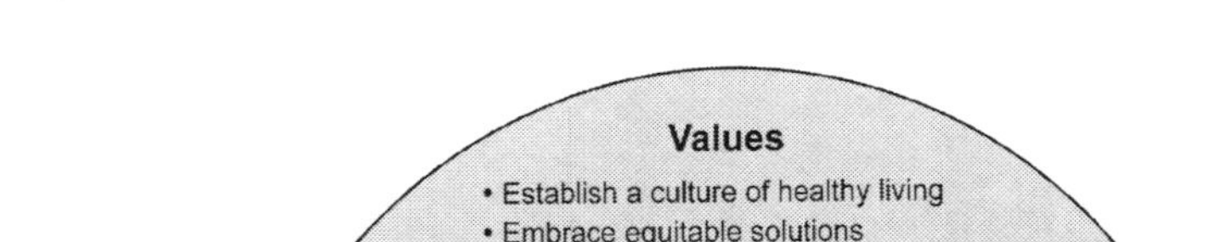
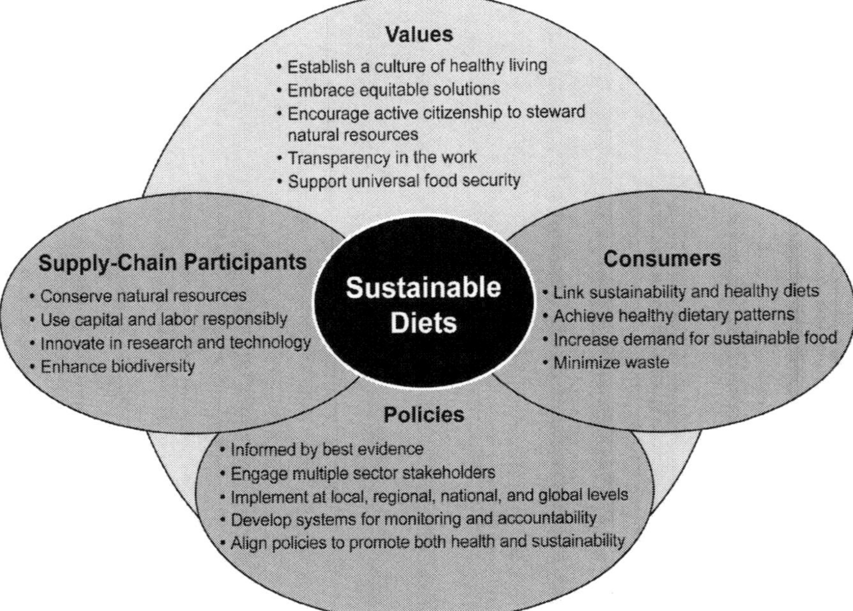

Although the addition of sustainability topics in the *Scientific Report of the 2015 Dietary Guidelines Advisory Committee* is new in 2015 it was acknowledged as a topic of strong relevance but not addressed by the 2010 DGAC. It has been a widely discussed aspect of nutrition policy for the past decade in countries such as Germany, Sweden and other Nordic countries, the Netherlands, Australia, and Brazil. For example, in the Netherlands, the Advisory report, *Guidelines for a Healthy Diet: The Ecological Perspective* focused on guidelines that inform both health and ecological benefits using an evidence-based strategy. Nordic countries, such as Sweden, have been researching sustainability and dietary choice since the late 1990s with the most recent edition of the Nordic Nutrition Recommendations (NNR) including an emphasis on the environmental impact of dietary recommendations. The German Dietary Guidelines developed a "sustainable shopping basket," which is a consumer guide for shopping in a more sustainable way. Overall, the environmentally sustainable dietary guidance from these countries includes elements identified in this DGAC report as consistent with the extant data: a focus on decreasing meat consumption, choosing seafood from non-threatened stocks, eating more plants and plant-based products, reducing energy intake, and reducing waste. Non-governmental and international organizations, such as the United Nations, the FAO, the Sustainable Development Commission in the United Kingdom (UK), the Institute of Medicine (IOM), the Academy of Nutrition and Dietetics, and the National Research Council have all convened working groups and commissioned reports on sustainable diets. Overall, it is clear that environmental sustainability adds further dimensions to dietary guidance; not just what we eat but where and how food production, processing, and transportation are managed, and waste is decreased.

The DGAC focused on two main topic areas related to sustainability: dietary patterns and seafood. The identification of dietary patterns that are sustainable is a first step toward driving consumer behavior change and demand and supply-chain changes. Furthermore, dietary patterns were an overall focus area of the 2015 DGAC and allow for a more comprehensive approach to total diet and health. This approach is particularly well suited for assessing overall environmental impacts of food consumption, as all food components of a dietary pattern are identified, and keeping within the context of health outcomes that have been documented for different dietary patterns. The topic area of seafood was chosen because consumption has well-established health benefits and the 2010 DGAC report highlighted the concern for seafood sustainability and called for a better understanding of the environmental impact of aquaculture on seafood contaminants. Meeting these recommendations, however, increases demand for seafood production and this, in turn, poses challenges, as certain seafood species are depleted and marine waters are over fished, while most other species are at the limits of sustainable harvesting. To meet these challenges, as world capture fisheries production has leveled off, aquaculture production has increased to meet demand. Therefore, building upon the 2010 DGAC report, the 2015 DGAC addressed the health benefits (nutrients) versus the risks (contaminants) of farm-raised (aquaculture) compared to wild-caught seafood and reviewed the evidence on the worldwide capacity to produce enough seafood to meet dietary guidelines. Overall, promoting sustainable fishing and aquaculture can provide an example for broader ecosystem stewardship.

Food Safety

Food safety was first introduced in the *2000 Dietary Guidelines for Americans*, and the recognition of the importance of food safety continued through the 2010 report. This chapter updates the 2010 DGAC report related to food safety behaviors in the home environment and evaluates new topics of food safety concern with very current and/or updated evidence. The current/updated topics include the safety of beverages, specifically coffee and caffeine, and food additives, specifically aspartame, in the U.S. food supply.

In 2015, the DGAC addressed new topics of concern. For the first time, the DGAC addressed the safety of coffee/caffeine consumption, as well as the safety of consuming higher doses of caffeine in products such as some energy drinks. The food additive, aspartame, has been the only non-nutritive sweetener to be completely re-evaluated in recent years and the results of this reevaluation were deemed important because it includes the most recent science on aspartame and health. These topic areas were chosen for consideration because they are of high public health concern and very recent evidence has been published that significantly updates the knowledge base on health aspects related to caffeine and aspartame in the diet.

For 2015, the DGAC brought forward the updated food safety principles to reduce risk of foodborne illnesses. These principles—Clean, Separate, Cook and Chill—are cornerstones of the Fight BAC! educational messages developed by the Partnership for Food Safety Education, a collaboration with the Federal government. These messages are reinforced by other USDA educational materials, including the *Be Food Safe* efforts; Is it Done Yet?; and *Thermy*, which outline key elements in thermometer use and placement to ensure proper cooking of meat, poultry, seafood, and egg products.…The DGAC brought forward the guidance for consumers that has been updated since 2010 on recommended procedures for hand sanitation, washing fresh produce, preventing cross-contamination, and safe meat, poultry, seafood and egg cooking temperatures and thermometer use from the FDA, the Center for Disease Control (CDC) and the Food Safety and Inspection Service (FSIS)….

List of Questions – Sustainable Diets and Dietary Patterns

- What is the relationship between population-level dietary patterns and long-term food sustainability?
- What are the comparative nutrient profiles of current farm-raised versus wild caught seafood?
- What are the comparative contaminant levels of current farm-raised versus wild caught seafood?
- What is the worldwide capacity to produce farm-raised versus wild-caught seafood that is nutritious and safe for Americans?...

Methodology – Sustainable Diets

The topic of Question 1 is new for a DGAC review and involves an emerging area of scientific investigation that is not readily addressed by traditional study designs such as randomized controlled trials and prospective cohort studies. The literature related to sustainable diets and dietary patterns involves a combination of food pattern modeling, Life Cycle Assessment (LCA) methodology (examines all processes in the life cycle of each food component - from farm to plate to waste), and determination of the environmental outcomes of the full LCA inventory....

Sustainable Diets

Evaluating the link between sustainability and dietary guidance will inform policies and practice to ensure food security for present and future generations. The DGAC concentrated its review on the inter-relatedness between human health and food sustainability, with a focus on dietary patterns, a theme of the 2015 DGAC.

Dietary Patterns and Sustainability

Question 1: What is the relationship between population-level dietary patterns and long-term food sustainability?...

Conclusion

Consistent evidence indicates that, in general, a dietary pattern that is higher in plant-based foods, such as vegetables, fruits, whole grains, legumes, nuts, and seeds, and lower in animal-based foods is more health promoting and is associated with lesser environmental impact (GHG emissions and energy, land, and water use) than is the current average U.S. diet. A diet that is more environmentally sustainable than the average U.S. diet can be achieved without excluding any food groups. The evidence consists primarily of Life Cycle Assessment (LCA) modeling studies or land-use studies from highly developed countries, including the United States. DGAC Grade: Moderate

Implications

A moderate to strong evidence base supports recommendations that the U.S. population move toward dietary patterns that generally increase consumption of vegetables, fruits, whole grains, legumes, nuts and seeds, while decreasing total calories and some animal-based foods. This can be achieved through a variety of dietary patterns, including the Healthy USDA-style Pattern, the Healthy Vegetarian Pattern, and the Healthy Mediterranean-style Pattern. Each of these patterns provides more plant-based foods and lower amounts of meat than are currently consumed by the U.S. population.

Sustainability considerations provide an additional rationale for following the Dietary Guidelines for Americans and should be incorporated into federal and local nutrition feeding programs when possible. Using sustainability messaging in communication strategies should be encouraged. The application of environmental and sustainability factors to dietary guidelines can be accomplished because of the compatibility and degree of overlap between favorable health and environmental outcomes.

Much has been done by the private and public sectors to improve environmental policies and practices around production, processing, and distribution *within* individual food categories. It will be important that *both* a greater shift toward healthful dietary patterns and an improved environmental profile across food categories are achieved to maximize environmental sustainability now and to ensure greater progress in this direction over time.

Consumer friendly information that facilitates understanding the environmental impact of different foods should be considered for inclusion in food and menu labeling initiatives.

Careful consideration will need to be made to ensure that sustainable diets are affordable for the entire U.S. population.

Promoting healthy diets that also are more environmentally sustainable now will conserve resources for present and future generations, ensuring that the U.S. population has access to a diet that is healthy as well as sustainable and secure in the future.

Review of the Evidence

A total of 15 studies met the inclusion criteria for this systematic review. The body of evidence consisted primarily of dietary pattern modeling studies that assessed related environmental outcomes. These studies were conducted between the years 2003 and 2014 in the U.S., the UK, Germany, the Netherlands, France, Spain, Italy, Australia, Brazil, and New Zealand. Dietary patterns that were examined included vegetarian, lacto-ovo vegetarian, and vegan dietary patterns; the average and dietary guidelines-related dietary patterns of respective countries examined; Mediterranean-style dietary patterns; and sustainable diets. The most frequent comparison diet was the average dietary pattern of the country, although numerous studies made additional comparisons across many of the above dietary patterns. Another approach was to examine diet "scenarios" that modeled different percentage replacements of meat and dairy foods with plant-based foods. The modeling studies used cross-sectional assessment of dietary intake from national nutrition surveys of representative adult populations; for example, the British National Diet and Nutrition Survey (NDNS) from studies in the UK, the National Nutrition Surveys (NNS) in Germany, or the Australian National Nutrition Survey were used to determine the observed average dietary patterns. The average dietary patterns were then compared with other modeled dietary patterns, such as vegetarian or Mediterranean- style patterns, as described in detail below. All of the countries were highly developed countries with dietary guidelines and, therefore, generalizable to the U.S. population. The study quality for the body of evidence ranged from scores of 7/12 to 12/12 (indicating the evidence was of high quality) using a modified Critical Appraisal Checklist.

Health outcomes associated with the dietary patterns were most often documented based on adherence to dietary guidelines-related patterns, variations on vegetarian dietary patterns, or Mediterranean-style dietary patterns. Diet quality was assessed in some studies using an a priori index, such as the Healthy Eating Index (HEI) or the WHO Index. In some studies, health outcomes also were modeled. For example Scarborough et al. used the DIETRON model to estimate deaths delayed or averted for each diet pattern. One study assessed the synergy between health and sustainability scores using the WHO Index and the LCA sustainability score to assess combined nutritional and ecological value.

The environmental impacts that were most commonly modeled were GHG emissions and use of resources such as agricultural land, energy, and water. In many studies, the environmental impact for each food/food category was obtained using the LCA method. The LCA is a standardized methodological framework for assessing the environmental impact (or load) attributable to the life cycle of a food product. The life cycle for a food typically includes agricultural production, processing and packaging, transportation, retail, use, and waste disposal. An inventory of all stages of the life cycle is determined for each food product and a "weight" or number of points is then attributed to each food or food category, based on environmental impacts such as resource extraction, land use, and relevant emissions. These environmental impact results can be translated into measures of damage done to human health, ecosystem quality, and energy resources using programs such as Eco-Indicator. In addition to the health assessment approaches listed above, some studies used LCA analysis with a standardized approach to determine damages from GHG emissions and use of resources; these damage outcome included human health as an environmental damage component, such as the number and duration of diseases and life years lost due to premature death from environmental causes.

Few studies assessed food security. These studies assessed food security in terms of the cost difference between an average dietary pattern for the country studied and a sustainable dietary pattern for that population. The basic food basket concept was used in some studies, representing household costs for a two-adult/two-child household.

Identified Dietary Patterns and Health and Sustainability Outcomes

Vegetarian and Meat-based Diets

Several studies examined variations on vegetarian diets, or a spectrum from vegan to omnivorous dietary patterns, and associated environmental outcomes. Peters et al. examined 42 different dietary patterns and land use in New York, with patterns ranging from low-fat, lacto-ovo vegetarian diets to high fat, meat-rich omnivorous diets; across this range, the diets met U.S. dietary guidelines when possible. They found that, overall, increasing meat in the diet increased per capita land requirements; however, increasing total dietary fat content of low-meat diets (i.e. vegetarian alternatives) increased the land requirements compared to high-meat diets. In other words, although meat increased land requirements, diets including meat could feed more people than some higher fat vegetarian-style diets. Aston et al. assessed a pattern that was modeled on a feasible UK population in which the proportion of vegetarians in the survey was doubled, and the remainder adopted a diet pattern consistent with the lowest category of red and processed meat (RPM) consumers. They found the combination of low RPM + vegetarian diet had health benefits of lowering the risk of diabetes and colorectal cancer, determined from risk relationships for RPM and CHD, diabetes, and colorectal cancer from published meta-analyses. Furthermore, the expected reduction in GHG for this diet was ~3 percent of current total carbon dioxide (CO2) emissions for agriculture. De Carvalho et al. also examined a high RPM dietary pattern with diet quality assessed using the Brazilian Healthy Eating Index. They found that excessive meat intake was associated not only with poorer diet quality but also with increased projected GHG emissions (~4 percent total CO2 emitted by agriculture). Taken together, the results on RPM intake indicate that reduced consumption is expected to improve some health outcomes and decrease GHG emissions, as well as land use compared to current RPM consumption. Baroni et al. examined vegan, vegetarian, and omnivorous diets, both organically and conventionally grown, and found that the organically grown vegan diet had the most potential health benefits; whereas, the conventionally grown average Italian diet had the least. The organically grown vegan diet also had the lowest estimated impact on resources and ecosystem quality, and the average Italian diet had the greatest projected impact. Beef was the single food with the greatest projected impact on the environment; other foods estimated to have high impact included cheese, milk, and seafood.

Vegetarian diets, dietary guidelines-related diets, and Mediterranean-style diets were variously compared with the average dietary patterns in selected countries. Overall, the estimated greater environmental benefits, including reduced projected GHG emissions and land use, resulted from vegan, lacto-ovo vegetarian, and pesco-vegetarian diets, as well as dietary guidelines-related and Mediterranean-style dietary patterns. These diets had higher overall predicted health scores than the average diet patterns. Moreover, for the most part, the high health scores of these dietary patterns were paralleled by high combined estimated sustainability scores. According to van Doreen et al., the synergy measured across vegetarian, Mediterranean-style, and dietary guidelines-related scores could be explained by a reduction in consumption of meat, dairy, extras (i.e., snacks and sweets), and beverages, as well as a reduction in overall food consumption.

Mediterranean-Style Dietary Patterns

The Mediterranean-style dietary pattern was examined in both Mediterranean and non-Mediterranean countries. In all cases, adherence to a Mediterranean-style dietary pattern—compared to usual intake—reduced the environmental footprint, including improved GHG emissions, agricultural land use, and energy and water consumption. Both studies limited either red and processed meat or meat and poultry to less than 1 serving per week, and increased seafood intake. The authors concluded that adherence to a Mediterranean-style dietary pattern would make a significant contribution to increasing food sustainability, as well as increasing the health benefits that are well-documented for this type of diet.

Diet Scenarios

Other studies examined different diet "scenarios" that generally replaced animal foods in various ways with plant foods. Scarborough et al. found that a diet with 50 percent reduced total meat and dairy replaced by fruit, vegetables, and cereals contributed the most to estimated reduced risk of total mortality and also had the largest potential positive environmental impact. This diet scenario increased fruit and vegetable consumption by 63 percent and decreased saturated fat and salt consumption; micronutrient intake was generally similar with the exception of a drop in vitamin B12.

Pradhan et al. examined 16 global dietary patterns that differed by food and energy content, grouped into four categories with per capita intake of low, moderate, high, and very high kcal diets. They assessed the relationship of these patterns to GHG emissions. Low-energy diets had less than 2,100 kcal/cap/day and were composed of more than 50 percent cereals or more than 70 percent starchy roots, cereals, and pulses. Animal products were minor in this group (<10 percent). Moderate, high, and very high energy diets had 2,100-2,400, 2,400-2,800, and greater than 2,800 kcal/cap/day, respectively. Very high calorie diets had high amounts of meat and alcoholic beverages. Overall, very high calorie diets, common in the developed world, exhibited high total per capita CO2eq emissions due to high carbon intensity and high intake of animal products; the low-energy diets, on the other hand, had the lowest total per capita CO2eq emissions.

Lastly, Vieux et al. examined dietary patterns with different indicators of nutritional quality and found that despite containing large amounts of plant foods, not all diets of the highest nutritional quality were those with the lowest GHG emissions.47 For this study, the diet pattern was assessed by using nutrient-based indicators; high quality diets had energy density below the median, mean adequacy ratio above the median, and a mean excess ratio (percentage of maximum recommended for nutrients that should be limited – saturated fat, sodium, and free sugars) below the median. Four diet patterns were identified based on compliance with these properties to generate one high quality diet, two intermediate quality diets, and one low quality diet. In this study, the high quality diets had higher GHG emissions than did the low quality diets. Regarding the food groups, a higher consumption of starches, sweets and salted snacks, and fats was associated with lower diet-related GHG emissions and an increased intake of fruit and vegetables, was associated with increased diet-related GHG emissions. However, the strongest positive association with GHG emissions was still for the ruminant meat group. Overall, this study used a different approach from the other studies in this review, as nutritional quality determined the formation of dietary pattern categories.

Sustainable Diets and Costs

Three studies examined sustainable diets and related costs. Barosh et al. examined food availability and cost of a health and sustainability (H&S) food basket, developed according to the principles of the Australian dietary guidelines as well as environmental impact. The food basket approach is a commonly used method for assessing and monitoring food availability and cost. The typical food basket was based on average weekly food purchases of a reference household made up of two adults and two children. For the H&S basket, food choices were based on health principles and environmental impact. The H&S basket was compared to the typical Australian basket and it was determined that the cost of the H&S basket was more than the typical basket in five socioeconomic areas; the most disadvantaged spent 30 percent more for the H&S basket. The authors concluded that the most disadvantaged groups at both neighborhood and household levels experienced the greatest inequality in accessing an affordable H&S basket. Macdiarmid et al. examined a sustainable diet (met all energy and nutrient needs and maximally decreased GHG emissions), a "sustainable with acceptability constraints" diet (added foods commonly consumed in the UK; met energy, nutrient, and seafood recommendations as well as recommended minimum intakes for fruits and vegetables and did not exceed the maximum recommended for red and processed meat), and the average UK diet. They found that the sustainable diet that was generated would decrease GHG emissions from primary production (up to distribution) by 90 percent, but consisted of only seven foods. The acceptability constraints diet included 52 foods and was projected to reduce GHG emissions by 36 percent. This diet included meat and dairy but less than the average UK diet. The cost of the sustainable + acceptability diet was comparable to that of the average UK diet. These results showed that a sustainable diet that meets dietary requirements and has lower GHG can be achieved without eliminating meat or dairy products completely, or increasing the cost to the consumer. Lastly, Wilson et al. examined 16 dietary patterns modeled to determine which patterns would minimize estimated risk of chronic disease, cost, and GHG emissions. These patterns included low-cost and low-cost + low GHG diet patterns, as well as healthy patterns with high vegetable intakes including Mediterranean or Asian patterns, as well as the average New Zealand pattern. The authors found that diets that aimed to minimize cost and estimated GHG emissions also had health advantages, such as the simplified low-cost Mediterranean-style and simplified Asian-style diets, both of which would lower cardiovascular disease and cancer risk, compared to the average New Zealand diet. However, dietary variety was limited and further optimization to lower GHG emissions increased cost.

Overall, the studies were consistent in showing that higher consumption of animal-based foods was associated with higher estimated environmental impact, whereas consumption of more plant-based foods as part of a lower meat-based or vegetarian-style dietary pattern was associated with estimated lower environmental impact compared to higher meat or non-plant-based dietary patterns. Related to this, the total energy content of the diet was also associated with estimated environmental impact and higher energy diets had a larger estimated impact. For example, for fossil fuel alone, one calorie from beef or milk requires 40 or 14 calories of fuel, respectively, whereas one calorie from grains can be obtained from 2.2 calories of fuel. Additionally, the evidence showed that dietary patterns that promote health also promote sustainability; dietary patterns that adhered to dietary guidelines were more environmentally sustainable than the population's current average level of intake or pattern. Taken together, the studies agreed on the environmental impact of different dietary patterns, despite varied methods of assessing environmental impact and differences in components of environmental impact assessed (e.g. GHG emissions or land use). The evidence on whether sustainable diets were more or less expensive than typically consumed diets in some locations was limited and inconsistent.

Three additional reports on the relationship between dietary patterns and sustainability were published after this systematic review was completed. Two of these reports were consistent with, and provided more evidence to support the Committee's findings that dietary guidelines-related diets, Mediterranean-style diets, and vegetarian (and variations) diets are associated with improved environmental outcomes. Tilman and Clark showed that following a Mediterranean, vegetarian (lacto-ovo), or pesco-vegetarian dietary pattern would decrease both current and projected GHG emissions and land use. Eshel et al. reported on the five main animal-based categories in the U.S. diet – dairy, beef, poultry, pork, and eggs – and their required feeds including crops, byproducts, and pasture. They found that beef production required more land and irrigation water and produced more GHG emissions than dairy, poultry, pork, or eggs. In addition, as a standard comparator, staple plant foods had lower land use and GHG emissions than did dairy, poultry, pork, or eggs. In contrast, a report from Heller and Keoleian suggests that an isocaloric shift from the average U.S. diet (at current U.S. per capita intake of 2,534 kcals/day from Loss-Adjusted Food Availability (LAFA) data) to a pattern that adheres to the *2010 Dietary Guidelines for Americans* would result in a 12 percent increase in diet-related GHG emissions. This result was modified, however, by their finding that if Americans consumed the recommended pattern within the recommended calorie intake level of 2,000 kcal/day, there would be a 1 percent decrease in GHG emissions. This finding reinforces the overriding 2010 DGA recommendation that all of the guidelines need to be followed, including appropriate calorie intake levels for age, gender, and activity level. Furthermore, in contrast to the findings of Eshel et al. regarding dairy, Heller and Keoleian suggest that increases in dairy to follow 2010 DGA recommendations contribute significantly to increased GHG emissions and counters the modeled benefits of decreased meat consumption.

Seafood Sustainability

Background

Seafood is recognized as an important source of key macro- and micronutrients. The health benefits of seafood, including support of optimal neurodevelopment and prevention of cardiovascular disease, are likely due in large part to long-chain n-3 polyunsaturated fatty acids (PUFA), docosahexaenoic acid (DHA) and eicosapentaenoic acid (EPA), although seafood also are good sources of other nutrients including protein, selenium, iodine, vitamin D, and choline. Currently, seafood production is in the midst of rapid expansion to meet growing worldwide demand, but the collapse of some fisheries due to overfishing in past decades raises concerns about the ability to produce safe and affordable seafood to supply the U.S. population and meet current dietary intake recommendations of at least 8 ounces per week. Capture fisheries (wild caught) production has leveled-off as a proportion of fully exploited stocks, and this is due in part to national and international efforts on seafood sustainably (e.g., the U.S. Magnuson-Stevens Fishery Conservation and Management Act (2006) mandating annual catch limits, managed by the U.S. National Oceanographic and Atmospheric Administration). In contrast, the increased productivity of worldwide aquaculture (farm-raised) is expected to continue and will play a major role in expanding the supply of seafood. Expanding farm-raised seafood has the potential to ensure sufficient amounts of seafood to allow the U.S. population to consume levels recommended by dietary guidelines. Productivity gains should be implemented in a sustainable manner with greater attention to maintaining or enhancing the high nutrient density characteristic of captured seafood. Consistent with overall sustainability goals, farm-raised finfish (e.g., salmon and trout) is more sustainable than terrestrial animal production (e.g., beef and pork) in terms of GHG emissions and land/water use. Currently, the United States imports the majority of its seafood (~90 percent), and approximately half of that is farmed. The major groups commonly referred to as finfish, shellfish, and crustaceans include more than 500 species, and thus, generalizations to all seafood must be made with caution.

Question 2: What are the comparative nutrient profiles of current farm-raised versus wild caught seafood?

Conclusion

For commonly consumed fish species in the United States, such as bass, cod, trout, and salmon, farmed-raised seafood has as much or more of the omega-3 fatty acids EPA and DHA as the same species captured in the wild. In contrast, farmed low-trophic species, such as catfish and crawfish, have less than half the EPA and DHA per serving than wild caught, and these species have lower EPA and DHA regardless of source than do salmon. Farm-raised seafood has higher total fat than wild caught. Recommended amounts of EPA and DHA can be obtained by consuming a variety of farm-raised seafood, especially high-trophic species, such as salmon and trout.

Implications

The U.S. population should be encouraged to eat a wide variety of seafood that can be wild caught or farmed, as they are nutrient-dense foods that are uniquely rich sources of healthy fatty acids. It should be noted that low-trophic farm-raised seafood, such as catfish and crayfish, have lower EPA and DHA levels than do wild-caught. Nutrient profiles in popular low-trophic farmed species should be improved through feeding and processing systems that produce and preserve nutrients similar to those of wild-caught seafood of the same species....

Question 3. What are the comparative contaminant levels of current farm-raised versus wild caught seafood?

Conclusion

The DGAC concurs with the Consultancy that, for the majority of commercial wild and farmed species, neither the risks of mercury nor organic pollutants outweigh the health benefits of seafood consumption, such as decreased cardiovascular disease risk and improved infant neurodevelopment. However, any assessment evaluates evidence within a time frame and contaminant composition can change rapidly based on the contamination conditions at the location of wild catch and altered production practices for farmed seafood.

Implications

Based on risk/benefit comparisons, either farmed or wild-caught seafood are appropriate choices to consume to meet current Dietary Guidelines for Americans for increased seafood consumption. The DGAC supports the current FDA and EPA recommendations that women who are pregnant (or those who may become pregnant) and breastfeeding should not eat certain types of seafood—tilefish, shark, swordfish, and king mackerel—because of their high methyl mercury contents. Attention should be paid to local seafood advisories when eating seafood caught from local rivers, streams, and lakes.

Based on the most current evidence on mercury levels in albacore tuna provided in the Report of the Joint United Nations Food and Agriculture Organization/World Health Organization Expert Consultation on the Risks and Benefits of Fish Consumption, 2010, the DGAC recommends that the EPA and FDA re-evaluate their current recommendations for women who are pregnant (or for women who may become pregnant) or breastfeeding to limit white albacore tuna to not more than 6 ounces a week....

Question 4: What is the worldwide capacity to produce farm-raised versus wild-caught seafood that is nutritious and safe for the U.S. population?

Conclusions

The DGAC concurs with the FAO report that consistent evidence demonstrates that capture fisheries increasingly managed in a sustainable way have remained stable over several decades. However, on average, capture fisheries are fully exploited and their continuing productivity relies on careful management to avoid over-exploitation and long-term collapse.

The DGAC endorses the FAO report that capture fisheries production plateaued around 1990 while aquaculture has increased since that time to meet increasing demand. Evidence suggests that expanded seafood production will rely on the continuation of a rapid increase in aquaculture output worldwide, projected at 33 percent increase by 2021, which will add 15 percent to the total supply of seafood. Distributed evenly to the world's population, this capacity could in principle meet Dietary Guidelines recommendations for consumption of at least 8 ounces of seafood per week. Concern exists that the expanded capacity may be for low-trophic level seafood that has relatively low levels of EPA and DHA compared to other species. Under the current production, Americans who seek to meet U.S. Dietary Guidelines recommendations must rely on significant amounts of imported seafood (~90 percent).

Implications

Both wild and farmed seafood are major food sources available to support DGAC recommendations to regularly consume a variety of seafood. Responsible stewardship over environmental impact will be important as farmed seafood production expands. Availability of these important foods is critical for future generations of Americans to meet their needs for a healthy diet. Therefore, strong policy, research, and stewardship support are needed to increasingly improve the environmental sustainability of farmed seafood systems. From the standpoint of the dietary guidelines this expanded production needs to be largely in EPA and DHA rich species and supporting production of low-trophic level species of similar nutrient density as wild-caught....

Review of the Evidence

The UN FAO report on *The State of World Fisheries and Agriculture* issued in 2012 formed the basis of the DGAC's evidence review on this topic. The FAO report addresses a wide variety of issues affecting capture fisheries and aquaculture, including economics, infrastructure, and labor and government policies. The DGAC focused on matters that directly address the world production of one important food—seafood—as a first attempt by a DGAC committee to consider the implications of dietary guidelines for production of a related group of foods.

The production of capture fisheries has remained stable at about 90 million tons from 1990-2011. At the same time, aquaculture production is rising and will continue to increase. FAO model projections indicate that in response to the higher demand for seafood, world fisheries and aquaculture production is projected to grow by 15 percent between 2011 and 2021. This increase will be mainly due to increased aquaculture output, which is projected to increase 33 percent by 2021, compared with only 3 percent growth in wild capture fisheries over the same period. It is predicted that aquaculture will remain one of the fastest growing animal food-producing sectors and will exceed that of beef, pork, or poultry. Aquaculture production is expected to expand on all continents with variations across countries and regions in terms of the seafood species produced. Currently, the United States is the leading importer of seafood products world-wide, with imports making up about 90 percent of seafood consumption. Continuing to meet Americans needs for seafood will require stable importation or substantial expansion of domestic aquaculture.

Access to sufficient, nutritious, and safe food is an essential element of food security for the U.S. population. A sustainable diet is one that assures this access for both the current population and future generations. This chapter focused on evaluating the evidence around sustainable diets and several topic areas of food safety.

The major findings regarding sustainable diets were that a diet higher in plant-based foods, such as vegetables, fruits, whole grains, legumes, nuts, and seeds, and lower in calories and animal-based foods is more health promoting and is associated with less environmental impact than is the current U.S. diet. This pattern of eating can be achieved through a variety of dietary patterns, including the "Healthy U.S.-style Pattern," the "Healthy Mediterranean-style Pattern," and the "Healthy Vegetarian Pattern." All of these dietary patterns are aligned with lower predicted environmental impacts and provide food options that can be adopted by the U.S. population. Current evidence shows that the average U.S. diet has a potentially larger environmental impact in terms of increased GHG emissions, land use, water use, and energy use, compared to the above dietary patterns. This is because the current U.S. population intake of animal-based foods is higher and the plant-based foods are lower, than proposed in these three dietary patterns. Of note is that no food groups need to be eliminated completely to improve food sustainability outcomes.

A moderate amount of seafood is an important component of two of three of these dietary patterns, and has demonstrated health benefits. The seafood industry is in the midst of rapid expansion to meet worldwide demand, although capture fishery production has leveled off while aquaculture is expanding. The collapse of some fisheries due to overfishing in the past decades has raised concern about the ability to produce a safe and affordable supply. In addition, concern has been raised about the safety and nutrient content of farm-raised versus wild-caught seafood. To supply enough seafood to support meeting dietary recommendations, both farm-raised and wild caught seafood will be needed. The review of the evidence demonstrated, in the species evaluated, that farm-raised seafood has as much or more EPA and DHA per serving than wild caught. Low-trophic seafood, such as catfish and crawfish, regardless of whether wild caught or farm-raised seafood, have less than half the EPA and DHA per serving than high-trophic seafood, such as salmon and trout.

Regarding contaminants, for the majority of wild caught and farmed species, neither the risks of mercury nor organic pollutants outweigh the health benefits of seafood consumption. Consistent evidence demonstrated that wild caught fisheries that have been managed sustainably have remained stable over the past several decades; however, wild caught fisheries are fully exploited and their continuing productivity will require careful management nationally and internationally to avoid long-term collapse. Expanded supply of seafood nationally and internationally will be dependent upon the increase of farm-raised seafood worldwide.

The impact of food production, processing, and consumption on environmental sustainability is an area of research that is rapidly evolving. As further research is conducted and best practices evaluated, additional evidence will inform both supply-side participants and consumers on how best to shift behaviors locally, nationally, and globally to support sustainable diets. Linking health, dietary guidance and the environment will promote human health and the sustainability of natural resources and ensure current and long-term food security....

Notes

1. What do you think of this advice to the Secretaries? If you were the decision maker on the Dietary Guidelines, what would you do?

2. Once the new Dietary Guidelines are final, may they be challenged in court? One federal district judge concluded that the 2010 Guidelines were not subject to judicial review. In Physicians Committee for Responsible Medicine v. Vilsack, 867 F.Supp.2d 24 (D.D.C. 2011), the court not only held that plaintiff (a nonprofit group promoting proper nutrition) lacked standing, but also held that the 2010 Dietary Guidelines were not even "agency action" reviewable under the Administrative Procedure Act (APA).

Section 704 of the APA provides for judicial review of "final agency action," which itself is defined to include "the whole or a part of an agency rule, order, license, sanction, relief, or the equivalent or denial thereof, or failure to act." 5 U.S.C. § 551(13). "Rule," in turn, is defined to mean "the whole or a part of an agency statement of general or particular applicability and future effect designed to implement, interpret, or prescribe law or policy of describing the organization, procedure, or practice requirements of an agency." 5 U.S.C. § 551(4). In response to plaintiff's argument that the Dietary Guidelines were a rule, the court held:

> The *Dietary Guidelines* ... is not an agency statement describing the USDA or DHHS organizations or the agencies' procedure or practice requirements. It is, in sum, a report containing 'nutritional and dietary information and guidelines for the general public.' 7 U.S.C. § 5341(a)(1). As the Nutrition Act makes clear, such dietary guidance 'does not include any rule or regulation issued by a Federal agency,' and thus, does not constitute 'agency action.' Id. § 5341(b)(3). Therefore, because plaintiff has not established that the *Dietary Guidelines* is actually subject to judicial review under the

APA, it has failed to state a claim upon which relief can be granted.

The provision quoted by the court, section 5341(b)(3), is part of a section (section 5341(b)) that requires the Secretaries' approval of any federal agency's "dietary guidance for the general population or identified population subgroups." This guidance must be consistent with the Dietary Guidelines for Americans or be "based on medical or new scientific knowledge which is determined to be valid by the Secretaries." 7 U.S.C. § 5341(b)(2)(A). The provision contains detailed instructions about how to proceed if the Secretaries find that an agency's proposed guidance is inconsistent with the Dietary Guidelines for Americans. 7 U.S.C. § 5341(b)(2). The Nutrition Monitoring Act makes clear, in other words, that the "dietary guidance" that is the subject of section 5341(b) is distinct from the Dietary Guidelines for Americans that are published by the Secretaries. Does this mean that the district court was wrong to conclude that the Dietary Guidelines are not "agency action" within the meaning of the APA?

3. If the Dietary Guidelines are indeed "agency action" within the meaning of the APA, what kind of action are they? Are they policy statements? Legislative rules? In thinking about this question, consider the fact that USDA personnel are required to follow the guidelines in developing requirements for, among other things, school lunches and breakfasts. Does this fact make the guidelines legislative rules rather than mere policy statements?

4. Is incorporating environmental considerations into dietary advice a promising way to promote food security? Does the answer depend on whether one takes a short- or long-term perspective on food security? If food security is relevant to the Dietary Guidelines, is there any reason to take a short- rather than long-term view of food security?

PART V

CHAPTER 12
REFLECTIONS ON FOOD LAW

The following materials offer ideas for you to consider as you reflect on the three substantive domains of Food Law: knowledge, safety, and security.

The Varieties and Limits of Transparency in U.S. Food Law

Lisa Heinzerling
70 Food & Drug L.J. 11 (2015)

Transparency is at once the oldest and the newest idea in the law of food. Roman civil law contained detailed rules against fraud in the sale of food. The Magna Carta required transparency in the weights and measures used by certain food sellers. The American colonies passed laws aimed at preventing deception in specific food markets. Today, dozens of federal statutes both constrain and compel statements about the identity, quality, and composition of our food. Regulations and guidelines issued by at least ten different federal agencies further refine the legal framework for representations about food. One cannot, in fact, look at the information provided on any package of processed food in the United States without seeing a highly refined product of the legal system. Indeed, I do not believe it is an overstatement to say that representations about the nature and quality of our food are among the most thoroughly regulated verbal expressions in the United States today.

Yet we remain dissatisfied, even deeply confused. When the great agrarian and essayist Wendell Berry urges us to remember that "[a] significant part of the pleasure of eating is in one's accurate consciousness of the lives and the world from which food comes," he is also reminding us how little we know about the food we eat: how it was grown, where it was grown, who grew it, how it was harvested or killed, how far it has traveled to reach us. In truth, we often do not even know what is in our food, much less how it has come to our table. The nagging, and growing, concern that we do not know nearly enough about our food has made transparency a core demand of the contemporary movement aimed at changing the industrial food system.

How can our highly refined legal system for food transparency leave us with such a deep sense that we lack crucial information about the food we eat? I offer two explanations for our continuing befuddlement, both grounded in law. The first is an observation internal to the existing regulatory system for representations about our food: in brief, this system is far less committed to transparency than it seems. The second explanation critiques the existing system from the outside, observing that current law does not even aspire to induce an "accurate consciousness of the lives and the world from which food comes," and indeed musters considerable effort to avoid such awareness.

In this article, I describe, in Part I, the federal legal regime regarding transparency in the U.S. food system. I turn, in Part II, to a discussion of how that regime--so seemingly robust and comprehensive--has fallen short. In Part III, I offer several observations about the way forward.

I. The Varieties of Transparency in U.S. Food Law

Close examination of the current regulatory system for food at first only deepens the mystery as to how we can remain perplexed about the food we eat. After all, a central goal of the federal legal system for food is to ensure the integrity of representations made by sellers of food about their products; in all of the major federal statutes on food, "misbranding" stands side by side with "adulteration" as a core concern. To achieve transparency, the law of food deploys three different kinds of regulatory strategies: prohibitions against fraud, compelled disclosures, and constraints on discretionary disclosures. One can only marvel at the apparent comprehensiveness of the system thus created, one in which false or misleading statements about food are forbidden, disclosures about a wide range of food properties are mandatory, and discretionary statements about many specific properties of food are tightly constrained. In principle, almost no imaginable food-related utterance, made in the food marketplace, can avoid this legal net.

All representations made in food labeling and advertising fall under generic federal prohibitions against misbranding, present in all of the major federal laws dedicated to food. Several of these laws define misbranding as statements that are "false or misleading *in any particular*." Under the Federal Food, Drug, and Cosmetic Act (FDCA), prohibitions against misbranding reach not only affirmative statements, but also material omissions. These prohibitions are backed by significant legal sanctions: depending on the specific statute, violators may face injunctions, of their products, fines, or even jail.

General laws on unfair competition contain similar prohibitions on misleading representations. The Federal Trade Commission Act (FTCA), for example, prohibits unfair or deceptive acts or practices in or affecting commerce. The Lanham Act creates a private cause of action for competitors harmed by deceptive representations about rival products. The Supreme Court recently gave the Lanham Act a boost in a case involving food, holding that the Lanham Act is not displaced by the FDCA--even where the Food and Drug Administration (FDA) has condoned a particular food-related representation.

Beyond the generic prohibitions on false or misleading representations about food lies a welter of highly specific, affirmative requirements of disclosure. Together, these requirements provide that we must be told the name of the food we are buying, name and address of the manufacturer, packer, or distributor of it, the ingredients in it (in decreasing order by volume), numerous facts about its nutritional content (including information on sodium, sugar, fat, cholesterol, fiber, calories, vitamins, and protein), the major allergens present in it, and the net weight of the product (in both English and metric units). For certain foods, we must also be given instructions for cooking and handling and be told the food's country (or countries) of origin. For alcoholic beverages, we must be told the alcohol content and warned of the consequences of abuse.

Behind each of these compelled disclosures is a phalanx of precisely rendered rules about the exact utterances required (and allowed). Developing rules for food names and identities alone occupied the Food and Drug Administration for the middle decades of the last century. The nutrition facts panel on food products has been made instantly recognizable not through some magical process of spontaneous clarity and uniformity, but through an intensely deliberate and intricate legal process. The seemingly straightforward requirement of identifying the place of origin of meat products--a requirement present in some form in federal law since the nineteenth century--has recently spawned regulatory and judicial proceedings stretching out over years and across continents. The law of food is thick, in other words, with both negative constraints--forbidding deception-- and a highly refined set of positive obligations of disclosure.

Federal prohibitions on deceptive food-related representations have led naturally to specific constraints on the kinds of representations that are likely to be highly enticing to consumers, and thus especially susceptible to abuse.

Claims about the superior nutrient content of food--its relative lowness in fat or sodium, or relative highness in fiber or calcium--are subject to a detailed legal structure specifying the exact food-content parameters that permit the claims. Claims about the disease-preventive properties of specific food products are likewise constrained by an intricate legal framework, one that even entails premarket review by the government. Lawful use of the one-word descriptor "organic" requires compliance with a dense code of specifications about the precise methods of food production that would warrant this term.

Collectively these constraints create an enormous legal structure governing representations about the food we eat. Upon surveying this structure, it would not be unreasonable to surmise that, when it comes to food, the American consumer must be the best-informed consumer (of any kind) in the world, perhaps in the history of the world. Every major legal strategy governing information has been deployed in the U.S. food system: prohibitions on fraudulent representations, affirmative obligations of disclosure, and specific constraints on especially alluring claims about the properties of particular foods. One might conclude that the U.S. food system is not just transparent, it is crystalline.

Yet, as I next explain, the transparency achieved by law is only partial, and indeed sometimes serves only to conceal a lie.

Ii. The Limits of Transparency in U.S. Food Law

Each of the regulatory strategies I have described--prohibitions on fraud, compelled disclosures, constrained claims--is weakened in practice by a set of problems well known to any observer of the modern regulatory state. Resource limits at federal agencies charged with regulating food hollow out enforcement programs aimed at false or misleading representations. Regulatory fragmentation ensures that agencies with very different cultures and missions preside, confusingly, over the transparency of the food system. Lopsided participation by food producers before the agencies works distortions in rules on mandatory disclosures. In all of these ways, the existing legal system for food fails to deliver the transparency it seems to promise. Moreover, the existing legal system does not even try to achieve the level of food-related awareness that many in the contemporary food movement would desire.

Consider first the problem of hollow government. Generic prohibitions on fraud, found in both food-specific federal laws and in general laws on unfair competition, are effective in promoting transparency only insofar as they are actually deployed. Here the story is not good. Through the better part of the twentieth century, the law on food fraud was primarily developed through case-by-case adjudication of claims brought by the government against specific food vendors on the basis of specific representations about their products. Working up individual cases in this manner is, needless to say, expensive and time-consuming. Moreover, in a food marketplace that offers tens of thousands of different products with different labels and claims, the prospect of achieving integrity of representations about food through case-by-case adjudication in the federal courts is daunting. The problem becomes even more severe when one considers the declining inspection-related budgets of the agencies with regulatory authority over food.

The relevant numbers on enforcement are striking, and sobering. Twenty years ago the Government Accounting Office, now the Government Accountability Office (GAO), estimated that together, FDA and United States Department of Agriculture (USDA) had legal authority over some 500,000 food labels, divided about equally between the two agencies. That number has certainly only grown in the intervening years; thousands of new food products enter the market each year. As of 2007, FDA itself had jurisdiction over the activities of some 65,000 domestic food firms. The agency has estimated that there are twice as many importers of food from abroad. Thus, over half a million labels, tens of thousands of regulated firms, and thousands of new products are present in the market every year. How does the government ensure compliance with the laws I have described, especially with so many firms and products to oversee?

The answer is simple: it does not. The ratio of enforcement-related activity (inspections, warning letters, court proceedings) to the universe of potential enforcement targets is vanishingly small. A food facility regulated by FDA can expect an inspection only about once every five years. A recent FDA oversight initiative on food labeling involved a mere seventeen warning letters. It is not clear that even these few letters sparked compliance from the relevant companies. The letters focused on potential infractions of only a tiny portion of the transparency-related legal requirements I have described. Most involved charges that the companies had unlawfully targeted dietary advice to children under two years old or that they had failed to list major allergens on their products' labels. The statistics are even less encouraging when it comes to enforcement actions filed in court. In a recent ten-year period, FDA managed to obtain only two court injunctions against food products on account of their misleading labeling. In a market with tens of thousands of sellers and hundreds of thousands of verbal claims, the sheer tininess of federal enforcement-related activity must give one pause.

Equally troublingly, the federal agencies charged with ensuring the integrity of food-related representations have become disinclined even to gather the kind of information that would facilitate enforcement or, at least, inform consumers as to the reliability of representations related to the nature and quality of their food. The USDA long ago abandoned any effort to conduct random sampling of food products to see whether these products are what they purport to be and contain what they purport to contain. The USDA also eliminated requirements for laboratory testing in 1993 with the explanation (in GAO's words) that "the agency believes that food companies should be responsible for the accuracy of the information on the labels." Almost twenty years ago, FDA likewise abandoned any effort to conduct random sampling and analysis. FDA explained that it preferred instead to conduct "targeted" testing. Its "targets" in this testing emerge when, for example, a candy bar's label does not list any fat or sugar. The agency has thus, inexplicably, decided that its laboratory testing and analysis will be deployed only in cases in which a moderately astute consumer could spot a problem without help from the government.

However, short of encountering self-contradictory labels--or conducting laboratory analysis on her own--a consumer cannot determine for herself whether food products actually contain the ingredients and nutrients they purport to contain. Yet the government has left the consumer to fend for herself in this domain. In response to a GAO report in 2008, FDA baldly stated that it had "no plans" for further random sampling of food products to test them against the representations made on their labels -- despite GAO's previous finding that laboratory analysis was the only way to verify the accuracy of food labels.

Evidence from tests conducted before FDA abandoned random sampling and analysis indicates the utility of such sampling in detecting food-related misrepresentations. After the labeling reforms of the Nutrition Labeling and Education Act of 1990, FDA conducted random sampling and laboratory analysis in 1994 and 1996 to determine whether products contained the level of nutrients that they purported to contain. Often, FDA found that the answer was no. In sampling conducted in 1994, FDA found that 48% of products sampled misrepresented the amount of vitamins A and C they contained, and 32% misrepresented the level of iron they contained. In sampling conducted in 1996, FDA found that 47% of products sampled misrepresented the amount of vitamin A they contained, 12% misrepresented the level of vitamin C, and 31% misrepresented the level of iron. In these respects, the labels were--in a word--false. This is the kind of violation that should be quite straightforward to attack; it does not depend on sometimes-controversial assumptions about exactly what words are misleading, nor does it engage the most speech-protective parts of First Amendment doctrine. Yet rather than taking these results as evidence of the necessity of continued vigilance over the integrity of food-related representations, federal agencies have simply stopped the kind of testing that produced these results.

The government has tried to minimize the vast disparity between the territory it is charged with overseeing and the territory it actually controls. High-level FDA officials have publicly acknowledged that they cannot adequately police food labels in this country, and that we must simply trust food companies to do the right thing. At the same time, however, such officials have also promised the public that the agency "has your back," that food labels cannot be false or misleading "in any way," and that the government will take "appropriate" action if it finds that labels violate the law. The latter comment seems almost designed to mislead. "Appropriate," of course, covers a world of passive sins, and the government will actually find that labels violate the law only if it is looking for such violations. For the most part, as I have said, it is not.

In a series of hard-hitting reports, the GAO has warned of the consequences of government passivity on food labeling. In 1994, after noting the government's plans for very limited laboratory verification of representations made on food labels, the GAO said bluntly: "Because of these limitations and the flexibility given food companies in developing the nutrient values on labels, the accuracy of the information provided on about 500,000 labels will depend largely on the food industry." In 2008, the GAO sounded an even louder alarm, warning that because FDA's "use of oversight and enforcement tools has not kept pace with the growing number of food firms," the agency "has limited assurance that companies in the food industry are in compliance with food labeling requirements, such as those prohibiting false or misleading labeling." Quoting a report from FDA's Science Board, the GAO stated that "the growing disparity between FDA resources and responsibilities" had made it "increasingly 'impossible' for FDA to maintain its historic public health mission." In 2011, the GAO reported that FDA had directed a substantial portion of its limited food labeling resources to evaluating qualified health claims, even while food companies were largely abandoning such claims in favor of less-regulated claims about the relationship between food products and the structure or functioning of the human body.

Compounding the problems caused by hollow government, regulatory fragmentation deepens the opacity of our food system. At least ten different federal agencies have some responsibility to ensure the integrity of representations about food. This fragmentation facilitates divergent and even conflicting messages from the government about the nature and quality of our food. The very same words can come to mean different things, depending on the locus of regulatory authority. The grocery store becomes--in the words of a former secretary of the Department of Health and Human Services--a modern-day "Tower of Babel," in which "consumers need to be linguists, scientists, and mind readers to understand the many labels they see."

Adding to the confusion, even the processes agencies use in pursuing transparency are different. The USD A reviews and approves the labels of the products it regulates; FDA does not. The result is a fractured process for ensuring transparency in the food marketplace. One agency reviews all labels before they are used; another rests with after-the-fact measures to correct misleading labels. Yet one would be wrong to conclude, from this structure, that the USDA process necessarily produces more transparent results. The USDA's filter has failed to catch patently misleading labels. Recently, for example, the USDA has acknowledged that the labels it has long allowed for "enhanced" meat products--products containing added solutions of water, salt, and other ingredients--are misleading insofar as they do not convey the loss of weight in actual meat or the gain in sodium associated with such products. The USDA has, in fact, decided that the labels it has long approved are so misleading that the agency has felt compelled to propose a new rule to prevent the use of the existing labels. A consumer who relied on the USDA's pre-approval regime as a sign of superior transparency in USDA-regulated products would thus be doubly misled, both by the implicit promise of government-backed transparency and by the dubious labels that have passed through the USDA's filter.

Different agencies may also embrace different interpretations of the very same words. The words "naturally raised" have a precise and approved meaning when they are applied to products regulated by the USDA, but the word "natural" has very little meaning when applied to products regulated by FDA. The USDA has stretched the approved meaning of the word "fresh" to cover a wide range of thoroughly worked-over products, including the now-infamous "lean finely textured beef" (aka "pink slime"). The USDA has also held fast to its position that poultry remains "fresh" down to an internal temperature of 26 degrees Fahrenheit and may be called "never frozen" all the way down to an internal temperature of 0 degrees Fahrenheit. The USDA will not, however, countenance the use of the term "fresh" for any product "treated with an antimicrobial substance or irradiated." FDA, for its part, holds that the term "fresh" may only be applied to "raw, unprocessed foods," and may not be applied to any food product that has "been frozen or subjected to any form of thermal processing," but it embraces the use of the term for produce that has been treated with "a mild chlorine wash or mild acid wash" and for foods treated with ionizing radiation. The combined consequence of these policies is that the same word, "fresh," has approved meanings that point in opposite directions, depending on the agency that is defining the word.

The confusing nature of officially-approved definitions of food-related terms also comes from compromises made within single agencies, compromises that are perhaps more often than not borne more of solicitousness toward regulated entities. Officially sanctioned descriptive terms hide a world of sins: "naturally raised," "natural flavors," "lean finely textured beef," and more are all euphemisms rather than aids to understanding our food. Moreover, FDA, after all, effectively gave us the now-infamous moniker, "pomegranate blueberry flavored blend of five juices," to describe apple and grape juice containing an eyedropper-full of pomegranate and blueberry juices. One needs a whole new dictionary (and a lawyer) to understand these terms, as remodeled by our regulatory agencies.

In these circumstances, one cannot help but turn to Lewis Carroll:

> "I don't know what you mean by 'glory,'" Alice said.
>
> Humpty Dumpty smiled contemptuously. "Of course you don't--till I tell you."

Officially sanctioned representations about food sometimes even include outright lies. When FDA required food labels to disclose the amount of trans fatty acids they contained, FDA allowed a report of "zero" for such ingredients so long as the actual amount in the food was 0.5 grams or lower. The agency explained that this compromise in accuracy was necessitated by practical concerns about detectability, and hence, enforceability. Considering whether this tradeoff was sanctioned for the benefit of consumers-- or for the benefit of industry--note that the agency has now proposed banning trans fatty acids in foods altogether, due to serious health risks presented even when the amount present in food is less than 0.5 grams. Similar to its decision on labeling trans fats, the FDA has allowed a "gluten free" label for foods containing up to 20 parts per million of gluten, again citing the challenges of detection. While FDA downplayed the significance of this shading of the meaning of "free," it also advised people with an extreme sensitivity to gluten (such as people with celiac disease) to read the ingredient list with care.

Given these FDA rules, a representation that a food contains "0" grams trans fat does not necessarily mean that it has zero grams of trans fat, and a representation that a food is "gluten free" does not necessarily mean that it is free of gluten. These foods can contain small amounts of trans fat and gluten and still use the terms "zero" and "free." The statements may thus be false, yet they are also officially sanctioned.

Of course, any regulatory regime must grapple with problems of administrability and practicality. An entire program cannot be condemned for minor deviations from the ideal. Yet, when it comes to a regulatory framework aimed at achieving transparency, permitting deviations from truthful statements--permitting, indeed, frankly untrue representations--can have an especially corrosive effect on public trust and in that way undermine the entire enterprise of transparency. If 'free" does not mean free, and "zero" does not mean zero, one might ask, what else does not mean what it seems to mean?

The government-distorted meaning of the seemingly absolute words "free" and "zero" becomes even more confusing when one considers FDA's approach to labeling genetically engineered foods. In that context, the agency has insisted on a very strict interpretation of the word "free," advising producers of foods made without use of genetically modified ingredients that they should steer clear of labeling their foods "GMO free" due to the difficulties of proving that foods are indeed GMO free and of avoiding, in food production today, the "adventitious" introduction of genetically engineered materials. These same concerns of administrability and practicality persuaded the agency to allow claims of "zero" and "free" for trans fats and gluten, even where such ingredients were deliberately introduced into a food product. However, when it comes to bioengineered ingredients, the agency forbids such absolute claims even with respect to food products deliberately formulated not to contain such ingredients. The American consumer, I believe, may be forgiven for being bewildered, and for suspecting that the information she is given about her food is often more a function of industry preference than of consumer protection.

So far we have seen that the large promises of transparency in U.S. food law fall short as a consequence of hollow government, regulatory fragmentation, and agency capture. Even if the existing regulatory regime for food-related transparency were fully functional, however, it would not meet the demands of many of the participants in the contemporary movement to transform our food system. These include demands for transparency of the kind Wendell Berry would counsel: transparency about the way our food is grown, where it is grown, who grows it, how it got to our table, and at what environmental and human cost. The truth is, the legal system does not even try to meet these demands.

There are no federally compelled disclosures on our food about the environmental origins and consequences of our food. Nor are there federally compelled disclosures about the human hardship or animal suffering involved in growing and raising our food. The USDA's National Organic Program, aims to provide a shorthand descriptor signifying a superior environmental profile, but use of the "organic" label--and agreeing to the conditions the USDA attaches to it--is discretionary, not mandatory, and in any event reflects only a partial accounting of the environmental consequences of food production and processing.

Indeed, in the domains of the environment, labor, and animal welfare, the federal regulatory apparatus has mostly avoided rather than embraced transparency. Federal agencies charged with ensuring the integrity of verbal representations about food have approved the use of terms that might signify environmental superiority--such as "fresh" and "naturally raised"--to describe the highly dubious products of an environmentally-degraded agriculture. Agencies have avoided even collecting information--for their own use--about the unwholesome practices of modern agricultural operations. States have piled on by passing laws forbidding speech documenting the unsavory practices of these operations.

I have described two different problems with the law governing food-related representations. The first is that while the law is mighty in theory, it is tame in fact. Legal prohibitions on false or misleading statements, legally compelled disclosures of many different qualities of our food, and constraints on especially enticing claims about the nature and quality of our food all look powerful on paper, but in practice they are severely undermined by hollow government, regulatory fragmentation, and agency capture. The second problem is that in many respects, particularly those relating to the environment, workers, and animal welfare, the law does not even aim to be mighty, instead lamely opting for secrecy over transparency. The combined result of these two legal gaps is sustained confusion and ignorance about the food we eat.

III. What Now?

There is no simple solution for the problems I have identified. Resource constraints at federal agencies, fragmentation of regulatory authority across multiple agencies, and capture of agencies by the industries they are charged with regulating are sad hallmarks of the modern administrative state. They are unlikely to disappear any time soon. Congress has shown no interest in increasing the funds of the agencies charged with regulating food; indeed, in the Food Safety Modernization Act passed in 2010, Congress gave FDA an enormous set of new responsibilities without providing any appreciable new funding to meet them. In addition, in the face of persistent critiques of regulatory fragmentation, both Congress and the White House have deepened rather than softened the split of food-related regulatory authority across multiple agencies. The continuing hold of industry over the regulatory agencies can be seen in current examples such as the failure meaningfully to address the problem of antibiotic resistance caused by the profligate use of medically important antibiotics in animal agriculture. Happily, there are counterexamples to the narrative of regulatory dysfunction, such as FDA's recent decision to finalize a strong rule on menu labeling. Even here, however, one must remember that a rule is only as strong as the resolve to enforce it. In this domain, as I have explained, the track record is not encouraging.

The stubbornness of the underlying problems of resource constraints, regulatory fragmentation, and agency capture makes me skeptical that the solution to the problem of opacity in the food system is to enact more rules requiring disclosure. For example, I am doubtful that the lack of transparency about the environmental and social consequences of our food will be solved with a new set of federal rules. I do not think adding another layer of legal rules, mandating additional disclosures about our food, will achieve the kind of transparency Wendell Berry and others have described. Such rules would suffer from the same resource constraints, regulatory fragmentation, and agency capture that have undermined the existing regime.

The problem of opacity is softened, but not solved, by private lawsuits aimed at food-related deception. The broad causes of action permitted by the Lanham Act against deceptive practices run only to competitors, not to consumers, and there is little reason to believe that competitors will pursue a broad, truth-based agenda to the benefit of consumers. To understand this point, one need only consider the deep irony of POM Wonderful's successful Supreme Court advocacy against Coca-Cola, which allowed POM's Lanham Act complaint about Coke's deceptive labeling and advertising of its "pomegranate blueberry flavored blend of five juices" to proceed. After all, POM had arguably created the very market it was trying to protect by engaging in equally dubious marketing strategies aimed at convincing consumers of the amazing, disease-preventive properties of pomegranate juice. At some point, makers of clean and wholesome food may well be able to use the Lanham Act to serve their own financial interests and the public interests of consumers, but the potential public-regarding consequences of Lanham Act enforcement have yet to emerge.

Likewise, litigation brought on behalf of consumers does not adequately fill the void left by the government in regard to fraud about food. The proliferation of state-law-based lawsuits alleging deceptive labeling, advertising, and marketing of food has been widely reported, and has likely contributed to some greater general awareness of the possibility of untruths in representations about food. However, the litigation to date has done relatively little to clear up generalized confusion about food. Some cases settle for no monetary relief and limited injunctive relief, while ensuring ample fees for plaintiffs' attorneys. Other lawsuits have succeeded in removing one particular deceptive claim--often the word "natural"--from a particular set of food products. Thus, although private lawsuits may have modestly increased our vigilance about food representations and have helped to end some egregiously deceptive claims, they have, to date, failed to correct for the government's retreat from the field.

Three changes, one each directed towards Congress, the agencies, and the food-consuming public would help. First, Congress should authorize citizen suits for violations of the federal laws aimed at ensuring the integrity of verbal representations about our food. In an age of declining government resources and expanding government responsibilities, the citizen suit would take some of the pressure off the government and would also draw upon the public-regarding purposes of federal law. A citizen suit for violations of food-related laws would offer a salutary complement to the cause of action now recognized for competitors under the Lanham Act.

The second change I recommend would come from the agencies that are charged with protecting the integrity of verbal representations about the nature and quality of our food. These agencies should stop claiming that they "have our back" and stop pretending that the law will protect us from lies and half-truths about our food. The only entities helped by the agencies' false promises of protection are the food companies themselves. They benefit from the illusion of federal oversight; they can reassure their customers that the government is on the job, while knowing full well that their representations about their food products are unlikely to draw a governmental response. The agencies charged with ensuring the integrity of verbal representations about food should ensure the integrity of their own representations about consumer protection itself. The agencies should not only cease to make false promises about the level of protection they afford the American consumer, but also loudly acknowledge (and bemoan) their own incapacity to provide the level of protection the consumer likely expects. When it comes to enforcement, the agencies charged with protecting the integrity of verbal representations about the nature and quality of our food have already beat a quiet retreat from their field of authority; they should make a noisy retreat as well.

Finally, consumers should be clear-eyed about the nature of the food label. Consumers should treat the food label like a legal document offered for their assent. It has been drafted by strangers, mostly for strangers' benefit. Every word, every number, even every font, has been parsed and negotiated and approved by strangers' lawyers. It is not a neutral document, and it is not authorless, even if it is anonymous. The ancient impulse of *caveat emptor* should activate, not recede, upon seeing a label on the food one is about to buy.

Why Healthy Behavior is the Hard Choice

Lawrence O. Gostin
93 Milibank Q. 242 (2015)

Science informs us that nutritious dietary patterns andphysical activity improve prospects for health and well-being. Yet pursuing a healthy lifestyle is incredibly difficult in a society designed to incentivize the opposite set of behaviors.

For example, individuals may know the value of physical activity, but there may be few parks, playgrounds, fields, and walking paths for exercising their bodies. In inner-city neighborhoods with hazardous, unlit physical environments, for example, parents, fearful of the dangers of firearms and illicit drugs, may not want to send their children out to play.

When it comes to our diet, we are constantly pushed toward unhealthy eating. Food manufacturers aggressively market hyperprocessed foods laden with saturated fat, salt, sugar, and refined carbohydrates. These companies put these unhealthy ingredients even in basic "healthy" foods, such as bread, granola, and yogurt. Advertisements for sugar-filled cereals and sodas are targeted to children. Fast-food chains collude with Hollywood and entertainment venues to give away toys in "meals" marketed for kids. It is little better for their parents. Consumers seeking whole, nutritious foods often find them inaccessible or unaffordable, driving many to buy convenient and cheap options.

Even the most informed consumer faces a confusing shell game— "low-fat" foods often contain high amounts of sugar and salt, while "low-sugar" foods often are filled with high amounts of saturated fats and calories. Serving sizes are not uniform, stymieing even the most mathematically gifted consumer when comparingproducts.

How can we structure society to make health the easier choice?

Four simple ideas could make healthy behaviors the "default" choice for most consumers. To be sure, the evidence for these interventions is mixed, mainly because they are rarely enacted, let alone rigorously evaluated. Although evidence for a given intervention is important, tobacco control has taught us that a suite of measures, working in combination over time, has the best chance of success.

Taxes/Pricing: Lower Demand/More Revenue

Higher prices for unhealthy products reduce demand, especially among youth and low-income groups, while generating revenue to increase access to and affordability of healthier alternatives. Of all the interventions to control tobacco, raising excise taxes on cigarettes translated into the greatest reduction in smoking. Modeling this success, Mexico levied a tax of 1 peso per liter on sugary beverages in 2013, resulting in a price increase of 10%. Modeling showed that the price increase would reduce consumption by 15%, thereby preventing 630,000 cases of diabetes by 2030, with early evidence demonstrating a 10% drop in soda purchases and a 13% rise in bottled water purchases.

In 2014, Berkeley, California, became the first US jurisdiction to adopt a soda tax, levying a penny-per-ounce tax on sugar-sweetened drinks. A recent European Commission Report lent support, concluding that taxes on sugar, salt, and fat reduce consumption, although consumers often switch to nontaxable foods, which might be equally unhealthy. Berkeley added the soda tax revenue to its general budget, but states could instead earmark food tax revenues to subsidize fruits, vegetables, and legumes, or for nutrition education campaigns.

Product Reformulation: Direct and Co-regulation

Industry adds copious amounts of fats, sugars, and sodium to foods, and consumer tastes have evolved to crave these additives. If companies gradually reduced these unhealthy ingredients, consumer tastes would adjust as well. For example, no one today misses artificial trans fatty acids (TFA) in their fried and baked goods. In March 2003, Denmark established a maximum of 2% TFA content in oils and fats; New York and other cities followed this model; and the US Food and Drug Administration (FDA) has proposed a national ban.

Co-regulatory strategies—voluntary industry compliance with government-set standards—can be a politically palatable alternative to mandatory bans. The United Kingdom, for example, set progressive targets for reducing sodium in 85 food categories and supported them through education campaigns. Companies voluntarily agree to both the targets and to front-of-pack labeling to alert consumers to high-salt products. Over a 7-year period, the program achieved a 15% reduction in the population's salt intake.

Disclosures/Advertising: The Informational Environment

Altering the informational environment shifts the political dialogue because few dispute the value of consumer awareness. In 2014, the FDA proposed rules for redesigning food-packet labeling, notably adding a separate line for added sugars and standardizing serving sizes. The United Kingdom's Food Standards Agency developed a voluntary "traffic light" system, with prominent green, yellow, or red lights for major nutritional groups like saturated fats, sodium, and sugar.

California could go further, with a proposed bill that requires warning labels on sugary drinks, including sodas, sweet teas, and sports and energy drinks. Sugar now has an air of comfort, but imagine the effect of this admonition on your beverage:

> STATE OF CALIFORNIA SAFETY WARNING: Drinking beverages with added sugar contributes to obesity, diabetes, and tooth decay.

Junk-food advertisements are even more ubiquitous than tobacco advertisements were in the years before tobacco control. In 1980, Quebec banned all commercial advertising aimed at children. The ban significantly reduced French-speaking children's exposure to food and beverage advertising. In the United States, the First Amendment poses a major obstacle to advertising bans. Nevertheless, in 2007 Maine became the first state to prohibit brand advertising of unhealthy foods and beverages in schools. The US Supreme Court is more deferential to government restrictions on advertisements targeting children, so regulating commercial messages in K-12 public schools remains a primetarget.

Built Environment: Healthy Food Accessibility

Visit any inner city in the world and witness food market globalization, with the same global "fast-food" brands populating the streets. What often is missing are supermarkets, farmers' markets, and greengrocers. Most urban settings are structured through market forces, but government can use zoning and licensing laws to limit fast-food outlets, while incentivizing vendors and stores to sell healthy products.

In July 2008, for example, the Los Angeles City Council passed a moratorium on new or expanded fast-food establishments in south- central Los Angeles, with plans to attract dining establishments and grocery stores.

That same year, New York City began its "Green Carts Scheme," creating 1,000 licenses for street vendors selling fresh fruits and vegetables in "food deserts." A 1-year evaluation found higher access to and more consumption of fruits and vegetables in low-income neighbor- hoods, with Green Carts being "a powerful tool . . . to combat obesity and poor nutrition." Minneapolis requires grocery stores to stock ample supplies of "staple foods" such as fruits and vegetables, while Philadelphia's Healthy Corner Store Initiative provides training and incentives for stores operating in food deserts.

The food industry lobbies hard to block these reform strategies, even though obesity is at epidemic levels. Tobacco control overcame key political obstacles—paternalism, the "nanny state," and personal responsibility—by demonstrating the harm of secondhand smoke and revealing industry deceit and recalcitrance. Certainly, the outcomes of unhealthy living (diabetes, cancer, and heart disease) pose real harms to families, the health system, and productivity. What is not as well under- stood is that the food industry behaves much like Big Tobacco, denying the health impacts and aggressively blocking taxes and regulations.

Choosing what to eat is not an unfettered personal choice. Poor diets have become the "default" behavior in a perversely structured society. Alas, in America, and throughout the world, living well is hard to do.

Diet for a Dead Planet

Christopher Cook

Beyond Organic – Community Food Security

Transportation is a central yet little-discussed part of the food system. According to research by David Pimentel of Cornell University, it takes roughly ten calories of fossil-fuel energy to produce, process, and transport a single calorie of food. Worldwatch Institute estimates that the average food item in the United States travels 1,500 to 2,500 miles from farm to table. As one writer explains, "While organic farming methods can save some energy in the production department, they don't have the same healthy effect on transportation; organic or not, oranges burn a lot of fuel on their way to Minneapolis." Zinn notes, "We're really shooting ourselves in the foot if our only focus is on organic. While are saving ourselves from ingesting all sorts of nasty synthetic chemicals, at the same time we are destroying the environment by [transporting] that clear across the country."

Even while organics' arrival in the mainstream—symbolized most potently by the 2002 adoption of (somewhat controversial) USDA organic standards—is celebrated, many group, such as the Washington, D.C.-based Center for Food Safety, are pushing for a system that is "organic and beyond." They advocate a more sweeping mission to "maintain strong organic standards and to promote agriculture that is local, small-scale, and family operated, biologically diverse, humane, and socially just."

It sounds wonderful, but what does it mean on the ground? Is it feel-good idealism for a privileged few or can it make a real difference? Actually, the goals and accomplishments of numerous "community food security" projects around the country reveal a movement that is striving to make local produced food less expensive and more accessible to urban and rural working-class and poor people. The national Community Food Security Coalition, bringing together antihunger, environmental, and sustainable-farming advocates, defines community food security as "all persons obtaining at all times an affordable, nutritious and culturally appropriate diet through local, non-emergency food sources." This means developing small farms near – and sometimes within – cities and towns, and prioritizing local food production over food banks, which however benevolent, feature mostly processed, nonorganic food made by large corporations. To achieve this, small (and poorly funded) independent groups are establishing real economic relationships between farmers and city folk, and creating exemplary models for sustainable food systems built around community resources and needs.

For the urban and rural poor, "beyond organic" takes on a different, more basic meaning, for many don't have access to decent food of any sort, organic, or conventional. Many inner-city poor are shut out of the supermarket: as studies document, either the produce store in their neighborhood charges much more than supermarkets in middle-class and suburban areas, or there is no food market at all. As detailed in Chapter 2; the only "food" readily available in many public housing communities is all-too-available McDonald's or Burger King, or a convenience store offering liquor, chips, and candy. Supermarket chains have become a meeting place for agribusiness conglomerates and middle- and upper-class consumers, leaving small farmers and rural and urban low-income groups hungry and out in the cold.

In response to this crisis in food security, a veritable cornucopia of innovations is taking hold. In Los Angeles, San Francisco, Denver, and other cities, urban gardening projects using city lands are producing fresh nutritious food for public housing residents, and offering paid job training for budding gardeners and landscapers. Some of these endeavors emphasize entrepreneurship, employing poor residents (many of them teenagers from public housing) to produce and market niche products. In the heart of the poorest neighborhood in Austin, Texas where more than 40 percent of the families live below the poverty line, residents and organizers have set up a community garden and farmers' market. It provides a hub for nutrition education and accessible food, as well as a direct market opportunity for local farmers, many of them organic.

Urban subsistence and market farming generates both dietary and economic nourishment, and creates at least the potential for community-based economic development and a local food supply in poor, isolated neighborhoods. But while individual projects create very real hope, they are no panacea for the immense problems of structurally entrenched poverty, malnutrition, and hunger. Many entrepreneurial efforts, ironically, involve selling pricey jams and sauces to "yuppie" markets. Such is the perverse economic trap for the poor within capitalism: the entrepreneurial path out of poverty enlists the poor to sell niche products to the middle and upper class. This may help a few individuals but it's an insufficient model for broad community sustainability.

In 1995, while the Republican-controlled Congress (with an ample assist from President Clinton) was vigorously attacking welfare and food stamp programs, an emergent grassroots movement gained passage of the Community Food Security Act, which provides funds for projects that address food, farm, and nutrition problems. It legislated the concept that the USDA could promote a whole different food system marrying the needs of small producers and low-income consumers. For the federal government, it was still mostly PR: Congress ladled out a meager $3.5 million in "seed grants" to thirteen community food-security projects that would ultimately have to become self-sustaining. Programs from Indiana to Montana to Maine to South Central Los Angeles would develop an array of rural-urban food links: community kitchens and gardens would be training grounds for public housing residents to produce food and sell it to local stores and restaurants; area urban-rural food policy councils would be set up to help develop new farmers' markets; local sustainable agriculture networks would bring together farmers and neighborhood gardeners to produce food for people in need. By 2003, the USDA was funding projects in twenty states to the tune of $4.6 million a year.

There also are ongoing efforts around the country to convince local institutions such as schools and hospitals to purchase locally produced and, when possible, organic foods. The California Food and Justice Coalition is promoting a statewide "farm-to-cafeteria" program in which schools would purchase foods from area farmers, to improve kids' nutrition and boost farmers' incomes. "To the farmers, it really means access to a market that was previously closed to them, particularly the smaller family farmer in California, which makes up the vast majority," says Karrie Steven Thomas, program director for Community Alliance with Family Farmers. "The food-service industry is typically only open to large-scale farmers."

With some help from USDA, small farmers in Florida, North Carolina, and Kentucky are selling fresh produce to nearby school districts. According to a USDA report, these farm-to-school marketing projects "typically yield concrete benefits to everyone involved in the program: school children can incorporate a greater volume and variety of fresh fruits and vegetables into their diets, local school districts can obtain products packed to meet their exact specifications without having to pay for long-distance transportation and handling costs, and local growers gain an addition – and generally stable – source of farm-based income.

One of the most promising trends in direct farm-to-consumer connections is the explosive growth of farmers' markets. By 2002 there were over 3,100 farmers' markets in the United States, according to the USDA, 79 percent more than in 1994. Nearly 20,000 farmers "reported selling their produce only at farmers markets," and 82 percent of the markets were self-sustaining, covering all their costs. Though on a limited scale, urban farmers' markets also improve food access for the poor: more than half the markets participate in the food stamps program, the federal Women, Infants and Children Farmers' Market Nutrition Program (WIC), and local or state nutrition programs. One especially promising effort the USDA likes to promote is its WIC coupon program, in which up to 2 million mothers on welfare in forty-four state can get special coupons to shop in farmers' markets. Since launched in 1992, the program has provided millions of welfare mothers with fresh fruits and vegetables and boosted earnings for thousands of farmers. There's just one problem: the program gives each recipient just $10 to $20 a year in farmers' market coupons. And even this tiny drop in a very big bucket is perennially under assault by antiwelfare budget cutters.

The Bigger Picture

This compelling array of alternatives provides at least a glimpse into how true food security could change our food system. Concrete examples are out there, and they're working. But there are serious limitations. First and foremost, the money devoted to these projects is a pittance, not much more than some of the largest subsidy payments made to individual big farmers. In addition, although farmers' markets and farm-to-school projects help small growers survive, they don't ensure that the food is organic or sustainably produced. Entrepreneurial projects help a few individuals and can symbolize progress in poor communities, but they don't challenge structural poverty and food corporations' astounding economic power. For those who can afford it, shopping organic is a fine individual investment in a healthier future. But we cannot simply eat our way to a better world: consumers and the various food-resistance movements must demand and pressure for sweeping policy changes concerning the many interrelated crises described throughout this book.

Food First's Peter Rosset is a trained agricultural ecologist and long-time food analyst (and activist). When asked about the way forward, he said: "We're not going to get [there] by just wishing or hoping that social change or popular culture will just come around. It requires policy change. The system we have right now is . . . the product of specific policies and policy biases. Policies by which 50 percent of American farmers, the smaller ones, get zero or only symbolic amounts of subsidies and the largest and richest 25 percent get almost all of it. That is a policy that is written in a particular way that could just as easily be written in reverse. And would produce the reverse. There's nothing inevitable about it."

The annual $20 billion bill for subsidies, if redirected to small, diversified agriculture, organics, and community food security projects, would go a long way toward making food more healthy, environmentally responsible, local, and economically sustaining. As the smallest of steps in that directions, says Michael Pollan, we could require that the USDA "turn back the clock a little bit and go back to the New Deal," when subsidies were far more equitable and were designed (in part) to keep farmers afloat. So subsidies are certainly one piece of the puzzle.

Another piece is the overwhelming, neat-total control of the food industry by a handful of corporations, most prominently ConAgre, Archer Daniels Midland, Tyson Foods, Monsanto, Cargill, Wal-Mart, Safeway, and Albertson's. Their grip on the entire food supply must be broken. In the lingo of an earlier age, the trusts must be busted.

The third piece of the puzzle, one with still broader implications, is the need for overt federal and local food policies that articulate and implement the goal that our food should, to the greatest extent possible, be locally, organically, and sustainably produced on small diversified farms that feed their surrounding economy. Federal rules should set far tighter standards for protecting food workers and farm ecologies; our tax dollars should be invested in community food security instead of corporate welfare; antitrust measures to prevent monopolies and at least diminish corporations' destructive market share must be strictly enforced.

On a local level, every community should have its own food policy as a central part of planning, of which food security is an intrinsic element. Cities and towns see it as their job to plan for housing, transportation, education of children, some social services, economic development, sewage and garbage collection, drinking water supply, and other essential services. But when it comes to food, the most basic and constant ingredient in our lives, we leave it up to the market and Band-Aid charity.

What kinds of measures could a local food policy incorporate? Many ideas are being tried, including convincing water agencies to donate water for community gardens and other urban agriculture ventures; offering tax incentives for sustainable agricultural land use; providing a site and other supports for a farmers' market; extending subsidies and other incentives to urban farms and small rural growers in the surrounding area; and providing purchasing incentives that entice restaurants, food markets, schools, and other food-services outlets to buy local organic produce. Local food policy would also use zoning and other policy devices to ensure that food markets are accessible and evenly distributed.

Numerous states and some cities have food policy councils that are bringing long-ignored groups such as low-income residents and small farmers to the table. The Hartford Food System, in Hartford, Connecticut, begun in 1978, addresses root cause of hunger and poverty and works with farmers, policy makers, antihunger groups, schools, and other institutions to establish "an equitable and sustainable food system that addresses the underlying causes of hunger and poor nutrition." The Arizona Food Policy Council, run by a group called Community Food Connections, emphasizes most of the core principles of community food security in statewide planning. The Minnesota Food Association has three main programs. It encourages communities and residents to "buy local," and provides directories to farmers' markets and Community Supported Agriculture (CSA) programs; it has helped more than 1,000 conventional growers make the move to organics; and it is working to help food banks purchase products from struggling small farmers, a policy that focuses on both hunger and the farm crisis. The list of individual programs and policy initiatives is hearteningly long.

Ultimately, however, we need to make a fundamental shift in our priorities. We must put healthy, accessible, sustainably produced food at the forefront of our society's political and economic agenda. What could be more important for sustaining both present and future generations than providing good food in a manner that sustains not only its consumers and its producers but also the planet itself? The answer will not come simply through boycotts of "bad" corporations, consumer revolts to reform McDonald's or Burger King, gentle antitrust reforms that essentially leave corporate power intact, or entrepreneurial niche marketing for the poor – though each of these steps plays an important role. There must be a larger commitment that encompasses all these hopeful parts, that takes into account the needs of the whole society – consumers, workers, farmers, the environment, and even animals – and not just the concerns of one group or another. Food is part of the web of life. How we produce and consume it is a measure of a people. We need to make a commitment as a society to change this diet for a dead planet – before it is too late.

Made in the USA
San Bernardino, CA
03 July 2018